p 74,191

The Illustrated Encyclopedia of

AIRCRAFT ARMAMENT

The Illustrated Encyclopedia of
AIRCRAFT ARMAMENT

A major directory of guns, rockets, missiles, bombs, torpedoes and mines

Bill Gunston

ORION
BOOKS
NEW YORK

A SALAMANDER BOOK

Published in the United States
in 1988 by Orion Books, a
division of Crown Publishers, Inc.,
225 Park Avenue South,
New York,
N. Y. 10003.

ORION is a trademark of
Crown Publishers, Inc.

Represented in Canada by the
Canadian MANDA Group.

ISBN 0-517-56607-9

This book may not be sold
outside the United States of
America and Canada.

Project Manager:
Philip de Ste. Croix

Editor:
Chris Chant

Designers:
Nick Buzzard
Carol Warren

Color artwork:
Michael Badrocke and
Terry Hadler
© Salamander Books Ltd

Diagram artwork:
Michael Badrocke and TIGA
© Salamander Books Ltd

Index:
Michèle Clarke

Filmset:
The Old Mill, England

**Color and monochrome
reproduction:**
York House Graphics Ltd,
England

Printed in Italy

All correspondence concerning
the content of this volume
should be addressed to
Salamander Books Ltd.

THE AUTHOR

Bill Gunston is a former RAF pilot and flying instructor, and
he has spent most of his working life accumulating a wealth
of information on aerospace technology and history. Since
leaving the Service, he has acted as an advisor to several
aviation companies and become one of the most
internationally respected authors and broadcasters on
aviation and scientific subjects. His numerous books
include the Salamander titles, *The Illustrated Encyclopedia
of the World's Modern Military Aircraft, Modern Fighting
Aircraft, American Warplanes, Modern Air Combat* (with
Mike Spick), *The Illustrated Encyclopedia of the World's
Rockets and Missiles, Soviet Air Power* (with Bill
Sweetman), *Modern Fighting Helicopters* (with Mike Spick)
and many of Salamander's successful illustrated guides to
aviation subjects. He has also contributed to the
authoritative *The Soviet War Machine* and *The US War
Machine,* by the same company, and carries out regular
assignments for technical aviation periodicals. Mr. Gunston
is also an assistant compiler of *Jane's All the World's
Aircraft* and was formerly technical editor of *Flight
International,* and technology editor of *Science Journal*.

PICTURE CREDITS

CONTENTS

1

2

3

4

5

DEVELOPING THE TECHNOLOGY

Surprisingly, only one large work on aircraft armament has been published since World War II, and that book dealt very sporadically with guns and bombs only. Today the subject has become so diverse that some of the more interesting historical facets have to be ignored or skimmed over, one obvious example being the development of gun turrets. One tends to think of turrets as being purely for the defence of large aircraft, but in fact many of the most powerful turrets were fitted to fighters. Today, though a few turrets are fitted to Soviet bombers and transports, most are found only on attack helicopters.

The author has often drawn attention to the fact that, it might be thought that things aeronautical would almost design themselves, the engineers having hardly any scope in reconciling the customer's demands with the basic difficulty of defeating gravity, in fact sheer fashion plays a very large part. In the early 1950s it was taken for granted that fighters would be made faster and faster, and projects were put in hand for aircraft able to fly at well over Mach 3, with fantastic powerplants. Some time later it was realized at such speeds you have to fly in a straight line, which is not very useful in a dogfight, and most modern fighters do Mach 2 or less. In the same way, fighters of the 1950s soon lost their guns; in the 1960s they began to be put back again.

Today we see a whole crop of new fighters fitted with guns, apart perhaps from the proposed European Fighter Aircraft where the opinion of at least some of the potential customers is that if any enemy gets within gun-firing range there is something wrong! Defence money is usually tight, and national treasuries are forever seeking ways to cut expenditure. If ever any kind of weapon is thought, rightly or wrongly, to be on the way out then the least that can happen is that no more money is made available for long-term research, though some may reluctantly be voted for ongoing procurement.

In the same way, the British appear slavishly to copy American developments and frequently adopt US hardware, but seldom copy the Soviet Union. Yet Soviet fighter pilots have for a quarter of a century taken it for granted that they will have a choice of AAM (air-to-air missile) guidance systems, either radar or infra-red, the particular method being selected according to the weather and other variables affecting each engagement.

This book has little chance to pontificate on such matters, because its pages are pretty densely devoted to outlining the

history of aircraft weapons and then to describing all current aircraft armament of which details are known. This main 'catalogue' section is subdivided according to class of weapon, and then further subdivided by country of origin. In almost every case the narrative text is preceded by a specification arranged according to a standard format, almost all the exceptions being for entries where no releasable numerical data may be published.

One of the biggest of the catalogue sections is entitled Unguided Ordnance. It is subdivided into Bombs, Rockets, Depth Charges and Mines (treated as one category) and a possibly unexpected category called Dispenser Systems. In fact the dispensers are one of the most important subsections in the entire book, partly because the fact that airfields ought never to be attacked by manned aircraft (a belief perfectly well understood 30 years ago) has today been forgotten, and no arms manufacturer seems to bear the thought of not joining the same lunatic bandwagon and designing dispensers for things that make pockmark craters in runways and airfield pavements. Admittedly some dispensers are also intended to drop things on top of hostile armoured vehicles, and this is a much more sensible idea. Indeed, whereas airfields are the ideal and obvious target for attack by missile – to the extent that each NATO airfield is today targeted by anything upwards of a dozen large Warsaw Pact missiles – moving armour is very hard to hit by any kind of long-range guided missile unless its

Left: Much technical effort is devoted to the armed helicopter. This is a French offering, the Aérospatiale SA 365M Panther. The Panther has capable sensors and exterior hardpoints for the carriage of different weapons, here a pair of podded 20mm cannon.

Right: The Hughes BGM-71 Tow is undoubtedly the West's most important anti-tank weapon, and has been extensively developed from the BGM-71A/B (left) via the probe-equipped BGM-71C to the larger-warhead BGM-71D (right). Further work is concentrated on means of defeating reactive armour.

Left: Currently the world's longest-ranged air-to-air missile, the Hughes AIM-54 Phoenix is matched to the AWG-9 radar and fire-control system of the F-14 Tomcat fighter. After launch it climbs to high altitude for long-range cruise before diving towards its target under control of its own active radar homing system.

Right: Much ingenuity goes into the development of dispenser weapons such as this large twin Hunting JP.233 installation under a Tornado. But the Tornado still has to overfly massively-defended targets to unload its submunitions.

Below: The West Germans have selected the American AGM-88 HARM in preference to the lighter but just as capable British ALARM as the primary anti-radar weapon of their Tornado ECR electronic warfare aircraft.

general whereabouts is known before the missile is launched. Even then a dispenser warhead, spewing various kinds of submunition, is by far the best kind of warhead to use against such dispersed yet hardened targets.

Under the heading ASMs (Air-to-Surface Missiles) the main known species in service or under development are listed. Subsections which follow the main ASM listing are concerned with torpedoes and with anti-tank missiles. The latter tend to form a special category with sharply defined characteristics. It might be thought that there should also be a separate subsection on anti-ship missiles, but a little thought will show that this is not possible to arrange. Though in some cases a missile cannot be used against anything but a ship, there are plenty of others – such as Gabriel III and Harpoon – which can also be used against other kinds of target including those on land thanks to their powerful warheads.

Air-to-air missiles are the decisive weapons of aerial warfare, and this fact is amply reflected in the diversity of such weapons catalogued in their own important section.

Had this book been written 30 years ago the catalogue section on Guns and Pods would certainly have been very much briefer. In the late 1950s there were few current varieties of aircraft gun, and the general consensus was that not many more would be produced. Future fighters were expected to be armed entirely with missiles, and the author can vividly recall a British civil servant who was one of the most senior people responsible for aircraft weapons saying 'There's not much doubt about it; the traditional kind of cannon or machine gun is as dead as the dodo where aircraft are concerned. Even bombers, if they have any defensive weapons, will use missiles.' He would surely be amazed to see the wealth of new guns in this book, just as the author is amazed to see such interest in such archaic weapons as the 'fifty calibre Browning', which dates from 1917. In World War II this gun played a gigantic role, but one has only to take a casual glance at the GECAL 50 to see what can be done today with the same ammunition.

In the introduction to the Guns and Pods section a brief survey is given of contemporary developments in guns and, especially, in ammunition. What is not mentioned is that with ever better miniaturized electronics, it is becoming increasingly possible to build a gun that can fire guided ammunition. For many years US Army artillery has had the Copperhead and Shillelagh guided missiles which are fired from regular guns. The job is much more difficult in smaller calibres, and in any case if a projectile is guided it is probably sensible to increase its calibre and cut down on the numbers fired. It looks doubtful to the author that any true gun ammunition is worth giving full self-homing capability. It makes much more sense to put the effort into guiding the gun, so that when each round is fired its barrel is pointing in the right direction to score a hit. At the same time, AAMs are likely to be developed with such violent launch acceleration that they virtually rival gun projectiles for brief time of flight.

DEVELOPING THE TECHNOLOGY

From a viewpoint in 1987 most of us would find it difficult to predict in any detail what aerospace warfare will be like in 2050. Trying to do so cuts us down to size and affords a proper perspective for considering what people had to say on the possibility of air warfare in the years before World War I.

There is a surprising amount of literature on the subect. Almost all the experts initially concentrated upon the fighting potential of airships as these were considered to be the only aerial vehicles able to carry both an aviator and weapons. The experts dwelt at length upon the fact that a strong wall no longer sufficed to keep out nasty objects (overlooking the fact that howitzers had been lobbing things over walls for centuries) and pontificated on the dreadful fact that even defenceless cities were now open to attack from above. Fred T. Jane, in the first edition of his famous annual in 1909, invited the most authoritative person he could imagine to contribute a special section on 'Aerial Warfare'. Vice-Admiral Sir Percy Scott KCVO wrote (and this is virtually his entire contribution), 'The heretofore only traversers of the air use beak and talon to destroy one another, the human aviator having neither beak nor talon, must be provided with some means of offence, it may be a gun, if it is, then the aviator will realise that his safety depends upon whether the projectile out of his gun hits the mark aimed at or not, and accurate gunnery, that is *quick hitting,* will in the air be as important as it is on land or on the sea in deciding a final issue. Whatever the weapons used are, practice with them will be necessary, and we may live to see two airships each towing a suitable target carrying out a test of their efficiency in *quick hitting.*'

Since then 'Jane's' has not only improved its standard of punctuation but has also recorded tens of thousands of kinds of aircraft armament. Perversely, the one tangible thing the admiral predicted (airships firing at targets towed by an accompanying ship) has never happened. The quotation is given to show how very difficult it was in 1909 to envisage air warfare. By 1915 such warfare was becoming reality, and the fact that the belligerents, even when spurred on by actual attack by hostile airships and aeroplanes, never did succeed in constructing what we today would consider any kind of plausible defence system ought not to be too astonishing. In any case, this book is concerned only with the weapons deployed by aircraft (fixed- and rotary-wing).

Claiming anything to have been an absolute 'first' is fraught with danger, but it is generally accepted that the first aircraft used in war was the tethered balloon *Entreprenant* manned by observer Capitaine Coutelle of the French republican forces during the Battle of Fleurus on 26 June 1794. The occasions on which a gun was first fired or a bomb first dropped from the air are more difficult to fix. In 1910-11 high-spirited young officers in the US Army did both. At Sheepshead Bay, NY, Lt Jake Fickel repeatedly hit a ground target with a rifle, despite the fact he was sitting on the bare leading edge of the lower wing with no way of holding on! A few weeks later, on 7 January 1911, Lts Beck and Crissy caused consternation by letting go of home-made bombs over the Tanforan racecourse at San Francisco! A more serious 'first' was the dropping of Cipelli grenades on Turkish troops on what is today Libya by 2nd Lt Giulio Gavotti, of the Italian air flotilla, on 1 November 1911. Nearly a year later the Bulgarian air regiment dropped the first purpose-designed bombs on Adrianople (today Edirne), and also fired hand guns at Turkish troops. Before that, on 2 June 1912, Captain Chandler of the US Army had

Above: In the absence of an interrupter gear, early fighters such as this Airco D.H.2 were designed as pushers to allow a nose-mounted gun.

Right: Typical defensive armament in World War I was one 0.303in Lewis gun, seen here on a Scarff mounting.

Below: Definitive fighter armament was two fixed guns. These are Sopwith Camels with two 0.303in Vickers guns.

fired the first Lewis machine-gun in the air, and another US officer, Lt Riley Scott, had developed the world's first accurate bombsight (but this book has no room for such adjuncts, vital as they are).

The remainder of this first, historical, section is subdivided according to class of weapon.

Primitive devices

There already existed *a wealth* of possible air weapons in the form of conventional small arms, grenades and artillery shells, as noted below. Several countries experimented with dropping heavy weights, including 1kg (2.2lb) weights from kitchen scales! These soon faded from the scene, but various forms of dart persisted for years. Some darts had a rear tubular portion while others had tail fins. The only standard mass-produced model used by the UK and France was the Fléchette (French for a small arrow or dart), a pointed steel rod 5in (127mm) long and 0.375in (9.5mm) diameter. Released from vertical canisters holding (typically) 250, a fléchette could penetrate steel helmets but was rightly considered an ineffective kind of scatter weapon. (The much bigger Ranken dart is described below under the heading 'Bombs'.)

One of the first kinds of armament considered long before 1914 was the grappling hook: not, like its naval forebear, for grasping the enemy over a period but merely in order to cause lethal damage to flimsy structures. Russian Staff Captain A. A. Kazakov was a famed exponent, while an officer of RFC No. 6 Sqn trailed a weight on a 150ft (46m) cable in the hope of ensnaring a few propellers. A bigger and more awesome device was the Fiery Grapnel, devised by the Royal Aircraft Factory at Farnborough. Carried in pairs but used singly, this was a big four-barbed anchor lowered on a long cable to rip an airship's envelope; an explosive charge was intended then to ignite the escaping hydrogen as it mixed with the air.

Hand guns

Many types of pistol, revolver, carbine and rifle were fired from aircraft in 1914-16 (rarely later). The German Mauser and Luger 9mm stocked pistols with a long barrel were favoured for their handiness and accuracy, while some aviators sought to overcome basic inaccuracy by using shotguns (in a few cases firing chainshot). At least six types of rifle grenade were also used. Favoured RFC weapons included the Martini and Lee-Metford carbines, SMLE rifle and 0.45in (11.43mm) Winchester, a few being clamped to the aircraft at various angles. Nobody came near emulating the success of Captain L. G. Hawker of RFC No. 6 Sqn who, on 25 July 1915, shot down three German aircraft, all with observers firing a machine-gun, using a single-shot Martini carbine fixed diagonally to clear the propeller of his Bristol Scout!

Machine-guns

The pioneer modern machine-gun was that invented by Hiram Maxim in 1882-3. Recoil-operated, belt-fed and water-cooled, this went into production in 0.45in (11.43mm) and 0.303in (7.7mm) calibres, both being widely used on aircraft. Essentially the same gun was the German MG.08, which in MG.08/15 form armed many aeroplanes and airships. Of 7.92mm (0.312in) calibre, the MG.08/15 had either a rear stock and pistol grip or twin handholds and a trigger at the rear. Without the 100- or 200-round web belt or cooling water the weight was about 36lb (16kg), and rate of fire usually around 500 rounds per minute. The original gun was used with minor modifications in fixed and movable installations, and was almost standard on airships. On aeroplanes the slipstream could cool the barrel, exposed by perforating the jacket, and this gun became commonly known as the Spandau, from the location of the factory. A considerable modification of this gun

Below: This Fokker E IV monoplane fighter was fitted with three 7.92mm MG. 08/15 guns, but its performance was degraded to an unacceptable degree by the extra weight.

DEVELOPING THE TECHNOLOGY

was the Parabellum, designed at the DWM by Karl Heinemann. This had a refined action and was also much lighter and faster-firing (700 rounds per minute). The 1913 model became the standard free gun for observers, fed by a fabric belt wound on a spool attached beside the gun, and often used in a staggered paired mount. The 1917 model had a smaller-diameter barrel casing.

In 1884 Maxim went into partnership with the British arms firm of Vickers, and the result was a classic belt-fed gun which served all British (and many other) services for over 70 years. Progressively improved, it was used by the RFC and RNAS chiefly in 0.303in (7.7mm) calibre, weighing about 32lb (14.5kg), the water cooling being eliminated in later marks with a perforated barrel jacket. The rate of fire was originally 500 rounds per minute, later raised to about 650. The Vickers Gun Bus of February 1913 had an infantry gun on a pivoted mount, but in most later installations the Vickers was fixed (at first in ways that cleared the propeller, though in Bristol Scouts it was common to count bullet holes in the blades and scrap the propeller if there were more than three), with Vickers, Dibovsky, Sopwith-Kauper or Constantinesco gear to interrupt the firing mechanism or synchronize the gun to the engine rpm. From 1918 the Constantinesco was standard in the RAF, in progressively improved versions.

For background interest, it is often thought, especially from the name 'interrupter gear' that the bursts of fire were intermittently halted to allow a propeller blade to pass through the bullet line. In fact the frequency of passing of the blades was always much higher than the cyclic rate of the gun, so what actually happened was that anything up to eight blades (depending on the number of blades on the propeller) might go by between the firing of successive bullets.

By 1914 the Vickers was being produced in several calibres, including particularly 11mm (0.433in), 0.45in (11.43mm) and 0.5in (12.7mm). All these heavier versions were used in aircraft, in both fixed and free installations. These guns had no kinship with the much heavier Vickers guns described under 'Cannon'.

The most important manufacturer of French aircraft guns was Hotchkiss, though this company's chief rifle-calibre weapon was also known (especially in the USA) as the Benét-Mercié (often mis-spelt Mercier), from its designers. An excellent gas-operated weapon with no barrel jacket, it was compact and reliable, firing at 500 rounds per minute from 30-round clips inserted from the side. The only real drawback was that this method of feed was bulky laterally and necessitated frequent insertion of fresh clips. The very first air victory brought about by gunfire is generally believed to have been gained on 5 October 1914 by the crew of Voisin V.89 whose observer had a Hotchkiss in the new 7.7mm (0.303in) calibre, the original bore being 8mm.

Above: Leading US ace of World War I with 26 'kills', Eddie Rickenbacker is seen with his Spad XIII, a sturdy fighter with two 0.303in Vickers.

Below: The true fighter was made possible by development of interrupter gear to allow a fixed gun to be fired directly forward without shooting off the propeller blades.

Sopwith-Kauper interrupter gear

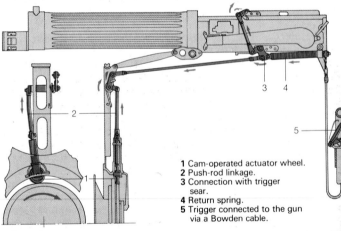

1 Cam-operated actuator wheel.
2 Push-rod linkage.
3 Connection with trigger sear.
4 Return spring.
5 Trigger connected to the gun via a Bowden cable.

Left: The Felixstowe F.2A could carry six Lewis guns for a very prickly defensive capability, and a pair of 230lb (104kg) bombs.

Above: The Fokker Eindecker was the world's first truly effective fighter. This is a single-gun E III over the Western Front in early 1916.

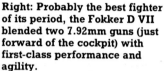

Right: Probably the best fighter of its period, the Fokker D VII blended two 7.92mm guns (just forward of the cockpit) with first-class performance and agility.

The same gun was also used by the US Army as the 'Benet-Mercier', and it continued in the handful of US armed aircraft in preference to the locally designed Lewis, which on almost every count was superior. Fed up, Colonel Lewis took his gun (in fact designed by Samuel Maclean) to Europe, where it went into production by FN and, after the German occupation of Belgium in 1914, by BSA in the UK. For the rest of the war it was virtually the standard observer gun of the Allies. Features included a rotating bolt driven forward by a spiral fusee spring and back by gas tapped from the barrel, air cooling (with or without a large-diameter casing which greatly altered the appearance) and feed from a drum in which the rounds were arranged radially and fed under continuous positive control, so that the gun worked equally well in any manoeuvres and in any attitude. The normal infantry gun had the cooling jacket and a 47-round drum, but in aircraft it became usual to omit the jacket and use a deeper drum of 94-97 rounds. These drums were very heavy and it was not easy to change drums in combat in freezing air at 20,000ft (6,095m), with the aircraft buffeting in all directions. On the other hand, once on the gun the drum stayed on, and Capt L. A. Strange, an RFC officer who did much to improve armament, saved his life in May 1915 by hanging on (entirely outside the aircraft) to a jammed Lewis drum on a Martinsyde S.1 while in an inverted spin! With jacket the gun weighed 27lb (12kg) and fired at 550 rounds per minute.

Towards the end of the war other guns came into use. Germany produced the Dreyse, a lighter and faster-firing replacement for the MG.08/15 the brilliant twin-barrel Gast and the powerful 12.7mm (0.5in) TuF (Tank und Flieger), which was almost a scaled-up MG.08/15. France developed the Darne, a notably neat and light gun put into production soon after the Armistice in the new calibre of 7.5mm (0.295in). Even more important was the series of machine-guns designed by the American John Browning. Starting with a water-cooled model for the US Army, these led in 1918 to a lighter air-cooled model using a disintegrating metal-link belt with standard 0.30in (7.62mm) rimless ammunition. Good features of this gun were a rate of fire over 1,000 rounds per minute and the kind of mechanical design which lent it self to easy mass-production. One of the first did well in a fixed installation between the cylinder blocks of an RAF Bristol Fighter in August 1918. By this time the much bigger 0.50in (12.7mm) Browning was also on test, but neither saw action in World War I. Both weapons were extensively developed in the interwar period, and were important in World War II.

Cannon

The author knows of no fully automatic large-calibre gun fitted to aircraft before 1916, but there were many semi-automatic or hand-loaded weapons. In terms of numbers the most important were the breech-loaded Hotchkiss guns, initially identical with those used on warships. A few were of 47mm calibre, but the only mass-produced Hotchkiss cannon were of 37mm size, firing ball, tracer, incendiary and armour-piercing ammunition (though not very effective in the AP role in the common short-barrel model). The short gun was refined from the mod"ele 1902, weighing 46.7kg (103llb) and fired a 0.45kg (1lb) shell at 400m (1,213ft) per second. The long-barrel Hotchkiss weighed 147kg (325lb) and fired a 0.7kg (1.54lb) shell at 860m (2,820ft) per second, but as the recoil travel was increased from 120mm to 600mm (4.7in to 23.6in) the recoil force stayed at around 1,200kg (2,645lb).

The Hotchkiss guns were aimed by observers who typically had about 50 rounds. In contrast the Puteaux arsenal developed an installation attached to the Hispano-Suiza geared V-8 engine, firing through the hub of the propeller. The aces Georges Guynemer and René Fonck used this *moteur canon* installation in their Spad XIIs, respectively scoring four and 11 victories with it, but cordite fumes proved a problem.

In the UK the Vickers 1.5-pounder 'pom pom' was installed experimentally in the 200hp (149kW) Sopwith seaplane No. 127 in May 1914, the same gun later being tested in Short S.81 No. 126. One report stated that firing the 265lb (120kg) weapon posed no problems, while another claimed that the recoil made the aircraft 'stop dead and drop 500ft'. Not much use was made of this gun, but later (1916) Vickers perfected an almost automatic 1-pounder which resembled a gigantic version of the company's machine-gun, firing 1.59in (40.39mm) shells from a 40-round belt. Carriers included an RAF F.E.2b, Martinsyde F. 1 and Vickers' own F.B.24E.

Certainly one of the first cannon installed in an aircraft was the COW (Coventry Ordnance Works) 1-pounder tested (but not flown) aboard the RAF F.E.3 in the summer of 1913. Two years later the famous COW 1.5-pounder appeared. This outstanding automatic gun had a calibre of 37mm and fired high-velocity shells of five species at the rate of 100 rounds per minute, though usually the feed clip held only five rounds. Such a weapon was fitted to two Airco D.H.4s in summer 1918, firing up and ahead at 65|, aimed by the pilot but fired and reloaded by the observer as an anti-Zeppelin weapon.

DEVELOPING THE TECHNOLOGY

Above: The 'large and small' of World War I bombs is exemplified by the 1,800lb (816.5kg) SN bomb and, at the foot of the ruler, a tiny incendiary with potentially just as devastating an effect.

Above: The weight and drag of even the small 14in (356mm) torpedo often gave machines such as the Short 184 marginal flight performance, but the type still proved useful.

Below: This SSW was a very ambitious stand-off glide weapon guided via wires and designed to split open near its target and deposit a torpedo into the water.

Germany produced several cannon, and one saw wide service as defensive armament for heavy bombers. This gun, the Becker, was about the simplest and lightest 20mm weapon that could be devised. Looking like a length of gaspipe topped by a 20-round box, it used plain blowback operation and fired at 400 rounds per minute. It was further developed post-war in Switzerland as the Semag. Another gun, produced only in prototype form by 1918, was the Rheinmetall 20mm known as the Erhardt after its designer. A high-velocity rapid-fire weapon, it became the post-war Solothurn.

An obvious problem with larger-calibre guns of conventional type was the recoil force imparted to the aircraft structure. In an endeavour to overcome this several inventors patented recoilless guns, one of which saw considerable service in British aircraft. This was the Davis gun, designed by Commander Cleland Davis of the US Navy. It consisted mainly of a normal rifled barrel whose rear end, instead of being closed by a bolt or breechblock, terminated in a plain open tube. Each round consisted of a conventional projectile at one end of the propellant case and a cylinder of lead shot at the other. On being fired, the shot accelerated out of the rear tube almost balanced the recoil of the projectile accelerated down the barrel. The Davis was put into modest production in three sizes, known as the 2-, 6- and 12-pounder. Ten rounds was a typical supply, unclipped and loaded by the gunner who also aimed the gun in pivoted installations. Many anti-Zeppelin nightfighters had these weapons fixed at a high angle to fire diagonally upwards, and this eliminated problems due to the blast and lead shot causing damage behind the gun. The Davis was claimed to be accurate to a range of 6,000ft (1,830m), and was tested from March 1915 with a view to its use against U-boats as well as against other aircraft. There is nothing wrong with the recoilless cannon in principle, and it found new expression in the MK115 of 1944, but by late 1916 the Davis had largely been abandoned.

Bombs

In August 1914 the heaviest aircraft bomb was a 50kg (110lb) weapon carried only by German navy airships; aeroplane bombs stopped at 22lb (10kg). At the Armistice the UK had a bomber able to carry two bombs each weighing 3,307lb (1,500kg). For the record, British bombs in World War I included the following sizes: 16lb (7.25kg), 20lb (9.1kg) Hale and Cooper, 27lb (12.2kg) Hale, 28lb (12.7kg) Analyte, 40lb (18.1kg), 50lb (22.7kg), 65lb (29.5kg) HE and flat-nose anti-submarine, 100lb (45kg), 112lb (51kg), 230lb (104kg) anti-submarine, 250lb (113kg), 336lb (152kg) heavy case, 520lb (236kg) anti-submarine, 550lb (249kg), 1,650lb (748kg) and 3,307lb (1,500kg). Incendiaries came in six patterns including the BIB (Baby Incendiary Bomb) carried in multiple boxes,

10lb (4.5kg), two Brock patterns and the 40lb (18.1kg) phosphorus. There were also incendiary darts and a variety of Carcass Bombs, which were tubes with triple hooks intended to snag on an airship's envelope. The commonest Carcasses were the 10lb (4.5kg) and 14.5lb (6.6kg) delivered through a 3.45in (88mm) tube incorporating electrical contacts which ignited the incendiary powder filling 20 seconds after passage down the tube. The dart named for Royal Navy Lt. F. Ranken was a small canister with a heavy pointed nose. After penetrating a Zeppelin it was arrested by sprung tail fins. The filling was HE and incendiary powder grains.

Other combatants deployed similar varieties of free-fall store, except for the USA which relied on Allied weapons. The heaviest non-British bomb was the German 1,000kg (2,205lb) type carried by Staaken R-types. Russian IM bombers carried 420kg (920lb) bombs by late 1915.

Torpedoes

Again British practice can be taken as typical. Pioneer trial with a 14in (356mm) weapon in July 1914 with Short tractor seaplane No. 121 led to widespread use of the much heavier Whitehead series of 18in (457mm) torpedoes, of which the chief models were the famed Mk VIII family (typically weighing 1,423lb, 645.5kg) and the shorter Mk IX weighing about 1,000lb (453.6kg).

Rockets

Despite centuries of regular use by armies and navies, the rocket saw rather limited use in World War I. By far the most numerous species were the simple devices designed by Lt. Y.P.G. Le Prieur of the French Navy. Almost all were of one

Right: Le Prieur rockets were fitted in quadruples on outer sets of interplane struts, and were electrically fired against airships and balloons.

Below: Though not produced to a common scale, these illustrations of World War I bombers provide a clear indication of basic weapon fits. The D.H.9 is typical of light bomber practice, with a fixed gun for the pilot, a ring-mounted gun for the observer and small bombs carried under the airframe. The larger bombers all feature heavier offensive loads and more comprehensive defensive armament.

Bombers of World War I

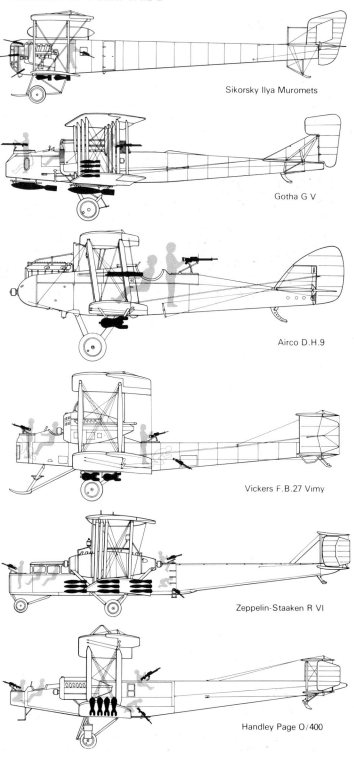

Sikorsky Ilya Muromets

Gotha G V

Airco D.H.9

Vickers F.B.27 Vimy

Zeppelin-Staaken R VI

Handley Page O/400

standard type resembling a Guy Fawkes rocket scaled up to carry a sheet-metal warhead. Le Prieur rockets were carried in groups of either four or five mounted one above the other on interplane struts (thus, eight or 10 per aircraft). The stabilising tail rod was simply inserted into ring eyes set to carry the rocket at a nose-up angle of 15°, and the electric firing squib connected. Rockets proved effective against observation balloons but never saw action against Zeppelins. In the UK the Vickers works at Crayford produced a technically interesting rocket gun which had much greater potential than Le Prieur installations. It was little more than a tube (in principle similar to the Bazooka and Panzerfaust of World War II), mounted on a cockpit pivot. The observer loaded rockets from the rear, aimed and fired.

Guided Missiles

Beyond doubt the most important programme of guided missiles before World War II was managed by the Siemens-Schuckert Werke (SSW) in World War I, chiefly for the Imperial German Navy. Dr Wilhelm von Siemens suggested a remotely controlled glide bomb as early as October 1914, and, as the company already had considerable experience of remotely controlled boats, progress was on a sound footing. Flight testing under Dipl-Ing Dorner began in January 1915, with gliders of increasing size. All were controlled by electrical command through fine copper wires unrolled from a spool. Servo controls, at first energized by a dry battery but by mid-1916 supplied by a windmill generator, operated a bang-bang rudder, self-centring after each command, and elevators which remained in the position last commanded. After many tests a method was perfected of making the left and right airframe halves — monoplane wings and half-fuselage — arranged to split open upon command to release a torpedo just above the water. Trials were flown from Siemens aircraft at Neumünster in the spring of 1915, and night testing began in August 1916. After 75 flights with larger biplane gliders the navy made an airship available, and flights with 300kg (661lb) monoplanes and biplanes were made from Zeppelin Z.XII near Hanover in April 1917. Then 300kg (661lb) gliders were flown from L.35 at Juterbog and Parseval PL.25 at Potsdam. L.35 carried numerous gliders of 500kg (1,102lb) size and a few of 1,000kg (2,205lb), the last flight being by an SSW Torpedo-glider No. 7 on 2 August 1918. It flew 7.6km (4.7 miles) from release at 1,200m (2,935ft) but the twin wires broke when the missile was just over the target at about 60m (200ft). At the Armistice SSW was starting more advanced trials at the airship base at Nordholz, using low-silhouette monoplanes of 4.2 to 5.0m (13.8 to 16.4ft) span. It was also hoped to release these pioneer ASMs from SSW bombers. There was inadequate ground clearance under the R.IV (R.4) but the R.VIII — the largest bomber of World War I — carried the impressive monoplane missiles beautifully. But they had not been released in flight when work was halted by the Allies in December 1918.

The UK and USA each developed many types of guided or preprogrammed cruise missile in the period 1915-18, but none was designed for aircraft launch.

DEVELOPING THE TECHNOLOGY

In the 30-year period between 1921 and 1950 almost every kind of aircraft armament that we know today was brought into existence, with the sole exception of directed-energy beams. Predictably, the Western democracies spent little on weapons until well into the 1930s, and any World War I pilot could have fought in any RAF fighter of 1935 without needing any instruction in new technologies other than a parachute, oxygen and radio. The armament remained two 0.303in (7.7mm) Vickers guns, and the Lewis guns and bombs carried by the bombers had invariably been made during World War I. In contrast, defeated Germany and the Soviet Union worked hard at developing new weapons, and so did smaller countries such as Switzerland and Denmark.

Thus, with the benefit of hindsight it is possible to come to the conclusion that the Western Allies won the 1939-45 air war with generally superior aircraft equipped with inferior armament. The reasons for this are hard to comprehend. British Air Staffs and the civilian 'boffins' at such places as the Royal Aircraft Establishment have a proud record of trying to look ahead and develop technology to meet predicted threats. To a fighting service there could hardly be a more basic need than its weapons, yet the RAF and Royal Navy fought World War II essentially with just two types of gun, one designed in the USA in 1914-16 and the other a French derivative of the German Becker 20mm cannon of 1913-14! When the Soviet Union was invaded in June 1941, it was smugly thought in the UK that its new ally had virtually no design capability in such an advanced field as aircraft weaponry, but in fact the boot was on the other foot. During the 1930s Soviet aircraft guns and rockets had led the world, and that country has never ceased to produce successive aircraft weapons of the highest quality and performance. Despite this, there was virtually no exchange of relevant armament information during the alliance years of World War II.

At the same time, whatever one may feel about the Nazi regime, full credit must be accorded the German designers who by 1945 had thrust far ahead in aircraft guns, air-to-air (but, oddly, not so much air-to-ground) rockets, and various kinds of guided missiles. Even today many gun designs of the wartime Germans stand alone, and have never been approached since. It may be that, had their designers had a little more time, these futuristic guns would have been seen to be flawed in various ways which did not show up in prototype

Below left: Well armed by Japanese standards, the Mitsubishi A6M5 carried two 7.7mm machine guns in the fuselage and two 20mm cannon in the wings.

Below: Seen on policing duties over Palestine in 1935, this Armstrong Whitworth-built Hart light bomber carries the World War I type armament of four 112lb (51kg) light bombs.

1920 TO 1950

Left: First of the British World War II fighters to carry bombs was the Hawker Hurricane. This Mk IIB is seen with two 250lb (113kg) bombs; on occasion bombs of twice this mass could be carried, and later versions could lift small bomb containers, smoke apparatus or eight rockets.

Below: The Luftwaffe gained vital combat experience in Spain. This He 111E-1 shows how eight SC250 (551lb) bombs were carried nose-upward.

Below: Three He 51A-1s come up astern of a Do 23G during 1935 exercises. These were the principal fighter and bomber types in the newly born Luftwaffe. The whole concept of air fighting was identical with that of 1918, with speeds slightly higher. The fighters had twin MG17s and the bombers three hand-aimed but essentially similar MG15s.

testing, but this is speculation. Equally, German missile aspirations were often far ahead of the real state of the art, but they showed everyone the way to go.

Primitive devices

Perhaps surprisingly, these abounded in World War II, especially in the UK. By 'primitive' is meant not necessarily simple of crude, but bizarre in concept and insufficiently thought through to prove a viable weapon in the long term.

Several combatant nations experimented with arrangements for harassed bombers to try to deter stern attacks by fighters through the use of devices to strew grenades or bomblets ('aerial mines') behind them. These devices included spring-powered catapults and spring- and pneumatic-powered tube launchers. One of the latter got into operational service in 1940 on the Heinkel He 111H-6 of the Luftwaffe.

An equally hit-or-miss weapon was the British Long Aerial Mine, abbreviated to LAM which, when pronounced as a word, resulted in the prolonged trials being codenamed 'Mutton'. The idea, which was originally suggested in 1929 by the great jet inventor Frank Whittle, but ignored at that time, was to try to fill the sky with vertical cables in the path of enemy bombers. In some schemes the cable remained attached to a night-fighter, being towed behind and below it; in others it was released to descend slowly on a parachute. On the end of the cable was an explosive charge (a No. 7 bomb). The idea was that when an enemy bomber flew into the wire the bomb would quickly be drawn up (or down, depending on the arrangement of the free-fall type of LAM) to explode when it struck the bomber. Experiments in autumn 1940 with Handley Page Harrows led to widespread trials with Douglas Havocs which lasted until November 1942.

In 1943 the Germans devised, but did not deploy, a scheme for firing canisters of coal dust into the sky near bomber formations. An HE charge was to disperse the particles into a giant cloud. This would be detonated. The idea is seen at work in today's FAE weapons.

DEVELOPING THE TECHNOLOGY

Machine guns

The UK showed almost total disinclination to advance the technology of aircraft guns from 1920 until 1935. The standard fighter armament in service remained two Vickers of 0.303in calibre, though the gun was refined through six marks and the fabric belt was exchanged for one with separate metal links. The only new gun introduced to RAF and Fleet Air Arm service was the Vickers GO (gas-operated), also known as the Vickers K. This drum-fed 0.303in weapon, used by observers, was simply a refinement of the 1908 Berthier, for which Vickers bought rights in 1923. The Browning guns are discussed later under the USA.

In France two indigenous guns went into general service in 7.5mm (0.295in) calibre, namely the gas-operated Darne and recoil-operated MAC 1934. Both were belt-fed, the belt often being packed in a drum, and the fast-firing (1,700-round per minute) Darne was used by observers as well as in fixed installations. Neither the guns nor the calibre survived World War II by any appreciable time.

In Germany the standard rifle calibre remained fixed at 7.92mm (0.312in), and gun development thrived despite the ineffectual restrictions of the Allied Control Commission. Oddly, it was a Swiss gun of 1929, the Solothurn M29, which via the MG30 led in 1932 to the MG15, or in Rheinmetall factory parlance the T6-220. It was an unusually neat weapon, looking like a piece of pipe (perforated over the barrel casing) with a 75-round saddle drum clipped on top, feeding alternately from left and right. There was also a T6-200 model for fixed installations, fed from either side by a distintegrating-link belt. The original design had a closed bolt, but to avoid 'cook offs' in an infantry version the action was modified to hold the bolt open. Almost all MG15 production from 1935 until 1942 was of the hand-aimed observer gun, with a pistol grip at the extreme rear and various sight systems. Without magazine or link bag a typical weight was 7.14kg (15.75lb), and length 1,079mm (42.5in). Typical cyclic rate was 1,000 rounds per minute and muzzle velocity 760m (2,493ft) per minute. The MG15 was the standard Luftwaffe observer gun until 1942, some installations (e.g. some Junkers Ju 88A-4s) having four on separate ball/socket mounts all reloaded and fired by just one very hard-pressed man!

In the MG17 for fixed installations the action was modified back to the Solothurn original, the bolt being locked by small rollers (a 'cook off' being considered no problem in fighters).

Below: Boulton Paul Defiant Mk Is. This two-seat fighter was based on the erroneous idea that a turret with four 0.303in Brownings would suffice as the armament of a day fighter. After summer 1940 the Defiant achieved limited success as a night fighter.

Above: After 1941 all US heavy bombers were defended by guns of at least 0.5in calibre. Most B-24 Liberators had a Consolidated tail turret with two 0.5in weapons. Other turrets were produced by Martin, Emerson, Motor Products and Boulton Paul.

Right: Douglas SBD Dauntless dive-bombers during the invasion of Saipan in June 1944. Each has one 1,000lb and two 500lb bombs (the wing bombs were usually of 100lb size). Each SBD had two 0.5in fixed and two 0.3in guns, the latter aimed by the observers.

Below: A classic piston-engine fighter, the Focke-Wulf Fw 190A-8 had two 13mm MG131s in the fuselage, two 20mm MG151/20s in the roots and two MG151/20s in the outer wings, the last replaceable by twin MG151 underwing packs.

Fighter firepower: Fw 190A-8

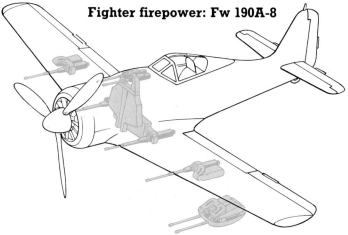

This facilitated synchronization with the engine. The feed was always a link belt, typically of 250 rounds. Without the pneumatic cocking and solenoid firing system a typical fixed MG17 weighed 12.5kg (27.56lb) and was 1,213mm (47.75in) long, the firing rate and muzzle velocity being as on the MG15 (cyclic rate rising to 1,100 rounds per minute when unsynchronized). Production continued until 1942.

In 1925 the great Mauser firm began designing the action of what became the superb MG34 infantry machine gun. This interested the Luftwaffe, and in 1939 production began of the MG81, using the same action but in a much shorter and lighter gun in the standard 7.92mm calibre. Compared with the MG15 and 17 the MG81 was much lighter (6.3kg, 13.87lb), handier, faster-firing (1,500 rounds per minute) and cost less than half as much to produce. Feed was by a steel link belt which always remained intact for refilling. As the neatest and smallest machine-gun ever used in aircraft, the MG81 was often installed in twin or even quad mountings, all aimed and fired by a single pistol grip. There were also a few fixed installations, but after 1943 the Luftwaffe showed little interest in calibres less than 20mm, recognizing (what may to some extent have been forgotten today) that firepower counts in the pressing conditions of real warfare.

In 1933 Louis Stange, at the Rheinmetall works, began the design of a totally new gun in 13mm (0.512in) calibre, and from 1938 this was produced in large numbers as the MG131, a standard fixed and free gun of the Luftwaffe. It had a rotating bolt, but its most notable feature was that the ammunition (five varieties) was fired electrically. This method made perfect synchronization possible, and was later judged essential for weapons of the largest calibres. The MG131 weighed 17kg (37.47lb), was recoil operated and fed from a disintegrating belt at 900 rounds per minute. Muzzle velocity was 710m (2,330ft) per second for AP and 750m (2,461ft) per second for ball ammunition. It was used in remotely controlled barbettes (as in the Messerschmitt Me 410) and in single, twin and quad turrets, as well as being fixed in many fighters.

In Italy the standard guns were the Vickers (fixed), Revelli (movable) and SAFAT, in either 7.5mm or 7.7mm calibre. In 1930 SAFAT was acquired by Fiat from the Breda company, and in World War II the Breda-SAFAT guns were virtually the only Italian machine-guns, in 8mm (0.315in) and 12.7mm (0.5in)

calibres. Both guns had belt feed, recoil operation and a rate of about 800 rounds per minute, respective weights being 12.5kg (27.6lb) and 28kg (61.7lb).

In Japan the Imperial army and navy used different weapons. The army machine guns were: the Type 89 (year 2589, our 1929), a light gas-operated 7.7mm weapon for observers, weighing 7kg (20lb) and fed from a 69-round drum at 750 rounds per minute; the Type 89 Model 2, almost identical to the Vickers 7.7mm, with disintegrating link belt feed at 900 rounds per minute; the Type 98, a copy of the MG15, retaining the German gun's calibre of 7.92mm; and the Ho-103, a 12.7mm weapon derived from the 0.5in Browning but rather lighter at 21.8kg (48lb), used in fixed and free installations fed from a disintegrating link belt at 900 rounds per minute. The navy guns were: the Type 92 (year 1932), an observer gun copied from the Lewis in 7.7mm; the Type 97, based on the Vickers 7.7mm but uprated to 1,000 rounds per minute; the Type 1, based on the MG15 and thus a 7.92mm weapon almost identical to the army Type 98; the 13.0mm Type 2, an observer gun copied from the German MG131, with identical characteristics; and the 13.2mm (0.52in) Type 3, a fixed gun weighing 30kg (66lb) and firing from a link belt at 800 rounds per minute.

In the terrible civil war surrounding the birth of the Soviet Union guns were used from every source available. Gradually the situation stabilized and by 1928 two aircraft guns were in production, both in 7.62mm calibre. The PV-1 (Pulyemet Vozdushnyi, or machine gun, aerial) was derived from the Vickers, weighing 14.5kg (32lb) and firing from a belt (fabric, then from 1932 metal links) at 780 rounds per minute. The DA (Degtyaryev Avyatsiya, or Degtyaryev aviation) was a locally designed observer gun, based on a neat gas-operated infantry weapon fed at 550 rounds per minute from a 47-round drum. In 1932 a superb new gun by B.G. Shpital'nyi passed its tests: this was the ShKAS (Shpital'nyi-Komarnitskii Avyatsionnyi Skorostrel'nyi, or Shpital'nyi-Komarnitskii aviation fast-firing). Thanks to lightweight action and brilliant design it weighed only 18kg (22lb), and fired 7.62mm ammunition from a link belt at 1,800 rounds per minute. This was the first of a long series of guns by different designers that have consistently put the Soviet Union ahead of the rest of the world. The next was the superb 12.7mm weapon designed by M.Ye.Beresin and put into service in 1940. Recoil-operated with gas assistance, it was much more compact than the Browning of the same calibre, but had higher performance. The UB (Universal'nyi Beresin) weighed 21.5kg (47.39lb) and fired 1,000 rounds per minute with a muzzle velocity of 860m (2,822ft) per second. Other versions weighed up to 25kg (55lb), including the UBS (synchronized), UBT (turret) and UBK (wing mounted) versions. Ahead of other countries the Soviet Union recognized that machine-guns simply lacked adequate firepower, and though the Beresin is still found on helicopters no new machine gun was developed for aircraft until the four-barrel 12.7mm helicopter gun listed in Section III.

There were at least 14 other types of machine gun developed by most other European countries and elsewhere in the world before 1950. The only make to achieve wide export sales was the Danish Madsen, a simple recoil belt-fed gun made in several calibres all firing at about 1,000 rounds per minute.

Cannon

Perhaps the best-known cannon of the period was the 'Hispano'. The full name of the company was Hispano-Suiza, meaning Spanish-Swiss, though the main factory was soon moved from Barcelona to Paris. Marc Birkigt, the famed Swiss founder, designed the aircraft engines in World War I which mounted the 37mm Hotchkiss-Puteaux cannon firing through the propeller hub. He was unimpressed by the gun, and in 1932 got round to designing a fully automatic cannon which he rightly thought would prove a best-seller. He did not hesitate to copy the best features of rival weapons, and he adopted the 20mm ammunition already in use with the Oerlikon F-series (a gun made under licence as the Hispano-Suiza Types 7 and 9), and almost exactly the same 60-round drum. The action, however, was quite different, a gas piston being used to push back two side plates and unlock the breechblock, which was then moved by blowback action. The result was light, efficient, reliable, fast-firing and perfectly designed for mass-production. Moreover the gun's power was much greater than that of the Oerlikon, muzzle velocity rising to around 800m (2,625ft) per second compared with about 550m (1,640ft) per second, at the cost of considerably greater gun barrel length and weight. On test in early 1935 prototypes performed so brilliantly that the French air ministry put a security clamp on the gun and on Birkigt. The latter, however, knew just about everyone, and within weeks the British Air Ministry was clamouring for a gun to test.

The request was eventually granted, and the upshot was that in 1937 Hispano-Suiza set up a British subsidiary, British MARC (Manufacturing and Research Co) at Grantham, solely to make the HS.404 cannon. As early as 1935 the British Air Ministry issued a specification (F.37/35) for a fighter to carry four 20mm cannon; this formidable armament was considered too heavy for any single-engined aircraft and the result was the Westland Whirlwind. By 1939 the Mk I gun was in production for a growing number of RAF fighters. In wing installations no change was envisaged to the drum magazine, but in the big Bristol Beaufighter the observer had access to the breeches and so racks were provided for 16 ammunition drums, four for each gun. Clearly this was a ludicrous arrangement. In night-fighters it made the observer leave his vital radar display, undo his harness and, possibly during violent manoeuvres, unlatch massive drums and exchange full for empty ones. Obviously the observer could not serve all four guns

Above: In the Hawker Typhoon Mk IB the four Hispano Mk II cannon had smooth fairings over the projecting barrels, early Mk IBs having had exposed barrels (like those of the Hurricane) with little effect on low-level speed.

simultaneously, so once the first drums were empty there could never be more than two or three guns firing at once. The Bristol Aeroplane Co designed a neat recoil-operated sprocket feed for a belt, but the British armament experts said it would not work. Just before France fell, in June 1940, two French officers escaped with drawings of a French Chatellerault belt feed. This was adopted at once, but it took until September 1941 to get it on the 401st Beaufighter off the line. When Bristol saw the French feed they realized that it was identical to their own rejected design, except that it withdrew rounds by pushing the nose instead of pulling the case. This caused problems with pointed AP rounds, so it was modified to make it exactly like the Bristol feed — which could have been on the first Beaufighter! Subsequently the belt feed became standard on later marks of Hispano, and from the Mk V the barrel was shortened to fit more easily inside fighter wings. Data for the most numerous (Mk II) gun include: length 2,360mm (92.9in), weight 43kg (95lb), cyclic rate 600 rounds

Left: An experimental Hawker Tempest Mk V, NV768 had a Napier Sabre IIB engine with an annular radiator. Usually it was unarmed, but in this picture it has four Hispano Mk Vs, two with projecting muzzles.

Right: A Bristol Beaufighter Mk IF in Malta. The red-doped fabric under the fuselage covers the 20mm Hispano cannon muzzles, while six 0.303in Browning MGs are fixed in the outer wings.

Below: PZ865, a Mk IIC, was the last and most famous of the Hurricanes. Note the unfaired barrels of the Hispano Mk II cannon in the wings.

Above: Final Hawker piston-engined fighter, the Sea Fury FB.Mk 11 had Tempest outer wings with the same short-barrel Hispano Mk V cannon. The ammunition feed blisters reveal the rear location of the gun breeches.

automatically at about 100 rounds per minute, the gunner being able to release the trigger after single shots. In the 1920s it was used as an offensive observer gun in several aircraft, for use particularly against bombers and submarines. It was also installed in fixed oblique mounts, firing upwards at 55|, in the Vickers and Westland fighters built to specification F.29/27. By this time (1930) the gun and its installations had become Vickers-Armstrongs products, and Vickers devised a 50-round feed box for its own fighter. In the Westland a 39-round drum dispensed rounds into a trough from which (in the heat of combat) the pilot had to grasp them and load them into the gun. What the author finds even stranger is that not only had British interest in weapons bigger than 0.303in calibre almost evaporated by 1932 but, despite the extensive British experience with upward-firing cannon in World War I and later, such armament used in Luftwaffe night-fighters in World War II was greeted with total disbelief by British intelligence as if it were a bizarre new idea! Thus, over 20,000 British heavy bombers were sent over Germany with a front turret, a mid-upper turret and a tail turret, but a defenceless belly, without even a small window through which the crew might have seen the upward-firing Messerschmitt Bf 110s and Junkers Ju 88s!

The last installations of the Vickers-COW gun were in a Bristol Blenheim I and Short Sunderland for use against U-boats (a scheme was studied in which two guns were aimed down through the big flying-boat's planing bottom, via watertight doors). By 1941 Vickers had completed the prototype of an improved gun of 40mm calibre known as the Type S, able to be installed in underwing pods with a 15-round belt feed. In April 1941 the Air Staff sanctioned a tank-busting Hawker Hurricane (Mk IID), and this was produced both with the Vickers S and with a rival (and in some ways better) 40mm gun developed by the Rolls-Royce Car Division at Crewe. The Rolls-Royce BF gun used the same armour-piercing ammunition with 12-round feed. In both versions of the Hurricane IID two 0.303in Brownings were used with a heavy loading of tracer ammunition for sighting purposes.

In April 1941 the versatile de Havilland Mosquito was selected to carry the Molins 6-pounder anti-tank gun, the basic gun installed being just as used by the army but with an automatic feed of 25 rounds of the 57mm AP ammunition. The objective was to pierce U-boats, and the resulting Mosquito XVIII proved able to fire with great accuracy. Amazingly, even the giant 3.7in (32-pounder) AA gun was considered for installation in the 'Mossie', with the complex Galliot muzzle brake! After 1945 German projects convinced the Air Staff that giant recoilless guns were worth trying, and the Royal Armament Research and Development Establishment at Fort Halstead developed a gun of 4.5in (114.3mm) calibre, to be installed in a fighter with one round 'up the spout' and seven more fed from a rotary drum magazine. The basic gun, with recoil-cancelling rear jetpipe, weighed a mere 1,440lb (653kg), or 140lb (63.5kg) less than the much smaller 6-pounder. Known only as the RCL (ReCoilLess), this impressive gun was never fired. Instead, British fighters were armed with the 30mm Aden which is described later on in the main part of this book.

per minute, muzzle velocity 880m (2,890ft) per second and recoil force 5,000kg (11,025lb). All seven types of projectile weigh around 138g (4.87oz). The Mk V gun is 2,052mm long and weighs 42kg with feed system, and maximum rate of fire is 640 rounds per minute.

Total production of 20mm Hispanos at Grantham was close to 99,000, and a further 134,663 were made under licence as the very similar M1 and M2 by US industry during World War II, plus over 50 million rounds of ammunition. A total of 32,426 guns were converted as T31 (locked bolt). Later HS guns are included in the main section of this book.

Much smaller numbers were made of another French design, the 25mm Hotchkiss. This gas-operated cannon was designed in 1928 and in its final form weighed 70kg (164lb) and fired at 180 rounds per minute from 10-round clips.

The massive British COW (Coventry Ordnance Works) 37mm gun was mentioned in the preceding section. Weighing 140lb (63kg), it fired clips of five or six rounds fully

DEVELOPING THE TECHNOLOGY

In the USA the Marlin was important in 1917-40 in both fixed and free installations in Army aircraft. Designed by the great Carl Swebilius, this 0.3in (7.7mm) gas-operated modification of the M1895 Colt weighed 22lb (10kg) and was fed from 250-round belts. Nevertheless, the Browning in both 0.3in and 0.5in calibres gradually became absolutely standard, and in World War II these guns were made in vast numbers (over 2,000,000 for the bigger weapon and a rather greater quantity for the rifle-calibre models). The basic lock followed the traditional Browning mechanism, recoil driving the barrel and locked breech block to the rear, the breech then being unlocked after a short travel and being flung aft by an accelerator before striking a rear buffer. Early guns had fabric belts with metal ends, but in the 1920s the lightweight aircraft guns switched to metal links. Standard ammunition was rimless 0.3in (or in British service rimmed 0.303in) and 0.5in, all the Brownings being capable of modification for fixed, fixed synchronized, hand-aimed or turreted installation. The rifle-calibre Browning weighed 24-26lb (10.9-11.8kg), had a length always close to 40in (1,020mm) and usually fired at 1,200 rounds per minute. The 0.5in gun weighed no less than 64lb (29kg) in fixed versions and about 68lb (30.9kg) in free models, was 54-57in (1,370-1,448mm) long and fired various kinds of projectile weighing 1.7oz (49g) compared with 0.5oz (14.5g) for the 0.3in weapon. Firing rate was 550-650 rounds per minute in early guns, rising to 800 rounds per minute in World War II and to 1,200 rounds per minute by 1948.

Among the several experimental US guns of World War II the only model produced in quantity was the 0.6in (15.24mm) weapon. This began as a copy of the first German MG151/15 to be captured, but after much unnecessary redesign it had become far inferior to the German original, and in particular lost all its reliability. Some thousands of the type were made in 1943, but the type was not released for service. There were also various 0.9in (22.8mm) cannon in the Army's T2 series, weighing 240lb (108.9kg) without the 48-round drum. On the other hand the Navy's 1.1in (27.94mm) weapon, which resembled the German MK103, and the 37mm guns produced by the AAC (American Armament Corporation) all failed to be accepted. The AAC cannon was derived in 1933 from the 1916 Puteaux with a very short barrel, for use in free or turreted installations. The action and ammunition were identical with those of the French original, the weight being 250lb (113.4kg) and the muzzle velocity a useless 1,250ft (381m) per second. All the projectile types weighed 1.1lb (500g) fed in clips of five, and the rate of fire was 90 or 100 rounds per minute.

Much more important, the Browning (Colt) was made in 37mm calibre as the M4, later refined as the M9 which was produced in quantity by the Oldsmobile division of General Motors. The M4 weighed only 248lb (112kg) and fired at 150 rounds per minute from a 30-round drum. The weapon was used in the Lockheed P-38 and Bell P-39 fighters, while some fighters of the 1940 vintage were intended to carry four or even six of these substantial cannon: for example the McDon-

nell XP-67 was to have had six, each with 45 rounds, in the Vultee XP-54 the entire nose was pivoted to assist aiming, while in the Curtiss XP-87 the battery of guns (37 or 20mm) could be aimed by remote control anywhere in the forward hemisphere, a reflection on the poor manoeuvrability of the fighter itself.

Biggest of the US guns was the modified 75mm (2.95in) M4 field gun, installed in the North American B-25G. This 900lb (408kg) piece of ordnance was loaded with single 15lb (6.8kg) rounds by the navigator/cannoneer from a 21-round magazine. To keep recoil forces modest the whole gun recoiled an awesome 21in (533mm). In the B-25H the gun was the lighter and more efficient T13E1 pattern, specially designed for aircraft.

In Germany there appeared a wealth of aircraft cannon between the world wars, including the Semag, Szakats, Lubbe, two Rheinmetalls, the Erhardt and a whole family of Krieghoffs. The first pattern adopted for the Luftwaffe was the 20mm Rheinmetall MG c30/L, based on the army Flak 30, weighing 95kg (209.4lb) with 100-round drum and firing 350 rounds per minute at the very high muzzle velocity of 950m (3,117ft) per second. Around 1937 a development of this gun, the Lb 204 (ST-11), followed it into limited service on the Dornier Do 18E and Blohm & Voss Bv 138 with weight reduced (at expense of muzzle velocity) and firing rate raised to 400 rounds per minute.

In 1935 the MG FF series was adopted as the standard Luftwaffe 20mm cannon, replacing the types just mentioned. They derived from the Becker, via Semag and the Swiss firm of

Below: Based on analysis of an aircraft captured by the Germans, this artwork shows the cones of fire for the defensive guns of a B-17F, which for the 1942-3 period was notably well protected.

Above: The Fiat G.55 was the best Italian fighter produced in quantity during World War II. This prototype has a single MG151 and two Breda-SAFAT 12.7mm weapons. Two wing MG151s were later added.

Boeing B-17F defensive armament and fields of fire

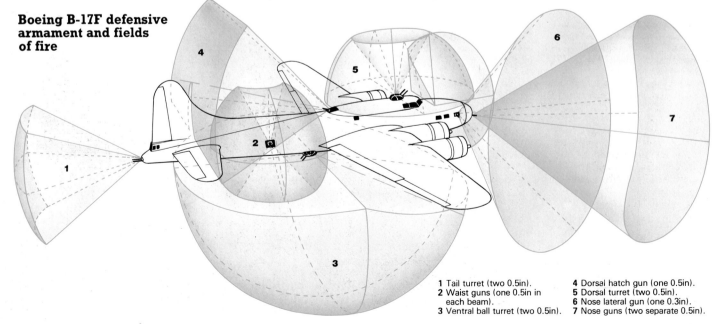

1 Tail turret (two 0.5in).
2 Waist guns (one 0.5in in each beam).
3 Ventral ball turret (two 0.5in).
4 Dorsal hatch gun (one 0.5in).
5 Dorsal turret (two 0.5in).
6 Nose lateral gun (one 0.3in).
7 Nose guns (two separate 0.5in).

Evolution of the bomber 1921-40

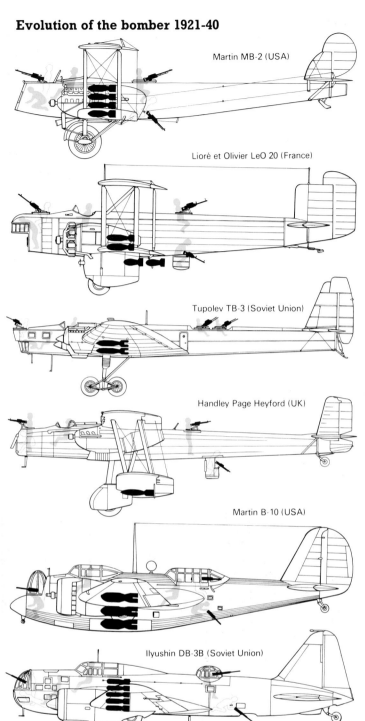

Martin MB-2 (USA)

Lioré et Olivier LeO 20 (France)

Tupolev TB-3 (Soviet Union)

Handley Page Heyford (UK)

Martin B-10 (USA)

Ilyushin DB-3B (Soviet Union)

Above: These drawings show how the basic concept for the bomber remained unaltered in the 20 years after World War I. Development concentrated instead on the aircraft itself. Thus while fabric-skinned biplanes gave way to stressed-skin monoplanes with many refinements, the basic arrangement of bombs, plus nose, dorsal and ventral machine guns, remained unaltered. The only unusual features in this selection are the twin dorsal gunners of the TB-3, and the Heyford's stowage of bombs in the thick lower wing. While the LeO 20 and Heyford had 'dustbin' ventral turrets, the B-10 (first of the sleek modern bombers) introduced the enclosed turret. Later bombers had power-operated turrets.

Oerlikon-Bührle, where the main development had been done in the 1920s. A very light and simple blowback weapon, the FF was produced by Ikaria-Werke of Berlin, and though initially there were three distinct models all the German Ikaria FFs were very similar. Feed was from a drum or box magazine, and about 99% of Luftwaffe guns used the T-6 drum of 60 rounds. Charging/cocking was electropneumatic and firing control electric, though standard percussion-cap ammunition was used. Typical data included: weight 28kg (61.7lb), length 1341mm (52.8in), firing rate 520-530 rounds per minute, and muzzle velocity 585m (1,919ft) per second. There were no production turreted installations, but very many fixed and free (hand-aimed) applications.

Subsequently more aircraft guns were developed in wartime Germany than at any other time or place. Most were designated according to a system in which guns up to 20mm were called MG (Maschinengewehr), guns over 20mm MK (Maschinenkanone) and large guns derived from ground artillery BK (Bordkanone). Originally the numerical suffix indicated the type of gun: thus, MG81 meant machine gun, 8 (7.92) mm, type 1, and MG151/20 meant first type of 15mm gun converted to 20mm calibre. From 1942 this system became unworkable, and in the new system a three-figure numeral was used, the first denoting maker (1 Rheinmetall, 2 Mauser, 3 Krieghoff, 4 Krupp) and the next two numbers being just a numerical sequence. The following text mixes up all systems in order to follow a strict numerical order.

The BK 3,7 was the 37mm Flak 18 anti-aircraft gun modified for use from aircraft such as the Junkers Ju 87G in the anti-

Below: Another World War II picture shows an SBD attacking Vunakanau airfield at Rabaul. The pilot had access to the breeches of the twin 'fifties' while the rear gunner had only twin 'thirties'.

Above: Loading the twin Breda-SAFAT 12.7mm machine guns of a Macchi M.C.202, the best Italian fighter of World War II to see wide service. Some also had 7.7mm wing guns and underwing MG151s.

DEVELOPING THE TECHNOLOGY

armour role. This Rheinmetall gun had a rotating bolt head, recoil operation and automatic fire from a six-round clip inserted from the side. Weight was 295kg (650lb), length 3,277mm (129in), muzzle velocity 798m (2,620ft) per second, and firing rate 180 rounds per minute for 2 seconds.

The BK 5 was an outstanding 50mm weapon for use against armour. Though a ponderous load at 531kg (1,170lb), it was far lighter than any previous gun with similar performance, the muzzle energy of each shot being 73 tonne-metres and muzzle velocity no less than 917m (3,010ft) per second. There was no normal breech; instead the mighty rounds were picked from an endless permanently attached 22-round belt and fed by a system of solenoid-governed pneumatic rammers, the breech being briefly locked by a small vertically sliding block. The rate of fire was 48-50 rounds per minute. The distantly related BK 7,5 was the most powerful gun ever installed in aircraft; indeed it was too much for the Henschel Hs 129 and Junkers Ju 88P, and even strained the Heinkel He 177A-3/R5! The gun weighed about 1,000kg (2,205lb), and fired a 3.3kg (7.28lb) AP shell at 933m (3,060ft) per second.

The MK101, first gun to have a 1942 designation, was an aviation derivative of the Rheinmetall (Solothurn) S-18 anti-tank gun, but scaled up from 20 to 30mm. It used a new high-velocity cartridge giving its AP round a muzzle velocity of up to 960m (3,150ft) per second, other projectiles being slower. The action used a typical lock-ring. Gun weight was 180kg (397lb), length 2,592mm (102in) and firing rate 250 rounds per minute from a 30-round drum.

The MK103 was one of the best and most important guns in the world in 1943-45. Rheinmetall derived it from the MK101 but it soon became a totally new weapon, with gas operation, sheet-steel construction, a recoiling barrel with horizontally moving locking lugs on swinging links, and left or right feed of 30mm ammunition with electric priming. The weight was 141kg (311lb), length without muzzle brake 2,350mm (92.5in), muzzle velocity 790 to 960m (2,592 to 3,150ft) per second (AP Tracer 860m, 2,822ft per second) and rate of fire 420 rounds per minute.

G 104 (Gerät, device 104) was the biggest gun ever fitted to aircraft. It was in effect a plain tube, open at both ends, with calibre of 365mm (14.37in). Without the streamlined weather-proof nose cap the length was about 10m (32.8ft). Roughly amidships was a reinforced breech section, wherein was installed a large armour-piercing shell and, behind it, a heavy metal shellcase housing two booster charges and two main propellant charges. The gun was to be housed inside the Junkers Ju 288G, and swung out on parallel arms beneath the aircraft for firing. With the aircraft diving at its target (such as a fort or ship) the gun was fired electrically, the shell's muzzle velocity being 470m (1,036ft) per second and the case departing to the rear, cancelling recoil, at 476m (1,050ft) per second. Large muzzle brakes at each end deflected gas blast sideways away from the fuselage. The barrel had right-hand rifling, both shell and case being pre-engraved.

The MK108 was a brilliant Rheinmetall compromise and made it possible for devastating, but quite low-velocity, ammunition to be fired from a compact lightweight gun able to fire through propeller hubs or be installed in multiple. Rounds were drawn from a disintegrating belt, usually with 60 links, the empty cases being reseated in the same links and emerging on the side opposite to the feed. The gun was made of cheap welded stampings and fired pneumatically from the rear-seared position, with electric ignition and simple blowback operation. The barrel was a mere 584mm (23in)

long, of which only 440mm projected, overall length being 1,050mm (41.3in). Gun weight was typically 60kg (132lb), rate of fire 600 rounds per minute and muzzle velocity 505m (1,660ft) per second.

The MK112 was if anything even more impressive, because in effect Rheinmetall just scaled up the MK108 to a calibre of 55mm (2.17in)! Each projectile weighed 1.5kg (3.31lb), had a muzzle velocity of 595m (1,951ft) per second and contained 420g (0.93lb) of explosive. The gun, 12 prototypes of which were tested, weighed 274kg (605lb) in final form and had a rate of fire of 300 rounds per minute. Overall length was 2,032mm (80in).

The SG113 was a novel Rheinmetall/Unterlüss recoilless gun intended to fire downwards at tanks or, in a few installations, upwards at bombers. Simpler than the G 104, it had a calibre of 77mm (3.03in) and each 1,580mm (62.2in) barrel contained a propellant charge, 45mm sabot AP projectile and rear counterweight, the two end-pieces being joined through the charge by means of a weak-link screwed rod. The empty 'gun' weighed 47.9kg (105.6lb) and muzzle velocity was 645m (2,116ft) per second. Focke-Wulf Fw 190F-8s had a pair well out on each wing.

The MK114 was a gun of tremendous power spurred by the need to engage bombers at ranges beyond their own defensive guns. Another Rheinmetall development, it was a great challenge because alloy steels were prohibited! Data included a calibre of 55mm, a projectile of 2kg (4.4lb) fired with muzzle velocity of 1,050m (3,446ft) per second, and a gun weight and length 700kg (1,543lb) and 3,480mm (137in). The type was a gas-operated gun and feeder, with sliding vertical wedge breech, with rate of fire of 150 rounds per minute.

The MK115 was a brilliant attempt to get MK114 performance with less shattering recoil and gun weight. Rheinmetall achieved a near-recoilless weapon with high rate of fire (300 rounds per minute) from a belt feed by designing a cartridge of 55mm calibre with a length of 0.5m (19.7in), the main length of whose cartridge case was made of compressed nitrated cardboard. When the round was fired the case vanished, admitting gas to the gun-operating piston underneath and (via a big upper pipe) to a divergent ejector nozzle at the rear to equalize the recoil forces. Despite this, muzzle velocity was 600m (1,969ft) per second. The gun was 3.3m (129.9in) long and weighed 180kg (396.8lb).

The SG116 (Sonder Gerät, or special device) was another multi-barrel recoilless weapon developed at the Hermann Goering Werke with Rheinmetall assistance. The normal form comprised an MK103 30mm barrel firing a 'mine shell' whose recoil counterbalanced by firing a steel slug out of an open rear barrel. In some Fw 190A-8s there were two rows of three SG116s aft of the cockpit, set at 72.5°, 73° and 74° on each

Right: A Junkers Ju 87R seen in service with the Italian Gruppo Tuffatori in winter 1940-1. This bomber could carry an SC500 (1,102lb) bomb, but was effective only against indifferent opposition.

Below: The sole Me 262A-1a which was test flown with the mighty Rheinmetall BK 5. Single shots were fired because of the huge smoke cloud produced by each round.

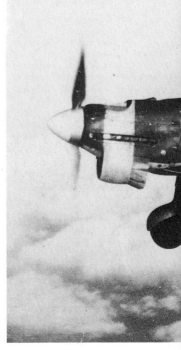

Above: The first production Bell P-59A-1, an advanced development of the XP-59A which was the USA's first jet aircraft. The armament was unusual: production machines had one 37mm (longest barrel) and three 0.5in weapons.

Left: All early variants of the Bf 110 had four 7.92mm MG17 machine guns in the upper part of the nose, and usually two 20mm MG FF cannon below them. The 7.92mm ammunition feeds can be seen in this crashed example.

Right: The ultimate Bf 110 night fighter was the G-4d/R3, seen here with low-drag SN-2 radar and other sensors. The nose armament was two 30mm MK108s above and two 20mm MG151s below, a vastly more effective combination than that of the original model.

side, triggered by a photocell as the fighter streaked past 50m (165ft) beneath a bomber, with 0.03-second delay between pairs of tubes. Each 'gun' weighed 32kg (70.6lb) and had a muzzle velocity of 860m (2,822ft) per second.

The SG117 was yet another cluster from Rheinmetall, this time consisting of seven MK108 barrels forming a giant 'pepperbox' and fitted behind an Fw 190 cockpit to fire at 75°. Each shot (muzzle velocity 505m, 1,657ft per second) pushed the whole installation downwards, its motion firing successive barrels at 0.0001-second intervals. The photocell trigger was in the cockpit. Two of these Rohrblöcke (tube blocks) were fitted to each fighter.

The SG118 and SG119 used the same SG117-type Rohrblöcke. The SG118 grouped three in a 21-barrel drum, two of which were to be installed firing ahead in the Heinkel He 162A, with SG117s under the wings. The pilot could select any group of Rohrblöcke, and thus could salvo 56 shells virtually simultaneously. The SG119 was a big (400mm, 15.75in diameter and 640mm, 2.1ft length) drum containing seven Rohrblöcke, giving a 49-shot salvo. Loaded weight was 200kg (441lb) and recoil about 6,000kg (13,228lb).

The MG151 was the most important Luftwaffe gun of World War II. Development started in 15mm calibre during 1935, the gun at the Mauser works at Oberndorf and special high-velocity electrically fired ammunition at DWM Lübeck. The action was by recoil and abounded in outstanding new features, with disintegrating link belt feed from either side

DEVELOPING THE TECHNOLOGY

and electric cocking. The long barrel resulted in a muzzle velocity of 850m (2,789ft) per second for AP shot and 960m (3,150ft) per second for ball, with very flat trajectory. Gun length was 1917mm (75.5in) and weight 42kg (92.6lb), firing rate being 700 rounds per minute. From late 1940 the gun was used in the Messerschmitt Bf 109F, but by 1938 it had been overtaken in development by a 20mm version with much greater destructive power. Still known as the MG151 (initially with suffix /20) this cannon was used in the majority of German combat aircraft until 1944. Weight remained 42kg, length was reduced to 1,767mm (69.6in), firing rate rose to 700-780 rounds per minute, and muzzle velocity fell slightly to 720-790m (2,362-2,592ft) per second. Belts came in multiples of 50 rounds. Synchronized, hand-aimed and turret installations were common.

The MG213 was a family of excellent guns resulting from a 1942 demand for a 20mm gun firing 1,000 rounds per minute with a muzzle velocity of 1,000m (3,281ft) per second. Hasag worked on high-performance electrically fired ammunition, while Mauser led on the gun. Development began using Krieghoff (MG301) action, but via several intermediate stages led in 1944 to the MG213C using the radical revolver principle. Devised by Anton Pölitzer (who was influenced by the Soviet ShKAS), this split the feed into three consecutive actions: stripping from the link, feeding into one of five chambers in a revolving cylinder, and presentation into the barrel. Case ejection was directly to the rear. This greatly speeded up rate of fire while reducing velocities and stresses, making possible use of inferior materials. The gun was gas-operated, pneumatically cocked and electrically fired. The calibre was soon changed from 20mm to 30mm (designation and specification remaining unchanged) and 10 prototypes were tested, one battery of four being fitted under a Bf 110C at Tarnewitz, initially 20mm with 120 rounds per gun, and later 30mm with up to 100 rounds per gun. Rate of fire was 1,400 rounds per minute in 20mm size, with a muzzle velocity of 1,050m (3,445ft) per second and 1,200 rounds per minute in 30mm size with muzzle velocity reduced to 530-570m (1,739-1,870ft) per second depending on type of projectile. In each case recoil force was 1200kg (2,646lb). This gun was the starting point for almost every new aircraft gun developed outside the Soviet Union after 1945.

The MK214 was a Mauser development, started in 1943, to convert the KwK39/1 tank gun to automatic fire for aircraft use. The result was an impressive 50mm weapon with simple recoil action, belt feed and a large muzzle brake. Initial cocking was by hand, followed by electric firing with pneumatic forward return of the recoiling barrel. Gun weight was 490kg (1,080lb), each round weighing 3.8kg (8.38lb) with a 1.54kg (3.4lb) projectile, and the overall length of the MK214A was 4.0m (13.12ft).

The MG301 was a Krieghoff 20mm gun with gas operation and electric ignition. It weighed 55kg (121lb) and fired at 1,000 rounds per minute with a muzzle velocity of 1,000m (3,281ft) per second.

The MK303 was a Czech (Brno) cannon developed in 1940 by Krieghoff. Gas-operated, it fired 30mm ammunition at 900 rounds per minute with a muzzle velocity of almost 1,000m (3,281ft) per second.

The MK412 was the only Krupp aircraft gun, firing 300 rounds per minute of 55mm ammunition with a muzzle velocity of 700m (2,300ft) per second.

Not fitting into any scheme, the HF15 was a unique gun invented by Schlitter in Hungary and developed by Gustloff Suhl Reichswerk. It comprised a single barrel with an enlarged chamber into which was loaded a single cartridge. The latter consisted of seven to nine projectiles, the centre one aligned with the 15mm barrel and the others wrapped tightly round it. After electric ignition the propellant fired all projectiles in succession, at a cyclic rate equivalent to 36,000 rounds per minute! The muzzle velocity, initially 1,000m (3,281ft) per second, fell towards the end of the burst. The designation meant Hohe Feuerfolge (high fire-follow).

After such a wealth of German guns everything seems anticlimax, but in fact the Soviet cannon were outstanding. Sadly, even today little is known of the experimental patterns, only of those produced in quantity being openly revealed. By far the most numerous, the 20mm (ShVAK (Shpital'nyi-Vladimirov

Above: As seen here, the Bristol Beaufort Mk I torpedo bomber had a single 0.303in gun, with four more guns of the same calibre added at a later date.

Below: The Cant Z.1007 bis often had a 12.7mm Breda-SAFAT or Scotti gun in a dorsal turret with a pivoted rod to provide aerodynamic balance for the gun barrel.

Aviatsionnyi Krupnokaliber, Shpital'nyi-Valdimirov aviation heavy calibre) was a neat gas-operated gun cleared for production in 1936. It had several features resembling the HS.404, but in most respects the action was superior and firing rate 800 rounds per minute. Gun length and weight were 1,760mm (69.3in) and 40kg (88lb), and the muzzle velocity 790m (2,592ft) per second. MP was the designation applied to pivoted and turreted versions of this gun, which was almost a scaled-up ShKAS. Almost equally important, because of its armour-piercing capabilities in the Ilyushin Il-2 Stormovik, the 23mm VYa (Volkov-Yartsyev) was a formidable gas-operated gun cleared for production in 1940. Weighing 68kg (150lb), it fired projectiles weighing 200.5g (7.07oz) compared with 96g (3.39oz) for the ShVAK. Moreover, muzzle velocity was no less than 920m (3,018ft) per second, firing rate from a link belt being equally impressive at 600 rounds per minute.

In 1942 the NS-37 entered service. This Nudel'man-Suranov design was not gas-operated but used short recoil. It was fully automatic, firing 37mm projectiles weighing 735g (25.9oz) at a muzzle velocity of 900m (2,953ft) per second and a cyclic rate

Above: The Mitsubishi Ki-46-III Kai was an improvised Japanese interceptor. Note the oblique 37mm Ho-103 as well as twin 20mm Ho-5 nose cannon.

Right: Hitler insisted on use of the Me 262 as a 'Blitz bomber', resulting in the Me 262A-2a with two SC250 (551lb) bombs. The four 30mm MK108 cannon were retained.

Below: Handley Page Halifax Mk II bombers had Boulton Paul nose, dorsal and tail turrets, but no belly protection.

serve in large numbers to this day as the NS-23 (various models for wing/nose, synchronized and turret mounting) and the NR-23 designed with A.Rikhter. The NR family retained Suranov's pneumatic feed but is faster-firing at 850 rather than 550 rounds per minute, the muzzle velocity remaining 690m (2,264ft) per second. Gun weight was a mere 37kg (81.5lb) for the NS and 39kg (86lb) for the NR, so both cannon are much lighter than the 20mm Hispano which has only 35% as much muzzle horsepower.

In Italy the only cannon of note was the German MG151/20, though there were prototype installations of the outstanding 1928-designed Scotti (the action of which was 'borrowed' by Hispano) and of the relatively primitive Breda CL.20 of the same 20mm calibre, fed by only 12 rounds in a clip. Mention must be made, however, of the Type 90/53 naval gun as an anti-ship weapon for the Piaggio P.108A four-engined bomber. This awesome 102mm (4.02in) weapon was installed at a negative angle (necessitating new firing tables for aiming) and with its long recoil system weighed about 1500kg (3,307lb). Each projectile weighed 13.75kg (30.3lb), and a magazine of 50 was provided, fed into 12-round drums before each firing run. The muzzle velocity was a modest but still useful 700m (2,297ft) per second.

Oldest cannon type in Japanese army air force service, the Type 97 (Ho-1 and Ho-3) was a 20mm gas-operated weapon firing at 400 rounds per minute: the Ho-1 was an observer gun weighing 32.5kg (72lb) with 15-round saddle magazine, and the Ho-3 a fixed gun weighing 43kg (95lb) with 50-round saddle magazine. Unquestionably a scaled-up Browning, the 20mm Type 1 (Ho-5) weighed 32.5kg (72lb) and fired from a belt at 850-960 rounds per minute. Put into production in 1944, the Ho-105 was a 30mm weapon weighing 44kg (97lb) and firing at 450 rounds per minute with a muzzle velocity of 716mm (2,350ft) per second. The 37mm Type 98 was based on the 1916 Hotchkiss and was hand-loaded with 610m (2,000ft) per second shells at the rate of 15 rounds per minute. It led to the Ho-203, weighing 89kg (196lb) compared with the old gun's 134kg (296lb), and firing 576m (1,890ft) per second ammunition from a 25-round box at 120 rounds per minute. The unique Ho-301 was almost a rocket gun because its 40mm shells contained their own propellant charge, expelled through 12 small holes in the base. Muzzle velocity was an unimpressive 232m (760ft) per second, firing rate being 450 rounds per minute; this close-range gun weighed 132kg (291lb).

of 250 rounds per minute. Armour penetration was seldom less than 40mm (1.57in) at 40° strike angle. Scaled up to 45mm in 1944, the resulting NS-45 was only fractionally heavier at 152kg (335lb), but fired 250 rounds per minute of 1.065kg (37.57oz) projectiles at 850m (2,789ft) per second with armour penetration of 58mm (2.28in). Even small Yakovler fighters also carried the mighty OKB-16-57 (57mm designed by OKB-16, i.e. experimental construction bureau 16), but recoil proved excessive. This 290kg (639lb) gun fired 2.78kg (6.13lb) shells with a muzzle velocity of 980m (3,215ft) per second.

In 1945 M.Ye.Beresin introduced improved versions of his UB series 12.7mm guns, and also the very neat B-20 cannon. This 20mm ShVAK replacement was gas-operated from a point well down the barrel. Weighing a mere 25kg (55lb) it fired standard 96g (3.39oz) projectiles at 800 rounds per minute with a muzzle velocity of 800m (2,625ft) per second. It was used in fighters and also in the quintuple twin-turret PV-20 defence system for the Tupolev Tu-4. Also in 1945 the Nudel'man-Suranov team scaled down the 37mm to take standard 23mm rounds and thus began a family of guns which

Above: A USMC Vought F4U-1 'softens up' Okinawa in 1944 with a salvo of 5in rockets. Four 20mm cannon were also carried, and the F4U-1D could lift two 1,000lb bombs.

Left: Seen here during the Korean War, the Boeing B-29 set new standards of defence with remote-control turrets.

Below: The Bristol Beaufighter Mk VIC was first armed with eight 3in rockets in 1942. Coastal 'Beaus' used these against enemy shipping.

The Imperial navy standardized on the 20mm Type 99, which owed much to the Hispano. Early models had a short barrel and 60-round drum, and later patterns had longer barrels and belt feed. Weight ranged from 23kg (51lb) to 37.5kg (82.6lb), and firing rate from 490 to 750 rounds per minute, and the Type 99 was found in fixed and movable variants. The same gun was scaled up to 30mm in the Type 5, with 42-round magazine. Weighing 70kg (154lb), it fired at 400 rounds per minute. Muzzle velocity is unknown.

Rockets

Simple unguided rockets — which in fact proved anything but simple to develop — were pioneered by the Soviet Union, which alone conducted research into such weapons from the 1920-22 civil war onwards. B.S. Petropavlovskii led the design of a missile at the GDL (gas dynamics laboratory) at the Peter and Paul Fortress, Leningrad, in 1929-32. The design featured a single skin of wrapped and welded steel, housing a nose fuze with windmill-unscrewed safety, powder warhead, powder propellant charge, rear divergent nozzle and four fins set at an angle to cause spin for stabilizing the trajectory. In 1933 the programme was transferred to the RNII (reaction-engine research institute) and upgraded to develop three weapons, the RS-75, RS-82 and RS-132, the numbers being the calibre in millimetres. Air firing trials began in April 1936 (first in the world) and in World War II vast numbers were produced: over 2,500,000 of the 82mm (3.23in) size alone. This rocket weighed 6.82kg (15lb) and was 864mm (34in) long. The other mass-produced rocket, the 132mm (5.2in) RS-132, weighed 23.1kg (50.9lb) and was 935mm (36.8in) long. Both were subsonic. By 1950 new designs with supersonic speed had been introduced, including the first 57mm (2.24in) series and the massive RS-182, TRS-190 and ARS-212.

British rockets were important in the Napoleonic wars, but from 1875 testing such weapons was made illegal! Fortunately — because the research took six years — in 1934 A.D. (later Sir Alwyn) Crowe, Director of Ballistic Research at Woolwich Arsenal, suggested the development of cordite rockets. After amazing difficulties a 2in (50.8mm) motor was perfected, and then a 3in (76.2mm) type. In July 1941 work was begun to adapt rockets to aircraft, and the first 3in RP (rocket projectile) was fired from a Beaufighter in October of that year. By late 1942 the 3in motor was in production for aircraft, fired from multiple rail launchers. Standard heads were a 60lb (27.3kg) semi-AP type with a large explosive charge, and a 25lb (11.3kg) solid

head. The former was used generally, while the 25lb 'spear' was used to puncture U-boats. Bigger 3-motor and 7-motor RPs remained experimental.

US aircraft rockets were based on British technology imparted in three reciprocal visits in 1941, plus a pilot production plant shipped from the UK. By late 1942 motors were being produced at Radford (Army), Indian Head (Navy) and Sunflower (Hercules Powder Co). At first the Army Air Force showed no interest, but in 1943 did adopt a version of the M8 4.5in (114mm) weapon for tube-firing from aircraft. This weighed 38.2lb (17.3kg) and was subsonic. A much more powerful 4.5in rocket, weighing 103lb (46.7kg), did not enter service. The Navy was more active, developing the 3.5in (89mm) rocket from late 1941, calling it the FFAR, at that time meaning Forward-Firing Aircraft Rocket. Developed in CalTech, it weighed 54.5lb (24.7kg). In 1944 the 5in (127mm) replaced the 3.5's original solid head with a big 50lb (22.7kg) explosive head. Soon this was followed by the formidable 5in HVAR (High-Velocity Aircraft Rocket), popularly called the Holy Moses. It was supersonic and weighed 134lb (60.8kg). Later in 1944 the fearsome Tiny Tim entered service. This Navy rocket had a calibre of 11.75in (298mm), a length of 10ft 3in (3124mm) and firing weight of 1,284lb (582.4kg). Like the original 5in type Tiny Tim was subsonic, but its 150lb (68kg) explosive charge was very powerful.

Germany put its Nebelwerfer (fog projector) into service as an artillery weapon in 1941. These surprisingly accurate spin-stabilized rockets came in various sizes, and the 210mm (8.27in) pattern was adapted to aircraft use for stand-off kill

Left: Incendiaries stream from a 'Special' Avro Lancaster with the tall masts of ABC (Airborne Cigar) radio jamming equipment. Lancasters delivered over 51.5 million standard incendiaries.

Above: A remarkably clear photograph shows a Japanese ship being hit by aircraft of the 823rd BS, USAAF, in a mast-height attack during June 1944. The 75mm gun of the B-25G/H was often used.

against heavy bombers. One hit was usually enough, but the massive single-tube loaded launcher greatly degraded aircraft performance, and once North American P-51s could go all the way with the bombers the weapon faded from the scene. For ground attack the Rz73, a 73mm (2.87in) member of the stumpy Föhn family, was used in large numbers. At the end of the war the R4/M came into use. This was a very fully engineered air-to-air rocket used mainly for air-to-air combat. A supersonic (500m, 1,640ft per second) weapon, it had a calibre of 55mm (2.17in) and weight of 3.5kg,(7.7lb), with a warhead closely related to aircraft gun ammunition of the same calibre. In the experimental stage was a shaped charge of larger diameter for piercing tank armour. A new feature was that each round was stabilized in flight by long narrow tail fins, usually eight in number, which were unfolded outwards from rear pivots after the rocket had left its launch tube. The first launcher housed nine R4/Ms all fired through a central tube to which they were fed from magazines at left and right by spring-driven levers, rate of fire being 300 rockets per minute. A later launcher fired at 400 rockets per minute with belts feeding twin central tubes. So far as is known the only installation used in combat, aimed ahead with the existing sight because the trajectory was similar to that of MK108 shells, was 12 rounds under each wing of the Messerschmitt Me 262A-1a, simply attached to a wooden tray scabbed on to the wing underskin. This rocket was the starting point for the USAF's postwar Mighty Mouse.

The Mighty Mouse was the only one of many postwar rocket developments in the USA to go into production as air-to-air armament (much later it was followed by the Genie, as noted in the next section). Though based on the German R4/M it was enlarged to a calibre of 2.75in (69.85mm, normally called 70mm), so that the warhead could be increased in weight to 7.5lb (3.4kg). This weapon is described in the next section.

Guided Missiles

It is a reflection on the changing fortunes of World War II that, while the German programmes for air-launched guided missiles began with ASMs (air-to-surface missiles) and quickly became concentrated entirely on AAMs (air-to-air missiles) to bring down Allied bombers, the Allied effort, which was entirely American, concentrated totally upon ASMs to hit enemy surface targets. Many types were used in action, but the only aircraft missiles to make an impact on the war were the first, the German Hs 293 and FX 1400.

Henschel Flugzeugwerke, formed in 1933 as the aircraft subsidiary of the great Kassel-based locomotive and truck company, was the first organization in the world to go into mass-production with guided missiles. The Hs 293 series was the most prolific and diverse in early guided-missile history, and large numbers made their mark on all kinds of enemy targets. The company got into the business in 1938, along with the Schwartz propeller firm and many other industrial concerns, with underpinning by the DVL.

In January 1940, Prof Dr Herbert A. Wagner left Junkers to head the Henschel missile teams. Work began on an air-launched sea-skimmer, probably the Hs 291, but this was dropped as too difficult. In its place the Hs 293 began in July 1940 as a glider bomb of aeroplane configuration, based on the SC 500 (500kg, 1,102lb) general-purpose bomb. Light-alloy wings and tail were added, with simple symmetric aerofoils, with solenoid-driven ailerons and an electric screwjack driving the elevator. A q-feel system, which measured dynamic pressure (varying with altitude and missile speed), altered the elevator gearing to minimize the effect of inaccuracy in applied angle. Early missiles of Hs 293 V2 type, dropped over Karlshagen about May 1940, were followed by V3 models in July with the definitive Kehl/Strassburg command link. By December 1940 the pre-production Hs 293A-0 was on test with an underslung pod containing a Walter 109-507B rocket burning T-stoff/Z-stoff fed by air pressure. This gave 600kg (1,323lb) thrust for 10 seconds, to drive the missile rapidly ahead where the controller in the launch aircraft could see it. Though at least 100 missiles were tested with Dortmund/Duisburg wire guidance (over the remarkable distance of up to 30km, 19 miles with wire fed from both the missile and aircraft) the radio link was standard, with a choice from 18 channels in the 48-50 MHz band, so that 18 aircraft could guide missiles simultaneously without the possibility of mutual interference.

The first carrier was the Dornier Do 217E-5 (and, with Rüstsätze kits, other versions), which equipped Ekdo 36 for trials over the Baltic in July 1943, and II/KG 100 which became operational at Cognac in the summer of 1943. On 27 August the Geschwader sank HMS Egret, a sloop, the first casualty in history to an aerial guided missile. Subsequently many vessels were sunk by hits from Hs 293A-1 missiles, including one Greek and four British destroyers. Procedure was to keep the missile warm in flight with hot air piped from the launch aircraft (an He 111 or 177, Do 217, Fw 200 or, rarely, other types) before release. Day or night flares in the missile

DEVELOPING THE TECHNOLOGY

tail ignited, guidance became operative, the operator gave the motor ignition command, and thereafter steered in a series of arcs using a two-axis miniature joystick on the sidewall of the bombardier's nose compartment. As the missile closed on the target the control demands became excessive, depending on dive angle, missile speed varied from 435 to 900km/h (270 to 559mph). Most attacks took place in the Mediterranean/Italian theatre, though a special KG 100 Geschwader was reformed in April 1945 to hit bridges across the Oder. Several thousand missiles were produced and at least 2,300 fired.

The Hs 293B had wire guidance on audio frequency. The Hs 293C had a conical fuselage for underwater attack and led to the Hs 294, a powerful missile with twin rockets of which some hundreds were made. The Hs 293D was a bold attempt at TV guidance, and Wagner himself guided many of about 70 test firings, but TV/radio range limitation of some 4km (2.5 miles) was prompting the use of wire signalling. Wingtip cones were drag bodies to restrict airspeed. The Hs 293F was a delta with two motors, made of non-strategic materials. The Hs 293G could be flown at very steep dive-angles. The Hs 293H was to disrupt 8th Air Force bomber formations. The twin-motor Hs 295 had an AP warhead, and the Hs 296 mated this warhead to an Hs 294 back-end and Hs 293 guidance.

The familiar 'V-1' flying bomb, more correctly called Fi 103 or FZG 76 (the latter a cover designation), was frequently air-launched from late models of the Heinkel He 111 bomber, such as the H-16. It is not included in this book, as it was not designed for air launching, a practice employed only because Allied troops had occupied the land launching areas within range of the UK.

Though the American ASMs gained little publicity, and had little effect on World War II, they were made in substantial numbers and many saw action. Later models in the VB series proved devastatingly effective in the Korean war of 1950-53.

In World War II both the USAAF and Navy developed ASMs in the Bomb Glider category, the intention being that they should be towed to the target area and then guided by remote (radio or other) control to the point of impact. The three USAAF models were the Fletcher XBG-1 (PQ-11 conversion), Fletcher XBG-2 and tail-first Cornelius XBG-3. The Navy types were the LB series: Pratt-Read (Gould) LBE (three built, BuAer Nos 85290-2), Piper LBP, and Taylorcraft LBT (BuAer 85265-85289). Many of these simple ASMs were called Glombs (glider bombs) though this name was also applied to other weapons such as the GB series.

Several primitive ASM projects were started in the United States in 1940-41, but most suffered from official disinterest, by emphatic belief by the operational staff that such missiles had no value, and by the fact that developing organizations were skilled either in electronics or in aircraft, but never in both. The only project that, by its very simplicity, did continue in 1941-42 was the GB-1, first of the Guided Bomb series in which the bomb was a glider supported by wings. GB-1 research began in March 1941, partly in industry and partly at the Air Technical Service Command and Air Proving Ground. It was a standard 2,000lb (907kg) GP bomb fitted with 12ft (3.66m) wooden wings, and twin fins and tailplane carried on twin booms. At the rear of the bomb was the radio receiver and control servo, which biassed a simple Hammond autopilot to

keep the bomb flying correctly and, in some versions, to impart course corrections. The original GB-1 had no guidance and was intended merely to be launched by the bombardier in the exact direction of the target at such a height and distance that it would reach the ground after travelling as far as the target — 20 miles (32 km) from 15,000 ft (4,570m). The advantage was that it kept the bombers out of the area of most intense flak. Production GB-1s were shipped to 8th Air Force bases in England in September 1943, but were not used. Then, as flak became more menacing, they were issued to the 41st Bomb Wing — the 303rd, 379th, and 384th Bomb Groups — each of whose Boeing B-17s were given two underwing GB racks. On 28 May 1944 Cologne Eifeltor marshalling yard was attacked by 109 bombs, with poor accuracy. Subsequently almost 1,000 were aimed at targets in Germany and Austria but accuracy was much worse than that of a free-fall bomb. GT-1 had a torpedo as payload. Later GB-2 to GB-15 versions incorporated improvements, and in some cases TV guidance. Only one saw combat service; in July 1944 the 388th BG set up a unit at Fersfield, called Project Batty, to operate the TV-guided GB-4. Potentially a pinpoint weapon, very successful

Below: Here carried by a test A-26, the USAAF's JB-3 Tiamat was a radar-guided rocket intended for AAM use, though most JBs (jet bombs) were surface-launched cruise missiles. This 283kg (625lb) weapon dated from March 1945.

Above: The Henschel Hs 293 was the world's first missile in wide service. Note the underslung rocket and, behind the tail, the guidance flare.

Right: As described overleaf, the US Navy's Bat was the first anti-ship cruise missile to use radar homing over 32km (20 mile) range.

in trials in California and Florida with AXT-2 vidicon camera, GB-4 sufferered severe difficulty in troops' hands in England and few found their targets. GB-4 weighed 2,500lb (1,134kg), glided at 240mph (386km/h) and achieved CEP averaging 200ft (61m). GB-6A was an excellent vehicle with the Offner IR seeker, flown many times before 1946. GB-8 was a direct visual-control glide bomb. GB-12 was an overwater light-contrast weapon. GB-13 homed on a bright flare. GB-14 was the first ASM to have active-homing radar guidance with BTL and NDRC radar equipment.

Unlike the GB family the VB (Vertical Bomb) weapons were free-fall missiles without wings, managed by Air Materiel Command at Wright Field. All the early models, at least up to VB-8, were based on existing bombs to which various types of guiding tail assembly were added. Some later models were ASMs with a complete airframe and separate warhead, with no vestige of bomb structure. Numerically the most numerous, and the only one to see widespread war service, VB-1 was called Azon, a contraction of Azimuth Only. It had guidance in azimuth (direction) but not in range, i.e. in vertical trajectory. Thus the bombardier could do no more than try to ensure that the line of the trajectory appeared to pass through the target; he could do nothing if the bomb fell short or over-shot. The basis was a 1,000lb (454kg) M44 to which was added a new cruciform tail with a radio receiver, tracking flare, vertical gyro (to stabilize the bomb right-side-up) and left/right rudders. In good weather one bombardier, using one radio frequency, could guide five Azons at once. Field commanders were unenthusiastic, and a prevailing view was that, while azimuth steering had not been proved to increase accuracy, it could be proved that bomber casualties would be increased by prolonging the bombing run until impact. The US 8th Air Force rejected Azon in February 1944 and first batches went to the 15th AF in Italy. The 15th AF bomb groups learned fast and scored direct hits on the Danube locks at the Iron Gates and on the Avisio viaduct south of the Brenner Pass. But on 31 May 1944 the Consolidated B-24 Liberators of the 458th BG from Horsham St Faith dropped 14 bombs against Seine bridges, scoring 14 near-misses. Previously, extensive US trials had shown Azon to be 29 times more accurate than free-fall bombs. Part of the trouble was lack of operator training, and the sheer difficulty of correctly sending left/right

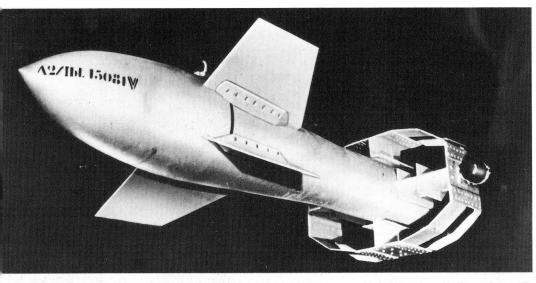

Left: Second of the mass-produced German guided bombs was the mighty FX 1400, usually carried by the Do 217K-2. Weighing 1,570kg (3,461lb), this weapon was an armour-piercing bomb with tail spoiler controls actuated by radio command from the launch aircraft. FX was first used on 29 August 1943 in the Mediteranean, 11 days later sinking an Italian battleship and crippling another.

Below: X-4 was the world's first AAM to enter mass production. Intended to help the Luftwaffe hack down US 8th Air Force bombers, it was launched by fighters and controlled via wires.

DEVELOPING THE TECHNOLOGY

commands to the distant spot of light. Azon's greatest success came in Burma on 27 December 1944, when nine VBs sufficed to demolish a rail bridge at Pyinmana that had been missed by literally thousands of bombs in the two previous years. The 493rd BS and other 7th BG units later destroyed 27 difficult bridge targets, using 493 Azons of which 12-15 per cent scored direct hits. VB-2 was a 2,000lb (907kg) bomb with similar guidance.

More ambitious, the later VBs had range as well as azimuth guidance and thus VB-3 (1,000lb) and VB-4 (2,000lb) were called Razon. Developed mainly by ATSC and Division 5 of the NDRC, Razon had a tandem octagonal ring-tail, which was also used on VB-5 to -8. Using similar roll-stabilization, radio and flare, it eventually gave excellent results but saw no action in World War II. Neither did the later and cleverer VBs, whose numbers multiplied the moment American staff heard of the Luftwaffe's use of ASMs in August 1943. VB-5 was a 1,000lb bomb with image contrast light seeker. VB-6 Felix was a 1,000lb bomb with the Bemis sensitive IR seeker cell in the nose which in 1945 demonstrated a CEP of 85ft (26m) in 12 drops. VB-7 and -8 were TV-equipped and radio guided. VB-9 to VB-12 used the NDRC ROC vehicle with an annular wing and fixed tail fins, 'rocked' in pitch and yaw for control whilst keeping wing angle of attack virtually constant. Douglas built them, VB-9 having radar homing (useless, because of ground reflections), TV, IR and direct visual control respectively. The final VB, VB-13 Tarzon, was a monster 12,000lb (5,443kg) missile 21ft (6.4m) long with a 54in (1.37m) annular wing. Built by Bell at Wheatfield, Tarzons destroyed such Korean targets as Hwach-On reservoir, Kanggye road bridge and Koindong railway bridge.

Undoubtedly the most sophisticated winged missile ever used in warfare before 1967, the Bat was a miniature aircraft designed as an anti-ship missile, and the first to have an Army/Navy missile designation. Its genesis lay in Dragon, begun in January 1941 by RCA who used their TV expertise to devise a TV-guided aerial torpedo for use against surface ships, with airframe by NBS (National Bureau of Standards). By late 1942, when the airframe had flown, the U-boat menace caused a change in direction. Dragon became Pelican and the payload a depth charge steered by semi-active radar homing, the radar being in the launch aircraft. By mid-1943 the U-boats had been defeated, the Pelican was again reorientated as an anti-ship missile, enlarged to carry a 2,000lb GP bomb and with RHB radar homing. In 1944 the fourth and final fresh start resulted in Bat, so named because like a bat it sent out pulses and listened to the reflections. Using the same NBS airframe Bat carried a Western Electric pulsed radar in the nose and homed on the reflections from the target ship. Like Gorgon it had four small windmill-driven generators, and the autopilot servos drove the tailplane (with fixed fins) and wing elevons. In the centre was a 1,000lb GP bomb. Bat was developed at the Navy Bureau of Ordnance in close collaboration with MIT whose Hugh L. Dryden won the Presidential Certificate of Merit for it. The Consolidated PB4Y-2 Privateer carried two Bats on outer-wing racks, and from May 1945 off Borneo took an increasing toll of Japanese ships, including a destroyer sunk at the extreme range of 20 miles (32km) — range being a function of release altitude. With modified radar several Bats successfully homed on bridges in Burma and other Japanese-held areas.

Under the US Navy flew a family of missiles and test vehicles of remarkable diversity in the eight years following World War II. The original members were all canard vehicles with the rear wing mounted shoulder-high. The first, Gorgon I KUM-1, was designed in 1946 at the Naval Air Modification Unit which occupied the former Brewster plant at Johnsville. NAMU became the Naval Air Development Station in August 1947, and two years later received its present title of NADC: Naval Air Development Center. Gorgon was one of its largest early projects, and though KUM-1 was intended as a SAM or SSM the later models were nearly all ASMs or AAMs, and increasingly served to provide the underlying basis of technology for later missiles. KUM-1 was designed for turbojet propulsion, but in late 1946 became KU2N-1 with a 350lb (159kg) acid/aniline rocket designed at the Naval Experiment Station. By early 1947 work embraced Gorgon IIA (CTV-4), IIC with provision for surface launch, and IV (PTV-N-2),

assigned to Martin, with the wing ahead of the tailplane and propelled by an underslung Marquardt ramjet. The final Gorgon was Mk V (XASM-N-5) also assigned to Martin.

The first missile by McDonnell Aircraft, the Gargoyle ASM, began life in November 1943 as an anti-ship glide bomb but at Navy BuOrd request was fitted with an acid/aniline rocket engine in March 1944. The compact airframe reflected sustained-cruise requirements, with fat fuselage, low wing and butterfly tail. A tracking flare surmounted the rocket nozzle, but, though many KSD-1 Gargoyles flew from December 1944, no definitive guidance system had been perfected when this vehicle was reduced to the status of a research project at the end of the war. It carried a 1,000lb (454kg) warhead at 690mph (1,100km/h) in typical ASM versions.

Bombs

At a rough count more than 500 types of free-fall unguided bombs were used in action in World War II, and probably as many again failed to reach operational units. All countries used small practice bombs weighing 10kg (22lb) or less, and GP (general purpose, i.e. high-explosive) bombs weighing up to 1,000kg (2,205lb). What follows are details relating to the more interesting species.

Above: The first atomic bomb was the 'Little Boy' dropped on Hiroshima. The weapon incorporated the first of many complex arming/fuzing systems (some of them linked to the B-29 launch aircraft) associated with nuclear weapons.

The UK conducted little bomb development until 1931, when a new range was designed in sizes 8.5lb (3.9kg), 20lb (9.1kg), 250lb (113kg) and 500lb (227kg) to replace obsolete World War I patterns. The new bombs had better ballistic properties, with finer aerodynamic form for greater speed and stability, with drum-type tails. In 1936 a 1,000lb (454kg) type was added, and in 1937 a 2,000lb (907kg) AP type, the latter with a parallel-sided central portion. The planned 4,000lb (1,814kg) bomb was cancelled in 1940 and replaced by a plain drum container of the same weight, but with HE charge increased from 2,900lb (1,315kg) to 3,690lb (1,674kg). Three fuzes were set at angles in each end, and ballistics no longer mattered as this, the first of the 'Blockbuster' LC (light-case) bombs, was for non-precision use against cities by night. The 4,000lb LC entered service in 1941, followed by the 8,000lb (3,629kg) and 12,000lb (5,443kg) types which were merely pairs or triplets of the 4,000lb type bolted together.

One of the toughest kinds of target for any bomb was the U-boat or E-boat pen, with a roof of reinforced concrete anything up to 7.0m (23ft) thick. No ordinary bomb could penetrate such a target, but the UK developed two types which could. One, the Disney Bomb, was the creation of Captain Edward Terrell RN. Weighing 4,500lb (2,041kg), it comprised an extremely strong AP bomb with a large rocket

Bomber development 1940-5

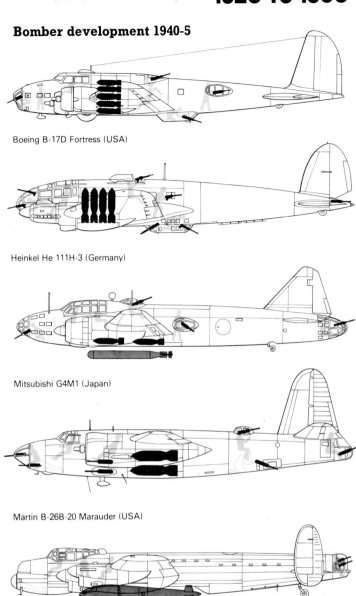

Boeing B-17D Fortress (USA)

Heinkel He 111H-3 (Germany)

Mitsubishi G4M1 (Japan)

Martin B-26B-20 Marauder (USA)

Avro Lancaster Mk I (Special) (UK)

Consolidated B-24J Liberator (USA)

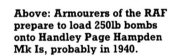

Above: Armourers of the RAF prepare to load 250lb bombs onto Handley Page Hampden Mk Is, probably in 1940.

Left: F4U-1 Corsair fighter-bombers head for the Marshall Islands in 1944. Each has a 1,000lb bomb on a locally constructed centreline rack.

These diagrams (like those on page 21 they are not to a common scale) show some contrasting World War II bombers. The first three are not fitted with power turrets, though such were fitted to later variants of all three. The He 111 shows how extra guns were stuffed into an under-armed aircraft as a result of combat experience. Like several US medium bombers the B-26 had rarely-used forward-firing 0.5in guns. The Lancaster normally had three power turrets, but two were removed from this special type.

Left: Loading the 12th 1,000lb GP bomb into the bomb bay of a Lancaster. A more common load was one LC 'blockbuster' plus incendiaries.

DEVELOPING THE TECHNOLOGY

1 SC50 (number is nominal mass in kg).
2 SD50 (splinter).
3 SD250.
4 SC250.
5 SD500E (piercing).
6 SD500ii.
7 SD500A.
8 SC500.
9 SC500 (no head ring).
10 SD1000.
11 SC1000L.
12 SC1000/1200.
13 SC1400.
14 SD1700 (splinter).
15 SC1800/2000.
16 SC1800 (head ring).

German bombs of World War II

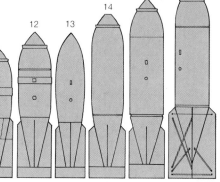

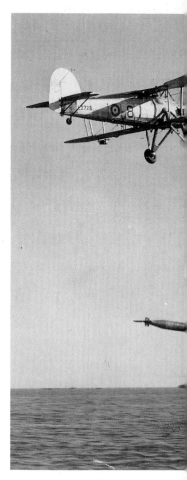

motor in the tail, the rear section having slightly greater diameter and six radial fins. After release at 20,000ft (6,095m), the bomb's rocket was fired barometrically at 5,000ft (1,525m), burning out near ground level at a speed of 2,400ft (732m) per second. The other bomb was the Grand Slam, or Earthquake, a Vickers-Armstrongs product designed by B.N. (later Sir Barnes) Wallis. Weighing an unprecedented 22,000lb (9,979kg), this was merely a finely shaped AP bomb stabilized by spin imparted by four canted tail fins of aeroplane construction. Its terminal velocity was about 1,300ft (400m) per second, faster than sound. Apart from U-boat shelters, this bomb was used against 'soft' structures, the most famous example being Bielefeld railway viaduct. On 14 March 1945 the massive structure was shaken down over part of its length by the tremors set up through the soil by an Earthquake dropped nearby. Wallis said this was the chief reason for developing this bomb: seismic waves cause more damage than direct hits.

Wallis's most famous bomb was codenamed 'Upkeep', and was desgined to breach giant concrete dams. The latter were protected by torpedo nets, so Wallis created a unique bomb in the form of a steel drum hung on trunnions with its axis transverse beneath a special Avro Lancaster bomber. An hydraulic motor spun the giant drum at 500rpm 'the wrong way' so that, when released 60ft (18.3m) above the water of the dam, it skipped across the surface over the nets. Slowing, it hit the rear face of the dam and rolled down it. At a depth of 30ft ((9.14m) hydrostatic pistols detonated the massive charge of 6,600lb (2,994kg) of RDX. Total weight of the 'Upkeep' bomb was 9,200lb (4,173kg). In parallel Wallis designed the smaller 'Highball' as a spherical skipping bomb originally intended to sink the battleship *Tirpitz*. De Havilland Mosquitoes carried two 'Highballs' in tandem, spun backwards at 700 or 900 rpm. Each bomb contained 600lb (272kg) of Torpex.

Among other British bomb types were the A/S (anti-submarine) retro, with a nose rocket to cancel forward speed and thus enable the bomb to fall straight down over a suspected target location. The standard incendiary, dropped by the million from large boxes, was a 4lb (1.8kg) magnesium rod of hexagon section for dense packaging.

Representative types of American bombs are discussed below. One unusual feature is that the commonest practice bomb was of no less than 100lb (45kg) size, with a 5lb (2.3kg) charge of black powder and large sand filling. The commonest model, the M38A2, was very cheap despite its size, and it was big enough to be of value in training not only bombardiers but also ordnance and armament crews in loading the aircraft. The standard HE 'demolition' bombs came in 100lb (45kg), 300lb (136kg), 600lb (272kg), 1,000lb (454kg), 2,000lb (907kg) and, very rarely, 4,000lb (1,814kg) sizes, though an experimental 42,000lb (19,051kg) bomb was developed in 1945. The commonest fragmentation bombs were of 20lb (9.1kg) free-fall, 23lb (10.4kg) parachute-retarded and 30lb (13.6kg) free-fall sizes, with their bodies made of thick steel grooved into 0.4in (10.16mm) fragmentation rings. There were several types of 30lb (13.6kg) chemical bombs in the M46 class, some (not used) containing persistent mustard liquid, while others (white phosphorus or titanium tetrachloride) produced dense white smoke. Incendiaries ranged up to 50lb (22.7kg), the 2.2lb (1kg) type being commonest. At first thermite compositions (iron oxide mixed with

Above: These diagrams of German bombs are to a common scale. There were also a vast number of special devices from 'butterfly' bombs to giant containers.

Right: An early-production Fairey Swordfish releases its 'tinfish' from a slightly higher than normal height. Note the 20lb practice bombs under the port wing.

Below: LS326 is today the only airworthy Swordfish. A Mk II, it has been carefully restored for the RN Historic Aircraft Flight.

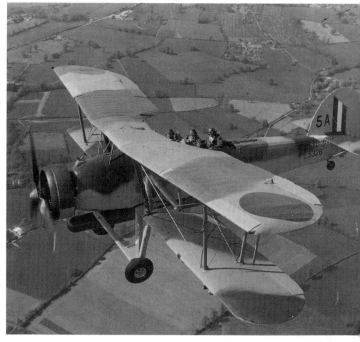

granular aluminium) were common, in various kinds of case. By 1943 the British magnesium hexagon was standard in the 8th and 9th Air Forces.

Among many unconventional bombs were several based on the so-called SBX (slow-burning explosive) principle. Large casings were filled with finely divided material such as coal dust or flour, with a small bursting charge in the centre. On detonation, the small charge would scatter the contents through perhaps 1,000,000cu ft (28,317m³) of atmosphere: this giant cloud would then be detonated causing a gigantic blast effect far greater than anything possible with a conventional bomb of similar weight. These FAE (fuel/air explosive) devices have remained important up to the present time, as noted in the main catalogue section. In 1944-45 they were considered to be no longer required in view of the imminent prospect of a workable 'atom bomb'.

first large nuclear reaction station in history. Previously, plutonium had never existed anywhere (at least, it is exceedingly unlikely). The vast Hanford works were built in 1944-45 to produce this dangerously toxic metal on a large enough scale for sustained atomic war, which has thankfully never happened. The second bomb, called Fat Man, weighed about 7,000lb (3,175kg) and contained a large sphere of Pu-239 which was just sub-critical. Surrounding it was a hollow sphere of very rapid-detonating high explosive. This focussed its blast inwards in what is called the implosion principle, exerting all round the Pu-239 mass a pressure far beyond anything normally attainable in a laboratory. This crushed the sphere inwards, increasing its density and causing it very suddenly to become highly supercritical. The second bomb was dropped on Nagasaki on 9 August 1945. In both cases the energy release was given as 20kT, the equivalent of 20 kilotonnes (20,000,000kg, 44,092,600lb) of TNT.

The Germans were less ambitious with bombs than with guns, but yet developed many types. Among the smallest dropped stores was the SD2 'butterfly bomb' which, dropped in tens of thousands with a fuze which (after initial ground impact) detonated on the slightest disturbance, at first cause large numbers of civilian casualties in the UK. Perhaps the smallest aerial weapon ever, the 'Crowsfeet' was an updated form of the traditional caltrops; one sharp prong always pointed upwards, ready to puncture tyres or shoes. A detail is that when the giant SC1800 (Spreng Cylindrisch 1800kg) was carried by the Fw 190, the downward-facing fin had to be removed to clear the ground.

Italy, Japan and the Soviet Union were all relatively unambitious in bomb design.

Torpedoes

Many countries used torpedoes derived from the classic British Whitehead of the 1870s. British air-launched torpedoes of the period included the standard 18in (457mm) Mk VIII, weighing 1,423lb (645.5kg), the shorter Mk IX (1,030lb, 467.2kg) or, from 1940, the Mk XII and XIV which were refinements of the Mk VIII and Mk IX. A few 21in (533mm) giants weighing around 3,000lb (1,361kg) were carried, e.g. by the Blackburn Cubaroo. All British torpedoes of the period were propelled by a Brotherhood-type piston engine running on compressed air. This was even then an archaic system with extremely low energy potential.

Most other countries were at least trying to do better, and the US Navy was fortunate to use the Bliss-Leavitt system in which compressed air was mixed with gasoline (petrol) or similar hydrocarbon fuel and fed through a gas turbine geared to contra-rotating propellers. In the late 1930s the Mk 13 torpedo was produced specifically for air dropping. It was relatively short but with a diameter of 22.4in (569mm), and weighed 1,927lb (874kg) with a 401lb (182kg) warhead. Though it suffered from the same depth-control and pistol problems as other wartime US torpedoes, the Mk 13 was nevertheless an important weapon.

Above: Mitsubishi G4M1 bombers attack US shipping off Guadalcanal. This large aircraft often served as a torpedo bomber, as did the German He 111 and Italian S.M.79 which, unlike the G4M, could carry two torpedoes.

Below: Though designed as a torpedo bomber, in combat the Fairey Barracuda usually dropped bombs. This Mk II is seen with a 735kg (1,620lb) version of the Mk VIII torpedo fitted with an air-launching tail.

The latter, the first of many hundreds of types of nuclear weapon developed subsequently, not only brought World War II to a swift conclusion but changed the world irreversibly. The basis is the energy released in an uncontrolled chain reaction of fissile (or, today, fusible) material. The 'explosive' used in the first bomb, dropped on Hiroshima on 6 August 1945, was uranium 235, the rare isotope of natural uranium which has to be separated out by a painstaking process (gaseous diffusion was used). This bomb, called Little Boy, weighed about 6,000lb (2,722kg) and contained a subcritical mass of U-235 plus a further mass of the same metal in the form of a slug fired from a special high-velocity gun into the centre of the first mass. At once the combined mass was supercritical, and chain-reacted uncontrollably. The subsequent bombs used a different 'explosive', plutonium 239, produced in the giant nuclear piles at Hanford, Washington, the

DEVELOPING THE TECHNOLOGY

The second half of the 20th century has seen no completely new air armament, but merely development and refinement of traditional weapons. As this is written, however, there is a chance that before the dawn of the next century there will be a new type of weapon. This is the DEW (directed-energy weapon), as most nearly realized in the ultra-high-power laser. Already this is important in space warfare, or at least in provision for it. In the atmosphere laser beams have to compete with all the other kinds of weapon.

The DEW does not appear in this book except in brief entries in the 'Guns' section of the main catalogue under the countries Soviet Union and USA. In space such devices are important because they can kill or destroy over great distances. In contrast, conventional explosives have hardly any effect, because a big bang in space is no 'bang' at all: it cannot be heard, and its effect is extremely local. Thus, the prospect of 'aerospace planes', such as are now being developed by the two superpowers, presages a perhaps more welcome kind of warfare which could have very little effect on our planet's ecology and environment, and would remain remote from humans dwelling on our planet's surface. It would be characterized by DEW engagements over distances of thousands of kilometres, and by ultra-fast missiles which to be effective had actually to hit their targets. NW (nuclear weapons) could also, unfortunately, be effective because of the ability of their emitted radiations to travel through a vacuum. Already the ER (enhanced radiation) weapon, more popularly known as the neutron bomb, is a weapon adapted for warfare in space.

Ordinary air warfare began around the lower levels of the atmosphere in the years before 1914, and then for half a century reached up to ever-greater altitudes. In World War II the ultra-high-altitude fighter became quite a specialized species, though nobody developed any special weapons for it. Then, quite suddenly after 1960, air forces woke up to what had been obvious since the 1930s, and which had actually been the subject of official 'requirements' from the late 1940s onward. This was the fact that it is possible to make life more difficult for defenders by flying as low as possible. This makes the defenders' task more difficult by reducing the amount of advanced warning available.

The subject is in practice a very complicated one. Real radars do not emit their waves or pulses along geometrically perfect lines of sight. Instead they usually send out lobes, the most powerful being in the centre along or close to the axis of the radar antenna, with the side lobes becoming progressively weaker. More recently it has been learned that, thanks to incredibly complex variations in the atmosphere (which change constantly, and can alter completely over a period of an hour), radar peformance varies greatly in different directions and is often subject to gross distortions called anomalous propagation. An air force clever enough to 'see' these regions could often come much closer to its targets, often without flying at treetop height, and still remain undetected.

The general picture, however, remains clear. Virtually all air warfare has moved back down to the lower reaches of the atmosphere, and the most important region of all is the lowest one, immediately above the land and sea surface. This must have profound effects on aircraft armament. The fact that virtually all future air warfare is going to take place at low levels

Above: Modern combat aircraft possess a versatile combat capability as they can carry a wide diversity of loads. These Douglas A-4s are being fitted with bombs and rockets.

Below: A major weapon that ultimately did not enter service was the USAF's B77 nuclear bomb, seen here under the wing of a General Dynamics F-111 during separation tests.

KOREA AND AFTER

Above: The efficiency of aircraft (and thus of their weapon-delivery capabilities) is boosted by the availability of force multipliers such as the Boeing E-3 Sentry warning and control platform.

Right: Another new 'weapon' is the battlefield helicopter such as this MBB BO105P anti-tank type with an armament of six HOT anti-tank missiles guided over long range via a stabilized sight.

means the atmosphere will be very dense, often warm, frequently wet and always filled with what is loosely called the weather, sometimes windy, and strongly influenced by turbulence from surface features. The proximity of the ground will exert a profound effect on line-of-sight propagation, for example of radar, laser and IR beams, and will exert a ceaseless mental stress on pilots who will never forget the relative effectiveness of things that can hurt them, often expressed as 'guns, 25%; SAMs, 50%; the ground, 100%'. In general the time available from first seeing a target to overflying it will be very brief indeed, often no more than four or five seconds, and special arrangements will have to be made to protect an aircraft from the explosions or ricochets of its own ordnance. Certainly the last thing a pilot wants is to direct a devastating device on a target immediately ahead, so that it explodes just as the target is overflown at very low level!

There are many other features that must characterise future air warfare at low level. In general, ranges will be shorter than before. If you are 'on the deck' you cannot see very far, and neither can an airborne sensor, unless by some miracle it becomes possible to devise OTH-B (over-the-horizon backscatter) radio/radar devices small enough to fit into aircraft. A great deal is heard about, for example, the ability of the AIM-54 Phoenix missile to intercept target aircraft from ranges handsomely in excess of 100 miles (160km), but this is possible only at medium to high altitudes. At sea level, not only can the missile not see its targets at such a range but its own flight range and speed are drastically cut by the dense atmosphere. In the author's view, far too much emphasis has continued (largely by inertia) to be devoted to traditional weapons intended for air combat of the Battle of Britain style. Snapshooting from the hip with a 'brilliant' (i.e. autonomous) missile is still thought of as a rather new idea, and even the obvious switchover from rockets to primarily air-breathing propulsion is a very slow and halting process.

It seems to be obvious that, to survive in any future war, aircraft will have to be of totally 'stealth' design, and to operate from almost anywhere on the land surface other than a known and targeted location, such as an airfield. Today's intercontinental and submarine-launched missiles are so formidable that airfields are obviously an archaic idea, no matter which country they are in. Secret and dispersed basing raises many problems, not least because the cleverest forms of reconnaissance sensors must be used to try to discover the locations of the hostile forces (including the enemy's airpower). Some reconnaissance cannot yet be done from very low level, and if the upper levels of the atmosphere are untenable (as they obviously must be) then the only alternative appears to be to have greatly improved coverage by satellites, which are themselves now becoming vulnerable.

There still remains the AWACS kind of aeroplane. This cannot operate at low level; indeed current examples, with the ability to climb to about 29,000ft (8,840m), fall far short of the ideal in their ability to lift a big surveillance radar high into the sky. It is surely extraordinary that no manufacturer should have been asked to build an AWACS able to climb twice as high. Even stranger, to the author at least, is the existence of such aircraft all all. Nobody has yet explained how they are supposed to survive in war. Proven beyond question to be a 'force multiplier', the AWACS aeroplane must surely expect to be a prime target of enemy attention, and by no stretch of the imagination can it be expected to protect itself merely by clever ECM (electronic countermeasures). These flying lighthouses, pumping out emissions of all kinds as well as pouring IR radiation from almost every nook and cranny (let alone the engines) would appear to have a life expectancy in warfare of precisely zero. As nations such as the UK are prepared to spend billions on them, there clearly must be some unannounced 'gentlemen's agreement' that in wartime they would not be destroyed!

As before, the following covers the main types of air weapon. Details of current hardware are not given, because all such equipment is included in the main Section 4 catalogue of current weapons.

DEVELOPING THE TECHNOLOGY

Guns

The preceding Section 2 (1920-50) made it clear that Nazi Germany showed an amazing capacity to invent new air weapons. Many may have been impractical, but one single type of gun, the Mauser MG213, can be considered to have made virtually all other aircraft guns obsolete overnight. The new feature of the MG213 was that it used a revolver-type cylinder to feed the rounds from the supply belt into the chamber and withdraw the empty cases. In the German gun the cylinder had five chambers, the barrel being in line with the top '12 o'clock' position. Rounds were fed in by belt feed sprockets rotating with the cylinder, plus an oscillating rammer which chambered each round in two stages and then shot the empties out directly to the rear on the left side of the gun. Features included gas operation and electric firing.

Most countries with an established air weapons capability studied the MG213C, the definitive model of the Mauser gun, with the most extreme care. Some, including the USA, appeared to wish to start with a clean sheet of paper, ending up with a gun as different as possible whilst reaping the maximum benefit from the revolver principle. The M39 series of guns which resulted from the US effort are, most remarkably, still in production in small numbers for the Northrop F-5E aircraft. This is remarkable because General Electric pioneered yet a further new form of gun, the modern 'Gatling', as described later, and in its turn this has to no small degree 'obsoleted' the single-barrel aircraft gun, at least in the USA.

In other countries the single-barrel gun still has anything from about 70 per cent (in the Soviet Union) to 100 per cent of the market. In the case of the UK and France the standard aircraft guns even today bear a very close resemblance to the MG213C, even to the extent of detail design of many of the parts — which is very surprising in view of the period of well over 40 years during which the British and French guns have been developed and refined. In both countries the decision was taken independently to adopt a calibre of 30mm. There were several reasons for this, the chief one being that it appeared to be the best compromise between such conflicting factors as single-shot kill probability, gun bulk and weight, ammunition bulk and weight, and rate of fire. The last factor then can be multiplied by the number of guns installed in the aircraft to give the predicted maximum number of strikes per second on the target assuming perfect aiming. Obviously, the heavier and bigger the gun, the fewer the number that can be installed and supplied with ammunition.

In the immediate post-war era most US fighters continued to be armed with the venerable 0.5in (12.7mm) Browning. The

Bombers of the Early Cold War

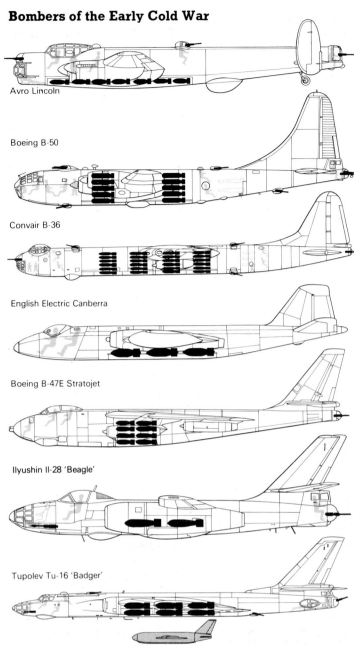

Avro Lincoln

Boeing B-50

Convair B-36

English Electric Canberra

Boeing B-47E Stratojet

Ilyushin Il-28 'Beagle'

Tupolev Tu-16 'Badger'

In the period immediately after World War II the major powers first soldiered on with World War II bombers and then, in the slightly longer term, with developments of these. Typical of the latter are the Lincoln (derived from the Lancaster) and the B-50 (derived from the B-29). The B-36 falls between these two camps, being a type conceived in World War II and then brought to mighty fruition after it. Next came the first jet bombers such as the simple Canberra and altogether more potent B-47 in the Western bloc, paralleled on the eastern side of the Iron Curtain by the sinple Il-28 and altogether more capable Tu-16. Both these aircraft still serve in substantial numbers.

Left: Though the MiG-19 has 'only' three 30mm cannon, these are far more powerful than Western 30mm equivalents, firing a larger shell at very much higher muzzle velocity for greater range, flatter trajectory and weightier impact.

Navy had pioneered the use of cannon with such piston-engined fighters as the Vought F4U-1C Corsair and Grumman F8F-1B Bearcat. The gun was the equally venerable M2, or Hispano, described previously. The newly formed (1947) US Air Force likewise adhered to the 'fifty-caliber', but did specify cannon for a very few production fighters, notably the big Northrop F-89 night fighter. By 1949 World War II had receded, and though money remained very tight it was possible to begin to look far ahead and plan what were to become known as Weapon Systems. Even the most perfunctory of analytical studies in the pre-computer era immediately threw up the answer that guns in general, and most certainly the 0.5in Browning, were gravely lacking in killing power. This was especially the case in the new era of transonic and supersonic jet aircraft, much larger and tougher than their predecessors.

By 1950 the USAF was making sweeping and fundamental changes which were to revolutionize the entire picture of air combat, especially the techniques of all-weather and night interception. To the crews the only change was the addition of a computer to carry out many calculations and give clear and unambiguous radar displays showing which way to steer to reach the enemy. Of course, by modern standards the computers were grotesquely bulky, accomplishing little more than a card-size calculator and needing a massive array of thermionic valves (tubes) with which to do it. This took much of the pressure off the interceptor crews at the most crucial time, but not much happened to the armament. Indeed, such was the weight of radar and other electronics in the Lockheed F-94B Starfire that, even though the engine had an afterburner, the armament was cut to just four 0.5in guns.

Above: By any standards a prodigious design success by contemporary standards, the

Myasishchyev M-4 possessed powerful gun armament but was well short of planned range.

These early Starfires were among the first aircraft ever to have an interception and fire-control radar (the Type E-1) by the infant Hughes Aircraft. Hughes was to be the pioneer in the development of ever more advanced fighter radars, a process which has continued right up to the present day. This is fine, but in the early years the Hughes work was allied to USAF concepts which, for many years, were to put guns out of business entirely.

The reasons were deep and often the result of both imperfect deductions and, to an even greater degree, a failure to dream up the right scenarios. Certainly the USAF never for a moment thought its next major war after Korea would be one in which its pilots would be forbidden to open fire until they had 'positively identified each target visually'. Thus, while AAMs were used in the Vietnam war, their full range capability was almost never called upon, whereas the absence of a gun was found to be an unexpectedly severe handicap.

Back in the 1950s the basic scenario, which not unnaturally worried most 'advanced' nations to death, was the threat posed by the single strategic bomber carrying a nuclear weapon. Suddenly single aircraft could destroy cities, or anything else, much more effectively than could giant formations of heavy bombers in World War II. It followed that, no matter how many hostile aircraft might be detected on radar, every single one had to be unfailingly destroyed; merely bagging a percentage (even a percentage previously judged to be improbably high) was quite useless. After prolonged and detailed study, very much deeper than anything accomplished in the other Western democracies, the USAF came up with the belief that the answer had to lie with the large, long-range interceptor. This aircraft had to have the highest possible flight performance and carry the most powerful radar and a fire-control computer. For the more distant future the most lethal armament appeared likely to be the AAM. Until this was ready, and possibly as a back-up to the future AAM-armed aircraft, the most lethal armament would be the air-to-air rocket, with calibre and hence warhead size considerably greater than anything possible with practical guns. A crucial factor was the ability of such rockets to be ripple-fired in extremely rapid succession or, better still, fired in simultaneous salvo. This form of armament is described under the separate heading 'Rockets'.

The Soviet Union keenly studied these decisions, but consistently came up with different answers. In particular, it never left guns off its fighters until later, from 1960, it produced extremely large 'strategic interceptors', deployed only by the IA-PVO (manned fighter branch of the air-defence of the homeland organization) whose sole purpose was to defend the

Left: The Soviet Union has never lost sight of the basic virtues of cannon. So while the Western nations were reducing such weapons in supersonic fighters, the MiG-19 (and its Chinese versions) featured three powerful 30mm NR-30 cannon.

Above: Aircraft such as the Soko G-2 Galeb are little more than World War II concepts with a jet engine and modern features. Evidence of this is provided by items such as the armament of 0.5in (12.7mm) guns aimed with a gyro or other simple optical gunsight.

DEVELOPING THE TECHNOLOGY

Left: The Emerson M28 chin turret offers the possibility of two 7.62mm Miniguns (seen here), or two 40mm grenade-launchers or, most commonly, one example of each weapon.

country's colossal length of frontier against large supersonic bombers flying at high altitude. These aircraft, such as the Yakovlev Yak-28P, Tupolev Tu-128 (28P) and Mikoyan-Gurevich MiG-25, were all armed with AAMs only, as were smaller dedicated interceptors used also by Frontal (tactical) Aviation, such as the Sukhoi Su-11 and Su-15/21 series.

Today the Soviet Union, perhaps realizing it had been right all along about the importance of guns, has restored internal guns to its newest fighters and added them to the little MiG-21 and, in the form of external pods, to the Su-21 (Su-15 derivative), previously a gunless interceptor. As explained earlier, the Soviet Union began to produce superior aircraft guns in 1933, and the coherence of this work has never suffered from the hiccups and reversals of policy that have afflicted gun designers in the USA and UK.

Unfortunately, little is known of Soviet aircraft guns designed more recently than 1959, when the GSh-23 series entered production. This gun naturally features in the main catalogue section, and is notable in being one of a rather rare group having twin barrels. The pioneer and ancestor of most twin-barrel guns was the outstanding German Gast, first produced in 1916 and in service in many aircraft by the November 1918 Armistice at the end of World War I. The firing of each barrel provided the energy to load, fire, extract and eject the round in the other barrel, which in turn did the same for its partner. There are many ways in which modern twin-barrel actions can be desgined, and the two modern twin-barrel guns could hardly be more different. The Soviet gun has barrels side-by-side firing alternately in a system generally reminiscent of the Gast. The American McDonnell Douglas Helicopters (ex-Hughes) Mk 11 is fed simultaneously by left and right belts which supply rounds to an eight-chamber revolver cylinder which fires two rounds at a time into upper and lower barrels. So far as is publicly known, the only twin-barrel gun at present under development is the General Electric GE 225.

By far the most important gun in the USA is the General Electric Project Vulcan family, including the M61, T-171 and GAU-4. These were the pioneer members of the 'Gatling' family which superficially follow the technology of the famous gun of around 1860 invented by Dr Richard Gatling. The original Gatling was not a true automatic weapon, in that rate of fire depended upon, and demanded, the turning of a hand-crank. The basic similarity between the old and new guns lies in the use of multiple barrels fired in a repeating sequence.

The advantages of the multi-barrel arrangement are numerous. One, surprisingly, is simplicity. The barrels, of

which there are six in the Vulcan family, rotate as a single unit together with a revolving breech rotor. As the latter spins inside its fixed housing, cam followers simply oscillate the bolt of each barrel to and fro, successively feeding, chambering, firing, extracting and ejecting each round, each action taking place at a different point in the rotation. Other advantages are long life achieved by improving heat dissipation and by firing only one-sixth of the rounds through each barrel.

Today there are many General Electric multi-barrel guns, most still covered by patents and nearly all originally designed for use in aircraft. Some have as few as three barrels, while others have as many as seven, and calibres range from 5.56mm to 30mm. Most are externally powered, by electricity, hydraulic motor, pneumatic motor or ram-air turbine drive. A few are self-powered, typically by bleeding gas from a proportion of the barrels. A major characteristic of these guns is that they can have an unparalleled rate of fire, and this has caused problems with traditional kinds of belt feed. Today most of these multi-barrel guns have GE's own patented linkless feed system which, whilst dispensing with links,

keeps every round under continuous positive control and, in twin-conveyor systems, returns spent cases to the ammunition tank so nothing need be ejected overboard.

As the speed of fighters has increased, so have the problems of ejecting anything from the aircraft. Even dropping bombs and firing missiles can cause severe difficulty: they can come back and hit the aircraft. In the case of the Hawker Hunter the problem was aggravated by the last-minute addition of a ventral airbrake which stood proud of the original fuselage underskin, and the adopted solution was to add chutes to eject cases well clear of the aircraft, as well as bulky boxes under the guns to collect the links. Called Sabrinas, after a 'starlet' of the mid-1950s, the curvaceous boxes were large enough to be a recognition feature, but like the airbrake they were an appalling admission of lash-up design.

The guns in the Hunter were four 30mm Adens, the British copy of the German wartime MG213C. The four gun bodies and their ammunition were packaged into a large container which could be winched up into the aircraft as one unit, and winched down again, on each occasion the barrels being disconnected and remaining in the aircraft. This bold arrangement proved popular in service. Each gun could be checked over and the freshly loaded belt offered up and the first round made ready for firing before the whole pack was reloaded. In other Aden installations, such as that of the English Electric Lightning, the guns stayed in situ and were cocked after reloading by a pneumatic ram. In the BAe Harrier and Sea Harrier the guns and ammunition are again packaged in demountable boxes, but in this case each container houses a single gun and is scabbed on beneath the fuselage. There were many other Aden installations, the Saab 35 Draken in Sweden, for example, having conventional wing mountings with ammunition boxes reloaded via hatches.

The French version of the same gun was the original DEFA. Hispano-Suiza also produced a derivative of the classic Mauser, and while the first Dassault jet fighter had 20mm Hispano guns, the next (the Mystère II) was tested with the DEFA and the Hispano revolver cannon. Subsequently the French were confused by the actions of their allies, so that while the Super Mystère B2 had two DEFA guns and a box of air-to-air rockets, the first Mirage was designed to have no guns at all but just a single AAM. Even the first production Mirage, the Mirage IIIC, entered service with no armament except a single and most unreliable AAM. If the booster rocket installation was removed it then became possible to carry ammunition for the two DEFA cannon in the wing roots, and of course this was increasingly done.

To this day there is little unanimity regarding fighter gun armament. The famous McDonnell F-4 Phantom II entered service with no gun, and no inbuilt gun was fitted until Vietnam fighting showed up the deficiency in the late 1960s. Ever responsive to a market, GE packaged the Vulcan series of

Above: The extemporized nature of the Hawker Hunter's initial cannon fit is revealed by the need for spent case chutes, though the installation was considerably improved and given greater tactical flexibility through the use of a winch-down pack for quick reloading. This Hunter GA.Mk 11 is firing unguided rockets from two underwing launchers.

Above: In support of ground forces the accurate delivery of 'dumb' weapons, such as the free-fall bombs and unguided rockets carried by this Douglas A-4 Skyhawk, is aided by good low-level handling at high speed and by capable weapon-aiming systems that have been steadily improved.

Left: This McDonnell Douglas F-4E Phantom shows the contrast of modern weapon types. It is releasing free-fall bombs in a shallow dive against an area target, and still carries a 'Paveway' laser-guided bomb for the accurate engagement of a point target.

Right: The last word in cannon capability is currently offered by the immense General Electric GAU-8/A Avenger, which fires enormous shells of depleted uranium to pierce tanks and set them on fire.

guns into external pods, so that in theory an F-4E could carry four such guns, three of them externally. This would probably make sense only for certain types of ground attack, especially when only one strafing run was possible. It is possible to instal external packaged guns in such a way that there is no serious effect on aircraft trim when the gun is fired, though aerodynamic drag is inescapable. A worse failing is an inherent lack of aiming accuracy, which is invariably superior with an internally mounted gun. In the McDonnell Douglas F/A-18 Hornet one of these guns is installed in the upper part of the nose directly ahead of the pilot, and the author has consistently looked askance at the F/A-18 pilots who insist that the gun can be fired at night without loss of night-adapted vision.

Where the gun is a conventional type with a single barrel a compromise has to be struck between strikes per second, which depends on the rate of fire, and on the number of guns and their consequent weight and bulk. It is instructive to look at some of today's aircraft and see how many guns are installed, and what rate of fire is achieved. This is done in an accompanying table, and not least of the odd features is that, while the IDS (attack) variant of the Panavia Tornado has two guns, the ADV (interceptor fighter) version has only one. This reflects the supposition that the RAF Tornado F.3 will always kill at a distance, using AAMs. This is just what the Americans thought about the Phantom until they actually went to war in Vietnam during the 1960s.

There is just as much divergence of opinion on the matter of gun calibre. Apart from the light trainer and COIN type attack aircraft, where rifle calibre (7.62mm or 5.56mm/0.3in or 0.22in) is common, everyone seems agreed that the ideal calibre for a fighter gun is not less than 20mm and not greater than 30mm. Indeed, even this statement is slightly open to question because in the USA, and doubtless in the Soviet Union, work is in progress on studies for guns both below and above these limits. The one thing everyone wishes to aim for is standardization of hardware and interoperability, and nowhere is this more important than in aircraft ammunition. Just to help things along, the RAF, today a relatively puny force, uses guns in the following calibres: 20mm, 25mm,

Above: A mere tithe of the McDonnell Douglas F/A-18A's capability is revealed in this illustration of a Hornet with six missiles (four Harpoon anti-ship and two Sidewinder air-to-air weapons) and a 20mm cannon with its nose port.

Below: Podded guns can add to the firepower of most tactical aircraft. This is a US Army 7.62mm Minigun pod. Note the six-barrel gun at the front, together with its motor, and ammunition tankage at the rear.

FIGHTER GUN ARMAMENT

Aircraft	Gun	Cal (mm)	No	Strikes per second	Mass (kg) per second
F-14, F-15, F-16, F-18	M61A1	20	1	100	10
F-5E	M39A2	20	2	53.3	5.3
Tornado F.3, JAS 39	BK27	27	1	28	7.35
Harrier GR.5	Aden 25	25	2	31	7.65
AV-8B	GAU-12/U	25	1	60-70	11.1-12.9
JA 37	KCA	30	1	22.5	8.1
Mirage 2000	DEFA 554	30	2	60	16.6
MiG-29	?	30	1	66.7	26.0
Su-21	GSh-23L	23	2	100	20

In a single-barrel cannon design a very high rate of fire can be achieved only by use of a revolver mechanism of the type brought to a high degree of perfection in the 27mm IKWA-Mauser BK27. This has a five-chamber cylinder that turns anti-clockwise. The cylinder's cycle is shown on the right. Following chamber no.1, we see the chamber empty (1), the chamber about to receive a round (2), the round being fully chambered (3 and 4), the round being fired (5) and the empty case being extracted (6) before being ejected as the chamber returns to the 6 o'clock position for the cycle to begin again with the loading of a new round.

Mauser BK27

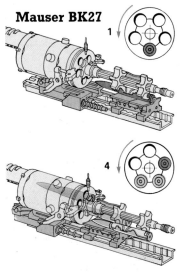
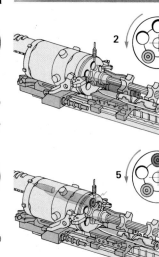
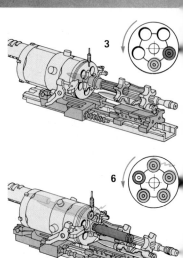

Left: Fitted with a nose-mounted sensor turret, attack 'helos' such as the Bell AH-1 HueyCobra are assured of great accuracy for weapons such as the drum-fed 40mm grenade-launchers.

Above: Rigorous trials were flown with the Fairchild YA-10 to prove the qualities of the devastating GAU-8/A anti-tank cannon, which has enormous recoil and generates great jets of muzzle flash.

27mm, 30mm and, if captured Argentine AA cannon are included, 35mm! This is clearly a ludicrous state of affairs, and with the Lucas chin turret for helicopters the 12.7mm calibre may soon be added. Comment is superfluous, beyond noting that the two newest guns in this spectrum of calibres are the 25mm and 27mm, which may suggest that nations are beginning to home in on some kind of optimum figure.

In the past 20 years there have been many other new developments in aircraft guns. Much effort has been expended in devising consumable cases, so far obviously without success because nothing has been published. The 25mm gun originally planned for the F-15 was to have used such ammunition. There are various ways of trying to 'consume' the case, most using a case of combustible material which can be burned rapidly enough for nothing to survive and cause problems when the next round is chambered. In theory it is possible to get fractionally greater muzzle velocity from the heat put out by the burning case, but of course the objective is merely to eliminate the problem of what to do with an empty case. Some of the latest ammunition uses advanced propellant ar-

rangements which need no case at all. Obviously this demands a propellant whose outer portion, at least, is weatherproof and hard enough to avoid superficial damage, and whose total bulk has the mechanical strength needed to hold the projectile under severe manoeuvring and vibration loads. Lacking such consumable-case ammunition, the best that can be done today is to use two much simpler new techniques. One is the rectilinear or square-section case. This obviously makes better use of the available ammunition space, and it is possible to achieve a volume fraction of 99.8 per cent, compared with about 78 per cent for typical aircraft ammunition. Equally obviously this shape of case is structurally weaker than a circular-section drum, but this need not cause problems. The other development is telescoped ammunition, in which the projectile is recessed inside the case instead of being cantilevered from it. This again greatly reduces bulk for a given muzzle velocity, and when the two techniques are combined it is possible to achieve dramatic advances in ballistic performance, rate of fire, total installed weight and quantity of ammunition.

To conclude this section it is worth briefly recapitulating some reasons why guns ought never to have been left off fighters. Even today AAMs are hard pressed to kill at extremely short ranges, against manoeuvring targets at the lowest altitudes. Guns are relatively cheap and simple to produce and deploy, and have much higher reliability than most AAMs. Depending on the choice of the fighter designer and customer, it is possible to carry sufficient ammunition for repeated engagements, giving superior combat persistence. Not least, gun projectiles cannot be deterred by decoys or countermeasures.

Rockets

In World War II most rockets were subsonic, and the standard British ground attack model had a warhead much greater in diameter than the 3in (76.2mm) motor. Just as the MG213C set a new fashion in guns, so did the German R4/M set a new fashion in rockets. Henceforth, the common air-launched rocket was to be supersonic, highly streamlined with an ogive nose leading to a constant-diameter body, and used not only for attack on surface targets but also for air-to-air combat. One of the remaining variables, however, is the use of fixed tail fins. Almost always such fins are needed for inflight stability, to get the projectile quickly pointing in the desired direction and to counter errors caused by inflight disturbances. Some rockets have simple fixed fins, which in many designs stabilize further by imparting spin. A few types, such as the Oerlikon SURA family, have a fin group amidships which before launch acts as the front suspension; on being fired, each rocket slides ahead through the fin ring until the latter comes up against the enlarged motor nozzle, the fins thereafter acting as fixed fins at the tail.

Like the pioneer R4/M, most modern rockets have folding fins, thus enabling them to be fired from compact multi-tube launchers, generally called 'pods'. The commonest fin type is that pivoted at the root end, opening either backwards or forwards. Most fins are arranged to impart spin, and in some rockets there are canted vanes in the motor nozzle, or multiple canted nozzles, or some other arrangement whereby the motor itself initiates and maintains spin. A small number of types, notably the Canadian CRV7, have wraparound fins hinged directly outwards from the tail of the body. In these rockets each fin is much larger, there being typically three or four instead of perhaps twice as many. The CRV7 is the highest-velocity aircraft rocket currently available. It has motor vanes to cause very rapid spin-up, and in turn this flicks the fins fully open within 360mm (14.17in) of the exit from the launch tube. Certainly there is every reason to increase the

speed of aircraft rockets, because this reduces flight time and dispersion of shot, improves accuracy, flattens the trajectory and greatly enhances impact energy.

Most manufacturers of rockets offer a range of warheads, such as: inert for training, smoke, flare, HE, HE/frag, armour-piercing and hollow-charge. The AP (armour-piercing) warheads typically have a single 'slug' of very dense material (such as tungsten, GEC Heavy Alloy or depleted uranium) to punch through the plate by sheer kinetic energy. Unfortunately, the greater the mass of the core, the lower the rocket burn-out velocity, and kinetic energy (for penetration) depends

Above: Rockets such as the 55mm (2.17in) S-5 type carried in the UV-57-32 pods of this Mil Mi-8, offer devastating area fire-suppression capability in support of infantry.

Below: A Canadian CF-188 Hornet in action with the CRV-7 unguided rocket, whose speed provides accuracy and significantly improved kinetic energy delivered onto the target.

Right: A salvo of rockets each carrying a submunition warhead offers enormous saturation capability to battlefield helicopters. Typical is the TBA Multi-Dart whose operation is shown here: a salvo of 22 rockets is launched at the target, bursting at a predetermined moment to release 792 armour-piercing steel darts over an area of 55,000m² (65,780 sq yards).

Multi-Dart Helicopter Anti-Armour System

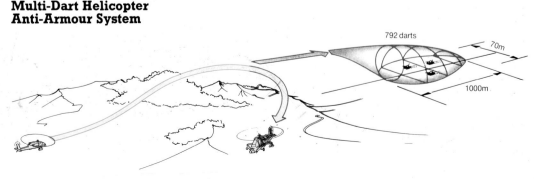

792 darts

70m

1000m

not on velocity but rather on the square of the velocity. Alternatively, the hollow-charge warhead can hit at quite low velocity, because it pierces through the armour by generating a jet of molten metal which travels ahead at such enormous speed that it punches clean through all known armour, the effect being gained by inwards focussing of the explosive charge. Penetration of a hollow-charge warhead depends on warhead diameter, and until rocket calibre reaches at least 100mm (3.94in) is unlikely to be effective against a modern tank of the heavier variety.

This leads straight to a vexed question of calibre, which is no nearer resolution with rockets than it is with guns. Obviously, a bigger rocket has far greater effect than a small one, but fewer can be carried. The most numerous air-launched rockets in the world are various Soviet and Eastern bloc weapons of 57mm calibre. Few popular rockets are smaller than this, though Brazil and Spain make 37mm types and 50mm or 2in (50.8mm) is a very common calibre (used, for example, by the Royal Navy). The commonest Western calibres are 68mm (2.68in) and nominal 70mm (2.75in, 69.85mm), while heavier calibres include the 75mm (2.95in) and 135mm (5.31in) Bofors and the 81mm (3.19in) SNORA and SURA. Soviet rockets range up to the 137mm (5.39in), 160mm (6.3in), 190mm (7.48in), 212mm (8.35in), 240mm (9.45in) and 325mm (12.8in), plus an alleged 220mm (8.66in). The biggest rockets are carried singly. Thus, there is a very wide range of sizes but the RAF appears to use only the French 68mm SNEB. Thus, again the disparity in policy between the UK and Soviet Union could not be more total.

In 1947 the newly created USAF was studying the problem of the all-weather and night interceptor. The conclusion was soon reached that the ultimate weapon would be the fully guided AAM, fired from an automated radar-equipped aircraft. Pending the availability of such armament, an interesting interim scheme was devised in which a single salvo of rockets was used to 'blanket an area of sky bigger than a football field', within which (if the aircraft's radar and com-

puter had done their stuff) would be the target aircraft at the same moment. The rocket was the 2.75in Mighty Mouse, one of the first of the new breed of supersonic rockets fired from a multi-tube launcher. Clearly the technique hinged on the capability of the radar and computer to steer the interceptor with precision in three dimensions of space and also in time. A major advantage was that this so-called 'collision course' method freed the fighter from the need to attack astern of the target. Instead it was vectored in from the side, where the target presents a much greater apparent size, increasing the chances of several hits with the spin-stabilized rockets.

The UK, France and some other countries also armed their fighters with air-to-air rockets, but failed to think the technique through. In such machines as the Super Mystère a box of rockets was mounted in what was effectively a day fighter, without radar, while the British Lightning F.1 and de Havilland Sea Vixen used boxes of rockets not linked to a computer-guided aircraft and with capacity so small that a hit would have been a sheer fluke. The Vixen's only inbuilt armament comprised two packs each housing 14 rockets, whereas the USAF's F-89 carried 104 rockets, and had an operative link between the radar and the computer governing the interception trajectory and completing the firing circuit only when the fighter was in the proper position relative to the target.

Predictably, this scheme was dropped as soon as guided AAMs became available. Subsequent history shows that it was abandoned rather precipitately, because reliability of the first few generations of AAMs was poor, except in the UK. A further severe drawback to some fighters at this time, 1953-73, was extremely limited combat persistence. As already noted, the British Lightning and French Mirage could respectively engage two targets and one target, respectively, and the collision-course technique also limited fighters to one target per mission, a ridiculous tactical limitation.

Guided missiles

Whereas in World War II the only reliable form of guidance for short-range missiles was direct command by a remote pilot, who sent his signals either via trailing wires or by radio link, by the 1950s the possibilities were almost embarrassing in their profusion. To all intents and purposes, however, the field became dominated by just two kinds of guidance, each offering its own advantages and disadvantages. These were passive infra-red homing on the heat emitted by the target, and semi-active radar homing in which the missile keeps steering towards the fighter's own radar signals reflected back from the target.

The first AAM to achieve fully operational status (in May 1956) was the first version of the Hughes Falcon, successively called MX-904, XF-98, GAR-1 and finally AIM-4. This had many advanced features, including clever packaging into an amazingly small airframe which made extensive use of glass-reinforced plastics. Aerodynamically, Falcon had four delta wings of extremely low aspect ratio, set at 90° to each other and each carrying a powered control surface downstream. Propulsion was by a high-impulse solid motor, giving tremen-

Above: Quite shattering close support capacity is offered by the load of this RAF-operated McDonnell Douglas F-4 Phantom, which carries an SUU-23 centreline pod, housing one 20mm Vulcan cannon, and no fewer than six pods, each for 19 2.75in (70mm) rockets, on triple racks attached to the inboard underwing hardpoints.

Right: Rocket pods are moderately heavy and fairly expensive, but light tactical aircraft can be given an attack capacity by use of SURA rockets of the type sported by this Cessna Skylane. These weapons clip together in a tier and can be carried by just about any aircraft.

DEVELOPING THE TECHNOLOGY

dous acceleration from launch up to a cruising speed of almost Mach 3, the speed then falling away rapidly after burnout. Effective range was about 4 miles (6.4km). Successive versions of Falcon were built with SARH or IR guidance, and with progressively higher performance.

Ultimately Hughes Aircraft, which also became a leader in fighter radars, developed the same aerodynamic configuration into very much bigger missiles with dramatically higher flight performance. The first was GAR-9, later redesignated AIM-47A, which was intended for such super-fast interceptors as the North American F-108 Rapier and Lockheed YF-12A 'Blackbird'. Though neither of these impressive machines entered combat service, the missile and associated ASG-18 pulse-Doppler radar were fully developed, and represented a massive thrust ahead into unknown areas. The UK had tried to do the same a little earlier with the Red Hebe and Red Dean missiles by Vickers-Armstrongs, for the even more advanced F.155/T interceptor, but the latter was cancelled along with all other new British fighter and AAM developments in April 1957, when the British government calmly stated that henceforth all fighters were obsolete and that no more would ever be needed. Such amazing counsel was ignored in other countries, and eventually AIM-47A became the foundation for AIM-54 Phoenix, which for the past 14 years has been in service with the US Navy's Grumman F-14 Tomcat, and will go on for at least a further 14 years.

A feature of all these monster Hughes AAMs is that, despite having pure rocket propulsion, they can travel more than 100 miles (160km) before completing the interception. Obviously this calls for very powerful and highly discriminating radar and IFF systems in the fighter, and it also demands extremely capable long-range guidance in the missile. Like almost all the longest-ranged AAMs, these types are initially told a predicted target position (at the future time of interception) and then fired off into the unknown. Over most of the mission the missile flies blindly, held straight and level, and the right way up, by a simple 'strapdown' inertial guidance system. As explained later, it would help greatly if, towards the end of this mid-course phase, the fighter could give a quick sweep with its radar and flash across an updated target position to the missile. Whether it gets such a helpful update or not (and no fighter in the past has been able to do this) the missile finally switches on its own active seeker. This could operate at various wavelengths, and indeed it could even be a passive IR seeker, but in the AIM-47A and the AIM-54 family it is a small radar. This provides increasingly sure and precise guidance as the missile completes the interception with a self-homing operation.

Like almost everything in the field of human conflict, AAMs of this type are a compromise between directly conflicting factors. The advantages need no emphasis, but the drawbacks are equally obvious. The missile has to be large,

Above: Seen in company with a Magic close-range dogfighting AAM under the starboard wing of a Dassault-Breguet Mirage 2000 attack fighter, the AM.39

Exocet is a combat-proved sea-skimming missile of the type that provides helicopters and fighters with a devastating anti-ship capability.

Above: Disappearing from operational use are first-generation missiles such as the AS.11. This was produced for anti-tank use but is now slow and short of range.

Right: The Sidewinder may be elderly in basic concept, but is still a potent weapon through constant development. This is an AIM-9J/N/P rebuilt from an obsolete AIM-9B/E.

Missile Homing Methods

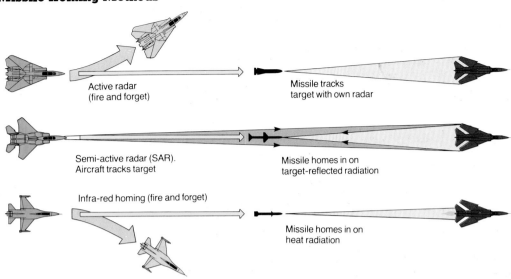

Active radar
(fire and forget)

Missile tracks
target with own radar

Semi-active radar (SAR).
Aircraft tracks target

Missile homes in on
target-reflected radiation

Infra-red homing (fire and forget)

Missile homes in on
heat radiation

Left: Larger medium-range missiles, such as this AIM-7 Sparrow being launched from an F/A-18 Hornet, are carried on underfuselage hardpoints and require a powered ejector mechanism to ensure clean separation.

Above: There are three homing methods for AAMs. The sequences are (top) active radar homing, a fire-and-forget method allowing the aircraft to break away after launching the missile, which homes onto the target using its own radar;

(centre) semi-active radar homing, in which the launch aircraft has to 'paint' the target with radar energy until the missile has detonated; and (bottom) infra-red homing, another fire-and-forget method best for short ranges.

Phoenix having a body diameter of 15in (381mm) and launch weight of 1,008lb (458kg). Each missile costs over $1 million, at a time when many other AAMs cost less than one-tenth as much. Not least, such weapons pose a formidable weight and drag burden to the fighter, and cannot be carried at all except by very special aircraft with matching radars and target-identification systems (Phoenix, for example, is carried only by the F-14). It is the penalty the US Navy is prepared to pay for the unique ability to kill at distances of 100 miles or more.

Ordinary fighters use smaller AAMs, of which by far the most important are AIM-7 Sparrow and AIM-9 Sidewinder. Both have a history dating back to 1950, both have been made in vast numbers and both have been widely copied. There all resemblance ceases, for while the Sparrow was the pioneer of the big medium-range radar-guided AAM, the Sidewinder was the pioneer of the small IR-homing missile for use only over shorter ranges. Indeed, the original development of Sidewinder was an extraordinary story of shoestring efforts without any proper funding, and literally using hardware rescued from scrap-heaps. The result looked rather like a length of 5in (127mm) gaspipe, with four tail fins and four delta control surfaces round the nose. The extreme nose houses the sensitive IR cell at the focus of a telescope to concentrate the weak radiation. The early models of Sidewinder were amazingly simple and cheap, and in favourable conditions demonstrated good reliability and lethality, but there were many deficiencies in performance, including the need to engage from within a narrow cone astern of the target and at a height as great as possible to avoid distractions by heat sources on the surface.

No AAM has ever been more developed, or over so long a period, and after 30 years the AIM-9L and AIM-9M offer capabilities of a totally different order. They can engage targets from any aspect, including head-on, and at any height above ground, and all flight-performance parameters have been improved dramatically. The increased-impulse motors and enhanced annular blast fragmentation warheads do not show externally, but the different shapes, areas and spans of the canard control surfaces have resulted in greatly increased manoeuvrability at all altitudes. A particular feature of this classic family of weapons is roll-stabilization by means of patented Rollerons, which are slipstream-driven gyro flywheels recessed into the tips of the tail fins.

In configuration the Sparrow family could hardly be more different. Much bigger than Sidewinder, because of the radar guidance, these impressive missiles have fixed tail fins but a cruciform of moving wings amidships. This is a powerful but

bold solution to the configuration problem, and many difficulties needed to be overcome. The earliest Sparrows were beam-riders: after launch they were slaved to fly along the centre of a narrow 'pencil beam' from the fighter's radar, locked on to the target. Missiles of this type can be identified by their tapering pointed nose, for perfect streamlining, because the guidance receiver antenna faces aft at the tail. The UK developed an early AAM in this class, called Blue Sky and later Fireflash, briefly used by the RAF for training in 1957. To avoid interference between the flame and ionized gas from the motor and the reception of the radar beam, this missile was made without a motor in the form of an unpowered dart which was accelerated away from the fighter by upper and lower cordite boost motors which quickly burned out and were jettisoned. No other AAM followed this curious configuration, and Sparrow I had a normal internal motor. Despite its size Sparrow I was carried four at a time by the Vought F7U-3M Cutlass and McDonnell F3H-2M Demon, typifying the lead of the US Navy in the AAM field.

Sparrow II did not enter production, and by far the most important Sparrows have been of the Sparrow III family, with SARH guidance. This naturally demands a forward-facing antenna to receive the radiation reflected back from the target, so the nose has to be relatively blunt. The fighter radar also has to have a continuous-wave mode to provide suitable guidance. Designated from AIM-7C to AIM-7M, the Sparrow III family has been developed almost to the same degree as Sidewinder, the latest version having solid-state Doppler radar guidance, a much bigger warhead and a more powerful motor increasing range at high altitude from 25 miles (40km) to 62 miles (100km). With a good guidance system and an 88lb (40kg) warhead, the latest Sparrows are formidable, but they are also quite heavy (503lb/228kg), impose a severe drag burden on small fighters, and are expensive.

For these reasons few countries have adopted such missiles. One of the exceptions is the Soviet Union, which has as a matter of policy tried always to arm its interceptors with both radar-guided and IR-homing versions of each AAM. The pilot has the choice of which type to use, depending on the weather, amount of cloud, day or night, altitude and many other variables such as type of target. For example, a small fighter in afterburner would rate an IR missile, while radar would be preferred for a large turboprop transport.

In the field of ASMs the choice of possible guidance methods is much wider. Nearly all the earliest ASMs used radio command guidance, the missile carrying bright tail flares which an operator in the launch aircraft tried to hold ex-

actly aligned with the target by means of a 'beep box' carrying a miniature joystick. This was no easy task, especially under fire, and it was perhaps too much to expect from the pilot of the launch aircraft (though the command-guidance Bullpup was carried by such single-seaters as the North American AF-1E Fury and Douglas A-4 Skyhawk, again from the US Navy), and in any case this form of guidance forced the attacking aircraft to cruise about close to the target all the time its missile was in the air.

By the 1960s many alternative arrangements had been developed, some of them offering so-called 'fire and forget' capability which enables the attacking aircraft to make itself scarce the moment the missile has been fired. No missile better illustrates the variety of possible guidance systems than the AGM-65 Maverick, one of the Hughes family of weapons which share broadly common aerodynamics (others being Falcon and Phoenix AAMs). The first production version, AGM-65A, has TV guidance. In the nose is a vidicon (TV camera) with a 5° field of view. The pilot or other crewman in the launch aircraft can 'see' the picture from this camera on a cockpit display and, by using a manual input and vertical/horizontal crosshair lines, lock it on the desired target. The missile can then be fired, thereafter homing on the target by means of a centroid tracker. This was improved in AGM-65B by means of a 'scene magnification' camera with a 2.5° field of view, and with clearer cockpit video symbols. AGM-65C, not produced in quantity, homed on laser light diffused and scattered from a laser-designated target. AGM-65D is IIR (imaging infra-red) Maverick, which has the same LAL (launch and leave) capability as other versions, but uses passive heat detection at much longer wavelengths to 'see' better through battlefield dust and smoke and also to spot heat-emitting targets that are camouflaged at visual wavelengths. AGM-65E is the production Laser Maverick, and an unusual feature of this is that the new 135kg (298lb) penetrator blast/frag warhead can be rendered instantly in-

ert during the flight of the missile to protect friendly troops in the event of any loss of lock between the missile and target (for example, if for any reason the designating laser fails or goes off-target). AGM-65F Navy Maverick has the IIR seeker but with modified algorithms (computer logic) for homing on warships, and with an anti-ship warhead which can be switched to explode either on impact or after passing through armour. AGM-65G is a land-attack IIR model with the bigger and considerably more effective warhead.

These seven versions of the same missile cover most of the possibilities for tactical ASMs, but for use against particular kinds of target there are several quite different families of weapon all of which have 'cruise' capability: in other words they have aerodynamic lift and can fly long distances and manoeuvre like aircraft. For use against ships a special class of cruise missile has been developed which, to have the best chance of escaping detection, approaches its target at the lowest possible height. This is possible because the ocean is sensibly flat and unobstructed, the actual height being set according to sea state to avoid passage through the crests of waves. For such a mission it is clearly preferable to use air-breathing propulsion, and the chief US weapon in this category, AGM-84 Harpoon, has a small turbojet fed from a kerosene tank. Future anti-ship missiles are likely to fly at supersonic speed on the efficient thrust of a ramjet, ramrocket or similar kind of propulsion system, but the only anti-ship missile to have seen much action (in the Falklands and Gulf wars) is the French Exocet which has relatively inefficient rocket propulsion.

For use against strategic targets, many kinds of cruise missile have been developed. In the 1950s the Soviet Union (mainly the MiG bureau) designed various extremely large turbojet- and rocket-powered cruise missiles for use against cities and major surface ships, and these are still in service augmented by nuclear warheads. The UK developed a massive supersonic rocket missile, Blue Steel, to carry a large

Left: Seven versions of AGM-65 with different guidance systems for different attack missions have been developed. Here AGM-65E, the production Laser Maverick, is loaded onto an AV-8B during the missile's certification trial programme.

Right: Evolved in France and West Germany for German and Italian use, the Kormoran is a potent anti-ship missile with a very advanced warhead type based on radial charges to pierce hull and bulkheads.

Below: The McDonnell Douglas Helicopters MD-500 series offers excellent capabilities despite its size. This example from an Italian line has two anti-submarine torpedoes and a magnetic anomaly detector.

Bombers up to the Present

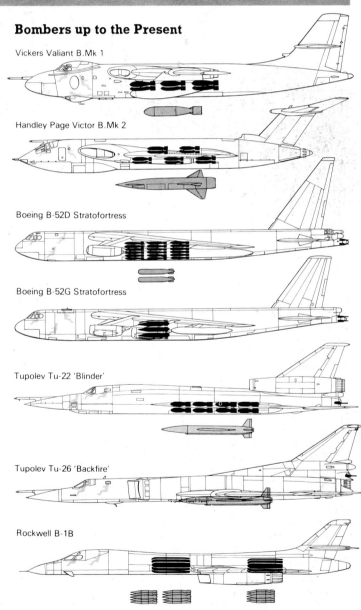

Vickers Valiant B.Mk 1

Handley Page Victor B.Mk 2

Boeing B-52D Stratofortress

Boeing B-52G Stratofortress

Tupolev Tu-22 'Blinder'

Tupolev Tu-26 'Backfire'

Rockwell B-1B

thermonuclear warhead at Mach 1.6 for 100 miles at high altitude. After 1962 it was easily switched to cruise at only 1,000ft (305m), but like most British major weapons all versions of this missile were cancelled. At just about the same time other nations, such as France and the USA, were recognizing that cruise missiles of this kind make sense. Indeed for some reason, when President Jimmy Carter cancelled the Rockwell B-1 strategic bomber in 1977 he presented the ALCM (air-launched cruise missile) as if it were a new idea, instead of something with a heritage of tens of thousands of examples going back to 1916. The USAF's ALCM is the Boeing AGM-86B, carried internally or externally by strategic bombers in multiple, and after launch arranged to unfold wings, tail surfaces and turbojet inlet to fly subsequently along various trajectories (in three dimensions) using an advanced mixture of inertial navigation and terrain-comparison techniques. Now under development is an ACM (advanced cruise missile) which, among other things, will have stealth design and thus be much more difficult to detect and shoot down.

There are many other kinds of ASM, some of which are only now being realized. Among the latter are the explicit anti-armour weapons, the latest forms of which can scatter large numbers of tank-destroying bomblets. Some of these are unguided and, if they miss a target, convert themselves into ground mines. Others have self-contained guidance, using various kinds of IR or millimetric radar sensor, and a few are designed to kill their targets either by punching straight through at ultra-high velocity or by exploding well above the target to create a hypersonic penetrating 'slug' of metal.

Another major weapon species is the ARM (anti-radar missile), many examples of which have been devised to home on hostile emitters such as air-defence radars. The ARMs are getting progressively more sophisticated, the British ALARM falling slowly by parachute whilst checking over the exact positions of its various targets and homing on the selected one even after it has been switched off.

The evolution of the bomber since the late 1940s has been enormous. The earlier machines were conceived to carry small numbers of nuclear weapons over long ranges at high altitude. They were then forced to fly at low altitude by the threat of surface-to-air missiles and air-defence fighters, and were largely reworked as tactical bombers with massive loads of 'iron' bombs pending the development of more advanced bombers. An interim measure was the use of stand-off missiles, but the latest bombers generally have variable geometry for range and low-level penetration at supersonic speed with nuclear weapons.

DEVELOPING THE TECHNOLOGY

As far as possible the remainder of this book, which is a structured catalogue of most current aerial weapons of which details are known in the West, includes information on new and projected types of armament for possible deployment in the next century. This is the real 'guts' of the book. While the long preceding sections provide essential historical background, the following pages describe in full available detail every known type of armament at present carried by aircraft, except for some Soviet and other Warsaw Pact equipment for which data are not yet available.

Soviet weapons are included to the fullest extent possible, of course, but the information often cannot be guaranteed. There have been countless instances where supposed facts, usually put out from Washington, have eventually proved to have been mere guesses or beliefs which are often highly coloured for propaganda purposes. There is often a yawning gulf between the long and informative articles signed by senior Soviet officers (rarely civilians) dealing with the modern techniques of warfare, which sometimes would cause envy if read by a NATO pilot, and the Western so-called descriptions of current Soviet weapons which appear to be based largely upon wishful thinking. One has always to bear in mind the period during which a particular hardware item was designed. For example, in 1976 Western analysts who were at last able to get their hands on a Mikoyan-Gurevich MiG-25 'Foxbat' appeared to be surprised at several primitive features, notably in the radar, and drew comparisons with Western counterparts of 1976, completely overlooking the fact that this aircraft was designed in 1958-60 to shoot down the North American B-70! The obvious Western aircraft able to stand comparison with the MiG-25 is the McDonnell F-4 Phantom. In the case of air-launched missiles the position is even harder, because we know little about when such Soviet weapons were designed beyond the obvious fact that it was long before any details or pictures began to appear in public.

Thus, in the late 1970s no information was available on Soviet tactical ASMs and, though commonsense logic decreed otherwise, many Western observers supposed that no such missiles had been developed. When at last a poor picture of the ASM called by NATO AS-7 'Kerry' became available, the type was hailed as a new development. Said to have radio command guidance, it was contrasted with the wealth of Western ASMs using later forms of guidance. This completely overlooks what seems to be plainly self-evident: that this particular missile was a contemporary of the American AGM-12 Bullpup, and very likely does employ similar radio command guidance. Such a missile by no means represents current Soviet capability, dating as it must from around 1955. Anyone who doubts this is referred to the numerous professional writings on current Frontal Aviation doctrine, which were describing the employment of laser-guided 'smart' weapons during the Vietnam war in the late 1960s, and have often discussed the use of ASMs with various other forms of

Above: The increased lethality of air-defence systems is such that even stand-off weapons such as the AGM-65A Maverick can be delivered by semi-expendible aircraft such as the BGM-34C RPV.

Right: Modern weapons can often give old aircraft a new lease of life. Older B-52s are thus being reworked as sea-control aircraft with mines or (as seen here) up to 12 AGM-84 Harpoon anti-ship missiles.

CURRENT SYSTEMS

guidance. All we have to do is keep on waiting for pictures to appear of what by now are weapons very well established in operational service.

The structure of the catalogue was not easy to arrange. One has always to try and serve the typical reader in the very best way possible. If all that any reader ever wanted to do was look up details of a particular weapon we might have made it one gigantic A-to-Z listing, jumbling up ASMs and torpedoes amongst rockets, bombs and guns. If all the reader wanted to do was read up about one particular country, and perhaps compare that nation with a rival, we would have presented the entire catalogue on a nation by nation basis, as for example is done in the case of the yearbook *Jane's Fighting Ships*. In the case of *Jane's All the World's Aircraft* all the factory-built aircraft are presented country by country, whereas another yearbook, *Jane's Weapon Systems*, is arranged totally subject by subject.

In the event it was decided preferable to subdivide the big section on unguided ordnance into sub-groups, successively Bombs, Rockets, Dispensers, and Mines and Depth Charges (one group), and to arrange entries nationally within each subgroup. The same policy has been adopted with Guns and Gun Pods, the section which comes last, and the preceding sections, Air-to-Surface Missiles (which includes anti-tank missiles and torpedoes) and Air-to-Air Missiles. Within the national entries in these Sections, missiles are arranged alphabetically by 'popular name' i.e. Sidewinder not AIM-9, Maverick not AGM-65.

Left: The latest Lynx-3 model by Westland sports a range of modern battlefield weapons such as Hellfire anti-tank and Stinger air-to-air missiles, and an Oerlikon 20mm cannon.

Right: The JP.233 dispenser system provides the Panavia Tornado with a useful anti-airfield capability — though only if it overflies the base and all its defences!

New developments

Many of the weapons listed are still under development, and a few (such as SRAM II) are still in the project or system-definition phase. They will not, therefore, become operational until at least well into the next decade, if not the next century. The length of time required for a new weapon to pass through all the various phases of study, feasibility, definition, engineering development and eventual ironing out of the faults and clearance for production is increasing all the time, and is now seldom less than 10 years for major weapon systems in a so-called 'advanced country'. This is largely because of the need to save money, so great care is taken to plan properly and avoid unnecessary expenditure, completely overlooking the fact that in an inflationary world the best way to save money is to do things more quickly. Of course, in any time of national emergency all such considerations go out of the window, and years of painstaking development are completed in weeks or even days. This was abundantly demonstrated during the South Atlantic campaign in spring 1982, when days sufficed to complete British develoment programmes that would otherwise have dragged on for years.

Some of the longer-term developments have not yet reached the point at which they can be included in this catalogue. In the field of guns, for example, there are many exciting new technologies which, even though some have been under research and development for as long as 20 years, have not yet been incorporated in a gun design for eventual produc-

DEVELOPING THE TECHNOLOGY

tion. Three of the new gun technologies are liquid propellants, electric acceleration and guided projectiles.

The use of liquid propellants has a long history, but only in test rigs and the laboratory. Many monopropellants and bipropellants (mixtures) have been used, the objective being to find a liquid, or combination of liquids, which can be stored safely and without tendency to freeze or decompose, yet which can be pumped in metered (precisely measured) doses into the gun at a rapid rate and which, on ignition, will burn with the greatest possible rapidity whilst leaving no non-gaseous residue. Some of the advantages are obvious: the only 'ammunition' to be supplied comprises the projectiles; and the propellant is stored in the most volumetrically efficient way possible for supply by pipe. Not least of the advantages is that in theory it is possible to obtain faster burning, higher chamber pressures and greater impulse from a given mass of propellant, and enhanced muzzle velocity. There are even sophisticated ways of feeding the propellant to slightly different places in the chamber, or at different rates, to enhance still further the resulting mean pressure acting on the base of the projectile.

Electric propulsion involves no combustion at all, at least not in the gun; it merely demands giant pulses of electrical energy. Often called 'rail guns', such devices have no normal breech and barrel but merely a way of feeding in the projectiles and accelerating them in an exactly controlled direction. This kind of device was conceived around 1950 as a means of propulsion for vehicles in deep space, but electric rockets, ion thrusters and arc-jets all accelerate high-velocity jets which contain no solid material. In contrast the rail gun has to fire tangible projectiles calculated to have sufficient kinetic energy to destroy the enemy. The projectiles can move so fast, say 23,000m (75,000ft) per second, that they can be quite small and still inflict serious damage. Most of the electric guns at present being considered fire projectiles resembling ball bearings, which are shot out linearly by exceedingly powerful electromagnetic fields. When 'firing', such a gun consumes energy at the rate of several thousand horsepower or kilowatts, so the electricity needed has to be stored beforehand in banks of capacitors. Probably the greatest advantage of this kind of 'gun' is that such problems as motion of the target, gravity drop, aim-off and similar causes of error can all be ignored, because the projectiles strike the target at essentially the same instant at which they are fired, having travelled in virtually dead-straight lines.

With an electric gun, which is particularly appropriate for aerospace warfare involving space as well as the atmosphere, there would probably be no need for each projectile to have any internal guidance system. With traditional guns guided projectiles look much more attractive, and in calibres of at least 30mm there is no technical barrier, other than cost. Guided shells would be wingless and finless, relying on body lift and probably some form of gas jet for trajectory control. Each shell would probably be a little longer than at present, and rings of gas jets might be arranged around the nose or tail, or at both nose and tail. There should be no need to effect major changes in trajectory, especially with the latest integrated fighter flight-control and aiming systems which even at near extreme range and with a crossing target can almost guarantee a high proportion of hits in a way never before seen. The main trouble to the slow realization of new technologies with guns has been persistent reluctance to comprehend that guns, as a class, are not obsolete. Even today the latest Western fighters, such as the McDonnell Douglas F-15C, General Dynamics F-16C and Grumman F-14D, still use the same M61A1 gun aimed by the pilot in more or less traditional ways. Many years ago computer links were available — Integrated Fire/Flight Control, IFFC — enabling a relatively unskilled fighter pilot to obtain almost 100 per cent hits with every burst fired, and this is a cheaper and much more attractive answer than developing self-guided gun projectiles, and technologically less demanding.

Right: Though based in aerodynamic terms on the R530, which can be regarded at best as a poor air-to-air missile, the Matra Super 530D is an altogether superior weapon. For reasons best known to the French, it was clearly designed to intercept the type of high-flying target that is becoming increasingly rare. The upper diagram details the 'typical' interception of a target flying at Mach 2.5 and 22,680m (75,000ft), while the lower diagram details a comparable interception at lower altitude, in this instance that of a Mach 1.5 target at 12,190m (45,000ft).

Below: Faster AAMs clearly possess tactical advantages. In the diagram the blue arrow shows the distance covered by an AIM-7 Sparrow at Mach 3 (ignoring acceleration from rest). The red arrow shows that in the same 3.8-second time a Mach 10 AAM could intercept a target 12.9km (8 miles) distant. But a Mach 10 AAM could not manoeuvre.

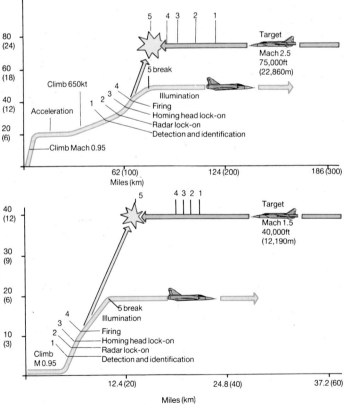

'Snap-up' AAM launch

Below: Much thought in current weapon programmes is devoted to increased stand-off range as a means of obviating the need for the launch aircraft to enter the target's air defence zone. This Hornet-carried AGM-84 Harpoon has a stand-off range of 105km (65 miles), well outside the range of the SAMs carried by all but the most important warships.

The Faster AAM

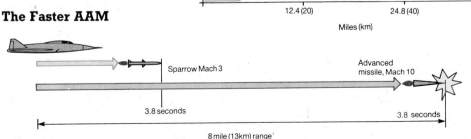

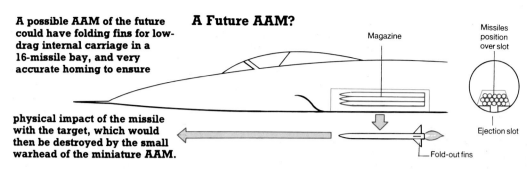

A possible AAM of the future could have folding fins for low-drag internal carriage in a 16-missile bay, and very accurate homing to ensure

A Future AAM?

Magazine

Missiles position over slot

Ejection slot

Fold-out fins

physical impact of the missile with the target, which would then be destroyed by the small warhead of the miniature AAM.

Below left: Under development in the UK and West Germany, the AIM-132 ASRAAM is schemed as a Sidewinder replacement, but appears to offer few real advantages.

Below: The venerable AIM-9 Sidewinder seems to go on and on as a viable weapon thanks to guidance, control and propulsion developments.

ASRAAM and beyond

With the AAM the West has spent most of the period 1975-95 going backwards with retrograde decisions. By 1995 the ASRAAM should at last be in service, offering a little more even than the latest competing Sidewinder such as AIM-9R, especially in all-round agility because of its different aerodynamic configuration. Unfortunately, and this can hardly be explained in the condensed catalogue entry, ASRAAM as now in full-scale development is in the author's opinion only a pale shadow of the original SRAAM of the early 1970s. The all-British SRAAM grew out of Hawker Siddeley's work on Tail Dog, the pioneer wingless and finless guided missile relying totally upon body lift and jet deflection. Obviously a missile devoid of any aerodynamic control surfaces (and thus looking like a length of pipe) is ideally suited to being carried in multiple and possibly fired from, say, a 12 to 20-round drum launcher inside the fuselage. Such an arrangement has many ob-

vious advantages. It gives great combat persistence (the ability to keep on engaging successive targets), reduces aircraft drag and thus enhances the fighter's flight performance, and not least enables the fighter to have good low-observables or stealth characteristics. Unfortunately it was decided to make ASRAAM fit existing Sidewinder launchers, which throws all the advantages away. It was also decided to reject the British solution of jet deflection and instead fit ordinary aerodynamic control fins at the tail. Such fins are ineffective during the vital first few metres of flight, before the missile has accelerated to high supersonic speed. In contrast, SRAAM could snap round a 90° turn the instant it left the launcher. One SRAAM tested from a Hawker Hunter only just missed clipping the fighter's nose as it shot round to engage a target far off to the opposite side of the line of flight!

Equally tragic, in the author's opinion, is the decision to equip ASRAAM only with an IR seeker. Marconi Defence Systems developed a virtually perfect miniature active radar for ASRAAM, fitting into the missile's homing head just 150mm (5.9in) in diameter. The company has decribed it as follows:

'The antenna is a twist cassegrain, based on the design used in the Sea Eagle seeker. It is lightweight, has a wide angle of look, and can be produced at low cost. The signal source, being frequency agile, significantly advances the successful glint reduction techniques employed in Sky Flash, and results in the achievement of guidance of extremely high accuracy. Frequency selection provides for a multiple fire capability by preventing mutual interference. The high signal purity, when combined with a unique waveform, results in good clutter rejection and the capability to engage and track manoeuvring targets close to clutter.

'A dominant factor in the advancement of radar guidance in the past decade has been the rapid development of semiconductor monolithic integrated circuit technology. The original discrete encapsulated diodes and transistors of the 1950s developed in the 1960s into integrated circuits (IC), containing a number of devices on a single semi-conductor chip and then in the 1970s to large scale integrated circuits (LSI) which have provided a quantum leap in signal processing capability. This has been fully exploited in the design of the microprocessor controlled LSI digital signal processor for the ASRAAM active anti-air radar seeker which provides very fast target detection and acquisition, and a rapid response to changing ECM threat scenarios by software changes.

'Our active radar seeker provided ASRAAM with a fire and forget, highly accurate, all weather, all aspect capability with excellent performance in short range engagements and against low flying targets, and with acquisition ranges and a

DEVELOPING THE TECHNOLOGY

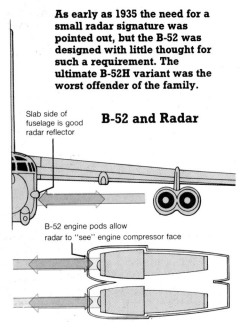

As early as 1935 the need for a small radar signature was pointed out, but the B-52 was designed with little thought for such a requirement. The ultimate B-52H variant was the worst offender of the family.

B-52 and Radar

Slab side of fuselage is good radar reflector

B-52 engine pods allow radar to "see" engine compressor face

The B-1 was planned with minimum radar signature, incident radar energy (pink) being scattered or diffused (blue). The B-1A's signature was one-tenth of the B-52H's, and the B-1B's one-hundredth.

Radar signal reduced by "ricochet" off B-1's curved surfaces

B-1 and Radar

Less radar energy is deflected directly back to radar antenna

Internal shape of B-1B inlet means radar cannot "see" compressor face and radar energy is diffused with inlet

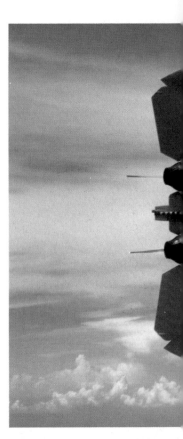

comprehensive performance which fully met the NATO operational requirements.'

To some readers this may all sound highly technical and rather academic, but most fighter pilots will realize the advantage of having a radar missile at once — unless they train at Nellis AFB or in Israel, where there is usually blue sky and sunshine! In the Falklands air fighting, though 16 Argentine aircraft were confirmed as shot down by Sidewinders, many more got away from the Royal Navy's Sea Harriers because they were able in seconds to pull up into thick cloud where IR-seeking missiles are useless. The UK, whose weather is notorious, is only too well aware of the need to offer fighter pilots a choice between IR and radar types of AAM, but apart from some French missiles the only country actually to do this is the Soviet Union, where it has been standard practice never to adopt just one kind of guidance on all the larger kinds of AAM carried by its fighter.

There was once a radar-guided Sidewinder (AIM-9C), but it was deployed only in small numbers by the US Navy and used SARH guidance. This semi-active kind of guidance demands that the launching fighter must illuminate the target all the time that the AAM is flying towards it, and thus any advantage gained by having a large long-range missile is thrown away. Indeed, nothing could be more suicidal than to carry an AAM which demands that, throughout its flight, the carrier aircraft must keep flying towards the enemy! It might be more sensible to fit the CW target-illumination radars at the back, so that the fighter can turn round and, whilst heading away, keep illuminating the target to provide a source of radiation on which its missile(s) can home. This has never been done, and even the latest F-15 and Tornado F.3 have to fly towards the enemy in order to enable their missiles to stay under guidance.

Fortunately, this ridiculous technique will become a part of history once AMRAAM (AIM-120A) takes its place in the squadrons to replace Sparrow and the various derived weapons such as Aspide and Sky Flash. AMRAAM, like the much earlier but very big and expensive Phoenix, has active radar guidance. Having its own radar in the nose of the missile makes it an autonomous LAL weapon. The new breed of AAMs, like most anti-ship missiles, cruise most of the way towards their targets stabilized (but not actually guided) by a simple 'strapdown' inertial reference system, which holds the missile the right way up and on course for the predicted future position of the target. As noted in an earlier section, it will help greatly if future fighter radars are fitted with a special AAM-update mode. When the missile is perhaps 70 per cent of the way towards the target's predicted future position, the fighter suddenly switches on its radar and, with a single sweep, discovers precisely where the target is at that moment, and the details of its trajectory in three dimensions. The fighter must then have an extremely powerful on-board computer which, armed with the new actual target position,

Right: The longest-ranged AAM in Western service is the mighty AIM-54 Phoenix, carried only by the Grumman F-14 Tomcat to a maximum of six missiles for the stand-off protection of US carrier groups.

Above: The AIM-120 AMRAAM is designed as the West's Sparrow replacement, and though good is perhaps not capable enough. It is also late to enter service and considerably more expensive than planned.

Right: Great hopes are pinned on the European Fighter Aircraft, planned for service in the mid-1990s and which will have exceptional agility and good avionics, but carry essentially the same sorts of weapons as its predecessors.

can calculate a new and much more accurate future target position at the time at which the missile can get there. It has perhaps half a second in which to work out the extremely complex calculations in order for the missile to arrive at the refined target position. The updated position is then flashed ahead to the missile by means of a secure jam-proof data link.

Immediately, the AAM is in a much happier position. Instead of having a target position which may be miles out (because the target, sensing illumination by the fighter's radar, may immediately have taken evasive action) the missile has a very much more accurate future position from which, in the second or two remaining before the missile switches on its own radar, the enemy cannot depart very far. Thus, as soon as the missile goes active, switching on its own radar, it knows almost exactly where to look. The possession of an updated target position also enables the missile to delay going active. The point in its flight at which the missile goes active is a compromise between conflicting factors: too early, and the missile's small radar may not be able to lock-on

positively to an elusive target, and it will itself give the target long warning of its approach, thus inviting retaliation by ECM jammers, rapid-bloom chaff and other countermeasures; or too late, and the target may not be anywhere within the missile's non-updated field of view. The situation could be eased by fitting a much bigger and more powerful radar, with a larger antenna having a wider scan angle and able to look up, down and to the sides to make quite sure it can lock-on to the enemy aircraft. But this just means a much bigger, heavier and more expensive missile, of which fewer can be carried. With an updated target position the missile can go active at the last possible moment and still be mathematically certain of locking-on to the target — and, because the target will be much closer, the lock-on will be highly positive.

Stealth

Everybody knows, or ought to know, that in future all combat aircraft and even cruise missiles will be total stealth designs. They will not merely pay lip service to the idea by having a few stealth design features or radar-absorbent material (RAM) coatings added, but will be designed as stealth aircraft from the outset. It is impossible not to draw the obvious conclusion from the fact that the winners of the vital and potentially enormous USAF ATF (Advanced Tactical Fighter) programme are Lockheed-California and Northrop, the winning prototypes being the YF-22A and YF-23A respectively. Why did these two companies win? Surely it was not mere coincidence that they are the world leaders in stealth technology, and the only prime contractors with actual experience of designing low-observable vehicles (LOVs)?

Identifying the Target

Above: To an IR-homing missile a target aircraft comprises just a few attractive local 'hot spots'. This fighter is shown as it would appear in subsonic cruising flight to an AAM tuned to a wavelength of 2-3 microns, which 'sees' high temperatures.

Above: This is the appearance to the same AAM of the same fighter, though in this instance making a supersonic dash in full afterburner. All the IR features are greatly strengthened, and the dominant areas are the inlet and afterburner nozzle.

Above: While IR detectors such as doped indium antimonide see in the 2-3 micron range, germanium and some others work best at 10.6 microns. This longer wavelength sees cooler areas, taking in virtually every part of the target.

Above: Operating at wavelengths about 10,000 times longer than IR seekers, radar can 'see' better through cloud and rain. It receives the strongest returns from flat surfaces and flat-surfaced junctions. Stealth designers must always bear this in mind.

DEVELOPING THE TECHNOLOGY

Above: The author is a keen proponent of STOVL and stealth for any combat aircraft able to survive in a 'real' war. The most obvious feature of this totally hypothetical design is stealth, though the conventional cockpit is retained. STOVL performance would reduce the chances of the aircraft being caught on fixed air bases. Internal sensor and weapon stowage would minimize drag, and it would also be vital to curtail all emissions.

Right: The interface between air and space is now becoming blurred by the development of weapons such as this Vought ASAT anti-satellite missile designed for carriage by the McDonnell Douglas F-15 Eagle air-superiority fighter.

This is inevitably going to influence future air weapons. Existing fighter radars will hardly notice future fighters, except at impossibly close ranges, and it will be even tougher for the active radars of such terminal-homing AAMs as AMRAAM and Phoenix. IR-homing missiles will have to rethink the operative wavelength, which again makes life much harder. Tomorrow's LOVs are not going to emit any radiation whatsoever at 'red heat' type wavelengths, so the IR seeker cells in tomorrow's missiles will have to peak in sensitivity at longer wavelengths, corresponding to lower temperatures. The total quantity of heat emitted by, say, a YF-22 will not be very much less than that from an F-15 in cruising mode, but it will be enormously diluted by cool air and there will be no direct line of sight from outside the aircraft to the hot parts of the engines. Using IR seeker cells tailored to lower temperatures naturally demands much greater discrimination in the guidance system to avoid unwanted distractions. To give a domestic example, it would be simple to design a seeker cell which, in a kitchen, would lock-on to a burning match or gas cooker flame. If one then had to design a seeker to lock-on to the same sources after they had been shrouded by relatively cool surrounding envelopes we should find it also showed an interest in a flat-iron, hair curlers, soldering iron and maybe even a hot coffee pot or overworked food mixer! Thus, tomorrow's AAMs will either have to have exceedingly clever radar or IR guidance or, more probably, they will need something more akin to human vision, because at optical wavelengths the LOV is usually not going to match the background except by chance and from particular directions. For example, a grey YF-22 will sometimes match grey clouds but not blue sky, and seen from above it will have to have self-changing chameleon properties to match desert, sea, green fields, snow and other backgrounds. In the author's view, it is impossible to rely on the target's noise, magnetic field or aerodynamic distur-

bance, and the visual aspect consistently returns as the one on which the weapon designers should really concentrate their major efforts.

These are, of course, fundamentals, based upon laws of physics. They will apply to all aircraft and all weapons, of all nations. There do not appear to be any ways of cheating or taking short cuts, though it may well be that some unsuspected phenomenon, which will give a perfect lock on a supposed LOV target and set at nought all today's stealth efforts, has been overlooked. Searching with a powerful pulsed laser might be one answer, because RAM coatings designed for radar wavelengths do not at present absorb laser wavelengths with anything like the same efficiency. Little purpose would be served by further discussion of vague possibilities in the all-stealth 1990s, though it is tempting to think of far-out homing systems, for example, supersensitive seekers able to detect a nearby aircraft's gravity field. The only things that appear obvious are that life is going to be harder for the weapon designers, which has always been the case, and all non-stealth aircraft will find the sky as perilous as being parked on a conventional airfield!

In conclusion, this overview of the contemporary weapon scene has to note that aerial ordnance is broadly categorized under three headings: dumb, smart and brilliant. Dumb means unguided. It is a rather derogatory term, as also is 'iron bomb' (aerial bombs are not normally actually made of iron, though their casings are often sheet metal). As in most things in life, dumb weapons are paradoxically often the hardest to counter. Many readers will have heard the story of the Luftwaffe night fighter pilot who was captured by the British after spending years on the Eastern Front. His captors were amazed to hear him say 'It was such a relief to fly against your Lancasters and Halifaxes. The Russians were so backward their aircraft had no radar or ECM systems, so at night we were

Left: The AGM-69 SRAM has a naturally good stealth shape, and this is to feature in the new AGM-131 SRAM II stand-off defence-suppression missile for carriage by the B-52 and, more importantly, the B-1B. Such weapons can have an offensive use, but are better employed to open the way for manned bomber penetrations.

Below: The smallest aircraft can now pack a considerable punch. This Aérospatiale SA 365F Dauphin 2, for example, has four AS.15TT lightweight anti-ship missiles (for use against smaller warships) and the appropriate Thomson-CSF Agrion 15 acquisition and guidance radar.

Above: The IAI Guillotine is a brand new laser-guided bomb, offering a stand-off point-attack capability with a weapon of modest size and comparatively modest cost.

eliminated. The laser designator has to be precisely matched with the receiver in the nose of the smart weapon. If they are incompatible, the bomb will be dumb (unguided after release from the aircraft).

Brilliant stores suffer from no such shortcoming. They are autonomous; in other words, the launch aircraft can toss them in the general direction of where targets are thought likely to be with the command 'There are some enemies out there. Have a good look, pick the most dangerous target and destroy it. Have a nice day.' A brilliant weapon could be launched from a de Havilland Tiger Moth biplane (if it could carry it). It needs no help from anyone. Its guidance system contains seekers that can find the enemy, distinguish friend from foe, pick out the best target, avoid any targets selected by accompanying brilliant stores (so our weapons do not all head for the same target, ignoring the others) and unfailingly clobber the item selected.

Some brilliant stores are of the LOBL (lock-on before launch) type, but most, especially those that have propulsion systems, are of the LOAL (lock-on after launch) variety. The attacking aircraft stands off perhaps 20 to 100km (12 to 62 miles), points in the direction of a battlefield or other place where enemies may be found, and releases one or more brilliant stores. They head in the right direction, hopefully by their totally stealth design avoiding detection, and, as they near the enemy, they start searching and taking decisions. If possible their brilliance has to be passive; if they start pumping out radar or laser signals they will say to the enemy 'Look out, we're coming, and this is our exact location.' At the same time, plain IR homing is far too crude, because it makes no distinction between a warship and a floating flare decoy, or between a battle tank and a camp fire. Readers may amuse themselves by designing a guidance system for a brilliant store that will really work. Who knows? This might prove a profitable excercise!

never able to find them.' Today's smart and brilliant stores are so clever they are vulnerable to various kinds of countermeasures, whereas a well-aimed dumb bomb is unstoppable!

What do we mean by smart and brilliant? A smart weapon is one which, with external help, can home on its target. Originally it referred specifically to conventional GP bombs to which had been added laser-homing nose seekers coupled to devices able to correct the trajectory. The best-known family of smart weapons are the Paveway bombs, but Matra in France makes its own series of laser-guided bombs (LGBs). When everything works perfectly a smart bomb is likely to hit its target, or miss by only a metre or so. The proviso takes into account the need to rely on laser illumination of the target, either by the launch aircraft or by an accompanying aircraft or, most commonly, by friendly troops on the ground who can use a laser to 'designate' the particular object they wish to be

UNGUIDED ORDNANCE

This is a 'portmanteau' section, into which are collected such diverse weapons as bombs, mines, cluster dispensers (free-fall and projected) and rockets. In the past by far the majority of all air-to-surface weapons have been unguided, but the onward march of technology is very gradually tilting the balance in favour of precision guided devices. Today miniaturized guidance can be built into explosive charges that could be carried in each hand, and when such bomblets are dropped in clouds hundreds at a time, possibly over hundreds of separate targets such as an enemy armoured division, the guidance systems have to key each bomblet to its own target and avoid several all trying to home on the same target whilst ignoring those around it.

Oldest of the unguided stores are bombs. These have been made in all shapes, sizes and types, ranging from small fragmentation or hollow-charge bomblets weighing about 0.45kg (1lb) up to the 10,000kg (22,000lb) Earthquake deep-penetrating bomb, which fell at supersonic speed, the mighty 5,443kg (12,000lb) thin-case blast bombs which could flatten two city blocks, and the B61, B83 and similar nuclear bombs used by Strategic Air Command which can eliminate a city. Newer species of free-fall bomb include ER (enhanced radiation) or 'neutron' bombs which kill humans beyond thick steel or concrete, binary chemical weapons (binary meaning that their filling comprises two types of material, each harmless in itself, which when mixed becomes unbelievably lethal), toxic dispensers, hollow-charge bomblets, FAE (fuel/air explosive) devices which can fill the sky with fine particles which are then detonated with cataclysmic power, retarded bombs whose airbrakes or parachutes slow them down very rapidly to give a low-flying bomber time to escape the explosion, and rocket-propelled penetrators which pierce and destroy sections of concrete runway.

For obvious reasons not much information is available on nuclear or chemical weapons, though both are covered as fully as possible in the section which follows. It will be noticed that, in any sensitive area such as these, virtually all the publishable information concerns American weapons. This does not mean that other nations do not make such weapons of mass destruction; indeed all the evidence suggests that the chemical inventory of the Soviet Union is very much greater than that of the rest of the world's nations combined, and its nuclear arsenal is also probably the world's largest. The only general trend that can be reported with absolute certainty is that all such ghastly devices are becoming ever more compact and portable for a given yield or lethality. For example, a 20-megaton bomb of the mid-1950s fitted the bomb bay of a B-52, while today it can be carried in multiple by a fighter.

Curiously, despite the wealth (if that is an appropriate word) of newer and more deadly bombs, nearly all those currently ready to be dropped are of completely traditional form, with technology little changed since 1918! All that has happened to GP (general purpose) bombs in the past 50 years or so is that they have become more reliable, more streamlined (to fit them better for external carriage under fast jets) and more reliable. The Falklands War also showed the need for faster-arming fuzes, so that bombs dropped at 500 knots at 15m (50ft) are ready to detonate when they encounter the target. On the other hand, too quick-arming a fuze can hazard the bomber, as many A-4, A-6, A-7, F-105 and similar aircraft discovered in Vietnam when clutches of GP bombs armed in seconds and, knocking against each other, exploded as a group perhaps 50ft (15m) below the aircraft that released them. It was partly to avoid being blown up by one's own bombs (but in this case nuclear)

that the technique of toss bombing was invented in about 1956. Here the bomber runs in as low as possible, to try to escape detection by enemy radars, and – either just short of the target or just beyond it – pulls up into an almost vertical climb. The bomb is released at the correct angle so that, after climbing far into the sky under its own kinectic energy, it falls back on the target, while the bomber puts as much distance as possible between itself and the big bang.

Above: An AH-64A Apache ripple-fires 2.75in rockets, one of the most cost effective solutions to effective area coverage without the expense of advanced weapons.

Below: Modern air-defence systems demand low-level delivery of weapons such as these 1,000lb bombs, with retarders to allow egress before weapon detonation.

2

Rockets are, in fact, many centuries older than aircraft. Thousands were used by the Chinese in the 13th Century, the Indians in the 17th and the British in the early 19th. In World War I several kinds of rocket were fired from aircraft, as noted in the first section of this book; yet in the early 1930s there were virtually no rockets in any of the world's air forces. These weapons were re-invented in the Soviet Union and put into production well before World War II. Britain re-invented them in 1939 but only for surface-to-air use. After Soviet air rockets had been studied, work began adapting the standard 76mm (3in) rocket, called a UP from 'unrotated projectile', for air launch, as noted earlier.

Until very recently the unguided rocket has been basically inaccurate. No matter how precisely the projectile might be aligned at the moment of firing, its point of impact could not be determined in advance because of irregularities in the motor and nozzle, the aerodynamics of the weapon, its mass distribution and the effectiveness of its spin-stabilization. Almost all air-launched rockets spin rapidly in flight, rotated by their motor nozzles or by external aerodynamic fins, or both, in order to keep pointing in the right direction without yaw/pitch oscillations which would make accuracy even poorer. Today excellent manufacturing quality control has ironed out most of the sources of error and made successive rockets from the same production line incredibly identical. Thus, when carefully aimed, they can be quite accurate, typical dispersion when fired from good fixed-wing aircraft or helicopters often being less than 1.8m (6ft).

Most rockets use a combination of kinetic energy and warhead power to achieve their effect. The same motor and tail section can usually be attached to any of as many as 18 different types of warhead, ranging from a hollow charge for armour penetration to fillings which generate smoke, poison gas, brilliant illumination or chaff to mask enemy radars!

Mines are not often thought of as air-launched weapons, but both tactical aeroplanes and helicopters are today often required to lay mines over the battlefield (and of course, sea mines have been laid, or 'sown', by aircraft for many decades). Several manufacturers have developed carefully engineered minelaying systems which often take the form of giant boxes into which can be laid large numbers of varying kinds of mine which are then released at very low level in a predetermined sequence. So far mines laid in this way have had no way of burying themselves, but lie in full view on the ground. Many scattered bomblets and anti-armour weapons are so arranged that, if they miss their intended targets, they lie on the ground and, sometimes after turning themselves so that a particular part is uppermost, act as mines with fuzes either triggered by the slightest jolt or, in some cases, not triggered until crushed by the tyre or track of a vehicle.

In the author's view, and as hinted in the opening paragraph, the remainder of the 1980s will see a dramatic falling away in the production of unguided ordnance. Random dispersion means that only a proportion of the devices used actually achieve the desired effect, and when the target is a large hunk of metal such as a tank or frigate the use of a bomb, bomblet shower or rocket appears to be lunacy. By about the year 2000 the precision-guided munition will cost only perhaps twice as much as the same device without any guidance, and instead of probably missing its target, it will hit it.

Above: Against less effective defences aircraft such as the F-15E interdictor can attack in a shallow dive, with their advanced weapon-delivery computers providing accuracy against small targets.

Right: Submunitions offer useful area-saturation coverage at modest cost. This is an HB.876 mine for the BL.755 and comparable weapons.

UNGUIDED ORDNANCE

Argentine bombs

Though major users of GP (general-purpose) bombs, the Argentine air force (FAA) and the air arm of the Argentine navy (CAN) have until now bought such weapons from abroad, mainly from the USA and Europe. Argentina intends to develop its own range of free-fall air ordnance.

Avibrás bombs

Origin: Avibrás, Industria Aeroespacial SA
Dimensions: see text
Weights: see text

Warhead: BAFG series, conventional high explosive; BI series, napalm
Users: Brazil and various export customers

The big Avibrás company produces a wide range of aircraft armament at Sao José dos Campos, in the same industrial complex as the prosperous EMBRAER aircraft company. Most of the weapons are copies of US originals, including five types of aircraft bomb. The BAFG-120 is equivalent to the American Mk 81 GP bomb of 127kg (250lb), length being 1,800mm (70.87in) and maximum diameter 230mm (9.06in). The BAFG-250 weighs about 250kg (551lb) and is equivalent to the Mk 82. Length is 2,200mm (86.6in) and maximum diameter 270mm (10.6in). The BI-200 is a napalm bomb weighing 177kg (390lb) and equivalent to the US 400lb (181kg) weapon. Length is 1,810mm (71.25in) and body diameter 420mm (16.5in). The BI-250 weighs 270kg (595lb) and corresponds to the American BLU-32, with a length of 3,460mm (136.25in) and a body diameter of 400mm (16in). The BI-375 weighs 362kg (798lb) and corresponds to the BLU-27, with a length of 3,630mm (143in) and a body diameter of 480mm (18.9in). Other types may be made later.

Above: The first production IA 58 Pucará, here in Argentine air force colours, is seen with CBUs (cluster bomb units) under the wings and six 125kg (275.6lb) GP bombs mounted in two triple arrangements under the fuselage.

Below: The three most common patterns of US 'slick' (low drag) bombs as made by Cardoen, the 1,000lb Mk 83 in the foreground, the 500lb Mk 82 in the middle, and the 250lb Mk 81 at the rear. The two outer Mk 82s are fitted with retarder tails for low-level use.

Cardoen bombs

Origin: Industrias Cardoen SA, Santiago
Dimensions: as for US Mks 81-83
Weights: as for US Mks 81-83
Warhead: standard GP explosive fillings in seamless forged steel body
Users: Chile and available for export

Cardoen is in production with bombs exactly equivalent to the standard US 'slicks', the Mk 81 of 113kg (250lb), the Mk 82 of 227kg (500lb) and the Mk 83 of a nominal 454kg (1,000lb). They have NATO standard 356mm (14in) suspension points, nose mechanical fuzes with fan-removed safety, and provision for two types of tail retarder.

Cardoen PJ-1

Origin: Industrias Cardoen SA, Santiago
Dimensions: length 500mm (19.7in); diameter 85mm (3.35in)
Weight: 3kg (6.6lb)
Warhead: high explosive (800g/1.76lb), with option of hollow charge

The PJ-1 is a neat bomb packaged in a drum from which it can be

FREE-FALL BOMBS

Above: Cardoen Mk 83 bomb, together with an imported US-type powered bomb loading trolley. The aircraft is an AMD-BA Mirage 50.

Right: The Cardoen version of the Snakeye retarded bomb with a metal tail brake. The four retarder fins open almost immediately upon release, and when fully deployed are perpendicular to the airstream.

removed and dropped by hand from light aircraft, transports or helicopters. Used chiefly against personnel, it has a warhead surrounded by 110 steel fragments which are lethal within a radius of 35m (115ft). The fuze is safe during the first three seconds after being released. For use against armour the head is either copper-covered or fitted with a hollow charge.

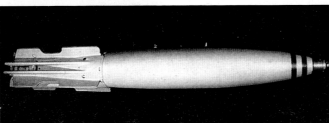

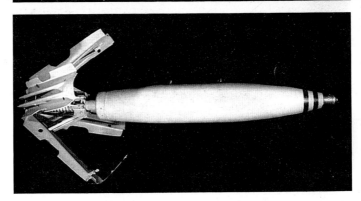

FAMAE bombs
(data for anti-personnel 3.5kg)

Origin: FAMAE Fabricaciones Militares, Santiago
Dimensions: length 429mm (16.9in)
Weight: 3.5kg (7.72lb)
Warhead: TNT, 0.4kg (0.88lb)

FAMAE makes a wide range of aircraft bombs, including standard low-drag GP bombs in nominal 113kg, 227kg, 340kg and 680kg (250lb, 500lb, 750lb and 1,500lb) sizes. These have nose and tail fuzes, the nose fuze being plugged for armour penetration. The 3.5kg (7.72lb) anti-personnel bomb shatters its heavy steel case into fragments, and has additional steel balls packaged along the centre of the charge. The contact fuze is armed after falling either 3 seconds or 5 seconds.

Type 2 bomb

Origin: NORINCO, Beijing
Dimensions: length (without fuze) 1,080mm (42.5in); diameter 280mm (11in)
Weight: 140kg (309lb)
Warhead: High explosive (TNT), 39.8kg (87.75lb)
Users: China and export customers including Pakistan

The People's Republic of China has for many years been in production with basic types of aircraft bomb. The original Type 1 is the '100kg' case but filled with a coloured pyrotechnic composition which burns for about 10 minutes with a white, red or green flame. The Type 1 weighs 80kg (176lb) and has a nose fuze only. The Type 2 GP bomb uses a generally similar case, with ring type cruciform tail and single-point suspension, but has an HE filling detonated by nose and tail Hang-Yin 1 fuzes each with ram-air propeller arming. Large numbers of the Type 2 have been delivered.

NORINCO Type 2

1 Windmill vane controller.
2 Nose fuze.
3 Booster charge (front).
4 Suspension lug.
5 Booster charge (rear).
6 Tail fuze.
7 Stabilizing tail.
8 HE filling.
9 Segmented steel body.

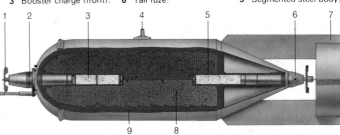

Left: A Chinese A-5C (Q-5 III) on display with Chinese 'slick' bombs of 125kg (275.6lb) size, shown without the nose fuzes being fitted.

Above: Longitudinal section through the NORINCO Type 2 bomb in nominal 100-140kg size. Note the use of separate nose and tail fuzes.

UNGUIDED ORDNANCE

125kg retarded

Origin: Thomson Brandt Armements, Paris and Boulogne Billancourt
Dimensions: length 770mm (30.3in); diameter of fins 310mm (12.2in)
Weight: 125kg (275.6lb)

The TBA close-support bomb comprises a Type 81A thick-wall bomb, which scatters fragments in the anti-personnel role, plus a special fuze and retarder tail. The FP78 fuze is super-sensitive and detonates the bomb at optimum height by means of a contact probe which extends 350mm (13.8in) ahead of the bomb body. At 925km/h (575mph) speed the fuze gives 7 seconds of safety time, initiated by pylon removal of a mechanical safety arm, followed by running of a faired air-driven internal motor plus an accelerometer locking device. The tail retarder is of the parachute type (deployed span 640mm/25.2in) and opens after a delay preset between 13 and 17 seconds. The final trajectory is almost vertical.

AN.52

No details have been released of this free-fall bomb, though it is the Armée de l'Air's standard tactical nuclear weapon. Carried by SEPECAT Jaguars of squadrons EC.1/7, EC.3/7 and EC.4/7, it weighs about 600kg (1,320lb) and has a yield probably selectable between 14kT and 18kT.

BAP.100

Origin: Thomson Brandt Armements, Paris and Boulogne Billancourt
Dimensions: length 1,780mm (70in)
Weight: 32.5kg (71.65lb)
Warhead: 18kg (39.7lb), with 3.5kg (7.7lb) explosive charge
Users: France plus five export nations

This is a runway cratering bomb, carried nine or 18 at a time (respectively using the 14-3-M2 or 30-6-M2 pylon adapter) in three layers each of three bombs. The BAP.100 is a slim tubular weapon retarded by a parachute which opens 0.5 seconds after release. The pyrotechnic train is aligned with the target 2.25 seconds after release, and the rocket boost burns from 3.75 to 4.05 seconds after release, giving a velocity of over 260m (853ft) per second. The bomb penetrates 300mm (1ft) of reinforced concrete, causing heavy damage over 40m² (430.6sq ft). A long delay fuze can be fitted.

Below: Longitudinal section through the BAP.100. This is delivered in a sequence of 18 weapons from a dispenser weighing 710kg (1,565lb).

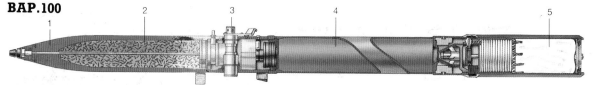

Above: A British Aerospace Hawk which cleared this type to use the BAT.120. Four clusters each of nine weapons are being carried.

BAT.120

Origin: Thomson Brandt Armements, Paris and Boulogne Billancourt
Dimensions: length 1,500mm (59,06in); diameter 120mm (4.72in)
Weight: 34kg (75lb)
Warhead: high-exlosive fragmentation, 24kg (52.9lb) containing explosive charge of 6kg (13.2lb)

BAP.100

1 Penetration warhead.
2 Warhead.
3 Suspension/ejection system.
4 Booster rocket.
5 Tail fin assembly and parachute.

Left: A SEPECAT Jaguar A of l'Armée de l'Air carrying a full load of 18 BAP.100 anti-runway weapons, which are released in tight sequence.

Below and right: Typical effects of French air-dropped anti-airfield and anti-armour bombs. Below, the crater and heave effect of a BAP.120 on a thick concrete runway. Right, the horizontal spray of fragments has passed right through this refuelling bowser, showing the fan of lethal splinters generated by a single BAT.120 bomb.

Users: France and 'several export customers'

BAT.120 is a Bombe d'Appui Tactique (tactical attack bomb) for use against such targets as aircraft, SAMs, vehicles and other not particularly hardened items. The bomb is carried in groups of 18 on the same adapter as used for the BAP.100 (see above), accurate spacing being assured by an intervalometer. A parachute retarder gives near-vertical impact at 20m (66ft) per second, fall time from 80m (260ft) being 6 seconds. Two types of this bomb are in service. AMV, for general use, scatters over 2,600 fragments in a horizontal sheet, each penetrating 4mm (0.16in) of steel at 20m (66ft) radius. ABL, for use against lightly armoured targets, scatters a sheet of about 800 main (and many secondary) fragments, each penetrating 7mm (0.28in) of steel at a radius of 20m (66ft).

Below: A longitudinal section through the BAT.120 anti-armour weapon. This is carried in groups of 18, each group being released in timed sequence to cover a half mile column of vehicles. A single pylon-load of 18 weighs 730kg (1,609lb) with all ancillaries. Note the two warheads.

BM.400

Origin: Thomson Brandt Armements, Paris and Boulogne Billancourt
Dimensions: length 3,200mm (126in); diameter 320mm (12.6in)
Weight: 390kg (860lb)
Warhead: three 100kg (220.5lb) modules (newer submunitions, see text)
Users: France and export

The BM.400 is an attack weapon for release in high-speed (650-1,110km/h; 404-690mph), low-altitude (30m-100ft) flight over high-value hardened targets including armoured vehicles, ammunition dumps, road or rail traffic and SAMs. On release it ejects at preset times three large parachute-retarded modules. This multi-munition bomb can be aimed by the toss method, giving a stand-off range greater than 5,000m (16,404ft) with a small rocket booster this stand-off range is doubled. Ground impact is sensibly vertical. Two modules are available: one ejects a horizontal sheet of 800 main fragments each able to penetrate 17mm (0.67in) of steel at 50m (165ft) and 12mm (0.47in) at 100m (330ft); the other ejects 1,500 main

fragments each able to penetrate 12mm (0.47in) at 50m (165ft) or 7mm (0.29in) at 100m (330ft). Two BM.400s can saturate an area 600m (655 yards) long by 100m (100 yards) wide (or considerably more if fragment density and penetrability are reduced). Two new submunitions may be in production by 1989; these are the SMABL from the BAT.120 bomb and the SMAP from the BAP.100 area-denial and cratering weapon described previously. SMABL weighs 20kg (44lb), has a

Above: Six BM.400s (plus two Magic AAMs and a tank) carried by a prototype Mirage 2000. Dropped in sequence by an intervalometer, such a load could decimate an armoured unit in march order.

length of 670mm (26.4in) and explodes into over 500 calibrated fragments. SMAP weighs 23kg (50.7lb) has a length of 1,000mm (39.4in) and has the performance described previously for BAP.100.

BAT.120

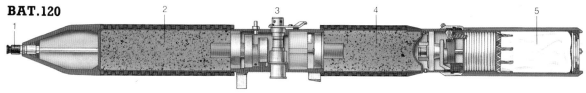

1 Sensitive piezoelectric fuze.
2 Front charge.
3 Suspension/ejection system.
4 Rear charge.
5 Tail fin assembly and parachute.

UNGUIDED ORDNANCE

Above: Six Durandals, plus two Magic AAMs and two tanks, carried by a Mirage F1C of the French Armée de l'Air. Timing is by intervalometer.

Above: Matra Durandal airfield-atack bombs carried in tandem by a USAF F-111A on test at Eglin AFB, Florida.

Above: The Mirage 2000 can carry up to 16 Durandals, and seven are visible here (so also is the muzzle of the Type 554 gun).

Below: A Mirage 5 on test with 14 GP bombs (ten 500lb, two 1,000lb, and two 250lb), plus two drop tanks each of 130 US gallons.

Durandal

Origin: Matra SA, Vélizy-Villacoublay
Dimensions: length 2,500mm (98.43in); diameter 223mm (8.78in); wingspan 430mm (16.93in)
Weight: 219kg (483lb)
Warhead: HE 100kg (220.5lb), with 1 second delay fuze for TNT charge of 15kg (33lb)
Users: France plus 11 export customers including USAF

Originally gaining notoriety in prototype form in 1967 as the 'concrete dibber' used by Israel, Durandal was developed in collaboration with SAMP as a weapon tailored to the task of causing maximum damage to concrete pavements and other hard targets such as concrete aircraft shelters. It is a simple tube which tactical aircraft can carry in multiple (16 on the Mirage 2000). After release at heights down to 75m (245ft) it is braked by Matra's standard parachute braking kit (45,000 delivered) and tilted nose-down before an internal rocket motor fires. Ac-

celeration is extremely high, ground impact, without ricochet, taking it through reinforced concrete 400mm (15.75in) thick before detonation of the warhead. Standard runway damage area is some 200m² (2,153 sq ft). A single run by two aircraft is claimed to neutralize runway, taxiway, manoeuvring aprons and numerous shelters. Delayed-action fuzing is an option. By late 1986 well over 29,000 rounds had been sold, and Durandal was the winner of a long competitive evaluation by the USAF.

SAMP bombs

Origin: Société des Ateliers Mécaniques de Pont-sur-Sambre, Pont-sur-Sambre
Users: France and many export customers

SAMP is the biggest manufacturer of free-fall bombs in

SAMP BOMBS

Type	Weight Nominal	Actual	Explosive content	Length	Diameter
2	2kg (4.4lb)	2.2kg (4.85lb)	—	489mm (19.25in)	98.5mm (3.9in)
6	6kg (13.2lb)	6.1kg (13.4lb)	—	489mm (19.25in)	98.5mm (3.9in)
7	7kg (15.4lb)	5.3kg (11.7lb)	—	610mm (24in)	98.5mm (3.98in)
8	8kg (17.6lb)	12.2kg (26.9lb)	—	610mm (24in)	98.5mm (3.98in)
BL.5	50kg (110.2lb)	50kg (110.2lb)	40%	1,320mm (52in)	176mm (6.9in)
BL.6	120kg (264.6lb)	118kg (260.1lb)	45%	1,778mm (70in)	228mm (9in)
BL.7	120kg (264.6lb)	115kg (253.5lb)	50%	1,660mm (65.35in)	228mm (9in)
EU.2	250kg (551.1lb)	250kg (550.1lb)	40%	2,253mm (88.7in)	273mm (10.75in)
25	250kg (551.1lb)	247kg (544.5lb)	50%	2,121mm (83.5in)	324mm (12.75in)
T.200	400kg (881.1lb)	345kg (760.6lb)	50%	2,195mm (86.4in)	403mm (15.9in)
EU.3	500kg (1,102.3lb)	452kg (996.5lb)	45%	2,855mm (112.4in)	356mm (14in)
BL.4	1,000kg (2,204.6lb)	1,000kg (2,204.6lb)	55%	3,500mm (137.8in)	457mm (18in)

LU250 EG-FT

Origin: Luchaire SA, Paris and Goodyear Aerospace, Akron, Ohio

Dimensions: length (conical fin) 2,154mm (84.8in) or (retarded) 2,162mm (85.1in); diameter 273mm (10.75in); fin span (conical) 380mm (14.96in) or (retarded) 385mm (15.16in)

Weight: (conical fin) 240kg (529lb) or (retarded) 254kg (560lb)

Warhead: HE charge with either mechanical or electrical fuzes at nose and tail

This bomb is a blast/fragmentation GP type based on the American Mk 82 low-drag type. It is in production either with a plain conical tail (and usually with mechanical fuzing) or with the Goodyear BSU-49/B ballute retarder (and usually with electrical fuzing). The ballute (balloon parachute) is housed in a tail container and, very shortly after release from the 356mm (14in) NATO suspension lugs, is rapidly deployed and inflated by integral ram inlets. With this retarder and Italian Borletti fuzes the LU250 is marketed by Consor, an Italian consortium.

Below: Jackie Swegar, a Goodyear chief inspector, checks BSU-49/B Ballute bomb retarders. The bomb is attached by the strops at the bottom.

Above: An early Jaguar on test with eight SAMP bombs of nominal 1,000lb (454kg) size. Note the aft-facing cameras under the nose.

France. The table gives brief particulars of some of the chief patterns. Types 2 to 8 are practice bombs, equipped with either a visual or acoustic spotting charge and compatible with any rack. Type 2 simulates anti-personnel and anti-matériel attack, Type 6 simulates retarded bombs, and Types 7 and 8 simulate low-altitude and dive bombing attacks. The 50kg (110lb) to 120kg (265lb) bombs are fitted with NATO 356mm (14in) lugs and a 50mm (2in) fuze well, and can be carried on multi-ejector racks or by light aircraft. The 250kg (551lb) to 500kg (1,102lb) bombs can have either the Matra Type 200 or Type SFA bomb retarding system, the SFA permitting release at lower speeds and from half the previous minimum height, as well as airburst detonations. The 1,000kg (2,205lb) bomb has 762mm (30in) lugs and can be fitted with Matra's LGB (laser-guided bomb) precision guidance system, as well as a tail retarder.

Thomson Brandt 74mm grenade

Origin: Thomson Brandt Armements, Paris and Boulogne Billancourt

Dimensions: individual cartridge 214mm (8.4in) long with diameter of 74mm (2.9in); grenade is 190mm (7.5in) long and 70mm (2.76in) diameter

Weight: cartridge 2kg (4.41lb); grenade 1.6kg (3.5lb)

Warhead: stand-off shaped charge plus fragments lethal within radius of 10m (33ft)

User: France, and export

The French air forces use a variety of standard launchers (Alkan Types 501, 530 and 5120) for 74mm (2.9in) cartridges for various purposes including electronic warfare chaff, jamming and IR flares. The TBA 74mm grenade is a parachute-retarded munition for use against armour. Normally released at 50m (165ft) at 650-1,110km/h (404-690mph), these grenades impact nearly vertically and penetrate 200mm of armour.

UNGUIDED ORDNANCE

Above: An assortment of American-supplied LAU-10 (5in) rocket launchers and free-fall ordnance going aboard an IAI Kfir C2 multirole fighter, which is also carrying a centreline tank. Israel has made strenuous efforts to become self-sufficient in weapons.

Below: The bombs displayed in front of this US-supplied F-4E Phantom II are mainly Israeli-made. The largest is the 3,000lb M118.

Israeli bombs

Nearly all free-fall bombs seen displayed with Israeli aircraft have been of either American or French patterns. No information is available on which models are produced in Israel.

Opher

Origin: Elbit Computers, Haifa
User: Israel

This is a passive IR homing head and canard flight-control system which can be attached to the front of a wide range of free-fall bombs, converting them essentially into smart weapons. The whole system geometry is similar to that of Paveway weapons, but a key feature is standardized design and low cost. The bomb can be released in a dive-toss or by ordinary CCIP (continuously computed impact point) aiming.

Warhead: cast steel body-with filling of Torpex 4B (practice version, HE substitute)

This is a standard general-purpose weapon, and other parts include a penetration nosecone and cup support, charging tubes for electronic nose and tail fuzes, and an arming wire for mechanical fuzing systems.

BRFA 330

Origin: Explosivos Alaveses SA, Vitoria
Dimensions: length 3,200mm (126in); diameter 300mm (11.8in); fin span 600mm (23.6in)
Weight: 330kg (727.5lb)
Warhead: HE filling 75kg (165.3lb)

This is an airfield attack weapon carried externally by high-performance aircraft. On release it is braked by a parachute to a near-vertical position over the target pavement, through which it is then driven by rocket motor to a depth of some 600mm (24in). Heave damage is caused over an area of about 180m² (1,937.6 sq ft).

Below: BRFA 330 deploys its braking parachute 2.5 seconds after release from the aircraft.

Above: Opher is one of the most sophisticated air weapons yet produced in Israel. Note the IR-transparent nose window.

Below: A complete attack on a tank target by an Opher (three frames chosen from many) dropped by an F-4E. Note that

the IR homing head has locked-on to the tank's hot engine compartment in the rear of the vehicle.

The seeker detects radiation from the target and corrects the bomb's trajectory to home on the sensed radiation. It is said to use 'the minimum smartness' to hit fixed or moving point targets.

Armscor bombs

Origin: Armscor, Pretoria, South Africa

12.5kg bomb
Dimensions: length 765mm (30.1in); diameter of bomb 95mm (3.74in)
Warhead: tail section contains 0.92kg (2.03lb) of pyrotechnic charge, with detonator or burster

This practice bomb simulates the 450kg (992lb) bomb and can be dropped at low altitude at up to Mach 0.95. It has a cast-iron body and vaned aluminium tail. The filling can generate a bright flash or smoke, according to whether use is by night or day.

120kg bomb
Weights: empty case 60kg (132.3lb); filled and assembled bomb 107kg (235.9lb) plus 8kg (17.6lb) tail section
Warhead: choice of 60/40 RDX/TNT, all-TNT or (practice model) HE substitute; SA771 mechanical nose fuze with instantaneous or various time delays; SA772 tail fuze with instantaneous action or various delays in the millisecond range

This is a standard GP bomb. It has a case or forged body and can be fitted with a penetration nosecone, or with a front and/or rear tube for electronic fuzes.

120kg shrapnel bomb
Dimensions: length and diameter of tail, 702mm and 325mm (27.6in and 12.8in)
Weights: bomb body, filled and plugged, 114.5kg (252lb); tail 7.5kg (16.5lb)
Warhead: normally contains 27kg of RDX/TNT (other choices available); around the HE core are packed steel balls cast in-resin within the glass-fibre skin, the choice being 42,000 balls of 6.7mm (0.26in) size, or 26,000 of 7.9mm (0.31in) size or 19,500 of 8.7mm (0.34in) size

This bomb is interchangeable in all respects with the 120kg GP,

but is for anti-personnel operations. It has the same ballistics, and the HE core is produced with charging tubes to accommodate fuzes with internal arming wires.

250kg bomb
Weights: empty case 116kg (255.7lb); assembled and filled 219kg (482.8lb) plus 9kg (19.8lb) tail section

This is a standard GP bomb, with NATO 500 lugs and carried externally by transonic aircraft.

250kg practice bomb
This large practice bomb has a case of glassfibre and polyurethane foam filled with steel balls giving ballistics identical to the GP 250kg. On impact the bomb breaks up, leaving nothing which could cause ricochets on subsequent sorties on the same aiming point.

480kg bomb
Weights: empty case about 225kg (496lb); assembled and filled 438kg (965.6lb) plus 28kg (61.7lb) tail section

Below: BRFA 330 can be released at heights slightly above 80m (260ft) and at any speed from 520-1110km/h (280-600 knots).

UNGUIDED ORDNANCE

BRP

Origin: Explosivos Alaveses SA, Vitoria

This range of parachute-retarded bombs was designed for low-level use from the fastest jet aircraft. All EXPAL GP bombs can be converted by fitting the BRP tail and a Kappa nose fuze. The tail is pulled open on release by arming wires, and safety devices prevent detonation if any part fails or if a minimum safe separation from the aircraft cannot be guaranteed. For use from the lowest heights a range of Super bombs (BRP.S) have rapid-action parachute tails.

EXPAL bombs

Origin: Explosivos Alaveses SA, Vitoria

This is the standard range of low-drag GP bombs used by the Spanish air force. All bombs can be fitted with nose and tail fuzes for impact detonation or various inbuilt delays. Carrier lugs can be single or NATO twin 356mm (14in). All bombs can be fitted with BRP tails, as noted above.

SWEDEN

HE bombs

Origin: FFV Ordnance, Eskilstuna

The standard bombs in service with the Swedish air force are: the M51 (120kg) type SB, the M50 (250kg) type SB, the M56 (500kg) type MB, and the M50 (600kg) type MB. In addition there is the Virgo M71 described below, and the M60 (80kg) type LYSB HE-fragmentation bomb for use against soft targets.

Below: A Saab AJ37 Viggen of the Swedish 7th Attack Wing, armed with eight pairs of FFV M51 (120kg) bombs.

BRP BOMBS

Type	Nominal wt	HE wt	Length	Diameter
500	500kg (1,102lb)	206kg (454lb)	3,000mm (118in)	360mm (13.2in)
375	375kg (827lb)	170kg (375lb)	2,855mm (112in)	330mm (13in)
250	250kg (551lb)	112kg (247lb)	2,285mm (90in)	290mm (11.4in)
50	50kg (110lb)	20kg (44lb)	1,425mm (56in)	180mm (7.1in)

Above: A CASA C.101CC Aviojet (light attack version of the Spanish jet trainer) with two EXPAL 50 bombs and four LAU-10 rocket launchers.

Below: A Mirage F1EE of the Spanish air force with a full load of eight BRP.S.500 para-retarded bombs. EXPAL also make anti-runway bombs.

EXPAL BOMBS

Type	Weight	HE wt	Length	Diameter
1000	1,000kg (2,205lb)	475kg (1,047lb)	3,820mm (150.4in)	460mm (18.1in)
500	500kg (1,102lb)	210kg (463lb)	2,940mm (116in)	360mm (14.2in)
375	375kg (827lb)	170kg (375lb)	2,805mm (110in)	330mm (13in)
250	250kg (551lb)	115kg (253.5lb)	2,150mm (84.6in)	290mm (11.4in)
125	125kg (275.6lb)	55kg (121lb)	1,820mm (71.7in)	240mm (9.45in)
50	50kg (110lb)	20kg (44lb)	1,395mm (54.9in)	180mm (7.1in)

M71 Virgo

Origin: FFV Ordnance, Eskilstuna
Dimensions: length (overall with fuze probe) 1,895mm (74.6in); diameter 214mm (8.42in); diameter of open parachute 530mm (20.9in)
Weights: total assembled bomb 121kg (267lb)

Warhead: RDX/TNT mixture charge 30kg (66lb), surrounded by steel fragments

This fragmentation bomb is designed to be carried externally at supersonic speed, and has single-point suspension and a glassfibre tail housing the retarder parachute. The long (945mm/37.2in) nose probe triggers an electronic proximity fuze which detonates the bomb a few metres above the target or ground vegetation. The bomb disperses a very large number of fragments of predetermined size.

SOVIET UNION

Soviet bombs

There are more than 1,000 types of Warsaw Pact free-fall store, more than three-quarters being of Soviet design. The most numerous are naturally the FABs (GP bombs), the main types being the FAB-100, -250, -500, -750 and -1000 (the numbers being the nominal drop weight in kg). There are at least 14 tactical TN nuclear bombs and an unknown (possibly larger) number of N strategic nuclear bombs. OFABs are HE fragmentation bombs, but many of these are strewn from dispensers. BETABs are retarded anti-runway bombs, two common sizes being the 250 and 500. Three known incendiary bombs are the ZAB-100, -250 and -1000. Many kinds of PLAB napalm store are available, as also are chemical bombs such as the AK mustard/Lewisite, KhAB or ChAB large phosgene, and SOV-AB and NOV-AB for persistent and non-persistent (respectively) Toxic-B fillings. FAEs are fuel/air explosive bombs, some being extremely large. DAP and DV-AB are smoke stores.

Below: An aged MiG-17F on a training mission with two of the unstreamlined FAB-250 (250kg) GP bombs.

Above: Trials and training in the UK are done at West Freugh bombing range in south-west Scotland. Here a

Tornado GR.1 from RAF No.9 Sqn at Honington 'lays down' a short stick of four 1,000lb (454kg) para-retarded bombs.

Below: The cluttered flight deck of HMS *Hermes* during the 1982 Falklands campaign, with Sea Harrier and Sea

Kings. Among the stores can be seen 1,000lb retarded bombs, rockets, torpedoes, depth charges and Sidewinders.

UNITED KINGDOM

British bombs

The known types of British bomb are GP high-explosive bombs weighing 245kg (540lb) Mk 1/2, and 454kg (1,000lb) Mks 2, 6, 6*, 7, 7*, 9, 10, 11, 11*, 12*, 13-16 and 19, those asterisked being compatible with the Hunting Engineering Type 117 retarder tail and the 245kg bomb being compatible with the Type 118 retarder. Both families of retarder have four airbrake panels hinged open from the rear and linked by drag ribbons. The Type 117 is used in two forms, Mk 3 for external carriage (open span 584mm/23in) and the Mk 4 for external or internal carriage (open span 419mm/16.5in). The open span of the Type 118 is 463mm (18.23in). WE.177 is believed to be a nuclear bomb.

UNGUIDED ORDNANCE

Free-fall bombs

US forces have in their inventories a vast number of free-fall ordnance items. These are designed for the whole range of tactical and strategic tasks likely to be demanded of US combat aircraft, but some of the earlier weapons (particularly those in the M series) are now comparatively rare. The following is an abbreviated list in strict alphanumerical order:

M30A1 general-purpose bomb, 45.4kg (100lb); M38A2 practice bomb, 45.4kg (100lb); M40A1 fragmentation bomb, 10.4kg (23lb); M41A1 and M41A2 fragmentation bomblet, 9.1kg (20lb) with a ribbon stabilizer and a shaped-charge/fragmentation warhead to penetrate 10mm (3.94in) of armour; M47 series incendiary or smoke bomb, 45.4kg (100lb) with various incendiary gel or plasticized fillings; M50 series incendiary bomblet, 1.81kg (4lb) mostly filled with magnesium thermite; M52 armour-piercing bomb, 454kg (1,000lb); M56 light-case demolition bomb, 1,814kg (4,000lb); M57 general-purpose bomb, 113kg (250lb); M58 semi-armour-piercing bomb, 227kg (500lb); M59 semi-armour-piercing bomb, 454kg (1,000lb); M64 general-purpose bomb, 227kg (500lb); M65 general-purpose bomb, 454kg (1,000lb); M66 general-purpose bomb, 907kg (2,000lb); M69 incendiary bomblet, 2.7kg (6lb); M70 persistent mustard gas or gel bomb, 52.2kg (115lb); M74 incendiary bomblet, 4.5kg (10lb); M76 incendiary bomb, 227kg (500lb) filled with 81.6kg (180lb) of petrol and magnesium; M78 non-persistent gas bomb, 227kg (500lb) with a

filling of AC, CK or CG; M79 non-persistent gas bomb, 454kg (1,000lb) with a filling of AC, CK or CG; M81 fragmentation bomb, 117.9kg (260lb); M82 fragmentation bomb, 40.8kg (90lb); M83 butterfly fragmentation bomblet, 1.81kg (4lb); M86 fragmentation bomb, 54.4kg (120lb); M88 fragmentation bomb, 99.8kg (220lb); M103 semi-armour-piercing bomb, 907kg (2,000lb); M104 leaflet bomb, 45.4kg (100lb); M105 leaflet bomb, 227kg (500lb); M109 general-purpose bomb, 5,443kg (12,000lb); M110 general-purpose bomb, 9,979kg (22,000lb); M113 persistent gas bomb, 56.7kg (125lb); M116 napalm bomb, 340kg (750lb) with 364 litres (80 US gal) of thickened fuel (in A1 to A23 versions 379 litres/100 US gal of thickened fuel); M117A series general-purpose bomb, 340kg (750lb); M117D destructor, as M117A but with tail retarder; M118 slick low-drag general-purpose bomb, 1,361kg (3,000lb); M121 general-purpose bomb, 4,536kg (10,000lb); M124 practice bomb, 113kg (250lb); M125 non-persistent gas bomblet, 4.54kg (10lb) filled with 1.18kg (2.6lb) of GB; M126 incendiary bomblet, 1.81kg (4lb); M129 leaflet bomb, 340kg (750lb); MC1 non-persistent gas bomb, 340kg (750lb) filled with 99.8kg (220lb) of GB; Mk1 demolition bomb, 907kg (2,000lb); Mk 1 Mod 1/1/3 armour-piercing bomb, 726kg (1,600lb); Mk 5 miniature practice bomb, 1.36kg (3lb); Mk 15 practice bomb, 45.4kg (100lb); Mk 23 miniature practice bomb, 1.36kg (3lb); Mk 33 armour-piercing bomb, 454kg (1,000lb); Mk 36 destructor, basically Mk 82 Mod 1 with acoustic thermal or seismic fuses to trigger the weapon as the appropriate vehicle passes; Mk 65 practice bomb, 227kg (500lb); Mk 66 practice bomb, 454kg (1,000lb); Mk 76 practice bomblet, 11.3kg (25lb); Mk 77 Mod 0 fire bomb, 340kg (750lb) filled with 416 litres (110 US gal) of petroleum oil; Mk 77 Mod 1 fire bomb, 227kg (500lb) filled with 284 litres (75 US gal) of petroleum oil; Mk 78 fire bomb, 340kg (750lb) filled with 416 litres (110 US gal) of petroleum oil; Mk 79 fire bomb, 454kg (1,000lb) filled with 424 litres (112 US gal) of

napalm and petrol; M81 slick low-drag general purpose bomb, 113kg (250lb); Mk 81 Mod 1 Snakeye high-drag general-purpose bomb, as Mk 81 but with a Mk 114 tail retarder; Mk 82 slick low-drag general-purpose bomb, 227kg (500lb); Mk 82 Mod 1 Snakeye high-drag general-purpose bomb, 254kg (560lb) as Mk 82 but with a Mk 15 or Mk 115 tail retarder; Mk 83 slick low-drag general-purpose bomb, 454kg (1,000lb); Mk 82 Mod 2/3 high-drag destructor, as Mk 83 but fitted with a MAU-91A/B tail retarder; Mk 84 slick low-drag general-purpose bomb, 894kg (1,970lb); Mk 86 practice bomb, 113kg (250lb); Mk 87 practice bomb, 227kg (500lb); Mk 88 practice bomb, 454kg (1,000lb); Mk 89 practice bomblet, 25.4kg (56lb); Mk 94 non-persistent gas bomb, 227kg (500lb) filled with 49kg (108lb) of Sarin GB; Mk 106 practice bomblet, 2.27kg (5lb); Mk 111 demolition bomb, 454kg (1,000lb); Mk 116 Weteye lethal chemical bomb, 340kg (750lb) filled with 182.8kg (403lb) of GB; and Mk 122 Fireye fire bomb, with a new filling mix.

Above: A remarkable load of 24 Mk 82 'slick' GP bombs (500lb nominal) let go by an F-111F then (1973) with the 366th TFW at Mountain Home.

Bomb Live Units

All prefixed BLU, these are basically submunitions designed for carriage as clusters or in a dispenser. As such, these weapons are not designed with aerodynamic factors primarily in mind: these are intended principally for area dispersal or parachute stabilization. The following is an abbreviated list in strict alphanumerical order:

BLU-1 fire bomb, 340kg (750lb) filled with 379 litres (100 US gal) of

napalm; BLU-3 Pineapple fragmentation bomblet, 0.79kg (1.75lb) with pop-out drag panels, 0.16kg (0.35lb) filling of Cyclotrol plus 250 steel pellets; BLU-4 anti-materiel bomblet, 0.54kg (1.2lb) with a spherical core that bounces to a height of 3m (10ft) on impact and then explodes; BLU-6 smoke bomb containing a TMU-10 smoke tank; BLU-7 paradropped anti-tank bomblet, 0.64kg (1.4lb) with a shaped charge; BLU-10 fire bomb, 113kg (250lb) with a filling of 125 litres (33 US gal) of napalm; BLU-11 fire bomb, 227kg (500lb) with a filling of 246 litres (65 US gal) of napalm; BLU-14 demolition bomb, a modified MLU-10 for low-level skip penetration; BLU-15 anti-materiel weapon; BLU-18 smoke bomblet, 0.73kg (1.6lb) with an M8 grenade and HC filling; BLU-17 smoke bomblet, 0.5kg (1.1lb) with an M15 grenade and white phosphorus filling; BLU-18 triangular miniature anti-personnel bomblet, 0.19kg (0.4lb) with a delay (booby trap) fuze; BLU-19/B23 chemical bomblet, with an explosive burster to disperse GB nerve gas; BLU-20/B23 parachute-retarded chemical bomblet, with a thermal generator for BZ incapacitant gas; BLU-21/B45 biological bomblet, with a dry biological agent; BLU-22/B45 biological bomblet, with a wet biological agent; BLU-23/B fire bomb, 227kg (500lb) filled with 254 litres (67 US gal) of napalm; BLU-24 Orange spherical anti-personnel fragmentation bomblet, 0.73kg (1.6lb) with plastic fins, a spin-

Below: A well-known F-15B (71-291) with an assortment of bombs, CBUs, Snakeyes, pods, tanks and a HOBOS (plus Sparrow and Sidewinder AAMs).

Cyclotrol filling and spin/impact fusing; BLU-65 fire bomb, 127kg (260lb); BLU-66 Pineapple spherical anti-personnel bomblet, 0.73kg (1.6lb) with plastic tail fins: BLU-67 cratering bomblet, 5kg (11lb); BLU-68 anti-personnel and anti-materiel (APAM) bomblet, 0.42kg (0.93lb) with a filling of zirconium sponge; BLU-60 spherical incendiary bomblet, 0.73kg (1.6lb); BLU-70 spherical anti-personnel and anti-materiel (APAM) incendiary bomblet, 0.4kg (0.88lb): BLU-72 Pave Pat I parachute-retarded fuel/air explosive (FAE) bomb, 499kg (1,100lb) filled with 450kg (992lb) of propane; BLU-73 fuel/air explosive (FAE) bomb, 60kg (132lb) filled with 33kg (73lb) of ethylene oxide and fitted with a long nose-probe fuse to detonate the weapon well above the ground after a parachute-retarded descent; BLU-74 modular fire bomb, 107kg (236lb) filled with Napalm-B; BLU-75 fire weapon; BLU-76 Pave Pat II fuel/air explosive (FAE) bomb, 1,200kg (2,646lb) and intended mainly for high-speed delivery but capable of low-speed dropping with the aid of a parachute retarder; BLU-77 anti-personnel and anti-materiel (APAM) bomblet with anti-tank capability, able to discriminate between soft and hard targets, and based on a shaped-charge warhead with a bounding fragmentation unit for anti-personnel capability; BLU-80 Bigeye chemical bomb; BLU-82 demolition bomb, 6,804kg (15,000lb) designed to clear instant helicopter landing zones in jungle; BLU-82/B 'Big Blue 82' refined version of the BLU-82 with 5,715kg (12,600lb) of GSX gelled slurry blast explosive triggered by a 970mm (38in) nose stand-off probe; BLU-86 fragmentation bomblet, 0.45kg (1lb) with a steel case and Composition-B or Cyclotrol filling; BLU-89 blast/fragmentation general-purpose weapon; and BLU-90 general-purpose weapon with a shaped-charge and blast-fragmentation warhead.

Above: Snakeye retarded bombs flick open immediately upon release from this A-7D Corsair II (with FLIR) from the 23rd TFW at England AFB (today an A-10A outfit).

Left: This crowded portion of the deck of the carrier _Saratoga_ (CVA-60) is occupied mainly by Mk 82 Mod 1 Snakeye retarded bombs.

ed with Napalm-B; BLU-57 fragmentation bomb, 230kg (507lb); BLU-58 general-purpose bomb, 230kg (507lb); BLU-59 version of the BLU-26 with shorter random-delay fusing; BLU-60 fragmentation bomblet, 5.9kg (13lb) with a filling of Cyclotrol; BLU-61 fragmentation/incendiary anti-materiel bomblet. 1kg (2.2lb) with a filling of zirconium and Composition-B; BLU-62 fragmentation bomblet, 0.43kg (0.95lb) based on the BLU-26 with Cyclotrol in a boundary fragmentation unit; BLU-63 spherical fragmentation bomblet, 0.43kg (0.95lb) with a scored steel case,

Below: F/A-18 Hornet pylons, one with a tank and the other with a twin ERU for 'crackle finish' Mk 82 bombs, which can be dropped separately.

delay fuze and filling of Cyclotrol; BLU-25 cylindrical anti-personnel fragmentation bomblet; BLU-26 Guava anti-personnel and anti-materiel (APAM) bomblet, 0.43kg (0.95lb) based on a 60mm (2.36in) steel sphere with a Cyclotrol A3 charge to disperse about 300 steel pellets; BLU-27 fire bomb, 340kg (750lb) filled with 379 litres (100 US gal) of Napalm-B; BLU-28 biological bomblet, with a filling of self-dispersing biological agent; BLU-29 anti-personnel and anti-materiel (APAM) flame agent canister bomb, 73kg (161lb); BLU-30 chemical bomblet, filled with a dry chemical agent; BLU-31 demolition bomb, 340kg (750lb) with an MLU-10 land mine as its core with acoustic and seismic sensors tuned to detonate the weapon when a tank passes within lethal distance; BLU-32 fire bomb, 227 or 268kg (500 or 590lb) filled with 254 litres (67 US gal) of Napalm-B; BLU-33 demolition bomb, 680kg

(1,500lb); BLU-34 hard-structure demolition bomb, 1,361kg (3,000lb); BLU-35 fire bomb, 113kg (250lb) filled with 140kg (309lb) of napalm; BLU-36 anti-personnel and anti-materiel (APAM) bomblet, 0.43kg (0.95lb) with random delay fuzes; BLU-39 chemical bomblet, 0.08kg (0.18lb) designed to bounce along the ground as the filling of CS burns; BLU-40 fragmentation bomblet, 0.78kg (1.7lb) with random delay fuzes; BLU-41 spherical fragmentation bomblet with spin arming and delay; BLU-46 anti-personnel weapon; BLU-47 general-purpose weapon; BLU-48 spherical fragmentation weapon; BLU-49 fragmentation bomblet, 6.1kg (13.4lb) with a ring tail and Cyclotrol 70/30 filling; BLU-50 chemical bomblet filled with BZ incapacitant agent; BLU-51 fire weapon; BLU-52 chemical bomb, 317.5kg (700lb) filled with 279kg (615lb) of CS gas; BLU-53 fire canister bomblet, 9kg (10.8lb) fill-

UNGUIDED ORDNANCE

Nuclear bombs

Early nuclear bombs retired from active service are: Little Boy and Fat Man (used in August 1945), Mk1*, Mk II, Mk III, Mk 5, Mk 6, Mk7, Mk 8*, Mk 11*, Mk 12, Mk 15*, Mk 17*, Mk 18, B20, B21, B24, B36, B39 and B41.

B28

This bomb was developed at Los Alamos Nuclear Laboratory (LANL) and entered USAF service (SAC) in 1958. It was subsequently produced in more variations than any other nuclear device, including W28 warheads for TM-76 Mace and AGM-28 Hound Dog missiles. Most versions have a common warhead section about 915mm (36in) long and of 508mm (20in) diameter, containing a thermonuclear implosion device using plutonium, lithium-6 deuteride and tritium as the fusion material, surrounded by Cyclotrol/PBX-9505 to provide the HE implosion. Different versions offer five yields, four of which are 70kT, 350kT, 1.1MT and 1.45MT. The original B28 was a strategic bomb carried chiefly by the B-52, usually in a quadruple 2x2 pack. Each Mod 0 bomb weighed 1,152kg (2,540lb), but Mods 0-3 have been withdrawn. Current versions are the Mod 4 B28EX, a streamlined bomb for external carriage at supersonic speed, radar fuzed for air or groundburst, length 4,318mm (170in) and weight 919-925kg (2,027-2,040lb); B28IN, most compact version, internally carried,

Below: Four strategic B28s are being loaded on a B-52G by means of special loading vehicle. They appear to be of the B28IN variant.

radar fuzed for air or ground-burst; Mod 5 B28FI, bluff cylindrical bomb for internal carriage with parachute, full fuzing including laydown mode (this is the only laydown version) and weight 1,061kg (2,340lb); Mod 4 B28RE, a streamlined bomb for external carriage, three-fin tail with parachute option, radar fusing for air or groundburst, length 4,216mm (166in) and weight 984kg (2,170lb); and (mainly withdrawn) B28RI, an internally

carried bomb with parachute option, retarded laydown fuzing (four of these were dropped on or offshore Palomares, Spain, in 1966 following a mid-air collision). From 1984 all B28s are being replaced, total numbers falling from about 1,200 to about 900 in 1987, the main replacement being the B83. Remaining bombs have warhead improvements with new electrics and HE more resistant to detonation in a crash or fire.

B43

This high-yield bomb was designed for strategic and tactical aircraft for use against high-value and semi-hardened targets. It is used by the Navy and Marine Corps as well as by SAC and TAC, but is being withdrawn from 1984. Most Mods are streamlined for external carriage, with cruciform fins. The warhead contains oralloy fissile material and lithium-6 deuteride and tritium for fusion, the yield being 1MT. Different models range in length from 3,658mm (144in) to 4,191mm (165in), the greater length being typical of later Mods. Drop weight varies from 934kg (2,060lb) to 962kg (2,120lb) for B43-1 and 971kg (2,140lb) for current Navy Mods. Different Mods were equipped for laydown delivery (minimum height 91m/300ft), or various toss techniques, or free-fall or retarded drop, with airburst or ground detonation. Some 2,000 were deployed in 1983, including a small number with NATO air forces; this may be halved by the time this book is published. Training versions are BDU-6, -8, -18 and -24.

B53

This is the largest bomb used by SAC. It entered service with the Boeing B-47, Boeing B-52 and Convair B-58 in 1962, and a very small number were still active with the B-52 force in 1987. The warhead, similar to the W53 of the now-withdrawn Titan II ICBM, is an all-oralloy device, with lithium-6 deuteride as fusion material, the yield being 9MT. It

Above: Complete stores and ammunition display for a Tactical Air Command F-111, showing the numbers that can be carried of each type. Reading from the centre, the pairs of nuclear weapons are: B43, B57 and B61. In the centre are Sidewinders.

is a cylindrical bomb, with four rectangular fins of broad wedge profile surrounding the bay containing five parachutes: one 1.52mm (5ft) pilot chute, one 4.88m (16ft) canopy and three 14.6m (48ft) canopies. It is possible to deploy and jettison these for a free-fall delivery. Normal delivery is by laydown or retarded drop, with airburst or contact fuzing. Length is 3,760mm (148in), diameter 1,270mm (50in) and weight 4,014kg (8,850lb). The B53's replacements are the B83 and ALCM.

B57
Though used primarily as a depth charge, this bomb has land applications also, being carried by a variety of Navy, Marine and NATO aircraft. A fission device with a yield of 5-10kT, the B57 is normally packaged in a streamlined four-fin container for external fixed-wing carriage, length in this configuration being 3.00m (118in) and diameter 375mm (14.75in). Weights vary from 231 to 322kg (510 to 710lb). Fuzing is provided for low (91m/300ft) laydown, toss delivery or loft, for air or surface burst or with depth pressure fuze in the ASW mode. In 1983 about 1,000 were in tactical use, about half being replaced by the B61 by 1967. The training versions widely used in peacetime are the BDU-12 and -19.

B61
Today the B61 is the most numerous nuclear bomb of the NATO air forces, including the US Air Force, Navy and Marines, Belgium, West Germany, Greece, Italy, the Netherlands and Turkey. A lightweight multipurpose weapon, the B61 can be carried externally at supersonic speeds as well as in the Boeing B-52 or Rockwell B-1B bomb bay. The basic device is all-oralloy, boosted by D-T (lithium-6 deuteride and tritium), and the

Below: A BDU-12, training version of the B57, installed on an F-16A Fighting Falcon parked on the flightline at Eglin AFB, Florida.

Above. The second B-1A (-0159) on weapon separation tests. The bomb is a special test (orange) B61.

surrounding HE is PBX-9404 in early Mods, and IHE (Improved HE, PBX-9502) from the B61-3 onwards. In the standard configuration the B61 is finely streamlined with a four-fin parachute tail. The length is 3,594mm (141.5in), the diameter 338mm (13.3in) and the weights typically 326-347kg (718-765lb). The yield varies from a maximum of 500kT to possibly a minimum of 10kT. The B61-0 entered service in January 1968 (production complete by June 1969); it has Cat-B PAL (permissive action link, triggering the weapon live from the cockpit). The B61-1 (no PAL) entered service in February 1969 and finished production in 1971. The B61-2 had Cat-D PAL and inertial command disable; it entered service in June 1975 and completed production in June 1979. The B61-3 has Cat-F PAL and command disable via a weak/strong link driven by a unique signal generator; it entered service in 1979 and is still in production. The B61-4 has the same features, and has been in production since 1981. The B61-5 has Cat-D PAL, nonviolent command disable and unique-signal weak/strong link; production took place in 1979-80 only. All versions can be delivered by laydown from as low as 15m (50ft) or by free-fall or para-retarded, with airburst or contact or time-delay fuze. In-

flight selection of yield and fuzing can be dialled in. All B61s are being upgraded at least to Dash-3 or -4 standard. Deliveries by 1987 were probably 5,000. Training versions are the BDU-36, -38 and -39E.

B83
This is a new high-yield bomb developed to increase the effectiveness of SAC's nuclear gravity bomb stockpile. Scheduled for deployment as the main bomb of the Rockwell B-1B, as well as the Boeing B-52 and General Dynamics FB-111A, it is the first megaton-class weapon designed for laydown from 46m (150ft) altitude at speeds exceeding Mach 1 in evasive flight, with groundburst fuzing to destroy ICBM silos and similar hardened targets (why manned aircraft instead of missiles should be used to attack fixed sites is not explained). The B83 in initial versions has a plutonium/oralloy mix with IHE, yield being in the low megaton range. The length is 3,658mm (144in) and weight 1,092kg (2,408lb). A new parachute system is designed to slow the bomb from Mach 2 to 90km/h (60mph). The weapon has a Cat-D PAL and weak/strong link disable, and very flexible fusing. Production may eventually exceed 2,500.

Below : A special test F-111A operating from Edwards on B83 carriage trials. One bomb is on the left wing and the other internal.

UNGUIDED ORDNANCE

Albatros CBAS-1

Origin: design CITEFA and manufacture EDESA, Buenos Aires
Dimensions: calibre 70mm (2.75in)
Weight: 8.7kg (19.2lb)
Warhead: anti-tank/anti-personnel 4.45kg (9.8lb), fragmentation 4.65kg (10.25lb), anti-personnel/anti-light matériel 4.8kg (10.6lb), training (smoke) 2.9kg (6.4lb)
User: Argentina (navy), and more than 78,000 exported

This rocket was designed for use from naval aircraft. It has an aluminium body, double-base extruded motor, and flick-open forged steel tail fins.

Below: This Argentine Pucarà, part-hidden among trees, is armed with CBAS-1 launchers.

Right: A Bell JetRanger, similar to the OH-58, of the Brazilian navy, armed with the Avibras SBAT-70 air-to-ground rocket system, and here using launcher LM 70/7. This fires seven rockets of the common 70mm calibre.

Below: This EMBRAER P-95 (commercial designation EMB-111 Bandeirante) of the FAB (Brazilian air force) 7th Aviation Group, 1st Squadron, is armed with Avibras SBAT-127 rockets of just 5in calibre. The lower rocket in each pair is suspended from the one above.

Avibras rockets

Origin: Avibras SA, Sao José dos Campos

This company produces three calibres of aircraft rocket, all based on US originals. The 37mm (1.46in) SBAT-37 is fired from the LM-37/7 launcher carried by light aeroplanes and helicopters. The 70mm (2.75in) SBAT-70 is made in large numbers in two versions: the M1 non-spinning type for high-speed aircraft, and the M2 spinning type which offers greater range and accuracy and can also be fired from low-speed aeroplanes and helicopters. Composite or double-base motors can be used, the former having greater impulse (burn time 1.2 seconds with thrust of 525kg/1,157lb). Seven warheads are available: AVC-70/AC, HEAT anti-tank; /AP, HE fragmentation anti-personnel; /AC/AP, combined anti-tank and anti-personnel; /F, flechette (multi-dart); /FB, white phosphorus smoke; /EF, practice smoke; and /E, inert dummy. By far the biggest of the rockets, the SBAT-127 is similar to the US Zuni and HVAR. It has fixed cruciform tail fins and the warhead weighs 20kg (44.1lb). It is carried in pairs or quads, whereas the common 70mm rocket is fired from launchers housing 2, 4, 7 or 19 rounds. Considerable exports have been achieved by Avibras rockets.

AERIAL ROCKETS

CRV-7

Origin: Bristol Aerospace, Winnipeg
Dimensions: calibre 70mm (2.75in); length (without warhead) 1,042mm (41in)
Weight: (without warhead) 6.6kg (14.6lb)
Warhead: kinetic-energy penetrators weighing 3kg (6.6lb), 4.5kg (9.9lb) and 7kg 615.4lb)
Burnout velocity: (3kg/6.6lb head) 1,500m (4,920ft) per second, or (4.5kg/9.9lb head) 1,250m (4,100ft) per second
Effective range: air/ground, 6,500m (21,325ft)

Developed by the Department of National Defense, the CRV-7 is the highest-velocity aircraft rocket known. Compared with the familiar 70mm (2.75in) Mk 4/40, the trajectory is flatter,

Above: High-speed photography captures the fastest aircraft rockets, CRV-7s, fired from a CAF CF-188 from Cold Lake CFB at Primrose Lake ranges.

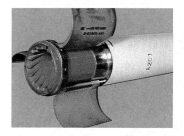

Above: CRV-7 has outward-opening fins and curved spinvanes in the motor nozzle.

range greater and impact energy three times as high. Accuracy is improved by more precise control of motor ignition and faster deployment of the outward-hinged curved fins. Spin is imparted by canted vanes moulded into the nozzle from the high-energy composite motor. The CRV-7 is fired from various launchers, the usual operational type being the 19-tube LAU-5003A/A. The rockets are used by Canada and six other countries.

57mm rocket

Origin: marketed by NORINCO, Beijing
Dimensions: calibre 57mm (2.24in); length (overall) 915mm (36in); span of deployed fins 230mm (9.06in)
Weight: 3.992kg (8.8lb)

Warhead: HE, 1.372kg (3lb)
Users: China and several export customers

Based on the Soviet rocket of the same calibre, this is the first weapon of its type produced in China, originally for loading into eight-tube launchers carried by the Shenyang J-6 (export F-6). Rockets may be fired electrically in rapid sequence or in salvo.

Below: This Chinese People's army air force A-5C (NATO 'Fantan') has launchers for eight Type 57-1 rockets on its inboard pylons.

UNGUIDED ORDNANCE

TBA rockets

Origin: Thomson Brandt Armements, Paris and Boulogne Billancourt
Data: see tables
Users: numerous countries; over 3,000,000 deliveries have been made since 1955 of the first-generation 68mm (2.68in) rocket, and production is in full swing on both calibres

TBA is in production with high-velocity aircraft rockets in two calibres, 68mm (2.68in) and 100mm (3.94in). The former is made in much greater quantities, for firing from various launchers such as TBA's own 12- and 22-tube helicopter launchers, and the Matra F1, F2 and F4 Type 155. In each case the rockets are produced in two basic series, the so-called '1st generation' rockets with conventional types of warhead (as listed in the tables) and the '2nd generation' rockets, which are appreciably longer, and which have warheads tightly packed with kinetic-energy darts of 10:1 fineness ratio which can pierce light armour. The darts are in two sizes (three in the case of the large 100mm rocket), with different penetrative capablity. A salvo of multi-dart rockets can blanket a large area ahead of the launch aircraft.

Above: The RAF's original Harrier GR.Mk 3s can carry the Matra 155 launcher, each firing 19 TBA 68mm rockets, of the 1st generation.

Above: SNEB 68 (TBA) rockets being rippled from four Matra launchers aboard one of the prototype Mirage 2000s. The Multi-Dart rockets look similar.

Below: A group of launchers for TBA rockets, mostly for the 68mm but including (right) a twin launcher for the big 100mm rocket.

68mm ROCKETS

1st generation (single warhead)

Type	Length	Weight	Warhead
253ECC	910mm (35.8in)	5.0kg (11lb)	Hollow-charge, pierces up to 400mm (15.75in) armour
256P.FAP	910mm (35.8in)	6.2kg (13.7lb)	GP HE/frag, 440 fragments
259L.LEM	1,170mm (46.1in)	6.2kg (13.7lb)	ECM chaff screening, multiband decoy
253.3XF2	910mm (35.8in)	5.0kg (11lb)	Inert practice round
252.5XF3	910mm (35.8in)	5.0kg (11lb)	Marking practice

The above all have Type 25 or 68F1B motor, and range 1,000-4,000m (1,095-4,375 yards)

2nd generation (multi-dart)

Type	Length	Weight	Warhead
261.8ABL	1,380mm (54.3in)	8.2kg (18.1lb)	Anti-armour, 8x13.5mm (0.53in) 190g (6.7oz) darts, pierce 10mm (0.4in)
261.36AMV	1,380mm (54.3in)	8.3kg (18.3lb)	Anti-armour, 36x9mm (0.35in) 35g (1.23oz) darts, pierce 8mm (0.3in)
269E.ECL	1,380mm (54.3in)	8.2kg (18.1lb)	Illuminating, marking, 1 million cp, 1 minute
262.6XF1	1,150mm (45.3in)	8.2kg (18.1lb)	Inert practice round
262.4XF4	1,150mm (45.3in)	8.2kg (18.1lb)	Marking practice

The above all have Type F2 motor, and range 1,200-4,000m (1,315-4,375 yards)

100mm ROCKETS

1st generation (single warhead)

Type	Length	Weight	Warhead
ECC	2,500mm (98.4in)	38.0kg (83.8lb)	Hollow-charge, pierces 500mm (19.7in) plus 1,300 fragments
DEM	2,500mm (98.4in)	42.0kg (92.6lb)	Demolition, 3m (10ft) soil plus 300mm (11,8in) concrete
EEG	2,500mm (98.4in)	42.0kg (92.6lb)	GP HE, pierces 100mm (3.9in) at 2,000m, (2,185 yards)
XFUM.F4	2,500mm (98.4in)	42.0kg (92.6lb)	Marking practice

The above all have F1 motor (100mm) and take seconds to reach 4,000m(4,375 yard) range

2nd generation (multi-dart)

Type	Length	Weight	Warhead
AB24	2,740mm (107.9in)	40.5kg (89.3lb)	Anti-armour, 6x24mm (0.94in) 1,650g (3.64lb), pierces 80mm (3.15in)
ABL	2,740mm (107.9in)	39.0kg (86.0lb)	Anti-armour, 36x13.5mm (0.53in) 190g (6.7oz) pierces 11mm (0.43in)
AMV	2,740mm (107.9in)	38.6kg (85.1lb)	Anti-armour, 192x9mm (0.35in) 35g (1.23oz) pierces 8mm (0.3in)

The above all have F1 motor (100mm), range 1,200-4,000m (1,315-4,375 yards) and hit at 500m (1,640ft) per second

(15.4lb). A bigger 10kg (22lb) sub-munition warhead is available containing 11 AT-2 anti-tank bomblets, and a head containing 11 AT-AP submunitions is under development. All 81mm rockets are 1,570mm (61.8in) long, weigh 15.9kg (35lb) with a 7kg (15.4lb) head, have burn time of 0.85 seconds and burnout velocity of 630m (2,067ft) per second.

The 122mm rocket is based on a field artillery system modified for use from 3- or 4-tube launchers, respectively for helicopters and aeroplanes. These large rockets are available either with single (HE or HEAT) warheads or with two types of submunition warheads, housing either 77 anti-personnel bomblets (Type APAMB) or six anti-tank mines (Type ATM). The submunition head increases overall length from 2.5m (8.2ft) to 3.0m (9.84ft), and weight from 60kg (132.3lb) to 66kg (145.5lb). This reduces burnout velocity from 750m (2,461ft) to 670m (2,198ft) per second.

Above: BPD rockets of the 50mm size, with different warheads, together with a single example of the larger 81mm family.

Below: BPD '2in' rockets are variously called 50 or 51mm. This Aerea launcher, mounted on an Agusta A 109A, fires a salvo of 14.

Above: The French SOCATA Guerrier light attack aircraft is seen here fitted with Matra F2 launchers, each for 6x68mm rockets, outboard.

ITALY

BPD rockets

Origin: SNIA BPD, Rome

This company is in production with aircraft rockets in three calibres, 51mm (nominal 2in), 81mm (3.19in) and 122mm (4.8in) all intended for use against ground targets. The 51mm rocket is available in two types, designated ARF/8M3 and ACR/M4, with 2.2kg (4.85lb) warheads of the following types: HEI, PFF, AT-AP (anti-tank, anti-personnel), SP (spotting), illuminating and practice (smoke, flash or inert). All have a length of 1,048mm (41.3in), weight of 4.8kg (10.6lb), burn time 1.1 seconds to peak velocity of 515m (1,135ft) per second. More powerful 3kg (6.6lb) warheads are being developed.

The 81mm rocket can, like the other models, be used by all aeroplanes and helicopters, and is available with the following warheads: HE, PFF, AT-AP and spotting, all weighing 7kg

UNGUIDED ORDNANCE

SPAIN

INTA rockets

Origin: design by INTA (MoD organization), Madrid

Standard rockets are produced in Spain under the designations S9 in 37mm (1.46in) calibre, S11 in the popular 70mm (2.75in) size and S12 in the big 100mm (3.94in) calibre. All are conventional single-warhead types with flick-out fins. The aircraft manufacturer CASA makes launchers: 18-and 54-tube for 37mm, 6- and 18-tube for the 70mm, and 6-tube for the 100, in all cases with electronic intervalometer. For light aircraft and helicopters CASA makes an external quad rack for 57mm or 80mm Oerlikon rockets.

SWEDEN

Bofors rockets

Origin: AB Bofors, Bofors

The Bofors company produces aircraft rockets in two standard calibres, 75mm (2.95in) and 135mm (5.3in). The former is available as the M57 with regular 7kg (15.4kg) HE warhead, the M57AC anti-tank with armour-piercing warhead, and the M57B with a fragmentation type warhead for use against personnel and soft targets. These rockets are all fired from 19-tube launchers or from single mounts.

Below: This AJ37 Viggen is armed with four launchers each housing six of the extremely powerful Bofors rocket of 135mm calibre.

The large 135mm rocket is extremely powerful. Known as the M70 system, it uses a standard 25kg (55.1lb) motor with a burn time of 2 seconds, giving a burnout velocity of 600m (1,969ft) per second. The GP warhead with fuze weighs 21kg (47.3lb) and contains a 3.7kg (8.2lb) charge; the AP fragmentation head weighs 20kg (44.1lb) and contains a 5kg (11lb) charge; and the practice head weighs 21kg (46.3lb). Earlier rockets of the 135mm calibre are the M56 and M60 series. All are fired from six-tube launchers or from single mounts. Small numbers are deployed in even larger calibres, including the 145mm (5.7in) M49 hollow-charge rocket for use against armour, and rockets reported to have calibres of 150mm (5.9in) and 180mm (7.09in).

SWITZERLAND

SNORA rockets

Origin: Oerlikon-Bührle Ltd, Zurich

These 81mm (3.19in) rockets are very widely used. They have a standard TWK 006 internal-burning motor, flick-out fins and the range of warheads and weights detailed in the table. SNORA rockets are fired from the following launchers: SAL-12-80 for all types of aircraft; SAL-6-80 for supersonic aircraft; AL-6-80 for low-performance aircraft; and HL-7-80 for helicopters (in each case the first number is the number of tubes).

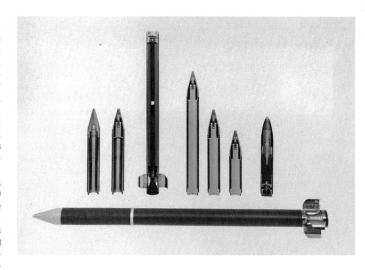

Above: Seen with a complete 81mm SNORA are (from left), trainer, marker, motor, 11kg, 7kg, 4.5kg ball-fragment and hollow-charge AT warhead.

Below: A special Swiss trials Mirage IIIS seen with the Oerlikon launcher for 12 SNORA rockets of the standard '80' (81mm) size.

OERLIKON SNORA ROCKETS

Type	Length	Weight	Warhead
RAK 022	1,548mm (60.9in)	15.7kg (34.61lb)	UGK 028 practice, 670m (2,198ft) per second
RAK 023	1,415mm (55.75in)	13.2kg (29.1lb)	SSK 031 fragmentation, 820m (2,690ft) per second 702 fragments
RAK 024	1,548mm (60.9in)	15.7kg (34.6lb)	SSK 029 fragmentation, 670mm (2,198ft) per second 1,215 spheres
RAK 025	1,783mm (70.2in)	19.7kg (43.4lb)	SSK 032 fragmentation, 520m (1,705ft) per second 2,133 spheres
RAK 026	1,510mm (59.4in)	13.2kg (29.1lb)	PHK 030 hollow-charge, 820 (2,690ft) per second 350mm (13.8in) penetration

SURA rockets

Origin: Oerlikon-Bührle Ltd, Zurich

These standardized 81mm (3.19in) rockets are unusual in that, instead of being fired from tube-type launchers, they are mounted externally hung one from another. A unique feature is that their cruciform 'tail' fins are initially arranged amidships around the body, the rocket being hung from the two upper fins and stabilized by a rear connection which incorporates the electrical firing socket. When the rocket is fired it initially travels straight ahead, guided by passing through its fin central drum. When the enlarged rear cone of the motor hits the fin drum it carries it ahead with it, disengaging its slots from those of the rocket from which it was hung. The system is deployed aboard all kinds of aircraft from supersonic to helicopters. Large numbers were delivered, to many countries, of the SURA Type FL. Current production is of the upgraded SURA-D, which has a TWK 007 motor weighing 8.4kg (18.5lb) and burning for 0.9 second to give burnout velocity (depending on warhead) of 530-595m (1,739-1,952 ft) per second. Overall rocket length varies from 1,077 to 1,212mm (42.4 to 47.7in) depending on warhead and launch weight from 12.7 to 14.2kg (28 to 31.3lb). Currently available types are: RAK 047 with PI-3 3kg (6.6lb) hollow-charge head; RAK

048 with UGK 033 4.5kg (9.9lb) practice head; RAK 049 with USK 035 4.5kg (9.9lb) marker; RAK 050 with SSK 031 4.5kg (9.9lb) HE fragmentation; RAK 051 with USE 3 3kg (6.6lb) practice head; RAK 052 with UIS 3 3kg (6.6lb) HE incendiary; and RAK 053 with US 3 3kg (6.6lb) HE fragmentation.

Right: The 81mm SURA family, showing a rocket with fins in flight position and (from left) 3kg and 4.5kg training, 4.5kg marker, motor, 3kg square fragment, 4.5kg ball fragment HE, 3kg HE incendiary and AT.

Below: BO 105 with SURA-D 81mm rockets.

Below: SURA rockets have been launched from a Lynx AH.Mk 1 of the British army. These rockets are far from being smokeless.

UNGUIDED ORDNANCE

Above: A captain in Soviet Frontal Aviation checking loading of a UV-16-57, the world's most numerous aircraft rocket launcher (on MiG-21).

Soviet rockets

It has been estimated that production of the S-5 series rocket of '57mm' calibre (actually 55mm/2.17in but fired from 57mm/2.24in tubes) is greater than that of all other aircraft rockets in the world combined. S-5s are conventional single-head folding fin rockets, with a typical burnout speed of 620m (2,034ft) per second. They can have any of nine types of head, including HE, antiarmour, fragmentation and chaff. The four standard launchers are the UV-8-57, UV-16-57, UV-19-57 and (most common on heli-

copters) UV-32-57, the first number denoting the number of tubes, loaded from the rear. Other rockets include the S-8 series of 80mm (3.15in), S-13 of 130mm (5.1in), S-16 of 160mm (6.3in), S-21 of 210mm (8.27in), S-24 of 240mm (9.45in), S-28 of 280mm (11.00in), and S-32 of 325mm (12.8in). Most of the heavy calibres are seldom seen, and there is even a report of a 'TRS-190' of 190mm (7.5in) calibre and an 'ARS-212' of 212mm (8.35in) size.

British rockets

The standard rocket family of the Royal Air Force is the SNEB 68mm (2.68in) type originally designed in France by Hotchkiss-Brandt and normally fired

from Matra type launchers. The SNEB, the immediate predecessor the TBA Types 252 to 259 described under Thomson Brandt of France, has eight fins which are pushed open by motor gas pressure, locked in position and have chamfered leading edges to induce spin. The usual Fleet Air Arm rocket is the 2in (50.8mm), of original French Matra design.

American rockets

By far the most common families of aircraft rocket are the 2.75in (69.85mm, commonly designated as 70mm) weapons made by various contractors to almost common designs. These usually have eight flick-out fins, and are all descended from the original Mighty Mouse air-to-air rocket of 1948. Various (nine types) of warhead are available, all in the 3.4kg (7.5lb) range. The earliest versions of the 2.75in rocket still in service are the Mk 4 and Mk 40, intended for use by high-performance fixed-wing aircraft and helicopters respectively. These belong to the original FFAR family, having folding fins that open to a diameter of 165mm (6.5in) after launch to provide maximum flight stability. In addition the Mk 40 has a scarfed rocket nozzle. The range of these two models is 500 to 6,000m (1,640 to 19,685ft). The two variants were then replaced by the Mk

Left: Principal weapons of the McDonnell Douglas AH-64A Apache include (blue) standard 2.75in rockets, seen with 19-tube launchers. Other items are 30mm ammunition, tanks and 16 Hellfires.

Hydra 70 Warheads

M261
The Hydra 70 is a proven system of 70mm (2.75in) folding-fin rockets. The M261 warhead contains ten high-explosive submunitions for use against armour, materials, personnel and many other targets. The M267 is a smoke-generating training version.

M247
The M247 is a shaped-charge marked for use against armoured targets. The charge is detonated on impact at the correct stand-off distance by an M438 base-mounted fuze. The only problem is that the rocket must strike the target.

M255
The M255 is a flechette warhead which contains approximately 2,500 28-grain flechettes plus three tracers for many missions including air-to-air as well as air-to-ground. The usual fuze for helicopter operations is the M439 airburst-type set to 500-6,000m height.

M264
Another warhead for the Hydra 70 family of rockets is the M264 smoke screen type. It provides up to five minutes of effective smoke screen for target marking or obscuration. In helicopter missions it would be triggered by an M439RC fuze, with airburst remotely set, giving variable range of engagement.

M262
The M262 is a specialized illumination warhead used against ground targets at night. It provides approximately one million candlepower illumination for a total time of roughly two minutes. This head is another usually fitted with the M439RC remote-set airburst fuze.

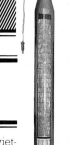

M?
The Department of Defense had not allocated a designation number to this warhed as this book went to press. It is a special long head packed with discs of radar chaff for jamming, decoy and effective countermeasure avoidance. It is another of the heads triggered by the M439RC fuze, though seven other fuzes are available, some of them nose-mounted.

Above: Dramatic picture of a 5in Zuni rocket being fired at Yuma from an A-4M Skyhawk II of Marine Attack Squadron VMA-324.

Below: Four blunt-nosed Zuni rockets can be seen in the launcher on this Bell AH-1T SeaCobra of the US Marines, which also has Sidewinders.

Right: Six types of warhead can be fitted to the Hydra 70 motor, the latter not being illustrated in this series of section drawings.

66, which introduced four wrap-round fins and spin-up while still inside the launcher for maximum flight stability (and accuracy) whether fired from rotary- or fixed-wing aircraft. This offers a complete flight-regime capability from the hover to high subsonic speeds, the rockets having a range between 500 and 8,000m (1,640 and 26,246ft). The family of warheads available to the 2.75in rocket maximizes the type's effectiveness in the air-to-surface role and, when launched from helicopters, the air-to-air role.

The warheads are the following: M151 HE, M247 HEAT, M255 flechette, M261 dispenser for nine M73 AT/AP submunitions, M262 illuminating, M264 smoke, M267 practice, and chaff. The highest-performance rocket of this family is the Hydra, now being marketed, which among other features has a high-impulse motor giving burnout speed in the region of 1,000m (3,280ft) per second. The Navy and Marine Corps still use the Zuni series of 127mm (5in) heavy rockets for air-to-ground use.

YUGOSLAVIA

Yugoslav rockets

Standard rockets are the Soviet-designed 57mm (called VRZ-57) and 130mm (VRZ-127).

UNGUIDED ORDNANCE

CB-130/CB-500 cluster bomb units

Origin: Industrias Cardoen SA, Santiago
Dimensions: length (130) 2,050mm (80.7in) or (500) 2,640mm (103.9in); diameter (130) 253mm (9.96in) or (500) 446mm (17.6in)
Weights: (130) 60kg (132lb) or (500) 245kg (540lb)

These CBUs are not very different in length, and both have NATO standard 356mm (14in) mounting lugs, but the CB-500 is very much fatter. Thus, while the 130 houses 50 bomblets, the 500 dispenses 240. The bomblets are 360mm (14.2in) long, 48mm (1.9in) in diameter and weigh 0.74kg (1.63lb). The CBU can withstand 6g while attached to the aircraft, and can be released over a wide range of speeds and heights, giving different elliptical bomblet patterns according to the delay (from 3 to 18 seconds) set on the electronically programmed fuze. Maximum ground coverage is 50,000m² (59,800 sq yards). When used against armour it is claimed that plate exceeding 230mm (9.1in) can be penetrated.

Below: General arrangement of the Cardoen CB-500 cut away to show the bomblets. The ghosted image shows the deployed position of the flick-out fins at the rear.

Above: A Chilean Mirage 50 loaded with two drop tanks and examples of both sizes of Cardoen CBU, the big CB-500 and the smaller CB-130.

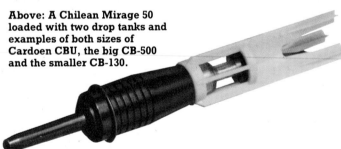

Above: A single 'bomba menor' or bomblet, carried in both sizes of Cardoen dispenser. The stand-off nose fuze probe ensures maximum armour penetration up to 150mm (6in).

1 Nose fuze (electronic timing).
2 Dispenser body.
3 Bomblets (in this case 240).
4 Suspension lugs (single UK, 250mm Warsaw Pact or 356mm/14in NATO).
5 Tailfins (fixed and retractable stabilizer fins).

Ferrimar cluster bomb system

Origin: Ferrimar, Santiago
Weights: fully loaded 227kg (500lb), 680kg (1,500lb) or 1,020kg (2,250lb) nominal

Ferrimar makes large CBUs in aluminium alloys, glassfibre, carbon fibre and moulded plastics. They each carry from 100 to 248 Avispa (wasp) bomblets, which have been developed in eight varieties with diameter from 48mm (1.9in) to 53mm (2.1in), with electronic fuzing. The varieties are: HEAT (high-explosive anti-tank), HEAT-AP30, HEAT-AP50, HEAD (HE area-denial), HEAD-AP30, HEAD-AP50, AP-Prox30 and AP-Prox50. The CBUs are suspended by either NATO 356mm (14in) or Warsaw Pact 250mm (9.84in) lugs. After release, tail fins flick open to spin the container to assist dispersion of the bomblets. Larger bomblets are being developed for use against such targets as ships and land fortifications needing larger warhead charges.

Cardoen CB-500

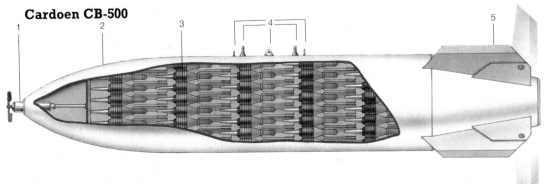

DISPENSER SYSTEMS

Alkan cartridge dispensers

Origin: R. Alkan et Cie, Valenton
Dimensions: vary with model
Weights: Model 500 (loaded) 74kg (163lb), and Model 530 (loaded) 135kg (298lb)
Users: France and export customers

The 500 series of dispensers are streamlined containers with side doors through which standard 74mm (2.9in) cartridges (described in the section on bombs) are loaded into sideways-firing tubes. The commonest production models are the Model 500, with a single block of 20 tubes, suitable for light attack and counter insurgency aircraft, and the Model 530, with two such blocks totalling 40 tubes for supersonic aircraft. Both dispensers are attached to standard NATO 356mm (14in) interfaces.

Giboulée

Origin: Thomson Brandt Armements, Paris and Boulogne-Billancourt
Dimensions: length 3,850mm (151.6in); width 400mm (15.75in); depth 700mm (27.6in)
Weight: loaded 490kg (1,080lb)
User: France (air force)

This bomblet dispenser was developed from 1966 by Thomson-CSF, Matra and LTE, principally to increase the effectiveness of low-level attacks on armour. The name means a sudden shower and, hence, a shower of blows. The dispenser consists of a streamlined box containing 12 or 24 tubes each housing five bomblets which are launched rearwards under electronic timing. The tubes are aligned in azimuth at different angles so that the shower of bomblets covers a chosen area; with 24 tubes and typical spacing the result is 120 bomblets distributed on a rec-

tangular mesh 4m x 3.3m (13.1ft x 10.8ft) over an area 20m (66ft) wide and 80m (262ft) long. The firing velocity is 230m (755ft) per second, or 835km/h (519 mph), and the objective is to match this with the aircraft speed to give zero bomblet ground speed. After leaving the tube each bomblet releases a coil spring which opens rear drag vanes which immediately stabilize the bomblet in a vertical attitude to fall at moderate speed. Each bomblet weighs 0.7kg (1.5lb) and contains 0.1kg (0.2lb) of explosive. Hollow-charge bomblets are used against armour, with penetration of 250mm (9.8in), and fragmentation bomblets can be loaded for attacks on personnel and softer vehicles. The pilot has control over the initiation point of the ejection sequence, the bomblet density and whether all or half the load is dispensed on each pass.

Belouga

Origin: Matra SA, Vélizy-Villacoublay, and Thomson Brandt Armements, Paris and Boulogne-Billancourt
Dimensions: length 3,300mm (129.9in); diameter 360mm (14.28in); fin span 550mm (21.6in)
Weight: loaded 305kg (672lb)
User: France and seven export air forces

This bomblet dispenser was developed as an improved successor to the Giboulée, with

reduced aerodynamic drag, the ability to be launched in attacking runs at greater speed and covering a larger ground area. The weapon is also known as BLG.66, and its name is that of the white whale. Each Belouga is supplied as a complete item of ordnance ready for use, loaded with 151 grenades. The latter are of 66mm (2.6in) calibre, weigh 1.3kg (2.9lb) each and are of three types: GP fragmentation, hollow-charge for use against armour and area-interdiction for use against road, rail and airfield areas. Belouga is attached as a single unit by NATO 356mm (14in) lugs. The pilot can select either of two ground patterns prior to release: 40-60m (130-195ft) wide by 120m (395ft) long,

Above: Belouga cluster munition dispensers carried by a Mirage 2000 of the French Armée de l'Air. Relatively light and with low drag, Belouga can be carried in multiple by most fighters.

or 40-60m (130-195ft) wide by 240m (785ft) long. On release, at any speed up to 1,020km/h (634mph) at a minimum height of 60m (200ft), the store is sharply braked to pull it back far behind the aircraft. It then strews the grenades at a regular rate to each side, and these also are individually braked to fall sensibly vertically in a regular pattern. Production began in 1979, and about 4,000 rounds have been delivered.

Above: A side elevation of Belouga. It is one of a diverse range of aircraft weapons produced by Matra and Thomson Brandt.

Below: The same basic principle of operation is used in both Giboulée and Belouga. The aircraft makes a fast low-level run across the target area and releases at least one store. The latter is braked by parachute and then dispenses its submunitions evenly to left and right.

Dispensing Sub-Munitions

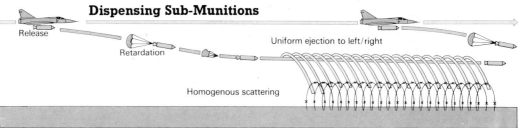

Release

Retardation

Uniform ejection to left/right

Homogenous scattering

UNGUIDED ORDNANCE

MDS

Origin: MBB, Munich
Dimensions: length varies from 2,500-4,500mm (98.4-177.2in); width 630mm (24.8in); height varies from 340-660mm (13.4-26in)
Weight: loaded varies from 500-1,750kg (1,100-3,858lb)
User: still under development (1987)

The Modular Dispenser System is planned by Messerschmitt-Bölkow-Blohm as a versatile weapon system able to be tailored to all kinds of tactical jet aircraft. It is a much more flexible system than MW-1 and in most installations has lower drag, although the bomblet capacity is usually smaller. As in the earlier weapon, the bomblet calibre is 132mm (5.2in), and different types of geometrically identical submunition may be loaded to fit the container for attacks on armour, personnel, runways, SAMs and any other tactical target. A proportion can be delayed-fuze submunitions for area-denial purposes. One typical MDS container, hung on NATO 762mm (30in) centres, has 42 double-ended tubes to project the submunitions in timed sequence to left and right. The key feature of MDS is that the container is assembled from modules of standard size, for example by superimposing from one to six layers of single-row double-ended tubes. The complete box then requires only a streamlined nose and tail. Limits of aircraft trajectory at release are a height of not less than 50m (165ft) and speed of between Mach 0.6 and 0.9. The submunition pattern can be selected for any of a range of automatically governed results. The discharged MDS container is normally not jettisoned but is returned for reloading.

Below: Experimental and test prototype of the MBB MDS dispenser mounted on a Northrop F-20 Tigershark.

MW-1

Origin: MBB, Munich
Dimensions: length 5,300mm (208.7in)
User: West Germany (air force)

The first dispenser of its kind to go into production, MW-1 (Mehrzweckwaffe 1) was developed by Messerschmitt-Bölkow-Blohm as one of the chief weapons of the Tornado aircraft in service with the Luftwaffe. It comprises up to four sections (two rectilinear centre sections and slightly streamlined nose and tail sections) which when fitted together form an enormous store carried under the aircraft fuselage and imposing a considerable aerodynamic drag penalty. Each section contains 28 double-ended tubes of 132mm (5.2in) diameter for submunitions of different types, including contact-fuzed hollow-charged bomblets for use against armour and other species. At present the MW-1 can be loaded with any of six types of submunition.

KB44 is a small subcalibre (44mm/1.73in diameter) armour-piercing bomblet weighing 0.6kg (1.3lb) and fitted with a hollow-charge head capable of piercing all known top and side armour. The MW-1 tubes are loaded with packs of seven, there being linear room for three packs on each side of the centreline; thus there can be up to 4,704 KB44 submunitions strewn by a single dispenser in one pass.

MIFF is a full 132mm (5.2in) calibre submunition weighing 3.4kg (7.5lb). It is a ground mine intended for use mainly against armour. Seven or eight can be loaded into each tube, resulting in a total load of 872 per MW-1 system. When fired (four different ejection charges being used, as with the other stores, to throw the mines different distances from the ground line of the aircraft track) the mine falls freely to the ground and radially-projecting spring struts tip it over and stabilize it so that either flat face is pointing upwards. The two internal plate charges are then detonated either by ground vibration or magnetically by the passage of a tank hull or other

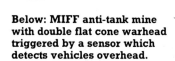

Below: MIFF anti-tank mine with double flat cone warhead triggered by a sensor which detects vehicles overhead.

Below: MUSA is an active area-denial mine developed jointly by MBB and RTG-Diehl. It is self-righting.

vehicle. MIFF can also be used against airfields, and is arranged to self-destruct after a preset time in the absence of a target.

MUSA is a 132mm (5.2in) fragmentation bomb weighing 4.2kg (9.25lb), and used against personnel and soft-skinned vehicles. Cylindrical, it is parachute retarded and self-righting on

reaching the ground where it detonates, its lethal radius being more than 100m (330ft). The total number of MUSA submunitions can be 648 (672 at six per tube throughout).

MUSPA is a 132mm (5.2in), 4.2kg (9.25lb) mine similar to MUSA but used with a delay fuze in an area-denial role. Intended particularly for use against airfields, it lies on the ground, stabilized face-upwards, and is triggered acoustically by the passage overhead of an aircraft on the runway or taxiway. To deter clearance, MUSPAs also self-destruct with random time delay.

STABO is a large (17kg/37.5lb) munition for penetrating and cratering runways. After ejection from the dispenser (which can carry 200, or 224 with every cell occupied), the STABO is stabilized vertically and parachute retarded to fall on the paved surface. As it falls, a small projecting sensor is activated, and as this

DISPENSER SYSTEMS

Above: Few aircraft weapons are as visually impressive as the MBB/Diehl MW-1, here seen in action with a Tornado.

Above: KB44 is a bomblet for use against armour. It also offers a fragmentation effect against soft targets.

Above: Biggest of the MW-1 submunitions, STABO is a parachuted device for cratering airfield runways.

Below: MUSPA is a passive mine which after settling right way up is triggered by aircraft taxiing overhead.

touches the ground it detonates a piercing charge. This blows a hole in the pavement through which a follow-through projectile is fired to detonate below the pavement to cause a crater and heave damage over a wide area. Repair is difficult.

ASW is an anti-shelter weapon very similar in concept to the STABO, and similar in size. Its operating sequence has three phases. After its stabilized para-braked descent it hits the earth covering a hardened shelter. This fires a boost rocket which drives the munition down until it is arrested by the concrete shelter structure beneath. This in turn detonates a shaped charge to pierce a hole through which a secondary projectile is accelerated to explode within the shelter.

Deliveries of MW-1 began to Luftwaffe JaboG 31 'Boelcke' in August 1984. About 1,400 systems should have been received soon after this book appears.

VEBAL/Syndrom

Origin: MBB, Munich
Data: not yet final
User: probably to be West Germany (air force)

With a name derived from Vertical Ballistic, this anti-armour dispenser uses an accompanying multi-sensor pod to sense and locate targets and ensure direct hits. Thus, the submunition pod can carry a smaller number of more powerful munitions. The sensors comprise an IR linescan, laser, radar and sensitive radiometer, the last being used to check the target's thermal characteristics and ensure positive identification. A fast microprocessor converts the information into precise aiming data. In operation, once activated, the system is autonomous and needs no pilot intervention. At a height of 76m (250ft) the sensor pod scans a swath 30m (100ft) wide. The accompanying VEBAL dispenser contains about 30 inclined tubes which fire large submunitions downwards and to the rear. With precise aiming and timing it can practically be guaranteed that each anti-armour bomblet will hit penetrating the tank's top armour. Extensive test flying, using a Luftwaffe McDonnell Douglas F-4F, is expected to lead to production by about 1989.

Below: VBW, a variant of VEBAL/Syndrom, is here seen mounted on an Alpha Jet, which is seen as one of the chief carriers. This particular dispenser is fitted with 18 inclined tubes only.

UNGUIDED ORDNANCE

CH-TABO

Origin: Federal Aircraft Factory, Emmen (Switzerland) in collaboration with Matra SA, Vélizy-Villacoublay (France), all marketing being by the French company
User: coming into production for several customers

This system comprises a pylon-mounted container for (typically) seven bomblet payloads for time release against soft or semi-hardened targets. Each bomblet comprises a spherical case containing an aluminium matrix, explosive charge and 8,000 cast steel balls. The bomblets are ejected from the container by dynamic air pressure, and are stabilized and braked by an integral cast aluminium tail fan which spins the bomb. Each bomb can be fitted with a sensitive mechanical fuze with a telescopic stand-off probe or with an electronic proximity fuze set to a chosen airburst height. With airburst fusing two CH-TABO containers can cover an area 200m by 50m (low level delivery at Mach 0.6-0.85) with a density of four fragments per square metre and penetration throughout of 5mm (0.2in) of steel plate.

LOCPOD

Origin: joint NATO programme by the USA, Canada, Italy and Spain
Propulsion: small solid-propellant rocket motor
Dimensions: (LD-LAD) length 4.17m (13.68ft); wing span about 1.57m (5.15ft); body cross section 660mm (26in) wide by 440mm (17.3in) deep
Weight: (LD-LAD) 1,020kg (2,250lb)
Performance: maximum speed 1,297km/h (806mph); maximum range unpowered 13km (8 miles) or powered 37km (23 miles)
Warhead: submunitions payload of 744kg (1,640lb)
Users: to developer countries

Above: LAD (Low-Altitude Dispenser) is the contribution of Brunswick Defense (USA) to the multinational LOCPOD. This LAD is on an F-16A.

The Low-Cost Powered Dispenser is being developed under a memorandum of understanding signed by the four nations in 1985. The principal candidate is the LD-LAD (Low-Drag Low-Altitude Dispenser) being developed by Brunswick (USA), Garrett (Canada), Agusta and OTO Melara (Italy) and ENSB and CASA (Spain). LD-LAD is compatible with the General Dynamics F-16 and similar aircraft and is offered as a replacement for SUU-54 and AGM-130, and as a near-term candidate for various NATO modular dispenser programmes including LOCPOD.

TAL-1 and -2

Origin: Rafael Armaments (MoD), Haifa
Dimensions: length (with fuze) 2.345mm (92.1in); diameter 406mm (16in); fin span 560mm (22.05in)
Weight: 250kg (551lb)
User: Israel

TAL cluster dispensers are identical except for payload, the TAL-1 (of 1981) being loaded with 279 bomblets each of 500g (17.6oz) and TAL-2 (of 1983) hav-

Left and below: TAL-1 is an Israeli anti-personnel cluster bomb available for export. It dispenses its bomblets by spinning centrifugal action, to cover the largest possible ground area. It is maintenance-free.

TAL-1

1 Nose fuze.
2 Nose section.
3 Arming wire.
4 Bomblets (279).
5 Suspension lug.
6 Container panels.
7 Tail section.

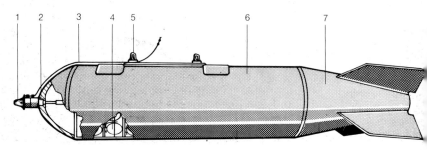

ing a payload of 315 bomblets each of 400g (14.1oz). In each case the submunitions have an HE content of about 160g (5.6oz) and generate about 1,800 fragments. The dispenser is attached singly or on multi-ejector racks via standard NATO 356mm (14in) lugs, and are safed by an arming wire to the nose fuze. On release the store is spun by its tail fins so that, when a safe distance from the aircraft, the case can be opened and the submunitions flung out over a wide area. Pattern size is governed by the timing of the fuze, and can reach a maximum of 53,000m² (63,400sq yards). The lethal radius of each bomblet is given as 8m (26.25ft), all exploding on impact.

Skyshark

Origin: Consorzio Armamenti Spendibili Multi Uso (a consortium formed by Aeritalia and SNIA BPD, Rome)
Dimensions: length 4,757mm (187.3in); wing span 1,500mm (59.05in); body cross-section 0.394m² (4.24sq ft)
Weights: payload 745kg (1,642lb); loaded weight glide

Left: The Skyshark was first test dropped in 1987 by an Italian air force Tornado IDS. Visible here in a separation trial is the excellent streamlining of this weapon, which has a low radar signature, and the dispenser tubes in its lower section.

Below: Seen displayed alongside an AMX, Skyshark can either glide to its target or be jet-propelled over much greater distances. Note the pitot head above the nose of this example, which was not fitted with propulsion.

1,050kg (2,315lb) and propelled 1,170kg (2,579lb)
Users: Italy and export customers

The first product of the CASMU consortium is yet another dispenser of various kinds of submunition for lateral ejection from a store released at high speed at low level during a pass over different kinds of tactical target, the nature of the target dictating the particular submunitions selected. Where CASMU hope to score over the many rival systems are in two areas: Skyshark is to have a very low radar cross-section, achieved by suitable shaping and use of radar-absorbent materials, and a

very advanced electronic fire-control system which includes onboard guidance. Small wings confer an extended glide capability, so that if released at low level at Mach 0.8 it can travel autonomously 6-12km (3.7-7.4 miles) to its target. A developed version with a small rocket motor would fly 20-25km (12.4-15.5 miles), and the intention is to develop a cruise version.

CB 470

Origin: Armscor, Pretoria
Dimensions: length 2,600mm (102.4in); diameter 419mm (16.5in); fin span 640mm (25.2in)
Weights: empty 170kg (375lb); loaded 450kg (992lb)
Users: probably South Africa and Zimbabwe

This dispenser and its associated bomblet stemmed from development in Rhodesia during the UDI era. An airburst anti-personnel munition was needed, but there was no possibility of developing the proximity fuze. Accordingly tests took place to perfect a spherical 'bouncing bomb' and this was eventually refined into the present pattern in which a rubber-coated steel case houses 1.4kg (3.1lb) of RDX/TNT, the bomblet weight being 6.2kg (13.7lb). On release the bomblets hit the ground, spin up and bounce forwards and upwards. Each bomb is detonated 0.65 seconds after ground impact, and even after striking mud or water this still results in a mid air burst at a height of 3 to 5m (10 to 16.5ft). Each burst scatters fragments at about 1,300m (4,625ft) per second. At first the bomblets, called Alphas, were scattered from basket trays carried in bomb bays. Development in South Africa led to their being packaged 40 at a time into the CB 470 dispenser pod. This can be carried on NATO 356mm (14in) or Warsaw Pact 250mm (9.84in) pick-ups, and is released at any speed between 850 and 1,100km/h (528 and 684mph) at a typical height of 30m (100ft), though the limits are 25m and 300m (82 and 985ft). On release, after 0.8 seconds the first radial row of four bomblets is ejected by cartridge, early radial rows being ejected at a velocity of 12m (39ft) per second falling with the final rows to 2m (6.6ft) per second. Each bomb is armed one second after being ejected, to avoid bombs being detonated by mutual collision. There are comprehensive safeguards. Each container covers an area from 30m (100ft) to 70m (230ft) wide by 250m (820ft) long.

UNGUIDED ORDNANCE

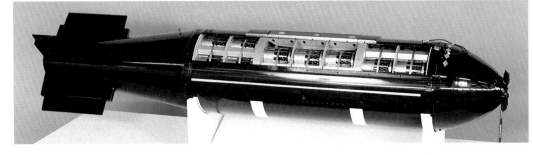

The Soviet Union was a pioneer of cluster dispensers, sophisticated designs being in use in the 1930s. Post-war types have included the PTAB-2, 2.5, 5 and 5/1, PTAB being the code for a hollow-charge bomblet and the number being the submunition weight; the PTK-250 is a modern dispenser of anti-armour bomblets, this number being the mass of the dispenser; the RPK-180 and -250 are dispensers of HE fragmentation bomblets; and the RRAB series dispenses incendiary munitions.

BL.755

Origin: Hunting Engineering, Ampthill
Dimensions: length 2,451mm (96.5in); diameter 419mm (16.5in); fin span 566mm (22.3in)
Weight: loaded 277kg (611lb)
Users: Royal Air Force, Royal Navy and export customers

Having the official MoD designation Cluster Bomb No 1, this pioneer weapon was designed for attack against a wide range of small hard and soft targets from low level, and strews submunitions over an area rather greater than the likely aiming error. Each store comprises a finned pod hung on either NATO 356mm (14in) or Warsaw Pact 250mm (9.84in) lugs and protected by various safety interlocks. Before take-off one of four time delays is selected to ensure safe separation from the aircraft before the primary cartridge is fired. Gas from this blows off the two panels forming the skin of the pod. The main cartridge is then fired,

blowing out 21 submunitions from each of seven compartments arranged in tandem, a total of 147 bomblets. Each submunition has a hollow charge for piercing armour (at least 250mm/9.84in) and also shatters the case into over 2,000 lethal fragments. BL.755 entered service in 1972, and was followed in 1987 by Improved BL.755. The second-generation weapon fires more powerful bomblets able to pierce thicker armour, using new-technology shaped-charge explosive held at almost a vertical attitude; the bomblet pattern takes into account the much greater accuracy of Tornado and other modern low-level attack aircraft, making possible far more accurate attacks on armour concentrations.

Right: Two BL.755 cluster dispensers belonging to a JaboG (fighter/bomber) unit of the West German Luftwaffe. This is one of very few British air weapons to have achieved wide export sales, partly because of its modest price.

Below: Tornado can carry eight BL.755s (these are Improved BL.755 type) without using any wing pylons. On an actual mission they would be dropped in fairly close succession across the target.

HADES

Origin: Hunting Engineering, Ampthill
Dimensions: length 2,451mm (96.5in); diameter 419mm (16.5in); fin span 565mm (22.25in)
Weight: 264kg (582lb)

The HADES (the name being an acronym from Hunting Area-DEnial System) combines the dispenser of the BL.755 bomb with the HB.876 area-denial minelets used in the JP.233 anti-airfield dispenser system. The weapon operates in exactly the same way as the standard BL.755, but the submunition

Above: Cutaway display model of BL.755 showing the seven compartments for submunitions. The nose windmill drives the arming system.

payload is made up of 49 2.5kg (5.5lb) minelets, which each have a diameter of 100mm (3.9in) and length of 150mm (5.9in). These submunitions fall freely to the ground after being dispensed in the air, then push themselves upright on their ring of radially-disposed spring-steel legs. Thereafter the minelets await detonation by any disturbance within their lethal radius. The individual minelets are designed to self-destruct after a variable but preset interval if not previously detonated.

Above: Improved BL.755 fires this design of armour-piercing bomblet, which falls in an almost vertical attitude on to a tank's top armour to be detonated at the correct stand-off distance.

JP.233

Origin: Hunting Engineering, Ampthill
Dimensions: (fuselage installation with one cratering and one area-denial dispenser) length 6,551mm (257.9in); width 840mm (33in); height 600mm (23.6in)
Weight: (Tornado dispenser, each) 2,335kg (5,148lb)
User: Royal Air Force

JP.233 is a weapon designed to increase the lethality of manned aircraft tasked with attacking fixed area targets such as airfields. By dispensing two types of submunition simultaneously (a concrete-heave munition and an area-denial munition to discourage runway repair) it is planned that JP.233 should put an airfield out of action for a significant period. Such a weapon is needed because the UK has no missiles suitable for use against airbases.

The SG.357 is a large (25.8kg/56lb) munition which after release is braked by parachute,

Above: The two types of submunition can be clearly seen dispensed by JP.233. The Tornado carries the largest size of JP.233 dispensers, in pairs.

Below: A single Tornado can dispense 430 of these HB.876 area-denial mines in a single pass. Each automatically rests this way up.

thereafter falling progressively more vertically until it strikes the runway. As in the West German STABO, a contact fuze probe is energized and this fires a shaped charge on contact with the paved surface. This punches a hole

through which a secondary charge is fired, to explode well below the surface and cause heave damage over a wide area.

The HB.876 is a much smaller (2.5kg/5.5lb) area-denial mine, strewn in larger numbers and falling freely. On hitting the ground and coming to rest the HB.876 is rotated into an upright position by a ring of sprung legs projecting radially all round. These stabilize the mine in the desired attitude. Here they remain until detonated by any local disturbance or until, after a preset period, they self-destruct.

JP.233 dispensers are available in different sizes for different aircraft, including the BAe Harrier, General Dynamics F-16 and General Dynamics F-111. The largest size, tailored to the Panavia Tornado, is carried in a side-by-side pair on the fuselage pylons. The forward compartments contain 215 HB.876s and the rear compartments 30 SG.357s. Hunting claim JP.233 to be 'typically, five times more effective per aircraft load than other systems', though the reasoning behind this claim is difficult to comprehend.

Above: An assortment of dispenser containers can be seen here in front of an AV-8B between the rocket launchers and the GP bombs.

Below: This A-4 Skyhawk at NATC Patuxent River was being tested with Fireye (Mk 122) incendiary containers (see section on bombs).

Cluster Bomb Units (CBUs)

There are more than 100 types of dispenser weapons in service with the US forces. The older weapons fall into the M and Mk series, while the newer weapons are generally listed as Cluster Bomb Units (CBUs), each comprising a dispenser (Suspended Underwing Unit, or SUU) or cluster adapter loaded with the appropriate Bomb Live Unit (BLU) or other submunitions. The following is an abbreviated list in strict alphanumerical order:

CBU-1 is the SUU-7 loaded with 509 BLU-4 anti-personnel bomblets; CBU-2/A is the SUU-7 loaded with 360 BLU-3 antimaterial bomblets; CBU-2B/A is the SUU-7 loaded with 409 BLU-3/B anti-materiel bomblets; 300kg (661lb) CBU-3/A is the SUU-10 loaded with 371 BLU-7A/B parachute-retarded anti-

tank bomblets; CBU-3B/A is the SUU-10B/A loaded with 352 BLU-7/A parachute-retarded antitank bomblets; CBU-5 is the M30 cluster adaptor with 57 M138 bomblets filled with BZ incapacitant gas; CBU-6 see CBU-13/A; CBU-7/A is the SUU-31/A loaded with 1,200 BLU-18/B antipersonnel bomblets; 390kg (860lb) CBU-8/A is the SUU-7A/A

loaded with 409 BDU-27/B spotting charges; CBU-9/A carries dummy bomblets; CBU-10 is the SUU-10 loaded with unspecified submunitions; CBU-11/A is the SUU-7B/A loaded with 261 BLU-16/B smoke bomblets; 290kg (640lb) CBU-12/A is the SUU-7B/A loaded with 261 BLU-17/B smoke bomblets; CBU-13/A is the SUU-7C/A loaded with 261

BLU-16/B and BLU-17/B smoke bomblets; CBU-14/A is the SUU-7B/A loaded with BLU-3/B antimateriel bomblets; CBU-14A/A is the SUU-14A/A loaded with BLU-3/B anti-materiel bomblets; CBU-15/A is the SUU-13/A loaded with BLU-19 GB (Sarin nerve gas) bomblets; CBU-16/A is the SUU-13/A loaded with CDU-9 clusters carrying BZ incapacitant gas bomblets; CBU-17/A is the SUU-13/A loaded with 1,200 BLU-34/B practice bomblets; CBU-18/A is the SUU-13A/A loaded with BLU-25/B anti-personnel bomblets; CBU-19 is a twin strong back dispenser supporting 16 modules each containing 33 BLU-39 CS gas bomblets; CBU-22/A is the SUU-14/A loaded with 72 BLU-17/B smoke bomblets; CBU-23/B is the SUU-31/B loaded with BLU-26/B fragmentation bomblets; CBU-24/A is the SUU-14/A loaded with BLU-24/B fragmentation bomblets; CBU-24/B is the SUU-30/B loaded with 670 BLU-26/B or BLU-36/B fragmentation bomblets; CBU-25 is the SUU-14 loaded with BLU-24 fragmentation bomblets; CBU-26 is the SUU-10/A loaded with 352 dummy fragmentation bomblets; CBU-27 is an empty canister for the Type 2 dispenser, becoming an ADU or CDU when filled; CBU-28 is the

Above: CBU-59/B is one of the family of Rockeye II dispensers. The tail fins flick open after release (in this case from an A-4).

Right: Avco's BKEP (boosted kinetic-energy penetrator) is dispensed in clusters (not fitting into the CBU system) for airfield attack.

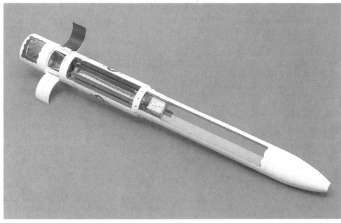

SUU-13 loaded with 40 CDU-2 clusters each of 120 BLU-43 mine submunitions; 380kg (838lb) CBU-29/B is the SUU-30/B loaded with 670 BLU-36/B fragmentation bomblets; CBU-30 is the SUU-13 loaded with 40 CDU-12 clusters each of 30 BLU-39 CS gas bomblets; 350kg (772lb) CBU-33/A is the SUU-36/A loaded with 30 BLU-45/B land mines; CBU-34/A is the SUU-38/A loaded with 10 CDU-18 or CDU-19 clusters each of 54 BLU-42 anti-personnel fragmentation bomblets; CBU-37/A is the SUU-13/A loaded with 40 CDU-3 clusters each of 120 BLU-44 anti-personnel mines; CBU-38/A is the SUU-13/A loaded with 40 BLU-40/B fragmentation bomblets; CBU-41/B is the SUU-51 loaded with 18 canisters of BLU-53 napalm fire bomblets; 380kg (838lb) CBU-42/A is the SUU-28/A loaded with 10 CDU-20 or CDU-21 clusters each of BLU-48 fragmentation bomblets; CBU-44 is loaded with unspecified anti-personnel fragmentation bomblets; CBU-45 is loaded with unspecified anti-personnel and anti-materiel (APAM) bomblets; 400kg (882lb) CBU-46/A is the SUU-7C/A loaded with 444 BLU-66/B anti-personnel bomblets; CBU-47 is the SUU-13 loaded with BLU-55 anti-personnel mines; 380kg (838lb) CBU-49/B is the SUU-30/B loaded with 670 BLU-59/B fragmentation bomblets; CBU-50/A is the SUU-13 loaded with 40 BLU-60 fragmentation bomblets; CBU-51/A is the SUU-13/A load-

ed with 40 BLU-67/B cratering bomblets; 350kg (772lb) CBU-52/B is the SUU-30B/B loaded with 254 BLU-61/B fragmentation bomblets; 370kg (816lb) CBU-53/B is the SUU-30B/B loaded with 670 BLU-70/B incendiary bomblets; 370kg (772lb) CBU-54/B is the SUU-30B/B loaded with 670 BLU-68/B incendiary bomblets; 230kg (507lb) CBU-55/B is the SUU-49 loaded with three BLU-73 fuel/air explosive (FAE) devices; CBU-57 is the SUU-14A/A loaded with 132 BLU-69/B incendiary bomblets; 370kg (816lb) CBU-58A/B is the SUU-30A/B loaded with 650 BLU-63/B

Above: This design of bomblet can be packaged 247 at a time into the familiar Rockeye II dispenser. The stand-off probe detonates the hollow charge above tank armour.

fragmentation bomblets; CBU-59/B is the Mk 7 Mod 3 Rockeye for seven PLU-77/B anti-personnel and anti-materiel (APAM) fragmentation bomblets; CBU-60 is the SUU-50 loaded with 264 BLU-24 fragmentation bomblets; CBU-61 is a dispenser for unspecified CS incapacitant gas bomblets; 380kg (838lb) CBU-62 is the SUU-30 loaded with 2,025 M38 fragmentation grenades; CBU-66 is the SUU-51/B loaded with CDU-24/B canisters of BLU-81/B minelets; CBU-68 is the SUU-30 loaded with BLU-48 fragmentation bomblets; CBU-70 is the SUU-30 loaded with unspecified submunitions; 370kg (816lb) CBU-71 is the SUU-30A/B loaded with 670 BLU-86A/B fragmentation bomblets; CBU-72 is the low-drag version of the CBU-55 fitted with retarder parachutes; CBU-75A/B is the SUU-54A/B loaded with 1,800 BLU-63/B or BLU-86/B fragmentation bomblets; CBU-76/B is the SUU-51B/B loaded with 290 BLU-61A/B fragmentation/incendiary bomblets; CBU-77/B is the SUU-51B/B loaded with 790 BLU-63/B fragmentation bomblets; CBU-78/B is the SUU-58/B loaded with BLU-91/B Gator anti-tank and BLU-92/B Gator anti-personnel minelets; CBU-83/B is the SUU-58/B loaded with BLU-91/B Gator

anti-tank or BLU-92/B Gator anti-personnel minelets; CBU-84/B is the SUU-54A/B loaded with BLU-91/B Gator anti-tank and BLU-92/B Gator anti-personnel minelets; CBU-85/B is the SUU-54A/B loaded with BLU-91/B anti-tank minelets; CBU-86/B is the SUU-54A/B loaded with BLU-92/B Gator anti-personnel minelets; M1A1 and M1A2 fragmentation cluster bomb, 45.4kg (100lb) containing six M41A1 fragmentation bombs; M1A3 and M1A4 fragmentation cluster bomb, 45.4kg (100lb) containing six M41A2 fragmentation bombs; M4 fragmentation cluster bomb, 454kg (1,000lb) containing three M40 cluster bombs; M12 cluster incendiary bomb; M13 cluster incendiary bomb, 227kg (500lb); M17 cluster incendiary bomb, 227kg (500lb); M19 cluster incendiary bomb, 227kg (500lb) containing 36 M69 incendiary bombs; M20 cluster incendiary bomb, 227kg (500lb), M21 cluster incendiary bomb, 227kg (500lb), M22 cluster incendiary bomb, 227kg (500lb); M26 cluster fragmentation bomb, 227kg (500lb); M28 cluster fragmentation bomb 45.4kg (100lb) containing 24 M83 fragmentation bomblets; M31 incendiary cluster bomb, 227kg (500lb) containing 38 M74 incendiary bomblets; M32 non-persistent gas cluster bomb, 454kg (1,000lb) containing 76 M125 gas bomblets; M34 non-persistent gas cluster bomb, 454kg (1,000lb) containing 76 M125A gas bomblets; M35 incendiary cluster bomb, 340kg (750lb) containing 57 M74A1 incendiary bomblets; M36 incendiary cluster bomb, 340kg (750lb) containing 182 M50A3 incendiary bomblets; M43 incapacitant gas cluster bomb, 340kg (750lb) containing 57 M138 BZ gas bomblets; M44 gas generator for BZ agent, 79.4kg (175lb); 270kg (595lb) Mk 12 Padeye dispenser with smoke or BZ incapacitant; Mk 17 Gladeye Mk 4 dispenser with seven bomblet dispensers; 370kg (816lb) Mk 21 Sadeye Mk 5 dispenser; 370kg (816lb) Mk 22 Sadeye Mk 5 dispenser; 249.5kg (550lb) Mk 44 cluster adapter M16 loaded with about 10,000 Lazy Dog shaped iron fragments.

YUGOSLAVIA

Yugoslav cluster bombs

The standard cluster bomb unit of the Yugoslav air force is the 150kg (331lb) DPT-150, loaded with 54 PTAB 1.5kg (3.31lb), or 44 RAB 2.5kg (5.51lb) or 34 RAP 3.5kg (7.72lb) fragmentation bomblets.

UNGUIDED ORDNANCE

AS-228

Origin: Cardoen Explosivos, Santiago
User: Chile and at least one export customer

This relatively small depth charge has very wide applications including aeroplanes and helicopters. It can even be rolled by hand through an aircraft doorway. The hydrostatic fuze, which is supplied as a separate unit, can be preset to any of 19 depths between 30 and 490m (100 and 1,600ft).

FRANCE

TSM series

Origin: Thomson-Sintra, Brest

This company makes most French sea mines, for deployment from aircraft as well as other vehicles. Several air-launched types are available, some having parachute-retarded descent both in the air and through the water. The same company manufactures depth charges, but details have not been published.

MR-80 Cutaway

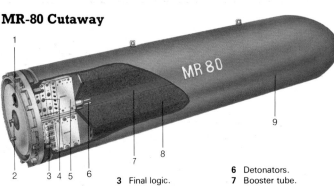

1 Sensitive transducer.
2 Safety/arming device.
3 Final logic.
4 Influence modules.
5 Batteries.
6 Detonators.
7 Booster tube.
8 Main charge (variable).
9 Glassfibre case.

ITALY

MR-80

Origin: Misar SpA, Brescia
Dimensions: length (Mod A) 2,750mm (108.3in), or (Mod B) 2,096mm (82.5in) or (Mod C) 1,646mm (64.8in); diameter 533mm (21in)
Weight: varies with Mod from 600 to 1,130kg (1,323 to 2,491lb)
Warhead: charge of from 400 to 920kg (882 to 2,028lb) of TNT, HBX-3 or similar explosive
Depth of use: from 8 to 300m (26 to 985ft)
Users: Italy and other countries

This is one of the commonest Italian sea mines, and it can be launched by aircraft as well as by

Below: Misar MR-80 Mod B mines awaiting delivery. The transducers, batteries and computer logic are grouped at the near end.

Above: The Misar MR-80 is a general-purpose ground influence mine produced with three different quantities of explosive. With very few metal parts it is considered to be highly resistant to MCM (mine countermeasures), and to have a very long trouble-free life in the sea.

ships and submarines. It is an advanced design, with an electronic module in which are assessed the signals received by various influence sensors which include magnetic, acoustic and pressure-variation signals in any combination. It can also be remotely controlled, by cable or otherwise. The cylindrical body is epoxy resin and glassfibre.

MRP

Origin: Misar SpA, Brescia
Dimensions: length 2,096mm (82.5in); diameter 533mm 621in)
Weight: 680-780kg (1,499-1,720lb)
Warhead: 530kg (1,168lb) TNT or 630kg (1,389lb) HBX-3
Depth of use: from 5 to 300m (16 to 985ft)
Users: Italy and possibly other countries

This mine is even more advanced than the MR-80, which it closely resembles. The main difference is the addition of a full microprocessor, offering a wide range of selectivity on the threshold, times, combination logic and localization logic. The central processor is used to compile the operator settings, mine programming and testing, and in action achieves the maximum effectiveness and discrimination of target countermeasures.

VS SM600

Origin: Valsella Meccanotecnica, Brescia
Dimensions: length 2,750mm (108.3in); diameter 533mm (21in)
Weight: approximately 780kg (1,720lb)
Warhead: charge of about 600kg (1,323lb) TNT
Depth of use: from 10 to 150m (33 to 492ft)
Users: Italy and probably other countries (production complete)

The SM600 can be laid by various means, including parachuting from aircraft. It is triggered by four types of sensor (magnetic, pressure, low-frequency acoustic and audio-frequency acoustic), and the sensor signals are fed to sophisticated processing electronics. Signatures of particular types of target are stored, and the mine can be tuned by local setting or remotely so that it is triggered only by the passage of a particular kind of target. The SM600 is said to possess good immunity to sweeping operations.

MULTI-NATIONAL

Air-sown land mines

Mines designed for use on the land battlefield are considerably smaller than their maritime counterparts: this results from the close proximity of the mine to the target that detonates it (requiring a comparatively small charge to inflict decisive damage), and also from the need to sow comparatively dense fields of mines that are difficult to detect and thus to neutralize. The two primary types of land mine are the anti-tank and anti-personnel varieties, generally laid in mixed fields to make it more difficult for the enemy's mine clearance crews to clear the anti-tank mines which are generally the main reason for the field. There is no doubt of the efficacy of such minefields in denying the enemy

MINES AND DEPTH CHARGES

terrain that is easily passable, so channeling his progress into areas better suited to the defenders' purposes, but the fields need to be large. These take time to lay and, though dummy or nuisance minefields can be useful, only a proper minefield, laid in the right density, depth and location, will usefully fulfil the defence's requirements. Such fields require considerable time to lay even with the aid of mechanized systems, and thus need to be laid in advance of the enemy's move, which may in the event bypass the main minefield. Here the air-laid minefield has its part to play, for comparatively large minefields can be laid as the tactical situation develops if the right launch platforms (helicopters) and delivery systems are available. Initial efforts in this direction involved the wholesale dropping of mines from transiting

helicopters, generally with adverse effects on mine density and fuze reliability even when the field was laid accurately. Next came ramp launchers derived from those used on ground minelayer vehicles. This technique was pioneered by the Soviets, who still use it for scattering the PGMDM anti-tank and PFM-1 'Green Parrot' anti-personnel mines. The PFM-1 has been extensively used in Afghanistan, where a less precise but nontheless effective laying system has been used: helicopter-carried packs are used to dispense cardboard or comparable frangible containers which carry substantial numbers of mines that fall onto guerrilla paths etc. The main tactical disadvantage of the system is that any helicopter fitted with a ramp launcher has to fly slowly and very close to the ground, mean-

Above: A Lynx-3, with KAD gun and 2.75in rocket launcher, lets go DAT mines from a Tecnovar Model A dispenser.

ing that mines cannot be laid close to obstacles such as trees, rocky outcrops, buildings etc. The West has progressed from this intermediate system in to differing forms epitomized by Italian and US laying techniques: the Italians have opted for the suspended magazine dispenser, and the Americans for the fixed tube dispenser. The Italian magazine system resembles a crate slung under the carrying helicopter, and the specially designed mines are dropped in pre-programmed or controlled sequences. The plastic-cased mines are very strong and difficult to detect, and are fitted with fuzes that are not armed until the mine has landed. The DAT system from Technovar uses the Model A dispenser, which can accommodate 64 magazines with a total of 1,536 anti-personnel scatter mines, or 32 magazines with a total of 128 anti-tank scatter mines, or a mix of 32 and 16 magazines with 768 anti-personnel and 64 anti-tank mines

respectively. The TS/50 anti-personnel mine weighs 210g (7.4oz) including 50g (1.8oz) of explosive, and the MATS anti-tank mine weighs 3.5 or 4.5kg (7.7 or 9.9lb) including 1.6 or 2.6kg (3.5 or 5.7lb) of explosive. The company produces a number of other mine types such as the VS Mk 2 anti-tank weapon, and Misar has the comparable SB-33 anti-personnel and SB-81 anti-tank mines. The US approach is epitomized by the Honeywell Volcano system designed for the Sikorsky UH-60 Black Hawk battlefield helicopter. The system comprises a rack of launcher tubes fitted in the cabin of the helicopter. From these are fired members of the 'Gator' family of mines: the helicopter flies fast and low over the target area, the mines being ejected laterally under the control of a microprocessor-based control unit in the cabin. Each mine is armed by an electrical pulse passed through the flexible strap separating the mines in the dispenser, the unwinding strap ensuring that the mines are randomly scattered within the designated target area. The West Germans have developed (but not yet adopted) a similar system under the designation MiWS (MinenWerfer System). This is very much a developing sector of the air armament field, and several other countries are working on air-launched mine systems for the modern battlefield.

Above: In January 1987 Honeywell and the US Army completed proof of concept tests with the Volcano mine delivery system on a UH-60A.

Below: Here the four racks are fired off. Each contains 40 canisters, each canister housing up to six anti-tank or anti-personnel mines.

UNGUIDED ORDNANCE

Soviet mines

The very wide range of Soviet mines can be subdivided into four categories: defensive moored, offensive moored, seabed and nuclear. In the first category is a wide range of small to medium devices which can be laid by light aircraft including helicopters. Most use an inertial pistol using mechanical, electrical or magnetic firing influences. The bigger offensive moored mines are a very large group, two of the three subcategories of which (known as rising mines) are laid by aircraft. Most members of this family are used chiefly in the ASW barrier role, with secondary anti-ship capability. Several members are believed to wait tethered until they recognize the signature (presumably chiefly acoustic) of a target; then they cut their tether and ignite a rocket motor, finally homing on the target in torpedo fashion. Two of the air-launched seabed (offensive bottom) mines are the AMD-500 and AMD-1000, the number being the mass in kilogrammes (according to some sources the air-launched versions are prefixed not AMD but KMD). These are produced in four main sub-variants: magnetic; LF and audio acoustic; pressure influence; and combined influences. Normal laying depth is 4-70m (13-230ft), but the 1000 size can be used in the ASW role down to 200m (656ft). Nuclear mines have yields believed to lie in the range 5-20kT. These are among the weapons carried by strategic naval aircraft including Tupolev Tu-26 'Backfires'.

Sea Urchin

Origin: British Aerospace, Bristol
Dimensions: length (SAP + 1 warhead) 1,442mm (56.75in) (2 warheads) 2,540mm (100in); diameter 533mm (21in)
Weight: (SAP + 1 warhead) 569kg (1,255lb) or (2 warheads) 1,058kg (2,332lb)
Warhead: 350kg (772lb) charge
Users: UK and export

This flexible mine system consists of a multi-sensor SAP (sensing and processing) unit and either one or two warheads attached in tandem. The mine,

which may be laid by transport type aircraft, has a processor giving programmable mission parameters for LF/audio acoustic signatures, magnetic and pressure influences, with individual or multi-influence activation, multiple-target count, selectable activation delay and selectable sterilization delay. It has advanced self-test, safety and arming procedures.

Stonefish

Origin: Marconi Underwater Systems, Waterlooville
Dimensions: length variable up to 2,500mm (98.4in); diameter 533mm (21in)
Weight: variable up to 990kg (2,183lb)
Warhead: variable up to 600kg (1,323lb)
Users: UK, Australia and possibly other countries

Below: Loading Stonefish mines into a Hercules C.1 of the Royal Air Force. It is a major Hercules mission.

The Stonefish family contains warshot, exercise and training mines, all having variable size and configuration, including versions specifically for dropping by aircraft. The modules include warhead, launch kit and tail section, the latter including the sensors, signal conditioning and processor package. The electronics includes signal conditioning and information processing, setting of threshold, logic and sterilization delay. A self-contained presetter can be used to change the programme. Stonefish mines are used at depths from 5 to 90m (16 to 295ft) and down to 200m (656ft) in the ASW role. They have a laid life of over 700 days.

Above: Side elevation profile of Stonefish, the 'intelligent' mine made by MUSL (Marconi Underwater Systems Ltd). It can be launched by a C-130.

Below: The family of Stonefish mines, all of which have the flat nose cap, various warhead modules and the electronics module.

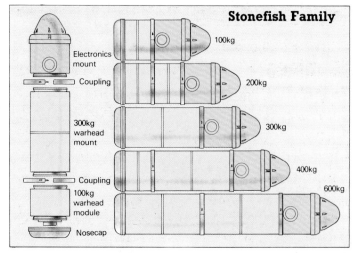

Stonefish Family

Electronics mount
Coupling
300kg warhead mount
Coupling
100kg warhead module
Nosecap

100kg
200kg
300kg
400kg
600kg

Mk 11 depth charge

Origin: British Aerospace, Bristol
Dimensions: length 1,390mm (54.7in) or without tail 970mm (38.2in); diameter 279mm (11in)
Weight: fully prepared 145kg (320lb)
Warhead: HE charge 80kg (176lb)
Users: UK and export customers

The current production version is Mk 11 Mod 3, with fuzing and safety mechanisms specifically tailored to launching from maritime patrol aircraft and helicopters. It can be used against surface vessels and submarines in shallow water. The assembly comprises a cylindrical steel case and a tail section which, on impact with the water, breaks off

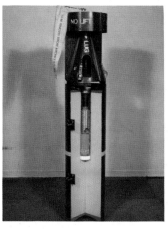

Above: The new Mk 11 Mod 3 depth charge was developed specifically for use from aircraft. This example has been sectioned.

Below: The Mk 11 Mod 3 can be carried by all Westland naval helicopters. This Sea King has two (plus two Mk 44 torpedoes).

to facilitate hydropneumatic arming and detonation. The fuze, inserted at the rear, comprises a valve, pistol, detonator placer and primer assembly. BAe also produce training versions of the Mk 11 Mod 3, one being for use by aircrew in carriage and release practice.

US mines

The US Navy uses a range of air-dropped munitions based on the standard 'slick' series of low-drag GP bombs, modified by the addition of a Mk 75 Mod 0 destructor kit. This can be added to the Mk 82 (227kg/500lb), Mk 83 (454kg/1,000lb) and Mk 84 (nominal 907kg/2,000lb) bombs to form the DST (destructors) Mks 36, 40 and 41, related to the mines described below. The latest air-launched mine family are grouped under the name Quickstrike. These are all bottom mines, using different size cases but sharing common target detection and classification systems. The first four members of the Quickstrike group, in production from 1982 to 1984, are the Mks 62, 63, 64 and 65. The first three are derived from the Mk 80 'slick' GP bombs, modified for use in water not deeper than 100m (330ft). The Mk 65, the first actually to enter production, is not a converted bomb but a new thin-case store, with a length of 3.3m (10.8ft), diameter of 734mm (28.9in) and very large charge of PBX explosive (907kg/2,000lb class). The next model in production was to be the Mk 64, in the same weight class and derived from the Mk 84 bomb, length being 3,800mm (149.6in) and diameter 633mm (24.9in). Most of the Quickstrikes will use the TDD-57 target detection device, employing influence mechanisms.

The chief mines currently in use are the Mks 25, 36, 39, 40, 41, 50, 52, 53, 54, 55, 56 and 115A. Of these the following are important aircraft weapons.

Mk 36

Dimensions: length 2,250mm (88.6in); diameter 400mm (15.75in)
Weight: (fixed conical fin) 240kg (529lb) or (tail retarder) 261kg (575lb)
Warhead: 87kg (192lb) charge of H-6
Depth of use: up to 91.4m (300ft)

This cylindrical mine is a standard aircraft-laid bottom (seabed) mine. Mods 0/3 have magnetometer actuation and Mods 4/5 a mix of magnetic and seismic (i.e. acoustic) actuation.

Mk 40

Dimensions: length 2,860mm (112.6in); diameter 570mm (22.4in)
Weight: (fixed conical fin) 447kg (985lb) or (tail retarder) 481kg (1,060lb)
Warhead: 204kg (450lb) charge of H-6
Depth of use: up to 91.4m (300ft)

This cylindrical mine is broadly like an enlarged Mk 36. It similarly has magnetometer sensing in Mods 0/3 and magnetic/seismic in Mods 4/5.

Mk 41

Dimensions: length 3,830mm (150.8in); diameter 630mm (24.8in)
Weight: (Mods 0/3) 926kg (2,041lb) and (Mods 4/5) 921kg (2,030lb)
Warhead: about 380kg (838lb) charge of H-6

This powerful mine is again fitted with magnetometer actuation in

Mods 0/3 and a combination of magnetic/seismic sensing in Mods 4/5. It is another aircraft-laid bottom mine.

Mk 52

Dimensions: length 2,250mm (88.6in); diameter 844mm (33.2in)
Weight: (Mod 1) 542kg (1,195lb), (Mod 2) 567kg (1,250lb), (Mod 3) 572kg (1,261lb), (Mod 5) 570kg (1,257lb), (Mod 6) 563kg (1,241lb)
Warhead: 270kg (595lb) charge of HBX-1
Depth of use: up to 45.7m (Mod 2) 183m (600ft)

This aircraft-laid bottom mine exists in five versions, with different sensing and actuation systems: (Mod 1) acoustic, (Mod 2) magnetic, (Mod 3) pressure/magnetic, (Mod 5) acoustic/magnetic and (Mod 6) pressure/acoustic/magnetic.

Mk 53

This is a standard cylindrical mine carried internally in P-3 and other aircraft. No data are available.

Mk 55

Dimensions: length 2,890mm (113.8in); diameter 1,030mm (40.6in)
Weight: (Mod 2) 589kg (1,279lb), (Mods 3/5) 992kg (2,187lb),

Left: Mine laying during Exercise Team Spirit '82. The aircraft are B-52Ds, a version of this bomber no longer in service, but the method of sowing is unchanged today.

Above: Many US aircraft-laid mines look similar. These Mk 52s were loaded aboard a B-52G during Exercise Team Spirit in 1985.

(Mod 6) 996kg (2,196lb), (Mod 7) 995kg (2,194lb)
Warhead: 576kg (1,270lb) charge of HBX-1
Depth of use: up to 45.7m (150ft) or (Mods 2/7) 183m (600ft)

This bottom mine exists in five versions with the following actuation: (Mod 2) magnetic, (Mod 3) pressure/magnetic, (Mod 5) acoustic/magnetic, (Mod 6) pressure/acoustic/magnetic, (Mod 7) dual-channel magnetic.

Mk 56 Mod 0

Dimensions: length 3,500mm (137.8in); diameter 1,060mm (41.7in)
Weight: 1,010kg (2,227lb)
Warhead: 159kg (350lb) charge of HBX-3
Depth of use: up to 366m (1,200ft)

This is an aircraft-laid moored mine with a strong case suitable for operations against submarines at the greatest depths. Its actuation sensing is total field, magnetic dual channel.

DST-115A

Dimensions: length 450mm (17.7in); diameter 620mm (24.4in)
Weight: 61kg (134lb)
Warhead: 24kg (53lb) charge of HBX-3

This aircraft-laid surface mine can be used against surface targets in any depth of water. It has magnetic/seismic actuation.

GUIDED WEAPONS

The first guided missiles used from aircraft dated from 1916-7, and they were of the ASM (air-to-surface missile) type. Some of these pioneer weapons were designed to carry air-launched torpedoes down to the sea. Perhaps oddly, no weapon in this class exists today; all aircraft torpedoes are dropped with no auxiliary device save a retarding parachute. But the wealth of ASMs today speaks for itself. This category also includes torpedoes and anti-tank missiles, though these are all listed separately because they are quite distinct classes.

One group which might be considered to be a distinct class comprises the specialist anti-ship missiles. These are, however, impossible to separate from other ASMs because many anti-ship missiles can be used against land targets, while (of course) almost any ASM could if necessary be used against a ship. The only kind that could not is the inertially guided kind of ASM, preprogrammed with the exact co-ordinate position of a fixed land target (and often with accuracy enhanced by a terrain-comparison system). Ships move about, so inertial guidance is no use, and the surface of the ocean is of little value to a terrain-comparison system.

This is a good place briefly to outline how the various ASM guidance systems work. The earliest ASMs all had manual command guidance, in which a human operator (almost always in the launching aircraft) steered the missile into the target. A few early ASMs used guidance commands transmitted along trailing wires, but today this method (which is almost immune to enemy counter measures) is found only in anti-tank missiles. By far the most common form of command guidance is now the radio link, though it is difficult to make this impervious to enemy jamming or other interference, with obvious tactical disadvantages.

An alternative method is semi-active radar homing, but this requires a target that stands out unmistakably as a radar reflector, such as a ship. Several of the smaller anti-ship missiles use SARH (semi-active radar homing), the launching aeroplane or helicopter 'illuminating' the target with a compatible radar and the missile having a receiver aerial (US=antenna) in its nose able to 'see' the reflected radiation, and sending signals to the guidance and flight-control system to make the missile home directly onto the apparent source of the signals.

Larger missiles, especially for use against ships, use active radar homing. The missile carries its own small radar along with it, and this sweeps ahead searching for a target that stands out sufficiently to be interesting. When it finds one, it locks onto this and thereafter steers the missile towards the object of interest. An active radar has the great advantage that it is self-contained. Once the aircraft has launched its missile it can turn away and, escaping from the scene, thus live to fight another day. Modern warplanes are too expensive for single-shot use!

Active radars have the drawback of alerting the target. But the radar is small, and packaged inside a small and hard-to-detect missile. If it is an anti-ship missile it is probably skimming just above the surface of the sea, holding its height accurately by use of a radio altimeter (which of course evens out the undulations of the waves to keep the missile just clear of th wave crests), and this increases the task of the defenders in spotting the oncoming missile and shooting it down. The latest active radars use frequency hopping methods, jumping randomly from one frequency to another to make their emissions harder to detect, and as they get nearer the target they grow quieter and quieter, needing only the occasional quick scan to check that they are still dead on course to intercept the target vessel.

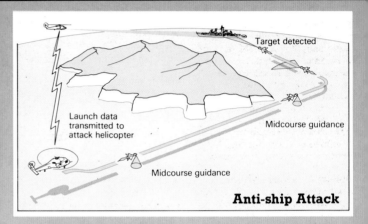

Anti-ship Attack

Above: In an attack on a surface ship, data can be provided by a specialist platform to a helicopter lurking behind a natural obstacle. This allows a Penguin missile to be programmed with the data for an attack including a dogleg so that the target is attacked from an unexpected direction.

Right: Last moment for a destroyer target about to be struck by a Kormoran, which will pierce the hull and explode its 16 radial charges to pierce bulkheads and bottom.

One special group of ASMs are the ARMs (anti-radar missiles), fired against hostile radars on land or in ships. These tend to survey (or 'surveil') a large tract of territory and notice any enemy radar thereon which happens to be working. The earliest ARMs, such as Shrike, were erratic in behaviour, and could be countered merely by switching off the radar on which they were locked. Modern ARMs, such as the British ALARM, are much cleverer. They can continue to home on the designated spot even after the radar there has been switched off, and there is not much the enemy can do about it.

Strategic missiles, fired against fixed targets, can have inertial guidance, which is totally self-contained. A few in the past even used stellar-inertial guidance, using the stars to update their inertial position as worked out by super-accurate gyros and accelerometers inside the missile. The gyros keep it flying exactly the right way up, so that Earth gravity acts precisely downwards (so-called 1g). The accelerometers then measure every change in acceleration as the missile undulates or changes course, even allowing for the gentle diving tendency caused by flying round the curvature of the Earth. When all the accelerations are added together and 'integrated' they give the missile's velocity across the planet's surface (speed and direction). When all the velocities are again integrated the result is instantaneous position. Provided the missile's exact launch position is known, it can be made to dive on a target at a precisely known location many thousands of miles away.

Even the best inertial systems have an accuracy not better than a few tens of metres, and for even greater precision it is possible to use a Tercom (terrain comparison, or terrain contour matching) technique. The missile's computer memory

Right: One of the most impressive of modern guided weapons, the ALARM is small enough to be carried in large numbers, yet sacrifices nothing in terms of electronic or warhead performance. The type can also be fired for a high-altitude loiter under a parachute before diving 'down the throat' of a radar unwary enough to resume operation.

Below: Controversy rages about the resistance of reactive tank armour to the shaped-charge warheads of anti-tank missiles, but there remains the strong possibility that combinations such as the Lynx helicopter and TOW missile can blunt any WarPac armoured thrust.

Bottom: Miniaturization has done much to advance the capabilities of advanced weapons. These six ALCMs on the starboard underwing launcher of a B-52 have miniaturized electronics, miniature warheads, small engines and compact dimensions with folding flying surfaces for multiple carriage.

stores not only the inertial co-ordinates of the target but also the precise variation of the ground along the route to the target. Suppose the inertially guided missile crosses an enemy coastline. Its Tercom system starts studying the rise and fall of the terrain below, and compares the results with the 'map' stored in its memory. It has enough information to say to itself 'We are a little to the left of the desired track, let's alter course slightly to the right.' This is a major technical achievement, and it is very difficult for the enemy to counter it. Eventually the missile is dead on track, and it flies to its target with such a small error that, it is said, it 'can enter by any particular window in a building'.

This kind of guidance is suitable only for the special class of ASMs called cruise missiles, which are lifted by wings and fly like small aeroplanes. Many other ASMs fly like supersonic or hypersonic projectiles, though with the vital ability of being able to change their trajectory. Some, such as the USAF's SRAM, can make dog-legs, dummy 'feint' attacks, zooms and climbs and finally run in to a target from an unexpected direction – all whilst under completely self-contained inertial guidance. To make life even harder for the defenders, the SRAM II (next generation) is to be a 'stealth' design, even more difficult than the original SRAM to detect and thus to intercept and destroy.

Anti-tank missiles are still usually guided by the manual command of a human operator, with signals passed along wires or a radio link. A few today have guidance by a laser beam or, like some AAMs, by homing on the IR (infra-red, or heat) emission from the target. In general, the greater the diameter of the warhead, the greater the thickness of armour it can penetrate.

GUIDED WEAPONS

Above: Martin Pescador attack missile being carried by an Aermacchi MB 326 of the Argentine Navy. The white object next to it is the associated radio command guidance pod.

Martin Pescador

Origin: CITEFA
Propulsion: single-stage solid motor
Dimensions: length 2,940mm (115.75in); body diameter 218.5mm (8.6in); span 730mm (28.75in)
Weight: at launch 140kg (308lb)
Performance: speed Mach 2.3; range 2.5-9km (1.5-5.5 miles)
Warhead: conventional 40kg (88lb) with DA fuze
Users: Argentina

CITEFA, the armed forces scientific and technical research institute, claimed to have completed development of this tactical ASM in 1979, and one was displayed alongside an Agusta A 109 helicopter at the 1981 Paris air show. Performance given in the table is for launch from fixed-wing jet aircraft; from hovering helicopter launch the range is 4.3km (2.7 miles). It has simple line-of-sight radio command from the launch aircraft. None was used during the Falklands conflict in 1982. The name means Kingfisher. A new version, with a heavier warhead, is under development.

C-601

Origin: available from CPMIEC, Beijing
Propulsion: liquid-propellant rocket engine
Dimensions: length 7.38m (24.2ft); body diameter 900mm (35.4in); wing span 2,400mm (94.5in)
Weight: 2,440kg (5,379lb)
Performance: cruising speed at low level Mach 0.9; maximum range 95-100km (59-62 miles)
Warhead: conventional, 500kg (1,102lb)
Users: PRC

Called CAS-N-1 by the NATO scheme, C-601 is a large anti-ship missile, two of which can be carried on underwing pylons by the Chinese H-6 (Tu-16 'Badger') bomber. The aircraft is fitted with a very large surveillance radar under the nose, with a rectangular antenna rotating inside a drum radome. The missile, which is a cross between the Soviet AS-5 'Kelt' and SS-N-2 'Styx' ship-launched missile, has delta wings and three tail surfaces set 120° apart. Midcourse guidance is by a strapdown inertial system, and the terminal phase switches on the missile's own active radar to pick out and home on the target.

C-801

Origin: marketed by the China Precision Machinery Import & Export Corporation
Propulsion: solid booster rocket and solid sustainer rocket
Dimensions: length 5,200mm (204.7in); span 1,000mm (39.4in)
Weight: about 1,000kg (2,205lb)
Performance: speed Mach 1.2; range not revealed
Warhead: semi-armour-piercing HE
Users: China, and possibly a small number of export customers

Below: A C-801, with tandem boost motor fitted. The sustainer motor fills the body aft of the wing leading edges.

The C-801 was introduced to Chinese service in 1983, and is an advanced anti-ship missile resembling the French Exocet in configuration and designed for launch by aircraft and ships. However, little is known with certainty about this weapon, which has a monopulse radar seeker in the nose, followed as one moves aft by the warhead, the forward electronics bay, the highly swept cruciform wings over the rocket section and, surrounding the rocket nozzle, the aft electronics bay and actuators for the small control surface indexed in line with the wings. Behind the missile proper is the jettisonable booster section with its large stabilizing fins indexed in line with the wings and control surfaces. The C-801 is said to be compatible with the fire-control system used with the Chinese HY-2 and FL-1 derivatives of the Soviet SS-N-2 'Styx' missile, and as well as aircraft and ships the missile can apparently be launched from shore batteries and surfaced submarines. The weapon cruises at a preset altitude of 20 or 30m (66 or 98ft), and is known to the Chinese as the YJ-6, YJ standing for Ying Ji (eagle strike).

HY-4

Origin: CPMIEC, Beijing
Propulsion: one turbojet with ventral air inlet
Dimensions: length 7,360mm (289.8in); diameter 760mm (29.9in)
Weight: 1,740kg (3,836lb)
Performance: cruising speed Mach 0.8-0.85 (at low level about 1,030km/h, 640mph); cruising altitude 70-200m (230-655ft); effective range 35-135km (22-84 miles)
Warhead: conventional, 500kg (1,102lb)
User: People's Republic of China

Derived from the earlier HY-2 family, this anti-ship missile is deployed as a ground-launched weapon with a solid rocket booster and as an air-launched version with no booster, dropped from H-6 bombers. In the nose can be an active radar or a passive IR homing system. The engine burns kerosene but no details of it are available. HY-4 can be programmed to have a

AIR-TO-SURFACE MISSILES

terminal pop-up mode to dive on its target from above; alternatively it can maintain low-level flight, dropping down in the terminal phase to impact obliquely. Single-shot hit probability is given as 70 per cent.

Armat

Origin: SA Matra, Vélizy-Villacoublay
Propulsion: SNPE high-energy solid-propellant rocket motor
Dimensions: length 4,150mm (163.4in); body diameter 400mm (15.75in); wing span 1,200mm (47.24in)
Weight: at launch 550kg (1,213lb)
Performance: speed typically Mach 0.9 (supersonic in a dive); range 15-120km (9.3-74.6 miles) depending on launch height and flight profile
Warhead: advanced HE blast/fragmentation, 160kg (353lb)
Users: initially France, Iraq and Kuwait

Armat (anti-radar Matra) is an advanced successor to the Anglo-French AS.37 version of Martel. Compared with its predecessor it has the same configuration and almost identical size and weight, but the motor has much greater impulse, giving considerably enhanced range, and the Electronique Serge Dassault homing head is a completely new 'fire

Below: Manhandling an Armat into position for loading on a Jaguar A of the French Armée de l'Air.

and forget' type able to select any target from a wide range of land and ship radars and home on it in the presence of 'enemy decoy tactics'. Armat has been in action from Mirage F1EQ aircraft of the Iraqi air force, and is also in service with French Mirage 2000s.

Above: An AS.11 wire-guided missile being fired from a Westland Wasp HAS. Mk 1 in service with Royal Navy No 829 Sqn at Portland, Dorset. Many incandescent particles can be seen in the motor jet.

Left: French ALAT (army light aviation) Alouette III helicopters can carry four AS.11s. Only two are on board.

AS.11

Origin: SNI Aérospatiale
Propulsion: SNPE boost/sustain solid motor
Dimensions: length 1,210mm (47.6in); body diameter 164mm (6.3in); fin span 500mm (19.7in)
Weight: at launch 29.9kg (65.9lb)
Performance: speed 580km/h (360mph); range 0.5-3km (1,640-10,000ft)
Warhead: choice of Type 140AP02, detonates 2.6kg (5.72lb) charge after penetrating 10mm (0.4in) armour; Type 140AC, hollow charge which pierces 610mm (24in) armour; or Type 140AP59, contact-fuzed fragmentation

Users: have included France, UK, USA (designation AGM-22A) and 26 other countries.

Derived from the SS.11 army anti-tank missile, AS.11 is one of the oldest missiles still in operation. Originally developed by Nord-Aviation in 1953-5 as Type 5210, it has been slightly improved over the years, notably by the 1962 introduction of the AS.11B1 with transistorized circuits and optional TCA semi-automatic IR-based guidance, and it stayed in production at Aérospatiale (into which Nord was merged) until late 1980, with deliveries exceeding 179,000 of all versions. The first trials of an air-launched version were undertaken in France with Alouette IIs and in Britain using Twin Pioneers, in 1958. The weapon system is similar to that of the SS.11 but needs a stabilized sight and preferably an image intensifier or other magnifying all-weather vision system. Carrier aircraft include most versions of Alouette and Gazelle, the British Army Scout, Navy/Marines Wessex and various STOL aeroplanes. Though now obsolescent, AS.11 has been fired in at least 14 wars or other local conflicts, possibly a record for any ASM.

GUIDED WEAPONS

AS.12

Origin: SNI Aérospatiale
Propulsion: SNPE boost/sustain solid motor
Dimensions: length 1,870mm (73.9in); body diameter (max at warhead) 210mm (8.25in); span 650mm (25.6in)
Weight: at launch 76kg (168lb)
Performance: speed 338km/h (210mph); range, max (measured relative to Earth) 8km (5 miles)
Warhead: usually OP.3C, explodes 28.4kg (63lb) charge after penetrating 40mm (1.57in) armour; alternative hollow-charge AP or fragmentation anti-personnel types
Users: include Abu Dhabi, Argentina, Brazil, Brunei, France, West Germany, Iraq, Iran, Italy, Ivory Coast, Libya, Netherlands, South Africa, Spain, Turkey, UK (RAF, RN), and other countires

Developed in 1955-7 by Nord-Aviation, this missile was a natural extrapolation of the original SS.10 and SS.11 weapons to a bigger weapon, with a warhead weighing roughly four times as much and suitable for use against fortifications or ships. Trials began in 1958, and production of surface-launched SS.12 started in late 1959, with AS.12 following in 1960, the original planned carrier aircraft being the French Navy Etendard and Super Frelon. AS.12 can be used with the APX 260 (Bézu) or SFIM 334 gyrostabilized sight and with IR night vision equipment, but the wire-transmitted guidance system is the basic CLOS type with optical (flare) tracking; the TCA semi-automatic IR command guidance system is not available with AS.12. Maximum airspeed at launch is 370km/h (230mph). About 8,100 missiles have been produced. AS.12 has been carried by the Alizé, P-2 Neptune, Atlantic, Nimrod, Alouette, Wasp, Wessex, Gazelle and Lynx. Several were fired by both sides in the Falklands war, one crippling an Argentine submarine at Grytviken.

Below: The Aérospatiale AS.12 is the largest member of one of the oldest and most widely used families of guided missiles in the world. This example is mounted on an Alouette III helicopter, but other AS.12s are fired from small warships. AS.12 is now generally being replaced by modern ASMs.

Above: As far as Aérospatiale is concerned the replacement for the helicopter-launched AS.12 is AS.15TT, developed with funding from the giant Sawari contract with Saudi Arabia. Here four are seen carried by a special trials AS.365F Dauphin helicopter, with Thomson-CSF Agrion 15 radar, with 360° scan.

Below: A different AS.365F Dauphin, at the moment of firing an AS.15TT anti-ship missile. Aérospatiale claim that absence of any form of homing guidance makes AS.15TT a relatively low cost missile. Instead the wings carry radar receiver pods, two white on the lower wings and black above.

AS.15TT

Origin: SNI Aérospatiale
Propulsion: SNPE Anubis, (Nitramite-filled) smokeless solid motor, 45.2 sec burn
Dimensions: length 2,300mm (90.55in); body diameter 188mm (7.4in); span 564mm (22.2in)
Weight: at launch 103kg (227lb)
Performance: speed 1,010km/h (628mph); range over 15km (9.3 miles)
Warhead: derived from AS.12, conventional, 30kg (66lb)
User: Saudi Arabia

Aérospatiale's older missiles with wire guidance could lose export sales to the British Sea Skua. To rival the British missile Aérospatiale has developed AS.15, in at least two versions, funded by the gigantic Sawari defence contract with Saudi Arabia of 1976. It has command guidance, and there are flip-out rear fins. It can be launched from existing AS.12 installations provided they have been updated with a stabilized sight and, preferably, FLIR or imaging IR. Like other Aérospatiale tactical missiles of this series the basic AS.15 has to be steered all the way to the target by the operator. AS.15TT (Tous Temps, all-weather), on the other hand, is a substantially different missile, though carrying the standard warhead. It is not roll-stabilized and is guided semi-automatically. The basic system depends on Thomson-CSF Agrion 15 radar (derived from the Iguane developed as a retrofit to the Alizé aircraft), with pulse-compression and frequency agility to improve behaviour in the presence of ECM. This radar continuously compares the sightlines to the target and missile, and a digital radio link drives the difference to zero. After a programmed descent to sea-skimming height on the radio altimeter the missile runs to within 300m (1,000ft) of the target and is then commanded to sink to immediately above the sea surface to be sure of hitting the target. AS.15TT has been integrated with the two Aérospatiale helicopters, Dauphin 365N and the Super Puma. Both thus acquire a long-range surveillance capability with auto-digital link to the missiles or surface vessels. The first complete air-firing test took place in October 1982 and the first of 220 missiles were delivered to Saudi Arabia in 1985.

AS.30/30L

Origin: SNI Aérospatiale
Propulsion: SNPE solid with composite boost and CDB sustainer (max time 21 sec)
Dimensions: length (X12 warhead) 3,839mm (151in), (X35) 3,885mm (153in), (AS.30L) 3,650mm (143in); body diameter 340mm (13.5in); span 1,000mm (39.4in)
Weight: at launch 520kg (1,146lb)
Performance: speed Mach 1.5; range up to 11.25km (7 miles)
Warhead: conventional, 240kg (529lb), with optional impact or delay fuzes.
Users: (AS.30) France, West Germany, India, Peru, South Africa, Switzerland, UK (RAF); (30L) France, Egypt, Iraq and probably other customers

Scaled up from the obsolete AS.20, this hard-hitting missile has a higher wing loading yet can be launched at Mach numbers down to 0.45 compared with the lower limit of 0.7 for the earlier missile. Originally the Nord 5401, it was developed in 1958 and disclosed on the Mirage III and Northrop N-156F in 1960. AS.30 was produced to meet a French DTE requirement for an ASM with range of at least 10km (6.3 miles) without the launch aircraft having to come within 3 km (1.86 miles) of the target (today unacceptably close). CEP was to be 10m (33ft) or less, and all these demands were exceeded. Early AS.30 missiles, tested from Canberras and Vautours at Colomb-Béchar and Cazaux, were aerodynamically similar to AS.20. The missile is not roll-stabilized and the sustainer motor is equipped with two nozzles, one on each side. The operator keeps tracking flares on the missile aligned with the target by a radio link which sends signals to bias two vibrating spoilers that intermittently interrupt the jets from the nozzles. The autopilot interprets the command to interrupt the correct jet to steer left/right or up/down. In 1964 an improved AS.30 was produced with four flip-out tail fins indexed in line with the wings, and without spoilers on the sustainer nozzles. At the same time the TCA semi-automatic guidance system was introduced, with a SAT tracker in the aircraft continuously monitoring an IR flare on the missile and the pilot keeping the target centred in his attack sight, an onboard computer zeroing any difference between the two sightlines without the need to work a pitch/yaw joystick control.

As as company venture, Thomson-CSF and Aérospatiale began to work on a laser-guided AS.30 in 1974 (Ferranti in Britain proposed this with company hardware almost a decade earlier). Using Martin-Marietta licensed technology Thomson-CSF developed the Atlis (automatic tracking laser illumination system) target-designation pod and a complementary Ariel seeker head able to fit any missile of 100mm (3.94in) or greater diameter. Aérospatiale produced the AS.30L (AS.30 Laser) to make use of this more modern guidance system. In late 1977 an Armée de l'Air Jaguar A tested an Atlis 1 pod at Cazaux, in the course of which unguided AS.30L prototype missiles were fired. These had roll-stabilization and were programmed to fly on a gyro reference in a pre-guidance phase, prior to picking up the radiation from the target. In 1980 trials began using pre-production missiles homing on radiation from targets illuminated by the Cilas ITAY-71 laser in the Atlis 2 pod, which also includes a TV tracker to assist accurate designation. In 1981 Aérospatiale claimed the system, linked with the Jaguar, was the only one in the world to allow autonomous firing with laser guidance from single-seat aircraft. Deliveries began in 1983, initially on 300 missiles to arm the last 30 Armée de l'Air Jaguars. Carriers in Egypt and Iraq are the Mirage 2000 and Mirage F1.

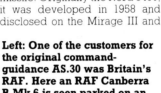

Left: One of the customers for the original command-guidance AS.30 was Britain's RAF. Here an RAF Canberra B.Mk 6 is seen parked on an airfield in Cyprus with these French missiles aboard.

Below: An orange AS.30L laser-guided missile, carried along with a white AS.30L by a special trials Jaguar equipped with cameras and instrumentation, as well as the Atlis 2 laser pod.

GUIDED WEAPONS

ASMP

Origin: SNI Aérospatiale
Propulsion: integrated rocket/ramjet, using SNPE rocket with Statolite smokeless filling and Aérospatiale advanced kerosene-fuelled ramjet
Dimensions: length 5.380mm (212in); body diameter about 420mm (16.5in); width across inlet ducts 820mm (32.2in)
Weight: at launch 900kg (1,984lb)
Performance: speed about Mach 3; range variable up to 100km (62 miles)
Warhead: CEA nuclear, 150kT
User: France

It is difficult to know whether to class this weapon as tactical or strategic, and the French are not sure themselves. Though it has a fair range, for the initials signify Air/Sol Moyenne Portée (medium-range air-to-surface), it has a nuclear warhead. ASMP was initiated in 1971 to arm whatever emerged as the next-generation Armée de l'Air deep-penetration aircraft, successively the Mirage G, ACF (Avion de Combat Futur) and Super Mirage. Cancellation of the last in 1976 reduced the pace of development, and no deep-penetration platform is now in prospect. Development was initially competitive between Matra with turbojet propulsion, and Aérospatiale with a ramrocket or ramjet. In March 1978 the go-ahead was given to Aérospatiale, with liquid-fuel ramjet propulsion. Today an integrated hybrid system has been chosen. Range specified for the

original (January 1974) ASMP was 80-150km (50-93 miles). This has since been more than doubled, because of the short range of the only available carrier aircraft (Mirage IVA, 2000 and Super Etendard) and the chief puzzle now is how the Antilope 5 radar can acquire targets at very long ranges. Mid-course guidance is pre-programmed, with Sagem playing a major role in the main inertial guidance. About FF4,000 million is to be spent on 100 missiles which have been carried by 18 Mirage IVP converted bombers from 1986. These are being supplemented by the Mirage 2000N. Further ASMPs are to be carried by Aéronavale Super Etendards.

Right: ASMP fires its rocket (top diagram), jettisons the rocket nozzle after burnout (centre) and then cruises on a ramjet engine.

Below: Cat launch of an Aéronavale Super Etendard carrying an ASMP nuclear cruise missile and drop tank.

Exocet, AM.39

Origin: SNI Aérospatiale
Propulsion: SNPE Condor 2-sec boost motor and SNPE Hélios solid (Nitramite-filled) smokeless 150-sec burn sustainer
Dimensions: length 4,690mm (184.6in); body diameter 350mm (13.75in); span 1,100mm (43.3in)
Weight: at launch 655kg (1,444lb)
Performance: speed high subsonic; range 50-70km (31-43.5 miles) depending on launch altitude
Warhead: Serat hexolite/steel block, 165kg (364lb), penetrates

ASMP Propulsion

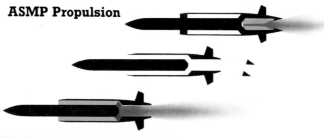

Above: The proposed Lancier, the attack version of the Alpha Jet, can carry a single AM.39 Exocet, balanced by a tank on the left wing as in the case of the Super Etendard. The Lancier prototype is seen here also carrying two Matra Magic AAMs for self-defence, plus a centreline gun pod with one 30mm cannon.

armour at contact angles to 70°, proximity and delay fuzes
Users: (air-launched) France and six other countries including Argentina, Iraq and Pakistan

Exocet was designed as a ship-launched sea-skimming missile, fed with target data before launch and provided with inertial mid-course guidance, flying at Mach 0.93 at a height of about 2.5m (8ft), and finally switching on the EMD Adac X-band mono-pulse active radar seeker to home on the ship target. Exocet was obviously a potential ASM and inert rounds were dropped by an Aéronavale Super Frelon in April 1973, followed by cut-grain powered launches in June of that year. In May 1974 the decision was taken to put the air-launched Exocet into production for the Aéronavale, and since then Aérospatiale has sold this missile to an increasing list of export customers. Originally almost identical to MM.38, and designated AM.38, the ASM developed into AM.39 with a new propulsion system (see data) and reduced overall missile length and weight giving increased performance. The wings and fins are reprofiled to facilitate carriage at supersonic speeds, and because of the greater range and flight-time the Adac seeker radar operates over a greater angular scan. AM.39 entered Aéronavale service in July 1977 carried aboard the Super Frelon (two missiles), followed by Pakistani

Above: An Aérospatiale AS.332F1 naval helicopter demonstrator armed with the maximum load of two AM.39 Exocet anti-ship missiles. The necessary targeting radar can be seen in the chin position ahead of the nose landing gear. One of the customers for this helicopter/missile combination is Kuwait.

Sea Kings. The Super Etendard followed in mid-1978 with either one or two on underwing pylons, and AM.39s fired from such aircraft of the Argentine navy gained world wide notoriety in the Falklands conflict (the missile which hit HMS *Sheffield* failed to explode, the ship being lost due

to a fire started by the still-burning sustainer). The successes have boosted an already good order book (900 rounds).

American reports claim that 52 of the first 53 fired by Iraqi aircraft in the Gulf War hit their civilian targets, two failing to detonate. Aérospatiale claims AM.39 to be the only long-range missile in the West that can be launched from helicopters (the latest platform is the Super Puma). A one-second delay allows the missile to drop clear before boost-motor ignition. French Aéronavale missiles are being updated with a Super Adac homing head, more resistant to countermeasures. A future replacement will be ANS.

French LGBs

Origin: SAMP and SA Matra
Propulsion: none
Dimensions: similar to Paveway
Weight: two production types have 1,000kg (2,205lb) warheads, others being smaller
Performance: typical effective range up to 10km (6.2 miles)
Warhead: usual sizes 250, 400 and 1,000kg (551, 882 and 2,205lb)
Users: France and several export customers

Since the late 1970s SAMP and Matra, assisted by Thomson CSF and other companies for guidance, have created French counterparts to the American Paveway series of LGBs (laser-guided bombs). All are matched to the Atlis II laser illuminator pod, and other lasers have been evaluated including types by Ferranti and Hughes. Seekers, packaged into the windvane-type nose guidance unit based directly on the Paveway weapons, include the Thomson-CSF Eblis and a Rockwell pattern. By 1981 large numbers of LGBs had been produced in France and production deliveries had begun. In all cases the front guidance kit and flip-out wings can be adapted to standard bombs. Improved tracking results in miss distances of around 1m (3.3ft) even at considerable lateral offsets and with flight times in the order of 30 seconds. Large numbers of the 400kg (882lb) size have been delivered, and the Armée de l'Air is receiving 100 of the 1,000kg (2,205lb) size for use with Mirage 2000s.

KDAR/PAB

Origin: Messerschmitt-Bölkow-Blohm, Bremen
Propulsion: one 16.5kW (22hp) Fichtel & Sachs two-cylinder piston engine
Dimensions: length 1,810mm (70.9in); body diameter 250mm (9.84in); span 2,260mm (89in)
Weight: empty 100kg (220lb), at launch 150kg (331lb)
Performance: speed 140-250km/h (87-155mph); cruise height to 3,000m (9,845ft); endurance stated to be several hours
Warhead: various conventional types
Users: West German army (PAD) and Luftwaffe (KDAR)

These are combat derivatives of MBB's big RT-900 Tucan (toucan) programme. KDAR (Kleine-Drohne Anti-Radar) and PAD (PanzerAbwehrDrohne) are different versions of a neat tailless, cruciform-wing RPV (remotely piloted vehicle) which could be air-launched. Up to 20 can be stored and launched from a standard container, thereafter searching for targets and attacking them. If KDAR finds a radar it can home on it, while PAD searches for armour. At any time an attack can be broken off if terminal sensors do not confirm the target's validity, and these small high-flying drones have proved difficult to shoot down.

Right: Lacking lift or any propulsion, an LGB has to be launched so that, without guidance, it would still fall fairly near the target.

Below: The pilot still has a wide choice of attack modes. Laser direction lines are chosen in blue.

Below: The French Matra family of LGBs are quite distinctive, being visibly different from the US Paveway series. Here a 400kg (882lb) LGB is seen under the wing of a Mirage F1C of the Armée de l'Air. Note the twin (diagonal) fins on the laser receiver nose.

Laser-guided Bomb Loft Trajectories

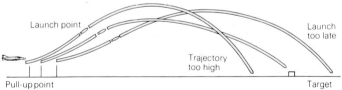

Launch point

Launch too late

Trajectory too high

Pull-up point

Target

Delayed Lasing

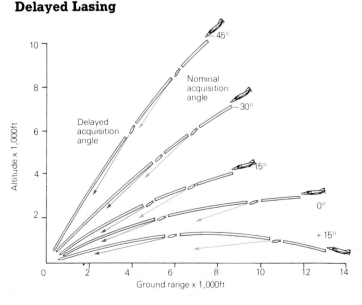

Altitude x 1,000ft

45°

Nominal acquisition angle

30°

Delayed acquisition angle

15°

0°

+15°

Ground range x 1,000ft

GUIDED WEAPONS

Kormoran

Origin: MBB
Propulsion: SNPE double-base solid motors, twin Prades boost motors and central Eole IV sustainer
Dimensions: length 4,400mm (173.2in); body diameter 340mm (13.4in); span 1,000mm (39.4in)
Weight: at launch Kormoran 1 600kg (1,323lb), Kormoran 2 630kg (1,389lb)
Performance: speed Mach 0.95; range up to 37km (23 miles), Kormoran 2 greater
Warhead: advanced MBB type, 160kg (352lb) with 16 radially mounted projectile charges and fuze delayed for passage through 90mm (3.54in) of steel plate
Users: West Germany, Italy; later probably other countries

The first major missile programme in West Germany after World War II, this began life in 1964 to meet a Marineflieger (navy air) requirement for a large anti-ship missile. Based on a Nord project, the AS.34, using the Sfena inertial guidance planned for the stillborn AS.33, it became a major programme in the new consortium. MBB, with Aéro-

spatiale participation. The basic weapon exactly follows Nord/Aérospatiale principles, but incorporates more advanced guidance. After release from the F-104G or Tornado carrier aircraft the boost motors give 2,750kg (6,063lb) thrust each for almost 1 second when the sustainer takes over and gives 285kg (628lb) for 100 seconds. Sfena/Bodenseewerk inertial midcourse guidance is used with a TRT radio altimeter to hold less than 30m (100ft) altitude. The missile then descends as it nears the pre-inserted target position, finally descending to wavetop height as the Thomson-CSF two-axis seeker (operating as either an active radar or passive receiver) searches and locks-on. Kormoran can operate in a range and bearing mode, or be fired optically without radar in a bearing-only mode. Impact should be just above the waterline, and the warhead projects liner fragments with sufficient velocity to penetrate up to seven bulkheads. Flight trials from F-104Gs began on 19 March 1970. The first of an initial 350 Kormoran production missiles was delivered in December 1977, and by mid-1978 the Marineflieger MFG2 at Eggbeck was fully equipped. The first Tornado-Kormoran unit was MFG 1 at

Leck in 1982. Kormoran is also carried by Italian Tornados.

Under government contract, MBB is developing Kormoran 2 with an entirely new radar seeker, strapdown inertial navigation system and digital signal processor. This new missile offers better target engagement, longer range, enhanced ECCM, better penetrability and a heavier (220kg/485lb) and more powerful warhead. It is compatible with the standard 1553B digital bus and is interchangeable with Kormoran 1. Guided rounds were on test with the manufacturer, MBB, by late 1986.

Above: A live Kormoran enters through the thin side plating of a destroyer target. The sustainer is still burning. Height above water: 3m (10ft).

Below: A pair of Kormoran missiles carried by a Tornado of the AMI (Italian Air Force). The aircraft flies from Gioia del Colle with the 156° Gruppo of the 36° Stormo (wing) in the anti-ship role. Tornados will eventually be rearmed with Kormoran 2, which is designed to be installationally interchangeable. Four can be carried.

ANS

Origin: joint programme by Aérospatiale, Chatillon, and MBB, Ottobrunn
Propulsion: launch and acceleration by integral solid-propellant rocket motor; cruise propulsion by high-energy rocket/ramjet (hybrid)
Dimensions: length 5,700mm (224.4in); body diameter 350mm (13.78in); wing span 1,100mm (43.3in)
Launch weight: 950kg (2,095lb)
Performance: sustained cruising speed Mach 2 at sea level, rising with height to Mach 3 at high altitude; range on all profiles not less than 185km (115 miles)
Warhead: conventional penetration/blast, 180kg (397lb)
Users: France and West Germany

ANS (Anti-Navire Supersonique) is a 50/50 programme between France and West Germany to develop an advanced replacement for Exocet. It followed the abortive three-nation ASSET/ASEM, but remains a NATO project. Among the assumptions made at the start are: such a missile needs air-breathing propulsion in order to provide much greater thrust over a much greater time in order to cruise faster and over greater range; air-breathing propulsion also provides the sustained thrust needed to maintain maximum manoeuvrability all the way to the target; it has to be a 'fire and forget' weapon; and there will be ship-and air-launched versions.

Features of the ANS include a large integral rocket motor to accelerate it to at least Mach 2 (see data); thereafter the propulsion system converts itself into a rocket/ramjet, the rocket providing fuel-rich gas which is then burned in the combustion chamber. MBB is responsible for the air-breathing propulsion, which

takes in air through four double-shock ram inlets, from which curved ducts lead to the central combustor where the oxygen-lean fuel grain containing boron is situated. This gives much higher-energy propulsion than hydrocarbon liquids. Aerodynamically ANS has four wings and four tail controls, all indexed in line with the inlets, and can pull 10g all the way to the target. Midcourse guidance is autonomous strapdown inertial; and terminal guidance is by a substantial active radar with a digital processor. ANS is expected to fly lower than any previous anti-ship missiles and to have exceptional ECM capability, besides giving defending crews much shorter warning of the missile's approach. All the indications are that ANS will be an even bigger export success than its predecessor, Exocet.

Above: A model of ANS, joint development by Aérospatiale and MBB, showing the four inlets to the single hybrid rocket/ramjet engine.

Apache/CWS Modules

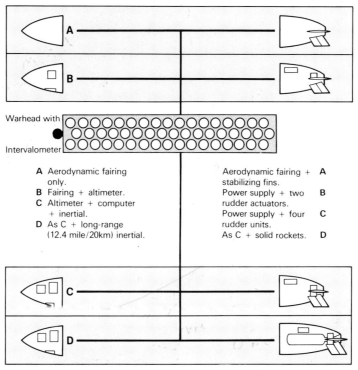

A Aerodynamic fairing only.
B Fairing + altimeter.
C Altimeter + computer + inertial.
D As C + long-range (12.4 mile/20km) inertial.

Aerodynamic fairing + stabilizing fins. A
Power supply + two rudder actuators. B
Power supply + four rudder units. C
As C + solid rockets. D

Above: Apache/CWS is to comprise a central munitions container plus various noses and tails depending on the guidance and range needed.

1 Possible active radar in some versions (or alternative nose sensor).
2 Nose fairing (common to all models).
3 Payload dispensers (various types of munition dropped or ejected laterally).
4 Common central payload container.
5 Standard NATO 356mm (14in) crutches (twin tandem).
6 Swing-out lifting wings.
7 Wing pivots.
8 Wing stowage recesses in top of central module.
9 Tail fairing (possibly containing propulsion and flight control units).
10 Powered rudders (not on all versions).
11 Hinge-down fins.

Apache/CWS

Origin: joint programme by SA Matra, Vélizy-Villacoublay, and MBB, Ottobrunn
Propulsion: (I) none, (II) solid-propellant rocket motor, (III) turbojet or turbofan
Dimensions: length 4,040mm (159.06in); width of body 630mm (24.8in); height of body 480mm (18.9in); span (wings deployed) 2,530mm (99.6in)
Weight: (I) 1,000kg (2,205lb), (II, III) 1,150-1,200kg (2,535-2,646lb)
Performance: launch speed up to Mach 0.95; flight speed Mach 0.95; range (I) 12km (7.45 miles), (II) 25-30km (15.5-18.6 miles) (III) 40-50km (24.9-31.1 miles)
Warhead: carries 750kg (1,653lb) payload of sideways-ejected submunitions (see text)
Users: initially France and West Germany

Apache and the Container Weapon System were respectively studied by the two partner firms which have now launched a joint programme. The basic vehicle is almost common to all three versions, with self-contained inertial guidance, pivoted flick-open wings and rear elevators, and twin ventral rudders. The midships section is a little more than 2m (6.56ft) long and can be configured for various modular payloads, which at least initially are to be the same submunitions as dispensed from the MW-1 (KB44, MIFF, MUSA, MUSPA and STABO). Thus the number carried for ejection to left and right along the flight path will depend on the mix of submunitions; diagrams show the numbers possible. The longest-ranged (air-breathing) version will have separate terminal guidance, but in all cases the submunition pattern size will be up to 350m (383 yards) wide (less from very low level) and 1,000m (1,094 yards) long. Functional prototypes were tested in 1985, tests with live submunitions were to take place in both countries in 1987 and initial operational capability aboard Tornado and Mirage 2000 is due in 1992.

Below: This artist's impression shows one form of Apache/CWS modular dispenser system. The tail now differs from that shown here.

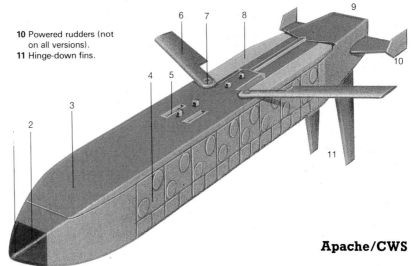

Apache/CWS

GUIDED WEAPONS

Right: A full-scale mock-up of the proposed LR-SOM at British Aerospace Air Weapons Division at Hatfield.

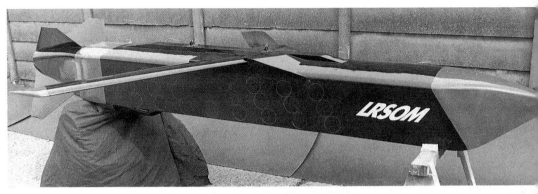

LR-SOM

Origin: competing tri-national teams, (1) Boeing Aerospace, British Aerospace, GEC Avionics and MBB, (2) General Dynamics, Hunting Engineering and Dornier

Propulsion: air-breathing turbojet or turbofan, competing teams are (1) Williams International, Rolls-Royce and KHD, (2) Teledyne CAE and Lucas Aerospace

Dimensions: not finalized

Weight: probably in the 750kg (1,653lb) class

Performance: cruising speed about Mach 0.9; range up to 600km (373 miles)

Warhead: large conventional, or clustered submunitions

Users: to be Britain, West Germany and USA

The three governments named above signed a memorandum of understanding on 12 July 1984 for the joint development of a Long-Range Stand-Off Missile. Competing teams have been formed for the missile and for its propulsion, and they are expected to propose contrasting guidance and control systems. Initial operational capability is scheduled for 1994, and carrier aircraft are expected to include the Tornado, B-1B, B-52, F-16 and F-111.

Martel

Origin: joint programme by SA Matra and British Aerospace Dynamics (previously HSD)
Propulsion: solid motor; (AS.37) SNPE Basile boost (2.4s burn) and Cassandre sustain (22.2s), both composite, (AJ.168) SNPE composite boost and cast double-base sustainer
Dimensions: length (AS.37) 4,120mm (162.2in), (AJ.168) 3,870mm (152.4in); body diameter 400mm (15.75in); span 1,200mm (47.25in)
Weight: at launch (AS.37) 550kg (1,213lb), (AJ.168) 530kg (1,168lb)
Performance: speed see text; range (treetop-height launch) 30km (18.6 miles), (high-altitude launch) 60km (37.3 miles))
Warhead: conventional 150kg (331lb) with DA or (AS.37) proximity fuze
Users: France (AS.37 only), UK

This excellent weapon grew from studies by HSD in Britain and Nord-Aviation and Matra in France in 1960-3. In September 1964 the British and French governments agreed to develop the weapon system jointly, in one of the first examples of European collaboration. In the event it was Engins Matra that became the French partner, responsible for the AS.37 anti-radar Martel. HSD developed the AJ.168 version with TV guidance. The name stems from Missile Anti-Radar TELevision.

Having a configuration similar to the AS.30, Martel has French propulsion. Flight Mach number is typically about 0.9, though this depends on angle of dive. Several sources state that Martel is supersonic.

The operator of AJ.168 studies the target area as seen on his control screen in the cockpit of the launch aircraft, fed by the MSDS vidicon camera in the nose of the missile. When he acquires a target he manually drives a small graticule box over it to lock-on the TV seeker before launch. The weapon is then fired holding height constant by a barometric lock, and steered by the operator's control stick via a streamlined underwing pod which also receives the video signals from the missile. Special features assist the operator to steer the missile accurately to the target.

AS.37 has an EMD AD.37 passive radiation seeker, with steerable inverse-Cassegrain aerial. If the rough location of a hostile emitter is known, but not its operating frequency, the seeker searches up and down a pre-set band of frequencies; when it detects the enemy radiation the aerial sweeps through 90° in azimuth to pinpoint the location. When it has locked-on the missile is launched, thereafter homing automatically. Alternatively, if the hostile radiation is known before take-off the seeker can be fitted with a matched aerial and receiver to pinpoint the source. AS.37 continues to home no matter how the hostile radiation may change frequency so long as it remains within the preset band.

Both versions of Martel have the same warhead. AS.37 having a Thomson-CSF proximity fuze. AS.37 is carried by Mirage III, Jaguar, Buccaneer and Atlantic; AJ.168 is used only by the RAF Buccaneers Production terminated in the late 1970s.

SR-SOM

Origin: Aérospatiale and Thomson Brandt Armements, and Diehl and Dornier
Propulsion: solid-propellant rocket
Dimensions: length (SOM 1) 3,400mm (133.85in); (2) 4,300mm (169.3in); wing span 2,600mm (102.4in)
Weights: (1) 720kg (1,587lb); (2) 1,400kg (3,086lb)
Performance: cruising speed (both) about Mach 0.8 at low level; range at low level (1) 20km (12.4 miles), (2) 40km (25 miles)
Warhead: large conventional or, in most cases, submunitions; weight (1) 350kg (772lb), (2) 900kg (1,984lb)
Users: France and West Germany

The Short-Range Stand-Off Missile is being developed by a Franco-German team led by Dornier for service in the 1990s. Dornier and TBA had previously conducted studies into such weapons, and these culminated in 1985 in the start of flight testing of SOM 1 dummies carried under the wings of an Alpha Jet. The eventual SOM does not have to be a dispenser, but most of the current work is directed towards MoBiDiC (Modular Bird with Dispensing Container). The two sizes are intended for (1) smaller aircraft with NATO 356mm (14in) ejector racks, and (2) larger aircraft (eg Tornado) with 762mm (30in) attachments. Dornier has proposed an 'intelligent sensor' midcourse guidance with high-precision terminal holding. Where submunitions are carried they will be for use against moving armour and aircraft in shelters. SR-SOM must be an all-weather fire-and-forget weapon.

Left: The two versions of Martel are visibly different. The British TV-guided version, AJ.168, has a bluff glass nose for the vidicon camera. The French AS.37 anti-radar model has a pointed nose radome.

Below: A Mirage IIIE of the French Armée de l'Air carrying a single AS.37 anti-radar Martel. France has never bought the British TV-guided version of this missile, supposedly a 50/50 joint programme.

Below: Dornier's SR-SOM, MoBiDiC (or MOBIDIC) is seen here in short form with a 1.6m (63in) payload bay, and with wings and tail deployed. The bigger version has a 2.5m (98.4in) payload container.

GUIDED WEAPONS

Gabriel III A/S

Origin: Israel Aircraft
Industries, Lod
Propulsion: boost/sustain solid
rocket motor
Dimensions: length 3,840mm
(151in); body diameter 340mm
(13.4in); wing span 1,100mm
(43in)
Weight: about 600kg (1,323lb)
Performance: speed transonic;
range basic version 40km (25
miles), extended-range version
(longer motor) 60km (37.3 miles)
Warhead: blast/frag, 150kg
(331lb), delay action fuze
User: Israel

The original family of Gabriel
ship-launched missiles stemmed
from various earlier weapons
which included an air-launched
version, and the wheel has now
turned full-circle with the perfection of Gabriel III A/S (air/sur-

face). Autonomous after launch, it
can be carried by A-4, F-4, Kfir or
Westwind Sea Scan aircraft, and
launched in either a fire-and-
forget or a fire-and-update mode.
In the latter the pre-programmed
point in the sea-skimming run (at
a height of 20m/66ft) at which the
inertial guidance is replaced by
active radar homing is delayed to
a point nearer the target, so the
active search covers a smaller
geographical sector and operates for a shorter time. IAI
emphasize the excellent ECCM
capability of Gabriel III and its
exceptionally low cruise height
which is set pre-launch according to sea state at 4, 2.5 or only
1.5m (13.1, 8.2 or only 4.9ft).
Gabriel III A/S is a major
technical achievement, and IAI,
backed by almost all Israel's
defence avionics industry, have
created a weapon with exceptional lethality and high accuracy
in the presence of hostile
countermeasures.

**Below: Two specially painted
Gabriel III A/S development
missiles carried by a trials
F-4E Phantom II of the Israeli
air force. Note the stores
pylons in Sparrow recesses.**

Marte Mk 2

Origin: OTO Melara, La Spezia,
and Sistel — Sistemi Elettronici
SpA
Propulsion: SEP 299 solid boost
motor (4,400kg/9,702lb for 1.6s)
and SEP 300 solid sustainer
(100kg/220.5lb for 73s)
Dimensions: length 4,700mm
(185in); body diameter 206mm
(8.1in); span 1,000mm (39.4in)
Weight: at launch 300kg (661lb)
Performance: speed Mach 0.74;
range over 20km (12.4 miles)
Warhead: semi-armour-
piercing, 70kg (154lb) with DA
and proximity fuzes
User: Italy

This ASM system was initiated by
the Italian navy in 1967 to give aircraft a fire-and-forget all-weather
attack capability against surface
warships. Sea Killer 2 was selected as the missile part of the

system, and Sistel was appointed
prime contractor. Major asso-
ciates are Agusta, which provides the helicopter platform,
and SMA for the MM/APQ-706
fire-control radar. Sea Killer is a
sea-skimming missile with various forms of azimuth and terminal
guidance. The usual carrier is the
Agusta-built Sikorsky SH-3D,
though Marte has been studied
for smaller helicopters, notably
the Italian navy's AB 212 (Marte
has been tested on AB 212s of the
Argentine Navy). Smaller helicopters would carry only one
missile and have no ASW capability. An SH-3D carries two
missiles, as also can the AMX and
MB.339 fixed-wing aircraft. The
Marte system weighs a total of
1,165kg (2,568lb) made up of
600kg (1,323lb) for the missiles,
400kg (882lb) for the launch
equipment and control console,
143kg (95lb) for sonar and 22kg
(49lb) for the optical sight. The
standard technique is for the
radar to acquire a target at maximum range, the helicopter then
descending to wave-top height
and flying towards the target,
finally popping up to re-acquire
the target and launch the missile
towards the hostile ship.

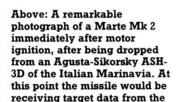

Above: A remarkable photograph of a Marte Mk 2 immediately after motor ignition, after being dropped from an Agusta-Sikorsky ASH-3D of the Italian Marinavia. At this point the missile would be receiving target data from the radar in the helicopter's nose.

Right: Loading a live Marte Mk 2 on to the right-hand missile attachment of the same ASH-3D helicopter. Note that stencilling on this Italian-built helicopter is in English. The size of the Marte means that two can be carried by medium helicopters.

JAPAN

ASM-1 (Type 80)

Origin: Mitsubishi Heavy Industries
Propulsion: Nissan Motors single-stage solid rocket
Dimensions: length 4,000mm (157.75in); body diameter 350mm (13.75in); span 1,200mm (47.25in)
Weight: at launch 610kg (1,345lb)
Performance: speed Mach 0.9; range, maximum 50km (31 miles)

Warhead: conventional anti-ship, 200kg (440lb)
User: Japan

Mitsubishi was selected as prime contractor for this large anti-ship missile in 1973, and after successful development the basic air-launched version was accepted by the Defence Agency in December 1980. Work has also begun on other versions, including a surface-launched variant with a tandem boost motor and an extended-range model with turbojet propulsion. The basic ASM-1 has mid-course guidance provided by a Japan Aviation Electronics strapdown inertial system, with a TRT radio altimeter which holds altitude just above the tops of the largest waves. Near the target the Mit-subishi Electronics active radar seeker is switched on to home on to the largest reflective target. Guidance tests were flown with a C-1 transport in 1977, and in December that year unguided rounds were fired from an F-1 over Waseka Bay. Guided flight trials began in July 1978, at which time a US report gave the estimated unit price as $384,000. Production was initiated in late 1979, and from 1982 about 30 rounds per year have been delivered to F-1 squadrons. Other possible carrier aircraft include the P-2J and P-3C patrol aircraft.

Below: Side elevation of the Mitsubishi ASM-1, which is designated Type 80 by the Japanese Air Self-Defence Force.

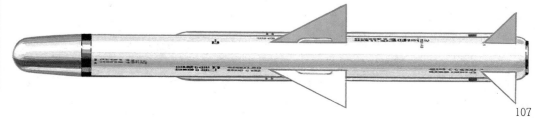

Above: A beautiful portrait of a live firing of a Penguin 3 from an F-16A of the US Air Force. This version has considerably smaller wings.

Below: The Penguin model optimized for carriage by helicopters is the Mk 2 Mod 7, seen here in a trial installation on board a naval Lynx helicopter. Note the large folding wings which deploy as the missile is released after the ignition of its rocket motor.

Penguin

Origin: A/S Kongsberg Väpen-fabrikk
Propulsion: Raufoss solid sustainer motor
Dimensions: length (2) 3,050mm (120in), 3,180mm (125.2in); body diameter 280mm (11in); span (2) 1,400mm (55.1in), (3) 1,000mm (39.4in)
Weight: at launch (2) 330kg (728lb), (3) 372kg (820lb)
Performance: speed over Mach 0.8; range variable with launch speed/height up to (2) 40km (25 miles) or (3) 27km (16.8 miles)
Warhead: as Bullpup, 113kg (250lb) bomb, DA fuze
Users: Norway, USA

Penguin was developed by Kongsberg and the Norwegian Defence Research Establishment as a ship-to-ship weapon in the 1960s. From it was derived Penguin 3 for air launching, with smaller wings, no booster motor and higher flight performance. It is basically a simple weapon, readily adaptable to fighter type aircraft and launched from a standard Bullpup pylon. Mid-course guidance is inertial, followed by

Right: Cutaway drawing of the helicopter-launched Penguin Mk 2 Mod 7, which has large folding wings and a boost rocket motor to facilitate launch from a helicopter.

Penguin Mk 2 Mod 7 Cutaway

1 Passive infra-red (IR) target seeker.
2 Canard.
3 Altimeter.
4 Control unit.
5 Inertial navigation unit.
6 120kg (265lb) warhead, DA fuze.
7 Fuze.
8 Solid propellant sustainer motor.
9 Folding wings.
10 Booster motor.

terminal homing by an IR seeker or a PEAB active radar. Another version is to home on hostile emissions using a passive seeker. BAe Sperry Gyroscope produce the canard actuation system and Saab-Scania of Sweden the launcher and system power unit to be installed in KNL (Royal Norwegian AF) F-16s which are to become operational with Penguin 3 in 1987. As initial development was completed in 1974, including carry trials on F-104Gs, this seems a very long time scale, but the missile itself has undergone successive modifications.

Meanwhile, the earlier Penguin 2, with larger wings for lower-speed launch, has been adopted by the US Navy as part of the LAMPS III system, carried by the SH-60B Seahawk helicopter. Penguin 2 Mod 7 is in production with US designation AGM-119, and it retains a tandem solid boost motor and folding wings, engineered by Grumman. Operational evaluation is due for completion in 1988, the production buy being 193 rounds.

AS-2 'Kipper'

Propulsion: one turbojet, believed to be a Lyul'ka AL-5F rated at about 4,450kg (12,015lb)
Dimensions: length about 10m (32ft 10in); body diameter 900mm (35.4in); span 4.88m (16ft)
Weight: at launch 4,200kg (9,259lb)
Performance: speed generaly considered to be marginally supersonic (Mach 1.2); range estimated from 185 to 200km (115 to 125 miles)
Warhead: generally believed to be conventional 1,000kg (2,205lb)
User: Soviet Union

First seen at the 1961 Soviet Aviation Day display, this large ASM has a more advanced aeroplane configuration than the preceding — and now obsolete — AS-1 and is considerably larger, the Tu-16 'Badger-C' and 'C-Mod' carrying

one missile on the centreline recessed into the weapon bay. Propulsion is by a turbojet (possibly a Lyul'ka AL-5) in a short pod underslung at the rear. In appearance this missile faintly resembles the defunct Hound Dog, but is utterly different in mission, it being intended to attack moving targets with large radar signatures. Guidance probably duplicates that of AS-1, the new missile merely increasing flight performance and payload. Thus, it is believed to have simple autopilot mid-course guidance, until when in line-of-sight distance of a ship (possibly other) target it could home by its own active radar. The warhead is conventional and very large. Cruising speed has generally been estimated at Mach 1.2 at high altitude.

AS-3 'Kangaroo'

Propulsion: one afterburning turbojet, possibly a Tumanskii R-11 or R-13 rated at about 6,800kg (14,991lb)
Dimensions: length about 14.96m (49ft 1in); body diameter 1,850mm (72.8in); span 9.15m (30ft)
Weight: at launch 11,000kg (24,250lb)
Performance: speed about Mach 1.8; range estimated about 650km (404 miles)
Warhead: thermonuclear, 800kT, or (unlikely) very large conventional, 2,300kg (5,071lb)
User: Soviet Union

Above: Seen over the Baltic near Sweden, this 'Backfire-B' bomber is carrying an AS-4 'Kitchen' cruise missile. Several different types of these missiles have been seen in recent years; this particular example is used for training in aircraft handling.

This missile was also disclosed at the 1961 Soviet Aviation Day display, when one was carried low overhead by a Tu-20 (Tu-95) 'Bear' bomber. This particular installation was probably a full-scale model to prove aircraft compatibility, the vehicle lacked many features seen in the actual missile, and a streamlined white nose appeared to be a temporary fairing forming part of the aircraft. This fairing is absent from some of the so-called 'Bear-B' and 'C' carrier aircraft, many (if not all) of which belong to the AV-MF, the Soviet naval air force. The missile is aerodynamically similar to Mach 2 fighters of the mid-1950s, and could well have been based on the Ye-2A 'Faceplate' by the Mikoyan bureau. This was powered by a Tumanskii R-11 two-shaft afterburning turbojet rated at 5,000kg (11,243lb), and this fits the missile perfectly. AS-3 has exactly the same wing, circular nose inlet, small conical centrebody, long instrument boom at the bottom of the nose, identical aerodynamic controls, and the same fuselage structure, and the ventral fin at the rear resembles that of the earlier Mikoyan Ye-50 prototype. The tips of the tailplane have anti-flutter pods similar to those flown on the MiG-19 fighter but not fitted to Ye-2. AS-3 is commonly described as 'operational since 1960' but was not seen in service until 1963. The main puzzle is how it steers itself to its target, because though it is easy to see how radio command/autopilot guidance could carry it up to 290km (180 miles) from the launch

Left: Release of a giant AS-3 'Kangaroo' from a Tu-95 'Bear-B' strategic bomber. Most of these aircraft have been converted to carry the higher-performance AS-4.

aircraft, despite cruising with full afterburner, the ultimate range is put by the DoD at 650km (404 miles), beyond the visual horizon.

A nuclear warhead is assumed, and this suggests inertial or preprogrammed guidance against cities, ports and similar large fixed targets. The 'Bear' carrier aircraft are being converted to carry the AS-4 'Kitchen', though a few AS-3s remained in service in 1987.

AS-4 'Kitchen'

Propulsion: rocket, believed to be liquid propellant
Dimensions: length about 11.3m (37ft 1in); body diameter 900mm (35.4in); span about 3.08m (10ft 1in)
Weight: at launch about 6,500kg (14,330lb)
Performance: speed up to Mach 3.5 at high altitude; range variable up to 460km (286 miles) on all high-altitude profile
Warhead: nuclear 350kT, or large conventional, 1,000kg (2,205lb)
User: Soviet Union

Yet another disclosure at the 1961 Soviet Aviation Day fly-past was this much more advanced and highly supersonic ASM, carried recessed under the fuselage of one of the ten Tu-22 'Blinder' supersonic bomber/reconnaissance aircraft that took part. This aircraft, dubbed 'Blinder-B' by NATO, had a larger nose radome, and other changes, as have several other Tu-22s seen in released photographs. Most aircraft of this sub-type have the outline of the AS-4 missile visible on their multi-folding weapon-bay doors, but the missile appears seldom to be carried today and in any case most remaining Tu-22s are of other versions, serving with the ADD and AV-MF. The missile itself has slender delta wings, a cruciform tail and, almost certainly, a liquid-propellant rocket. Prolonged discussion in the West has failed to arrive at any degree of certainty concerning the guidance, though the general consensus is that it must be inertial, possibly with mid-course updating by a Tu-95 or other platform. A homing system is obviously needed for moving targets such as ships. Both versions of the swing-wing Tu-26 'Backfire' multi-role platform are believed to have carried this missile, probably in AV-MF service. Surprisingly, AS-4 has been seen on these new bombers frequently, whereas the later AS-6 has been seen more often on aged Tu-16 'Badgers'. The general belief today is that the missiles carried by ADD aircraft are strategic and either have no terminal homing (and 350kT warhead) or passive anti-radar homing and an HE warhead for defence-suppression. AV-MF anti-ship missiles have active terminal radar.

believed to possess terminal homing. According to the DoD one version has an active radar, while another homes on enemy radar signals. Area-correlation has been suggested as a third (unconfirmed) possibility. Development appears to have been protracted, and though reported prior to 1972 AS-6 was still not in wide service in 1975. By 1977 it was carried under the wings of both the Tu-16 'Badger-G' and Tu-26 'Backfire'. User services certainly include the AV-MF and possibly the ADD. Launched at about 11,000m (36,090ft), the missile climbs rapidly to about 18,000m (59,055ft) for cruise at about Mach 3. It finally dives on its target, or it can approach just above the sea or surface of the land. This missile is probably still in production.

AS-5 'Kelt'

Propulsion: single-stage liquid-propellant rocket with pump feed
Dimensions: length about 8.59m (28ft 2in); body diameter 900mm (35.4in); span 4.30m (14ft 1in)
Weight: at launch 3,400kg (7,496lb)
Performance: speed Mach 1.2 at high altitude (subsonic at low level); range up to 230km (143 miles) at high altitude or 180km (112 miles) at low altitude
Warhead: conventional, 1,000kg (2,205lb)
Users: Iraq, Soviet Union

First seen in a released photograph of September 1968, showing one of these missiles under the wing of a Tu-16, AS-5 is based on the airframe of AS-1 and some may even be rebuilds. In place of the turbojet and nose-to-tail duct there is a rocket with extensive liquid-propellant tankage. In the nose is a large radome. Superficially the nose and underbody fairing appear to be identical to those of the ship-launched SS-N-2 'Styx', and AS-5 thus is credited with the same choice of active radar or passive IR homing, having cruised to the vicinity of the target on autopilot, with initial radio-command corrections. By the early 1970s deliveries are thought to have exceeded 1,000, all of them carried by the so-called 'Badger-G'. This launch platform has the same pylons as the 'Badger-B' and a nose navigator compartment.

In the early 1970s about 35 of these aircraft, plus missiles, were supplied to the Egyptian air force, possibly with Soviet crews and specialist tradesmen. In the Yom Kippur war in October 1973 about 25 missiles were launched against Israeli targets. According to the Israelis 20 were shot down en route, at least one by an F-4; five penetrated the defences. A

supply dump was one of the targets hit, but at least two AS-5s homed automatically on to the emissions from Israeli radar stations. All the missiles were released at medium height of some 9,000m (29,530ft), reaching a speed of about Mach 0.95; in the denser air at low level speed fell to about 0.85. AS-5 has been progressively put into storage, but at least 50 have been delivered to Iraq.

AS-6 'Kingfish'

Propulsion: liquid-propellant rocket motor
Dimensions: length about 10m (32ft 10in); body diameter 800mm (31.5in); span about 2.5m (8ft 2in)
Weight: at launch about 5,000kg (11,023lb)
Performance: speed (DoD estimate) Mach 3 at high altitude; range (DoD) 250-560km (155 to 350 miles)
Warhead: nuclear, 350kT or 1,000kg (2,205lb) conventional
User: Soviet Union

Above: A Tu-16 'Badger-G' bomber of the Egyptian Air Force carrying two AS-5 'Kelt' rocket missiles. Similar aircraft remain in service with Iraq, but the Egyptian force is inactive.

At first thought to be a development of AS-4, this completely new missile gradually was reassessed as the first Soviet ASM publicly known that offers precision guidance over long ranges. It is still largely an enigma in the West, but has a slim fuselage with pointed nose, low-aspect-ratio delta wings and quite small cruciform tail controls, with a folding ventral fin. AS-6 is appreciably smaller than the earlier AS-4 missile, and has a slimmer ventral instrumentation fairing and no blister on the underside amidships. Propulsion is by an advanced rocket, and key features of AS-6 are much higher flight performance and dramatically better accuracy than any previous Soviet ASM. It clearly reflects vast advances in inertial guidance and nuclear-warhead design, and it is generally

AS-7 'Kerry'

Propulsion: rocket, said by DoD to be single-stage solid-propellant
Dimensions: length 3,500mm (137.8in); body diameter 305mm (12in); fin span 950mm (37.4in)
Weight: at launch 400kg (882lb)
Performance: speed Mach 1; range up to 11km (6.8 miles)
Warhead: (DoD) conventional 100kg (220lb)
Users: Soviet Union, India, Yugoslavia, Iraq and other countries

Though the Soviet Union has clearly been testing tactical ASMs for at least 20 years, not one is known to have entered service until the late 1970s, a very strange fact. AS-7 was still almost completely unknown in the West

Below: A close-up of the massive AS-6 'Kingfish' carried by a supersonic 'Backfire-B' bomber, probably serving with Soviet naval aviation. This particular missile is for training.

in 1981, though for more than a decade it has been reported to be carried by the Su-24 'Fencer', and it is still probably part of the armament of the MiG-27 and several other FA (Frontal Aviation) types. Guidance was originally thought to be radio command, an outdated method which normally requires the directing aircraft to loiter in the vicinity of the target. A later DoD opinion was that AS-7 is a beam rider, though whether the beam is radar or laser has not been divulged. The traditional form of beam-riding guidance is a most odd choice for a missile intended to attack battlefield targets.

As this book goes to press it appears safer to regard the question of guidance as unknown. According to some reports it is carried by the Yak-38 'Forger', in this case presumably against ship targets. It has also been exported.

AS-8

Dimensions: unknown, but length in region of 1,800mm (7in); body diameter 140mm (5.5in)
Weight: possibly about 32kg (70.5lb)

This designation apparently refers to the AT-6 'Spiral' when used in the air-launched mode (see Anti-tank Missiles section).

AS-X-9

Propulsion: rocket motor (no details available)
Dimensions: length about 6,000m (236.2in); body diameter 300mm (19.7in); wing span no data
Weight: no information, but obviously about 650kg (1,433lb)
Performance: speed Mach 0.8; maximum range given as 88km (55 miles)

Warhead: conventional blast/fragmentation
User: Soviet Union

This is described as an anti-radar missile, carried by the Su-24 'Fencer' (and, doubtless, other aircraft). No other details have been disclosed.

AS-10 'Karen'

Propulsion: internal solid-propellant rocket motor
Dimensions: length 3,500mm (137.8in); body diameter 305mm (12in); fin span no data
Weight: in the 400kg (882lb) class
Performance: speed transonic, range given as 9.6km (6 miles)
Warhead: conventional, about 100kg (220lb)
Users: Soviet Union, and possibly other countries

This missile is said to be a precision laser-guided weapon derived from AS-7 'Kerry'. It is carried by all Soviet tactical aircraft, and probably by the Yak-38 'Forger'.

AS-12 'Kegler'

No details are available of this ASM beyond the fact that it is tactical in nature and may be a stand-off dispenser system.

AS-14 'Kedge'

Propulsion: solid-propellant smokeless rocket motor
Dimensions: length about 4,500mm (177.2in); body diameter 450mm (17.7in); wing span 1,300mm (51.2in)

Below: The only photograph known in the West of the big AS-14 'Kedge' attack missile, carried here by a MiG-27. The pod under the belly almost certainly contains a pivoting cannon.

Above: Crude US Defense Department artwork showing the AS-15 'Kent' cruise missile being launched from a 'Bear-H'. Not much reliance should be placed on the detail features of the aircraft or missile.

Weight: about 600kg (1,323lb)
Performance: speed transonic; range probably about 20km (12.4 miles)
Warhead: conventional, probably about 300kg (661lb)
User: Soviet Union

This precision attack missile has large rear wings indexed in line with canard nose controls, all surfaces having sharp taper on the leading edge and a very broad tip. It is said to be laser guided, and associated with a separate laser carried in a pod under the launch aircraft (MiG-27 and many other tactical types).

AS-15 'Kent'

Propulsion: air-breathing (turbojet or turbofan, possibly even a ramjet)
Dimensions: length about 7m (23ft); body diameter about 650mm (25.6in); span of deployed wings 3.25m (10ft 8in)
Weight: in the 1,500kg (3,307lb) class
Performance: cruising speed about Mach 0.9; range in excess of 1,200km (746 miles)
Warhead: normally thermonuclear, probably in the 200kT class
User: Soviet Union

Carried initially by 'Backfire' and 'Bear-H', this cruise missile is also expected to be carried in multiple groups by the 'Blackjack' bomber. It was tested over full range in 1978 (and announced by the US DoD in February 1979), and became fully operational in 1984. According to the DoD it has Tercom type guidance in order to achieve a CEP (circular error probability) of only about 45m (148ft). It is expected to be the first of a new generation of long-range air-launched missiles.

BL-10

Propulsion: air-breathing ramjet or rocket/ramjet hybrid engine
Dimensions: length about 7m (23ft)
Weight: probably about 2,000kg (4,409lb)
Performance: crusing speed supersonic (at least Mach 2); range about 3,220km (2,000 miles)
Warhead: thermonuclear, 200kT category
Users: to be Soviet Union

Virtually everything known about this new 'supercruise' missile is listed above, apart from the fact that it is expected to be of stealth low-observables design. The carrier aircraft will be the 'Blackjack' supersonic bomber now in production as the Soviet Union's counterpart to the USA's Rockwell B-1B.

GUIDED WEAPONS

RB 04

Origin: Saab (now Saab Missiles)
Propulsion: solid rocket motor with boost/sustain charges fired consecutively
Dimensions: length 4,450mm (175.2in); body diameter 500mm (19.7in); span (RB 04C,D) 2,040mm (80.3in), (E) 1,970mm (77.5in)
Weight: at launch (C,D) 600kg (1,323lb), (E) 616kg (1,358lb)
Performance: speed high subsonic; range variable with launch height up to 32km (20 miles)
Warhead: unitary 300kg (681lb) conventional, DA and proximity fuzes
Users: Sweden

This hard-hitting ASM has enjoyed one of the longest active programmes of any guided missile, for the requirement was finalized in 1949, and missile hardware was being manufactured for 28 years (1950-78). Planned as a primary weapon to be carried by the Saab A32A Lansen, this missile was originally designed and developed by the Robotavdelningen (guided-weapons directorate) of the national defence ministry, whose first missile, RB302, was flight-tested in 1948 from a T18B bomber. The original RB (Robot-

byran) 04 was made large enough to carry an active radar seeker, giving all-weather homing guidance earlier than for any other ASM apart from Bat. The configuration is of aeroplane type, with a rear delta wing with end fins and four control fins around the forebody. The two-stage solid cast-DB motor is by IMI Summerfield Research Station in Britain. The radar is by PEAB (Swedish Philips) and the autopilot, originally the XA82, is a Saab design with pneumatically driven gyros and surface servos. The first launch took place from a Saab J29 fighter on 11 February 1955. and following very successful development the first production version, RB 04C, entered service with the Swedish air force in

1958, equipping all A32A aircraft of attack wings F-6, -7, -14 and -17. In the early 1960s the Robot-avdelningen developed a version with improved motor and guidance, RB 04D, which was in production in the second half of that decade. On 1 July 1968 the bureau became part of the Air Materiel Department of the Försvarets Materielverk (Armed Forces Materiel Administration, FMV), and the ultimate development of this missile, RB 04E, was assigned to Saab (then Saab Bofors). Produced mainly to arm the AJ37 Viggen, which carries up to three, RB 04E has a reduced span, modernized structure and more advanced guidance. All versions have the same very large fragmentation warhead.

Above: An RB 05A attack missile on its transport trolley beside an AJ37A Viggen. The pylon adapter shoe is already installed on the missile, ready for fixing to the hardpoint.

RB 05A

Origin: Saab Missiles Corporation
Propulsion: Volvo Flygmotor VR-35 liquid rocket motor, 2,550kg (5,620lb) boost, 510kg (1,124lb) sustain
Dimensions: length 3,600mm (141.75in); body diameter 300mm (11.8in); span 800mm (31.5in)
Weight: at launch 305kg (672lb)
Performance: speed supersonic; range up to 9km (5.6 miles)
Warhead: conventional warhead by Forenade Fabriksverken, proximity fuzed
Users: Sweden

When the decision was taken to restrict what had been the Robotavdelningen (guided weapon directorate) to R&D only, Saab was the natural choice for this missile, prime responsibility for which was placed with the company in 1960. Originally known as Saab 305A, RB 05A is a simple command-guidance weapon readily adaptable to many types of launch aircraft. One unusual feature is supersonic flight performance, conferred by advanced aerodynamics and a pre-packaged liquid motor fed with Hidyne and RFNA, pumped by a gas-pressurized piston and collapsible aluminium bladder from each side of the missile's centre of gravity to burn rapidly in a boost phase and slower in the sustainer mode. Motor performance is independent of missile attitude or acceleration, and there is no visible smoke. The missile rapidly overtakes the launch aircraft and automatically centres itself dead ahead; it is then steered by a microwave link from the pilot's miniature control stick. The guidance is claimed to be highly resistant to jamming, able to control the missile at low altitudes over all kinds of terrain, and able to attack targets at large offset angles. RB 05A is carried by the AJ37 Viggen and can be carried by other Swedish aircraft including the SK60 trainer. Production was completed in 1977.

Above: The AJ37A Viggen attack version can carry three RB 04E missiles. This one is hung under the right wing pylon, on a special adapter.

Below: An AJ37A Viggen from wing F15 at Söderhamm armed with two RB 04E heavy attack missiles. A large drop tank is carried on the centreline.

RBS 15F

Origin: Saab Missiles
Corporation
Propulsion: Microturbo TRI 60-2
Model 077 turbojet, sea-level
thrust 377kg (831lb)
Dimensions: length 4,350mm
(171.25in); body diameter
500mm (19.7in); span 1,400mm
(55.1in).
Weight: at launch 598kg (1,318lb)
Performance: speed high
subsonic; range 'considerably
more than 70km' (43.5 miles)
Warhead: large FFV
blast/fragmentation with DA
and proximity fuzes
User: Sweden

RBS 15 was designed as a ship-to-ship weapon for use aboard the 'Spica II' FPBs. In August 1982 Saab Bofors announced a Swedish defence matériel administration (FMV) order, worth some SK500 million, for the RBS 15F air-launched version, for use by Viggens and the forthcoming JAS 39 Gripen. The 15F has no launch canister or boost motors, but is carried on external pylons and launched when over the horizon from the target. A fire-and-forget weapon, it has a pre-programmed mid-course guidance and an advanced radar seeker by PEAB with digital processing and frequency agility, selectable search patterns and modes, target-choice logic (to pick the most important of a group of hostile ships) and variable ECCM facilities. Saab claims all-weather RBS 15 will have fast reaction and a high kill probability. Service entry is due in 1988.

Above: An RBS 15F new-generation anti-ship missile carried by an AJ37A Viggen of the Swedish air force. A natural successor to the RB 04E, it is closely similar to the earlier weapon in size, but has much greater range conferred by an air-breathing turbojet engine.

Above: A full-scale model of the proposed AALAAW as displayed by British Aerospace. The remarkably stubby box-like appearance belies this missile's high speed.

UNITED KINGDOM

AALAAW

Origin: British Aerospace,
Hatfield
Propulsion: none
Dimensions: length about
2,000mm (78.7in); body cross-section 320mm (12.6in) square;
wing span about 1,000mm (39.4in)
Weight: not disclosed
Performance: range about 8km
(5 miles) at high subsonic speed
Warhead: large number of
TGSMs (terminally guided
submunitions)
Users: see text

Since about 1984 the UK has had a Staff Requirement (Air) SR(A).1238 for a completely new anti-armour weapon with which to arm tactical aircraft. Despite the wealth of similar devices, a study was completed by British Aerospace in partnership with Shorts and GEC Avionics, in competition with a rival study by a team led by Hunting, producer of the RAF's existing dispenser munitions. AALAAW (advanced air-launched anti-armour weapon), as displayed in mock-up form by BAe, is a box of submunitions formed into a glider with twin fins on the tips of aft-mounted wings, and with rudders at the tail. Features were said to include TGSMs with millimetre-wave radar guidance and large shaped-charge warheads. As this was written, work was held up pending some kind of international collaborative development programme.

Below: The prototype of the Saab JAS 39 Gripen was rolled out in April 1987, though it had not then received camouflage paint as shown in these drawings. The new Swedish multirole fighter is depicted here carrying two RBS 15F attack missiles, with Sidewinders on the wingtips.

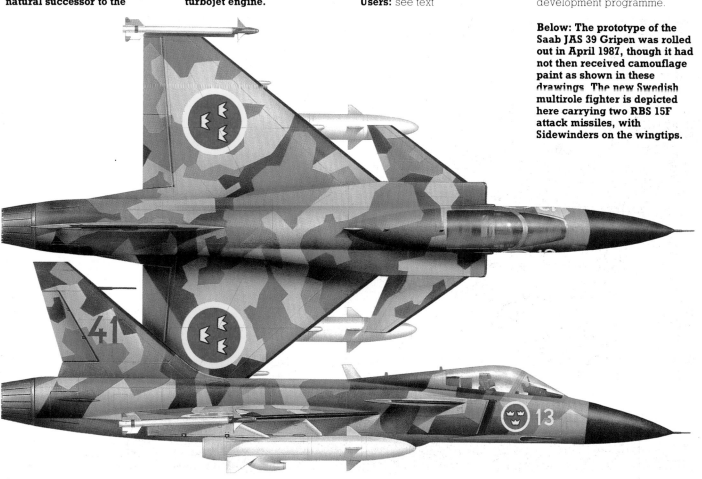

ALARM Pylon Interface

1 Streamlined nose.
2 Spring-loaded mounting for umbilical connector.
3 Cable connector.
4 Forward cable loom.
5 Standard attachments (NATO 14in/356mm or 30in/762mm).
6 Rear umbilical connector.
7 Rear cable loom.

8 Main electrical and control box.
9 Shoe to mate with missile.
10 Forward umbilical connector.

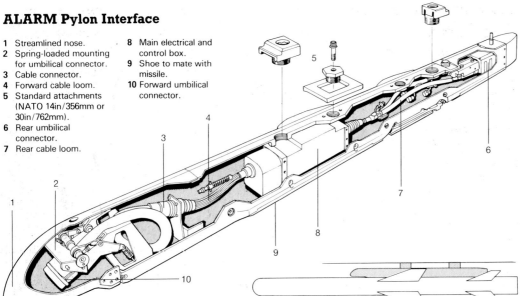

Above: The RAF Tornado GR. Mk 1 can carry nine ALARM missiles and still leave the outer pylons free for ECM pods or other stores. ALARM is not only more sophisticated but much smaller than rival anti-radar missiles.

Left: Like nearly all of today's sophisticated missiles ALARM needs a special shoe to serve as an interface between the store and the pylon or aircraft structure. This cutaway shows main elements of the ALARM interface, with a small inset showing how it links the missile to the pylon or aircraft.

Below: This British IDS Tornado was on test in 1985 with seven ALARMs, two drop tanks, a Sky Shadow jammer pod and a BOZ chaff dispenser, both essential ECM items.

ALARM

Origin: British Aerospace, Hatfield
Propulsion: MoD (ROF) Nuthatch solid rocket motor (but see text)
Dimensions: length about 4,000mm (157.5in); body diameter 230mm (9in); wing span 730mm (28.75in)
Weight: 300kg (661lb)
Performance: varies greatly with operational mode, see text
Warhead: advanced MBB (West Germany) HE warhead with precision laser proximity fuze by Thorn EMI giving autonomous classification of targets and exact trigger-point selection
Users: UK, Saudi Arabia and later other countries

By far the most advanced anti-radar missile in the world, the Air-Launched Anti-Radiation Missile was developed to meet the British AST (Air Staff Target) 1228 requirement, to increase penetrative capability of the Tornado in deep strike and interdiction missions. After competing against the American HARM, ALARM was selected in July 1983, chiefly because compared with the older weapon ALARM is much more capable, much more versatile and so much smaller and lighter that it can be carried in multiple without interfering with the aircraft's normal external stores spectrum. It had been hoped to use the Sky Flash airframe, but this proved fractionally too small and ALARM is an exactly tailored weapon with a range of operating modes. At the front is the Marconi Defence Systems seeker, which has a fix-

ALARM Indirect Attack Mode

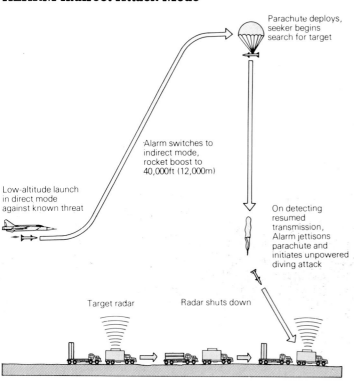

Parachute deploys, seeker begins search for target

Alarm switches to indirect mode, rocket boost to 40,000ft (12,000m)

Low-altitude launch in direct mode against known threat

On detecting resumed transmission, Alarm jettisons parachute and initiates unpowered diving attack

Target radar

Radar shuts down

Above: ALARM can be used in an unusual indirect mode in which it essentially hovers, passive and undetectable, whilst searching for the best target. The enemy can never be sure when an ALARM will strike home.

ed four-sided nose carrying four spiral helix broadband antennas. Signals from these are passed to a digital processor incorporating the latest LSI (large-scale integration) techniques and new microwave integrated-circuit materials. The seeker software can be reprogrammed in flight to take care of different target lists and assign different priorities. The associated broadband microwave receiver uses the same RF processing techniques as in advanced EW homing and warning systems. The MBB warhead is a new design, with an extremely advanced Thorn EMI fuzing subsystem. The whole missile has almost total autonomy, and makes no significant demands on the launching aircraft; thus it can be carried by almost all fixed-wing machines and by helicopters.

Among the several operating modes is a loiter mode in which the missile climbs for altitude and then deploys a parachute from which it hangs whilst studying the terrain below and picking out suitable targets. After deciding on the most important target the parachute is jettisoned and the missile homes in free fall. The operational date was to have been early 1987, but this has been delayed by protracted problems with the Nuthatch motor. Some ALARMs have been tested with alternative motors, and as this was written it was uncertain which motor would be used in the main run of production missiles.

Sea Eagle

Origin: British Aerospace, Hatfield
Propulsion: Microturbo TRI 60-1 Model 067 turbojet, sea-level thrust 357kg (787lb)
Dimensions: length 4,140mm (163in); body diameter 400mm (15.75in); span 1,200mm (47.25in)
Weight: 601kg (1,325lb)
Performance: speed Mach 0.85; range more than 110km (68 miles)
Warhead: ROF product (over 227kg/500lb) able to disable the largest surface warships
Users: UK, (RAF, RN), India

Originally designated P3T, Sea Eagle is an over-the-horizon fire-and-forget missile developed from Martel by switching to air-breathing propulsion and adding active radar and sea-skimming capability. Launched to meet Air Staff Requirement 1226, it progressed swiftly to the project definition phase in 1977, and development has been remarkably trouble-free. The airframe is basically that of Martel, with an underbelly air inlet. Guidance is initially on autopilot, with the on-board microprocessor storing the target's last known position and velocity, and height maintained by a Plessey radar altimeter just above the waves (or following a programmed profile). The target is then acquired by the very advanced MSDS active radar seeker. Electric power comes from Europe's first production lithium batteries. Features include full night and

Below: RN Sea Harriers are being updated to carry Sea Eagle anti-ship missiles.

Above: Westland Advanced Sea King Mk 42B of the Indian Navy, with two Sea Eagles as well as advanced electronics.

all-weather capability against the most powerful and electronically sophisticated targets, low life-cycle costs and 'round of ammunition' storage and maintenance. Launch trials began in November 1980, and a full-range sea-skimming flight was made in April 1981. In early 1982 a £200 million production contract — fixed-price incentive agreement — was announced. Sea Eagle entered service in 1986, initially on RAF Buccaneers (four missiles) and RN Sea Harriers (two). It can be carried by all other tactical aircraft and is almost certain to be issued to RAF Tornado GR.1 squadrons. It is also in service with Sea King helicopters of the Indian navy.

Sea Skua Cutaway

1 Fixed fins.
2 Sustainer nozzle.
3 Gyros and gyro-drive gas bottle.
4 Electronic pack.
5 Warhead with DA fuze.
6 Radome.
7 Semi-active radar receiver aerial.
8 Homing electronics.
9 Moving wings.
10 Thermal battery bay.
11 Radar altimeter.
12 Sustainer motor.
13 Boost motor.

Sea Skua

Origin: British Aerospace, Hatfield
Propulsion: BAJ Vickers solid boost/sustainer motors
Dimensions: length 2,502mm (98.5in); body diameter 250mm (9.75in); span 720mm (28.5in)
Weight: at launch 147kg (325lb)
Performance: speed high subsonic; range over 15km (9.3 miles)
Warhead: blast/frag, exploded within ship hull
Users: UK (RN), Brazil, West Germany, Turkey

Originally known by its MoD project number of CL.834, this missile is significantly more advanced than the comparable French missiles being developed as successors to AS.12. Instead of having wire or radio command guidance, Sea Skua is based on semi-active radar homing, and in its first application aboard the Lynx helicopter the target is illuminated by the specially developed Ferranti Seaspray overwater radar. The RN Lynx is equipped with this surveillance/tracking radar, as

Sea Skua Attack Profile

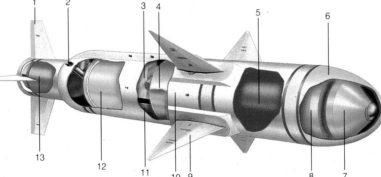

Radar illuminating target

Missile drops to intermediate sea-skimming height

Missile drops to terminal sea-skimming height

Radar reflected from target

Above: This photograph emphasizes the agility of the Lynx helicopter even when carrying four Sea Skua missiles. No other missile combines the qualities of the Sea Skua, which has been bought by several customers including the Royal and Federal German Navies.

Left: Cutaway drawing of the Sea Skua, using colour to clarify the internal parts. The sustainer nozzles are upstream of the boost motor.

Left: A typical Sea Skua attack profile shown in a diagrammatic form, exaggerating the Earth's curvature. The helicopter (1) sees a target on radar, drops below the horizon, closes the range (2) and launches a missile.

well as fire-control equipment and launchers for four missiles.

The weapon system is intended to confer upon helicopter-armed frigates and similar surface ships the capability to destroy missile-carrying FPBs, ACVs, PHMs and similar agile small craft at ranges greater than that at which they can launch their own missiles. This range is

Left: Sea Skua carried by a Westland Sea King of the Federal German navy. It is the newest helicopter-launched sea skimming missile in use.

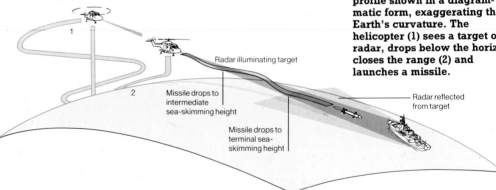

also said to be great enough to provide the launch helicopter with considerable stand-off protection from SAMs. The Decca TANS navigation system of the Lynx can combine with ESM cross-bearings to identify and fix the target, backing up the position on the Seaspray display. The Sea Skua, treated as a round of ammunition needing only quick GO/NO GO checks, is then launched and swoops down to one of four preselected sea-skimming heights, depending on wave state, using a BAe-manufactured TRT radio altimeter. Near the target a pre-programmed or command instruction lifts the missile to target-acquisition height for the MSDS homing head to lock-on. Guided trials began in 1978 and BAe has privately financed studies matching Sea Skua to other aircraft (including fixed-wing) and in coast-defence installations. BAe expects that this missile, roughly one-tenth as heavy as Exocet but able to cripple the radars and weapon launchers of all known targets, and to destroy ships of 1,000 tons with one shot, will find very wide use. In the Falklands on 2 May 1982 two Lynxes each ripple-fired a pair of Sea Skuas, sinking an 800-ton warship and crippling another, in bad weather.

ACM

Origin: General Dynamics Corporation, Convair Division, San Diego
Propulsion: one Williams F110 high-bypass-ratio turbofan (thrust classified)
Dimensions: not released, but probably similar to ALCM
Weight: probably about 1,500kg (3,307lb)
Performance: classified, but cruising speed about 800km/h (500mph), and range not less than 2,750km (1,700 miles)
Warhead: initially a W80 of selectable yield to over 200kT; later, probably a new W-series warhead
User: to be USAF (SAC)

In 1977 the USAF began the ACMT (advanced cruise-missile technology) programme to provide a technical foundation for a new cruise missile to augment and later to replace the ALCM in Strategic Air Command. The four broad goals of ACMT were: use of low-observables or 'stealth' technology to decrease the possibility of missile detection and greatly enhance penetrability; use of a new engine, possibly associated with new fuel, to give enhanced thrust with reduced specific fuel consumption; in-

crease in survivability through incorporation of sophisticated countermeasures (electronic and IRCM); and the incorporation of new software and microprocessors for better mission planning flexibility and improved trajectory control.

After many alternatives had been studied and rejected, the decision was taken to terminate plans to produce improved ALCMs and improved F107 engines, and instead to go ahead with an all-new missile and engine having the highest possible penetrability and flexibility. In April 1983 it was announced that the prime contract had been awarded to Convair, which already produces the SLCM and GLCM (Tomahawk) cruise missiles, with Williams International providing the F112 engine. Thanks to its extremely advanced aerodynamic and structural design the ACM (advanced cruise missile) will have a lower radar and IR cross-section than any previous flying vehicle (except possible miniature RPVs weighing less than 1 per cent as much), whilst still flying at about the same speed as ALCM. Range will be 'at least 10 per cent greater' and manoeuvrability will be much greater, partly because of much lower wing loading. Though details are classified, it seems reasonable to believe that the importance of near-zero IR emission is much greater than the attainment of greater thrust or reduced consumption. The programme has moved very rapidly, and ACM is regarded as a weapon for the B-52 and B-1B rather than for the

future B-2 (Northrop ATB). Operational capability may well have been achieved by the time this book appears. The SAC requirement had previously been put at 'at least 2,000', but the most recent estimate of ACM production (specifically for the B-52 and B-1B) is 1,261.

ADSM

Origin: General Dynamics, Pomona
Propulsion: similar to, or derived from, that of Stinger: high-thrust launch motor and main-body sustain motor
Dimensions: not defined but rather longer and heavier than Stinger-POST
Weight: at launch about 13.6kg (30lb)
Performance: not defined
Warhead: modified from that of BGT Viper
Users: could eventually include most NATO countries

ADSM (air-defence suppression missile) is a further variant of the infantry-fired Stinger SAM, and uses the same helicopter or fixed-wing launch installation as the Stinger MLMS. The missile itself differs in having an extended nose guidance section with the POST (passive optical seeker technique) modified to use two-

Below: A Bell 406 with (in the left foreground) twin launchers for ADSM Stinger missiles. Also visible are FFV and Aerea gun pods.

Above: Two AGM-130A missiles mounted on the swivelling wing pylons of an F-111 of the US Air Force. These missiles have only a single rocket motor, hung underneath the body.

colour IR-plus broadband RF aerials in two projecting probes extending well ahead of the glass seeker cover. The RF target designation system provides radar warning to the pilot of hostile radiating targets and cues the passive missile guidance on to that target. The complete dual-mode seeker had been fully tested by mid-1982, but funding for full development was still being sought. ADSM could be carried in groups of four by all tactical aircraft, a normal load being eight or 16 missiles.

AGM-130A

Origin: Rockwell Missile Systems Division, Duluth, Georgia
Propulsion: twin long-burn solid propellant rocket motors
Dimensions: length about 5,000mm (196.85in); diameter 457mm (18in); fin span about 1,400mm (55in)
Weight: about 1,400kg (3,086lb)
Performance: burn-out speed Mach 1; range (wide band of heights) 24km (15 miles)
Warhead: Mk 84 GP bomb, nominal 907kg (2,000lb)
User: US Air Force

Derived from the GBU-15(V), this stand-off weapon has added propulsion to give enhanced stand-off capability. The weapon is redesigned aerodynamically, with a longer and more tubular body, larger canard nose fins and smaller rectangular tail fins with control surfaces. Almost the entire drop and firing trials programme was completed in calendar 1986, and Fiscal 1987 included appropriations for the first 159 AGM-130As for the inventory. A plan to deploy a dispenser version, SUU-54 with eight or 16 BKEP (airfield-attack boosted kinetic-energy penetrators), may be resurrected if funding can be found.

Above: The first Strategic Air Command unit to receive the AGM-86B was the 416th BW at Griffiss AFB in 1981. Here a B-52G of this wing is seen having its missiles loaded; five are in place on the left pylon and the sixth and last is ready for installation.

Below: An AGM-86B awaiting recovery after a 4h 26min simulated combat mission over the Primrose Lake Air Weapons Range in northern Alberta, Canada. It was launched by a B-52G of the 319th BW from Grand Forks AFB, North Dakota.

ALCM, AGM-86B

Origin: Boeing Aerospace Co
Propulsion: one Williams F107-101 turbofan with sea-level rating of 272kg (600lb)
Dimensions: in cruise configuration length 6,325mm (20ft 9in); wing span 3,660mm (12ft); body diameter 620mm (24.5in)
Weight: at launch 1,452kg (3,200lb)
Performance: cruising speed typically 805km/h (500mph); range varies with profile up to maximum of 2,500km (1,550 miles)
Warhead: W80 oralloy/ supergrade Pu with tritium/IHE, yield selectable up to 250kT
User: USAF (SAC)

Today potentially one of the most important weapons in the West's inventory, ALCM (air-launched cruise missile) was presented by President Carter as a new idea when he terminated B-1 as a bomber; he even said B-1 had been developed 'in absence of the cruise missile factor', whose presence in 1976 made the bomber unnecessary. This is simply not true. The cruise missile never ceased to be studied from 1943, and — apart from such USAF examples as Mace and Snark — it was cruise-missile studies in 1963-6 that led to AGM-86 SCAD (subsonic cruise armed decoy) approved by DoD in July 1970. This was to be a miniature aircraft powered by a Williams WR19 turbofan, launched by a B-52 when some hundreds of miles short of major targets. Like Quail, SCAD was to confuse and dilute hostile defences; but the fact that some or all would carry nuclear warheads — by 1963 small enough to fit such vehicles — meant that SCAD could do far better than Quail. No longer could the enemy ignore the decoys and wait and see which were the bombers. Every SCAD had to be engaged, thus revealing the locations and operating frequencies of the defence sites, which could be hit by surviving SCADS, SRAMs or ARMs. SCAD was to be installationally interchangeable with SRAM, with a maximum range of around 1207km (750 miles). SCAD then ran into Congressional opposition, but the USAF knew what it was about and in 1972 recast the project as ALCM, retaining the designation AGM-86A. SCAD had had only a secondary attack function, but ALCM is totally a nuclear delivery vehicle, and like SRAM has the ability to multiply each bomber's targets and increase defence problems by approaching from any direction along any kind of profile. Compared with SRAM it is much easier to intercept, being larger and much slower, but it has considerably greater range and allows the bomber to stand off at distances of at least 1609km (1,000 miles).

The original AGM-86A ALCM was interchangeable with SRAM, so that a B-52G or H could carry eight on the internal rotary launcher plus 12 externally, and an FB-111A four externally plus two internally (though the latter aircraft has never been named as an ALCM carrier). This influenced the shape, though not to the missile's detriment, and necessitated folding or retracting wings, tail and engine air-inlet duct. Boeing, who won SCAD and carried across to ALCM without further competition, based ALCM very closely on SCAD but increased the fuel capacity and the sophistication of the guidance with a Litton inertial platform (finally chosen as the P.1000) and computer (4516C), updated progressively when over hostile territory by McDonnell Douglas Tercom (DPW-23). In 1976 the decision was taken to aim at max-

Above: Pushing away staging after completing the task of loading six AGM-86B cruise missiles on a B-52G of the 416th BW, US Air Force.

Right: A simplified 'exploded diagram' of the AGM-86B. Note the large size of the fuel tank, which gives the necessary range.

AGM-86B ALCM

1 Radar altimeter.
2 Flight control system.
3 Inertial navigation system.
4 Air-data computer.
5 Umbilical receptacle.
6 Suspension lug.
7 F107 engine.
8 Thermal batteries.
9 Taileron power units.
10 Wing deploy actuators.
11 W80 warhead.
12 Pitot head.

imum commonality with AGM-109 Tomahawk, but the guidance packages are not identical. The engine in both missiles is the Williams F107 of approximately 272kg (600lb) thrust, but in totally different versions: the ALCM engine is the F107-101, with accessories underneath and different starting system from the F107-400 of AGM-109. The warhead is W80, from SRAM-B.

AGM-86A first flew at WSMR on 5 March 1976. Many of the early flights failed — one undershot its target by a mile because its tank had been underfilled! — but by the sixth shot most objectives had been attained and 1977 was spent chiefly in improving commonality with Navy AGM-109, in preparation for something unforeseen until that year: a fly-off against AGM-109 Tomahawk in 1979 to decide which to buy for the B-52 force. It was commonly said Boeing were told to make AGM-86A short on range to avoid competing with the B-1. In fact no more fuel could be accommodated and still retain com-

patibility with SRAM launchers, and in 1976 Boeing proposed an underbelly auxiliary fuel tank for missiles carried externally.

A better answer was to throw away dimensional compatibility with SRAM and develop a considerably stretched missile, called AGM-86B. This has a fuselage more than 30 per cent longer, housing fuel for double the range with a given warhead. Other changes include wing sweep reduced to 25°, thermal batteries for on-board electrical power, all-welded sealed tankage, improved avionics cooling and

Below: Air-to-air view of an AGM-86B on test, flying over the Utah Training Range.

10-year shelf life. President Carter's decision to cancel the B-1 in June 1977 opened the way for Boeing to promote this longer missile, which could still be carried externally under the wings of a B-52 but would not have fitted into the weapon bays of a B-1. From July 1979 Boeing's AGM-86B was engaged in a fly-off against GD's AGM-109. Results were hardly impressive, each missile losing four out of 10 in crashes, quite apart from other mission-related failures, but after a long delay the USAF announced choice of Boeing on 25 March 1980. A month later it was announced that the USAF/Navy joint management was dissolved and that the USAF Systems Command would solely manage 19 follow-on test flights in 1980 and subsequent production.

ALCM is preprogrammed to attack any of up to 10 targets, to which it is steered in three dimensions according to a pre-programmed flight profile. In plan view the trajectory is governed by an inertial navigator updated with ever-greater accuracy by the terrain correlation system. This has software which compares the outputs of the iner-

tial platform, air-data system and radar altimeter with a stored terrain elevation map. This provides a very accurate axis-position update. It also progressively refines the alignment of the inertial platform (which is initially done by Kalman filtering from the carrier B-52's OAS (offensive avionics system) or the B-1B computers. Terrain following for very low-level flight is performed using an analog/digital system fed with signals from the inertial, air-data and radar-altimeter systems.

It was planned to procure 5,369 ALCMs, but the number was curtailed at 1,730 in order to switch deployment to the ACM (advanced cruise missile), the last being delivered in early 1986. The first missiles joined the 416th Bomb Wing at Griffiss AFB in January 1981, since when the 173 surviving B-52Gs have been converted to carry pre-loaded underwing pylons each with six missiles in tandem triplets (12 per aircraft). Strakelet fairings were added to the wing-root leading edges to identify CMC (cruise-missile carrier) B-52s in satellite imagery. The 96 surviving B-52H bombers have been converted with both wing pylons and the eight-shot rotary launcher in a rebuilt bomb bay. The same rotary launcher is carried by the B-1B, which can also carry 14 ALCMs in tandem twin or triple racks along the underside of the wing roots. From 1985 ALCMs have been upgraded with ECM packs giving better penetrability against advanced defence networks.

Brave 3000

Origin: Boeing Military Airplane Co, Wichita
Propulsion: Noel Penny Turbines NPT 171 or 301 turbojet, 91kg (200lb) static thrust
Dimensions: length 3,500mm (137.8in); span 2,260mm (89in)
Weight: 238kg (525lb); fuel 56.7kg (125lb) and max payload 31.5kg (290lb)
Performance: cruising speed 703km/h (437mph); range up to 500km (311 miles)
Warhead: various payloads including large conventional warheads
User: not yet developed

Following the earlier propeller-driven Brave 200, this 'miniature cruise missile' is a versatile multimission robotic air vehicle capable of operating autonomously. It can be ground-or air-launched (in the former instance, with a launch booster rocket), and is normally regarded as expendable. The unswept wing is pivoted at the centre and when folded lies along the top of the body, swinging round to 90° immediately prior to launch. Brave 3000 could be a dispenser of submunitions or fly reconnaisance missions.

Left: The four chief members of the Bullpup family are (front to rear): ATM-12A Trainer, AGM-12D (former GAM-83), AGM-12B (Bullpup A) and AGM-12C (Bullpup B).

AGM-12B in 1962, it was put into second-source production by W.L. Maxson, since 1963 US prime supplier for missiles, terminating at 22,100 rounds in 1970. Over 8,000 were built under licence by a European consortium headed by Kongsberg of Norway. Chief carrier aircraft included the USN/USMC A-4, A-6, F-4 and P-3, and in Europe the F-4, F-5, F-100, F-104 and P-3.

In 1959 Martin Orlando developed an improved version for the Air Force with radio guidance that freed the operator from the need to align the target with his sight, allowing guidance from an offset position. This was produced as GAM-83A, and used by TAC. At the same time Martin developed two new versions. For the Navy ASM-N-7B (AGM-12C), Bullpup B, was a larger missile with 454kg (1,000lb) warhead, wings greatly extended in chord and Thiokol LR62 liquid motor; 4,600 were delivered. The Air Force adopted GAM-83B (AGM-12D) using an airframe closer to the original but with an increased-diameter centre section able to house either a conventional or nuclear warhead. The TGAM-83 (ATM-12A/B/D) Bullpup Trainer developed by Martin's Baltimore Division was later replaced by firing surplus AGM-12Bs with inert warheads. The final model was AGM-12E, briefly (840 rounds) built for the Air Force by Martin, with an anti-personnel fragmentation warhead.

CSW

These initials stood for Conventional Standoff Weapon, which in 1980-4 was a USAF study and feasibility programme linked with the Pave Mover synthetic-aperture battlefield radar in an endeavour to find an improved weapon for use against large formations of armour. CSW was also seen as possibly having a defence-suppression role, but as this book was written in 1987 the project was no longer active.

GBU-15, CWW

Origin: Rockwell International
Propulsion: none
Dimensions: length 3,910mm (154in); body diameter 457mm (18in); span 1,499mm (59in)
Weight: at launch 1,187kg (2,617lb)
Performance: speed subsonic; range typically 8km (5 miles) but highly variable with launch height and speed
Warhead: Mk 84 bomb, 907kg (2,000lb) or CBU-75 cluster dispenser
User: USA (AF) initially

The CWW (cruciform-wing weapon) is the modern successor to the Vietnam-era Pave Strike HOBOS (homing-bomb system), of which GBU-8 (guided-bomb unit) was the chief production example. Like GBU-8, GBU-15 is a modular system comprising standard GP (general purpose) bombs to which a target-detecting device and trajectory-control fins are added. The full designation of the basic production missile is GBU-15(V)/B, and it is also called a modular guided glide weapon system. Though the payload and structural basis may be the CBU-75 cluster munition the normal basis is the Mk 84 907kg (2,000lb) bomb. To the

Left: A Rockwell GBU-15(V) with short-chord wings, on an F-4E trials aircraft of the USAF 3246th Test Wing with TISEO camera fitted.

Below: Cutaway drawing of one of the original HOBOS (Homing Bomb System) family, predecessor of GBU-15.

Bullpup, AGM-12

Origin: Martin Marietta (also Maxson and Kongsberg)
Propulsion: prepackaged storable liquid rocket
Dimensions: (AGM-12B) length 3,200mm (126in); body diameter 305mm (12in); span 940mm (37in)
Weight: at launch (B) 259kg (571lb)
Performance: (B) speed Mach 2.5; range 11.3km (7 miles)
Warhead: conventional, 113kg (250lb) GP bomb
Users: UK, USA

During the Korean War the US Navy urgently needed a precision ASM capable of being launched by carrier-based aircraft, and RFPs were issued in 1953. Martin Orlando Division's offering was chosen in May 1954, and subsequently was developed as ASM-N-7 Bullpup. It comprised a 113kg (250lb) bomb inside a roll-stabilized airframe with Aerojet-General solid motor, fixed rear wings, four pneumatically actuated nose control fins and twin rear tracking flares. The operator in the launch aircraft acquired the target visually, fired the missile and used a radio command joystick to impart left/right and up/down directions whilst keeping the flares as seen through his gunsight. It became operational in April 1959.

The existence of this primitive weapon at a price near $5,000 resulted in very wide acceptance. In 1960 it was replaced in production by N-7A, with Thiokol prepackaged LR58 acid/amine motor, extended-range control and a new warhead. Re-styled

HOBOS Cutaway

1 EO window.
2 Seeker optics.
3 Guidance section.
4 Four boresight adjusters.
5 Mk 84 bomb body.
6 Strakes.
7 Strake bands.
8 Suspension lug.
9 Umbilical.
10 Thermal batteries.
11 Hinged controls.
12 Pneumatic drive.
13 Data link.
14 Autopilot.
15 Fuze conduit.

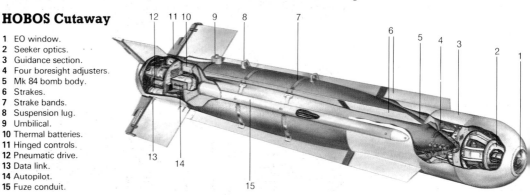

front are added an FMU-124 fuze, a tubular adapter and either of two target-detecting devices, TV or IIR (imaging infra-red). The TV missile is GBU-15(V)1/B and the night-attack IIR type GBU-15(V)2/B. At the rear are added an autopilot, displacement gyro, primary battery, control module and data-link module, and the weapon is completed by attaching four canard fins and four large rear wings with powered control surfaces on the trailing edges. (An alternative PWW, planar-wing weapon, by Hughes, is no longer active.) GBU-15 is launched at medium to extremely low altitudes. In the former case it is guided over a direct line of sight to the target. In the latter it is launched in the direction of the target, while the carrier aircraft gets away at very low level. It is steered by a data-link by the operator in the aircraft who has a display showing the scene in the seeker in the nose of the missile (TV is the usual method). The missile climbs until it can acquire the target, and then pushes over into a dive. The operator has the choice of steering the missile all the way to the target or locking-on the homing head. Extensive trials from F-4, F-111 and B-52 aircraft are complete and substantial deliveries had been made by early 1983, the IIR version following in 1987.

HARM, AGM-88A

Origin: Texas Instruments Inc
Propulsion: Thiokol single-grain (127kg/280lb filling of non-aluminized HTPB) reduced-smoke boost/sustain motor
Dimensions: length 4,170mm (164.5in); body diameter 254mm (10in); span 1,130mm (44.5in)
Weight: at launch 366kg (807lb)
Performance: speed over Mach 2; range/height variable with aircraft to about 16km (10 miles)
Warhead: fragmentation with proximity fuze system
Users: USA and West Germany, with several NATO countries in negotiation

Neither Shrike nor Standard ARM is an ideal air-launched ARM and in 1972 the Naval Weapons Center began R&D and also funded industry studies for a High-speed Anti-Radiation Missile (HARM). Among the objectives were much higher flight speed, to lock-on targets before they could be switched off or take other action, and to combine the low cost and versatility of Shrike, the sensitivity and large launch envelope of Standard ARM, and completely new passive homing using the latest microelectronic digital techniques and interfacing with new aircraft systems. In 1974 TI was selected as system integration contractor, assisted by Hughes, Dalmo-Victor, Itek and SRI (Stanford Research Institute). The slim

Below: Three HARMs, minus aerodynamic surfaces, trundle over a carrier deck. TI also make the FLIR pod seen on the A-7E in the rear.

AGM-88A missile has double-delta moving wings and a small fixed tail. The TI seeker has a simple fixed aerial (antenna) yet gives broadband coverage, a low-cost autopilot is fitted, and Motorola supply an optical target detector forming part of the fusing for the large advanced-design warhead. Launch aircraft include the Navy/Marines A-6E, A-7E and F/A-18, and the Air Force APR-38 Wild Weasel F-4G and EF-111A, with Itek's ALR-45 radar warning receiver and Dalmo-Victor's DSA-20N signal analyser both interfaced. Proposed carriers include the B-52, F-16 and Tornado. HARM can be used in three modes. The basic use is Self-Protect, the ALR-45 detecting threats, the launch computer sorting the data to give priorities and pass on to the missile a complete set of digital instructions in milliseconds, whereupon the missile can be fired. In the Target of Opportunity mode the very sensitive seeker locks-on to 'cer-

Above: AGM-88 HARM being fired from a prototype two-seat F/A-18B Hornet. Note spaced shock diamonds from the missile motor.

tain parameters of operation and also transmissions associated with other parts of a radar installation' which could not be detected by Shrike or Standard ARM. In the Pre-Briefed mode HARM is fired blind in the direction of known emitters; if the latter are silent the missile self-destructs, but if one of them radiates, HARM at once homes on to it. Test flights began in 1976; redesign followed and following prolonged further tests delivery to user units began in early 1983. About 2,900 are being supplied to US units, a few being used against Libyan radars on 24 March 1986. West Germany has ordered 368 plus a further 576 on option. It is a much heavier and technically earlier ARM than the British ALARM.

Harpoon, AGM-84A

Origin: McDonnell Douglas Astronautics
Propulsion: one Teledyne CAE J402-400 turbojet, sea-level thrust 300kg (661lb)
Dimensions: length 3,840mm (151in); body diameter 343mm (13.5in); span 914mm (36in)
Weight: 519kg (1,145lb)
Performance: speed Mach 0.75; range (A) over 92km (57 miles), (B) 120km (75 miles)

Warhead: NWC 221.5kg (488lb) penetration/blast with impact/delay and proximity fuzing
Users: USA (AF, Navy, Marine Corps); surface-launched and submarine versions widely exported, but no foreign sales announced for AGM-84A

Below: The McDonnell Douglas F/A-18A Hornet is the only fighter routinely to fly with the AGM-84A Harpoon cruise missile. This particular Hornet is a Navy aircraft. Note that the wing leading edges are slightly depressed to give extra camber.

This important weapon system began as an ASM in 1968, but three years later was combined with a proposal for a ship- and submarine-launched missile system. McDonnell Douglas Astronautics (MDAC) was selected as prime contractor in June 1971. The main development contract followed in July 1973, and of 40 prototype weapon systems 34 were launched in 1974-5, 15 being the RGM-84A fired from ships (including the PHM *High Point* whilst foilborne) and three from submarines, the other 16 being air-launched. At first almost wholly trouble-free, testing suffered random failures from late 1975, and the clearance for full-scale production was delayed temporarily. Production of all versions amounted to 315 in 1976, and about 2,100 by early 1983.

Target data, which can be OTH if supplied from a suitable platform, are fed before launch to the Lear-Siegler or Northrop strapdown inertial platform which can steer the missile even if launched at up to 90° off the desired heading. Flight control is by cruciform rear fins. A radar altimeter holds the desired seaskimming height, and no link with the aircraft is required. Nearing the target the Texas Instruments

Right: A B-52G of the US Air Force operating from Loring AFB, Maine, in the sea-control role. Its primary armament comprises 12 AGM-84A Harpoons carried externally.

Below: A cutaway drawing of the AGM-84A Harpoon, with colour used to clarify the various parts, and the internal configuration.

Bottom: Close-up of the AGM-84B Harpoon missiles on a B-52G. Some of these are training missiles. Note that the engine air inlets are closed by a sprung door.

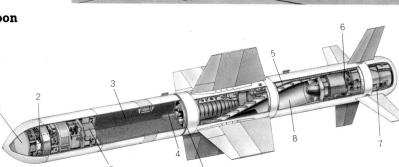

AGM-84A Harpoon

1 Flat-plate scanner.
2 Radar and radar altimeter bay.
3 Warhead.
4 Fuze system with safe/arm mechanism.
5 Fuel tank.
6 J402 turbojet engine.
7 Control actuators.
8 Air inlet duct.
9 Silver/zinc battery.
10 Midcourse guidance.

sion for the US Navy; and AGM-84D is the current production version, with increases in range (about 120km/75miles), waypoints and selectable terminal trajectories. Advanced versions are on test, including one with IIR (imaging infra-red) seeker (see SLAM).

Harpoon is also carried by two squadrons of USAF B-52Gs operating from Loring and Andersen AFBs in the sea-control role, each carrying up to 12 missiles externally. Harpoons can also be carried by Nimrod MR.2s of the RAF.

HVM

Origin: Vought Corporation
Propulsion: extremely rapid burn boost/sustain solid motor
Dimensions: not disclosed
Weight: under 27kg (50lb)
Performance: speed 5,472km/h (3,400mph) within 0.6s of launch
Warhead: none
User: not yet marketed

Though primarily a ground weapon, the Hyper-Velocity Missile could later be fired from tactical aircraft, including helicopters. An anti-armour weapon, it kills purely by kinetic energy, the forebody containing a penetrator designed to pass through multiplate and other forms of advanced armour. The multi-tube launcher is boresighted on the target by an electronically scanned lidar (laser radar), and the extremely high missile speed reduces flight time to below 1 second, minimizing errors due to target motion or countermeasures. The system is all-weather.

Vought is working under a 1981 USAF contract, using pods of about 40 rounds guided by CO_2 laser giving 3-D range and Doppler information. The limit of range in tests has been about 6km (3.7miles), and the penetrator has usually been a long rod of depleted uranium. A major advantage seen for HVM is low cost, hoped to be under $5,000 per round.

Below: An HVM is 'stopped' by a high-speed camera as it blasts away at well over 5,000km/h (3,100mph).

PR-53/DSQ-58 active radar seeker searches, locks-on and finally commands a sudden pull-up and swoop on the target from above. The Naval Weapons Center and MDAC are also studying possible versions with supersonic speed, torpedo-carrying payload, imaging IR homing, passive radiation homing, nuclear warhead, vertical launch, midcourse guidance updating and other features.

MDAC expects to make at least 5,000 systems by 1988 despite the delayed start. Of these well over 2,000 will be for the US Navy, for surface ships, submarines, and

P-3C, A-6E, S-3B, A-7E and F/A-18A aircraft, all of which cleared to use Harpoon by the end of 1987. The S-3 carries two missiles and the other types four. Production is at the rate of 40 missiles per month. Among the aircraft systems is a missile firing simulator.

Four air-launched versions have been announced: AGM-84A incorporates a terminal pop-up manoeuvre to counter close-in defences and enhance warhead penetration; AGB-84B eliminates the pop-up and has improved low-altitude penetrability; AGM-84C is an improved pop-up ver-

Maverick, AGM-65

Origin: GM-Hughes, Tucson
Propulsion: Thiokol boost/sustain solid motor, from 1972 TX-481 and from 1981 TX-633 with reduced smoke
Dimensions: length (A) 2,489mm (98in); body diameter 305mm (12in); span 719mm (28.3in)
Weight: at launch (AGM-65A, shaped-charge) 210kg (463lb), (65E, blast/frag) 288kg (635lb), (65D) 220kg (485lb), (65E) 307kg (677lb)
Performance: speed classified but supersonic; range 1-16km (0.6-10 miles) at sea level, up to 40km (25 miles) after Mach 1.2 release at altitude
Warhead: choice of Chamberlain shaped charge (37.6kg/83lb charge) or Avco steel-case penetrator blast/frag
Users: include Egypt, Greece, Iran, Israel, South Korea, Morocco, Saudi Arabia, Sweden, Turkey, USA, West Germany, Italy and six other countries.

Above: AGM-65E Laser Maverick serves with the US Marine Corps. Here Maj John P. Bland inspects the first missile to be fired by the corps (from an A-4M). As well as having exceptionally precise homing guidance it has a heavier warhead.

Smallest of the fully guided or self-homing ASMs for US use, AGM-65 Maverick was approved in 1965 and, following competition with Rockwell, Hughes won the programme in June 1968. An initial 17,000 missile package was fulfilled in 1975, and production was continued at reduced rate on later versions. The basic missile, usually carried in triple clusters under the wings of the F-4, F-15, F-16, A-7, A-10 and Swedish AJ37A Viggen, and singly by F-5 and the BGM-34 RPV, has four delta wings of very low aspect ratio, four tail controls immediately behind the wings, and a dual-thrust solid motor.

The pilot selects a missile, causing its gyro to run up to speed and light a cockpit indicator. The pilot then visually acquires the target, depresses his uncage switch to remove the protective cover from the missile nose, and activates the video circuitry. The TV picture at once appears on a bright display in the cockpit, and the pilot then either slews the video seeker in the missile or else lines up the target

Above: For comparison, this was a test example of the original AGM-65A, seen carried by a US Air Force Phantom II. An inert Maverick is visible on the inner shoe of the triple pylon mount. The AGM-65A has TV (video) guidance.

Pave Penny Attack

Below: Attack scenario for an A-10A Thunderbolt II on a target designated by a friendly laser (ground or heli-borne). The A-10A's Pave Penny laser detects the illuminated target, but Laser Maverick is not carried. Instead the pilot fires AGM-65A, B or D.

in his own gunsight. He depresses the track switch, waits until the cross-hairs on the TV display are aligned on the target, releases the switch and fires the round. Homing is automatic, and the launch aircraft at once escapes from the area. Unguided flights began in September 1969. AGM-65A has been launched at all heights down to treetop level. In the 1973 Yom Kippur war it was used operationally, in favourable conditions. It requires good visibility, and the occasional $48,000 A-model breaks its TV lock and misses its target — for example, because of overwater glint.

AGM-65B, Scene Magnification Maverick, has new optics, a stronger gimbal mount and revised electronics. The pilot need not see the target, but instead can search with the seeker and cockpit display which presents an enlarged and clearer picture. Thus he can identify the target, lock-on and fire more quickly and from a greater slant range. AGM-65B was in production (at up to 200 per month) from May

Left: Launch of an AGM-65A from a US Air Force F-4E in 1973. Several thousand of these missiles have now been fired.

1980 to May 1984, total A/B production being 31,022.

AGM-65C Laser Maverick was for close-air support against laser-designated targets, the lasers being the infantry ILS-NT200 or the airborne Pave Knife, Pave Penny, Pave Spike, Pave Tack or non-US systems. Flight testing began in January 1977, using the Rockwell tri-service seeker. Troop training has established the method of frequency and pulse coding to tie each missile to only one air or ground designator, so that many Mavericks can simultaneously be homed on many different sources of laser radiation. AGM-65C was replaced by AGM-65E with tri-service laser tracker and digital processing which in 1982 was entering production for the US Marine Corps with heavy blast/frag warhead. Westinghouse tested Pave Spike with the Minneapolis-Honeywell helmet sight for single-seat aircraft.

In May 1977 engineering development began on AGM-65D IR-Maverick, with Hughes IIR tri-service seeker. Considerably more expensive than other versions, the IIR seeker — especially when slaved to an aircraft-mounted sensor such as FLIR, a laser pod or the APR-38 radar warning system — enables

Above: A-10A Thunderbolt IIs seldom behave like this, and in target areas never get so far from the ground! This example is carrying four AGM-65D infra-red Mavericks, plus an ALQ-119A ECM pod.

Low-level Maverick Delivery

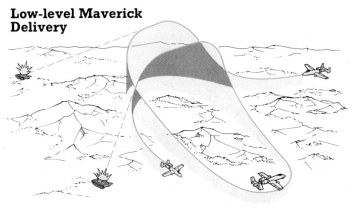

the Maverick to lock-on at least twice the range otherwise possible in north-west Europe in mist, rain or at night. Of course, it also distinguishes between 'live targets' and 'hulks'. Using the centroid seeker in place of the original edgelock optics, AGM-65D was tested from an F-4 in Germany in poor weather in January-March 1978. While Hughes continues to produce the

Below: A-10A pilots try to use terrain masking (flying in the 'nap of the Earth' for protection) before zooming up to 150m (500ft) to fire Maverick missiles. They then smartly get back down again 'in the weeds'.

common centre and aft missile sections, delay with the laser-seeker E-version means that AGM-65D got into pilot production first.

All AGM-65A Mavericks have the same 59kg (130lb) conical shaped-charge warhead, but different warheads are in prospect. The Mk 19 113kg (250lb) blast/fragmentation head is preferred by the Navy and Marines

giving capability against small ships as well as hard land targets, and may be fitted to C and D versions with new fuzing/arming and a 102mm (4in) increase in length. The AGM-65E and G warhead weighs 136kg (300lb), while in December 1976 the Air Force expressed a need for a nuclear warhead.

By far the largest numbers are expected to be of the IR Maverick, AGM-65D, of which 58,864 rounds for the USAF alone are predicted at a rate of 500 per month. Prolonged tests have confirmed the long range, which at last matches the flight limitations of the missile itself, and an AGM-65D is the standard missile for use with the Lantirn night and bad-weather sensor system now being fitted to F-16s and A-10s. The Navy uses AGM-65F, which is almost the same missile but fitted with the heavy penetrator warhead of AGM-65E, and with modified guidance software exactly matched to give optimum hits on surface warships. The USAF AGM-65G has the IIR Seeker and big warhead.

With this missile family Hughes has achieved a unique capability with various guidance systems and warheads, resulting in impressively large production and interchangeability.

Paveway LGBs

Origin: Texas Instruments
Propulsion: none
Dimensions: as for original bombs plus from 152 to 508mm (6 to 20in) length and with folding tailfins
Weight: as for original bombs plus about 13.6kg (30lb)
Performance: speed, free-fall; range, free-fall so varies with release height and speed
Warhead: as in original bombs
Users: including Australia, Canada, Greece, South Korea, Netherlands, Saudi Arabia, Taiwan, Turkey, UK (RAF, RN), USA (AF, Navy, Marines) and eight other countries

This codename identifies the most diverse programme in history aimed at increasing the accuracy of tactical air-to-surface weapons. The USAF effort linked more than 30 separately named systems for airborne navigation, target identification and marking, all-weather/night vision, weapon guidance and many other functions, originally for the war in SE Asia. In the course of this work the 'smart bombs' with laser guidance managed by the Armament Development and Test Center at Eglin AFB, from 1965, were developed in partnership with TI, using the latter's laser guidance kit, to form an integrated family of simple precision weapons. The first TI-guided LGB was dropped in April 1965.

By 1971 the Paveway I family of guidance units had expanded to eight, in six main types of which the three most important were the KMU-388 (based on the 227kg/500lb Mk 82 bomb), KMU-421 (454kg/1,000lb Mk 83) and KMU-351 (907kg/2,000lb Mk 84).

All these bombs are extremely simple to carry, requiring no aircraft modification or electrical connection; they are treated as a

Above: An early Paveway I series (KMU-351) drops away from an F-15A over the Eglin Gulf Test Range. The aircraft carries special cameras.

Below: Twin Mk 82 LGBs of the folding-fin Paveway II series carried on a twin Alkan Type 4036 stores carrier on an F-16A.

round of ordnance and loaded like a free-fall bomb. Carrier aircraft have included the A-1, A-4, A-6, A-7, A-10, A-37, F-4, F-5, F-15, F-16, F/A-18, F-100, F-105, F-111, AV-8A, B-52 and B-57. Targets can be marked by an airborne laser, in the launch aircraft or another aircraft, or by forward troops. Like almost all Western military lasers the matched wavelength is 1.064 microns, the usual lasers (in Pave Knife, Pave Tack or various other airborne pods) being of the Nd/YAG type. More recently target illumination has been provided by the Atlis II, LTDS, TRAM, GLLD, MULE, LTM, Lantirn and TI's own FLIR/laser designator.

In all cases the guidance unit is the same, the difference being confined to attachments and the various enlarged tail fins. The silicon detector array is divided into four quadrants and is mounted on the nose of a free universal-jointed housing with an annular ring tail. As the bomb falls this aligns itself with the airstream, in other words the direction of the bomb's motion.

The guidance computer receives signals from the quadrants and drives four control fins to equalize the four outputs. Thus, the sensor unit is kept pointing at the source of laser light, so that the bomb will impact at the same point. Electric power is provided by a thermal battery, energized at the moment of release, and power to drive the fins comes from a hot-gas generator.

Above: A GBU-10C, one of the folding-fin Paveway II guided bombs, about to go through the cab of a truck target at Kirtland AFB. Such accuracy is common.

Users include the RAF with Mk 13/18 454kg/1,000lb bombs carried by Buccaneers, Tornados and Jaguars. Total production of Paveway guidance units has been very large: in the early 1970s output was at roughly 20,000 per year at a unit price of some $2,500, and the 1987 total exceeded 150,000.

Since 1980 the Paveway II weapons have been in production including a simpler and cheaper seeker section, and a folding-wing aerofoil group. Portsmouth Aviation has integrated the system with RAF bombs used from Harriers over the Falklands.

Paveway III has flick-out lifting wings and a microprocessor, and can be dropped at treetop height. BAe Bracknell supplies the Dart precision gyro for Paveway III's digital autopilot, which enables this new series to operate in poor visibility and with a very low cloudbase. Mk III bombs can be released in dive, level or loft trajectories, and they have proportional terminal guidance 'shaped' to achieve optimum impact angles. By 1987 the first were coming into use.

Shrike, AGM-45A

Origin: Naval Weapons Center (NWC), with production by TI
Propulsion: Rockwell (Rocketdyne) Mk 39 or Aerojet (ATSC) Mk 53 (polybutadiene) or improved Mk 78 (polyurethane, dual-thrust) solid motor
Dimensions: length 3,048mm (120in); body diameter 203mm (8in); span 914mm (36in)
Weight: at launch (approximately depending on sub-type) 177kg (390lb)
Performance: speed Mach 2; range 29 to 40km (18 to 25 miles)
Warhead: blast/frag, 66kg (145lb) with proximity fuze
Users: include Iran, Israel and USA (AF, Navy, Marines)

Based in part on the Sparrow AAM, this was the first anti-radar missile (ARM) in the US since World War II. Originally called ARM and designated ASM-N-10, it was begun as a project at NOTS (later NWC) in 1961, and in 1962 became AGM-45A. Production by a consortium headed by Texas Instruments (TI) and Sperry Rand/Univac began in 1963 and Shrike was in use in SE Asia three years later with Wild Weasel F-105Gs and EA-6As. Early experience was disappointing and there have since been numerous models, identified by suffix numbers, to rectify faults or tailor the passive homing head to a new frequency band identified in the potential hostile inventory.

Carried by US Navy/Marine A-4, A-6, A-7 and F-4, the Air Force F-4 and EF-111, and the

Israeli F-4 and Kfir, Shrike is switched on while flying towards the target and fired as soon as the TI radiation seeker has locked-on. After motor cutoff Shrike flies a ballistic path until control-system activation. The seeker has a monopulse crystal video receiver and continually updates the guidance by determining the direction of arrival of the hostile radiation, homing the missile into the enemy radar with its cruciform centre-body wings driven in 'bang/bang' fashion by a hot-gas system. There were at least 18 sub-types in the AGM-45-1 to -10 families, with over 13 different tailored seeker heads, of which the USAF bought 12,863 by 1978 and the Navy a further 6,200. In the Yom Kippur war Israel used Shrike tuned to 2,965/2,990 MHz and 3,025/3,050 MHz to defeat SA-2 and SA-3 but was helpless against SA-6. In 1978-81 additional procurement centred on the -9 and -10 for the USAF to be carried by F-4G and EF-111A platforms, together with modification kits to equip existing rounds to home on to later SAM and other radars.

Above: A Shrike carried on one of the deep pylons of an A-7E Corsair II aboard USS *Saratoga* in the Mediterranean in 1986.

Below: An F-4G Wild Weasel Phantom II of the USAF 37th Tactical Fighter Wing, from George AFB, California, with an exceptional array of stores.

Reading from left wing to right are: an AGM-88A HARM, an AGM-65 Maverick, an ALQ-119(V) ECM pod, an AGM-78 Standard ARM and a Shrike.

Sidearm, AGM-122A

Origin: US Naval Weapons Center and Motorola
Propulsion: Naval Propellant Plant solid rocket motor
Dimensions: length 2,870mm (113in); body diameter 127mm (5in); fin span 630mm (24.8in)
Weight: 88.5kg (195lb)
Performance: speed Mach 2.3 on level, more in dive attack; range varies with target, but typically 17km (10.6 miles)
Warhead: blast/fragmentation 4.5kg (10lb)
Users: US Navy, Marine Corps

Motorola produced the AIM-9C Sidewinder as the only semi-active radar guided member of this famous AAM family, to arm the F-8 Crusader. Not wholly successful, the -9C was soon withdrawn, but after some argument has been used as the basis of the AGM-122A Sidearm self-defence anti-radar missile for AH-1J SeaCobra helicopters and AV-8B Harrier IIs of the Marine Corps, and possibly also of Navy aircraft. The first 168 Sidearms were procured with $20.5 million in Fiscal 1986, and a total of 885 (all the stored stock of -9Cs) are to be converted, mainly by Motorola. The seeker is new, but requires cueing by the carrier aircraft's radar homing and warning system. It is possible that larger numbers may be procured of a purpose-built form of Sidearm.

Skipper II, AGM-123A

Origin: US Naval Weapons Center and Emerson Defense Systems
Propulsion: ATSC Mk 78 improved smokeless solid-propellant rocket motor
Dimensions: length 4,300mm (169in); body diameter 356mm (14in); deployed wing span 1,600mm (63in)
Weight: 582kg (1,283lb)
Performance: speed transonic; range limited by guidance system to 16.5km (10.25 miles)
Warhead: Mk 83 GP bomb, 454kg (1,000lb)
Users: USA (Navy, Marine Corps)

This precision attack missile is similar in principle to the Paveway III series of laser-guided bombs, and uses a broadly similar form of add-on guidance and control package to a standard Mk 83 bomb. The major difference is addition at the tail of a rocket motor similar to that used for Shrike. Designated AGM-123A, Skipper II went into production by Emerson in 1986, with an initial 925 rounds for deploy-

Above: Two AGM-123 Skipper IIs drop from a Navy A-6E Intruder. They resemble Paveway II LGBs but with the important addition of a rocket motor.

Right: About to load a live AGM-69A SRAM from off its twin ground transporter trolley. As no tail fairing is fitted it is destined for a rotary dispenser (see overleaf for picture). Note the prototype Rockwell B-1A in the background.

ment aboard A-6, A-7 and F/A-18 aircraft aboard carriers. The propulsion greatly eases the task of the launch aircraft in doubling the bomb's range and permitting launch to be made at very low level. Emerson expect to make several thousand Skipper IIs, and also to modify Paveway II LGBs of customers around the world.

SLAM

Origin: McDonnell Douglas Astronautics
Propulsion: Teledyne CAE J402 turbojet of 300kg (661lb) thrust
Dimensions: length 4,500mm (177in); body diameter 343mm (13.5in)
Weight: 628kg (1,385lb)

The Standoff Land-Attack Missile is a multi-mission derivative of Harpoon, planned for deployment by US Navy carrier aircraft. It would mate AGM-84A with the Maverick Imaging IR seeker and the Walleye data-link for precision attack on land targets out to ranges exceeding 92km (57 miles).

SRAM-A, AGM-69A

Origin: Boeing Aerospace
Propulsion: originally Lockheed Propulsion Co two-pulse solid motor; Thiokol is in low-rate production with a long-life motor with numerous improvements
Dimensions: length (with tail fairing for external carriage) 4,830mm (190in), (without fairing) 4,270mm (168in); body diameter 444.5mm (17.5in); span (three fins at 120°) each tip is 381mm (15in) from axis of missile
Weight: at launch 1,012kg (2,230lb)
Performance: speed Mach 2.8-3.2; range (very variable depending on launch height and selected profile) 59 to 169km (35 to 105 miles)
Warhead: nuclear W6, 200kT, air burst and DA fuzes
Users: USA (AF)

Throughout the 1950s nuclear warheads became ever smaller, and by 1960 studies showed that a missile that could be carried by a fighter could deliver a large nuclear warhead from a range exceeding 160km (100 miles). In the event SRAM (short range attack missile) has not been used by fighters, but by aircraft of SAC, primarily to neutralize potential hostile defences such as radars, SAMs and other AA systems. The adjective 'short-range' has taken on a new meaning, while the compact light-weight design of this high-performance weapon multiplies in dramatic fashion the number of targets that one bomber can engage. Boeing, the final prime contractor, began SRAM studies in December 1963, ahead of the drafting of SOR-212 in 1964 which resulted in the establishment of WS-140A. A keen competition followed in 1965, with selection in November 1965 of Boeing and Martin and final choice of Boeing (now Boeing Aerospace Co) on 31

October 1966. A dummy SRAM was dropped from a B-52 in December 1967, live flights began in 1969, and IOC was reached in early 1972. Production of 1,500 AGM-69A missiles was completed in July 1975, the missile then equipping 18 SAC bases operating the B-52G and H and FB-111A.

Originally there were to be different guidance systems, Sylvania supplying a radar-homing version and an IR-homer also being required. These were not procured, and AGM-69A has only inertial guidance by Singer-Kearfott, with a Delco on-board computer to command very varied flight profiles. Four basic trajectories are semi-ballistic; terrain-following; pull-up from 'under the radar' followed by inertial dive; and combined inertial and terrain-following. The small, almost perfectly streamlined missile is said to have a radar cross-section 'about as large as a bullet'.

The B-52 can carry eight SRAMs on a rotary launcher reminiscent of a revolver cylinder in the aft bomb bay (exceptionally, and at the expense of other loads, it can carry three such launchers internally), plus two tandem triplets on each former Hound Dog pylon, modified for SRAM compatibility, a total of 20 missiles. The FB-111A can carry up to six, four on

Above: Tail fairings are fitted to SRAMs carried externally. These are seen on a swing-wing General Dynamics FB-111A of Strategic Air Command's 509th Bomb Wing.

Below: More tail-faired AGM-69A SRAM attack missiles, carried 12 at a time on the pylons of a special test B-52H, final version of SAC's main heavy bomber.

swivelling wing pylons and two internally. The bombardier selects each missile in turn, checks the updating of the KT-76 inertial guidance and lets it drop. The motor accelerates it to about Mach 3, fast enough to fly and steer with body lift and three tail fins (there are no wings). Nearing the target the second propulsion stage is ignited.

About 1,300 missiles remain available to SAC's dwindling forces. AGM-69B, an improved missile with nuclear hardening throughout, the W80 warhead, a completely new Thiokol HTPB-propellant motor and greatly increased computer memory, was almost ready for production for the B-1, which could have carried 32; AGM-69B was cancelled in 1977 following discontinuance of the production programme for B-1. The remaining A-series missiles must, however, be fitted with the new Thiokol motor, because of ageing problems, and computer-memory as well as nuclear-hardening improvements are also projected. There is no money for production of new missiles, despite attractions of large carrier aircraft such as the 747-200F which could carry 72 internally. Originally the size of SRAM dictated the dimensions of ALCM, which is now longer.

Since the announcement of SRAM II AGM-69A has generally been known as SRAM-A.

Left: Pictures of the planned AGM-131A SRAM II were not available as this book went to press, but the new missile will broadly resemble the beautiful shape of the original SRAM. Three of the latter are seen here loaded on to the eight-station rotary launcher of a Strategic Air Command B-52.

SRAM II, AGM-131A

Origin: Boeing Aerospace, Kent
Propulsion: two-pulse advanced solid-propellant rocket motor
Dimensions: 'About two-thirds the size of SRAM-A'
Weight: about 700kg (1,543lb)
Performance: speed highly supersonic; range greater than that of SRAM-A
Warhead: as yet unannounced W-series thermonuclear in the 175-150kT class
Users: USA (AF)

For many years USAF Strategic Air Command studied an ASALM (Advanced Strategic Air-Launched Missile), most forms of which would have had hybrid or ram-rocket propulsion. By 1985 these plans had been overtaken by a belief in a new-generation SRAM and, following an industry competition between Boeing, McDonnell Douglas Astronautics and Martin Marietta, the award went to Boeing in December 1986. The programme at that date remained subject to a Congressional order that SRAM II should be compared for cost-effectiveness against modifying the old AGM-69As, notably by fitting new rocket motors. SRAM II, if built, will have broadly similar aerodynamics to SRAM-A but be smaller, yet warhead effectiveness — especially against hardened targets — will be greater. Guidance will be by ring-laser inertial system. SRAM II, designated AGM-131A, will be used mainly in the defence suppression role ahead of manned bombers. Great care will be taken to maximize 'stealth'

features of all kinds, especially radar cross-section

Boeing Military Airplane Co at the same time was awarded the go-ahead for production of the CSRL (Common Strategic Rotary Launcher). This will take SRAM II, SRAM-A, ALCM and all nuclear bombs. CSRL enters service in the B-52H in mid-1988, and will also fit weapon bays of the B-1B and ATB. Total procurement of AGM-131A is expected to be 1,633. Boeing's initial contract covers low-rate production of the first 100 followed by full production of 300 Lot 1 missiles from 1989. The AGM-131A should enter service on the B-1B in 1992.

SRARM

Origin: study programme led by British Aerospace and including BDM (USA), AEG (West Germany), Hollandse Signaalapparaten (Netherlands), MBLE and Philips (Belgium), SNIA-BPD (Italy) and Garrett (Canada)

For many years the USAF has believed that Sidewinder is inadequate for use as the basis of a (Sidearm-type) anti-radar missile, and has deeply studied short-range ARMs for self-defence of tactical aircraft. What is needed is something much newer and smaller than HARM. Though ALARM would seem the obvious choice, it is hoped that by taking a further 15 months to study the situation something else might be invented, and the seven-nation team were, in September 1985, told to do just that. The time was up in November 1986, but as this book went to press there has been no further announcement. Contracting authority is the Armament Division of USAF Systems Command. As the requirement is a NATO one, merely to adopt ALARM is clearly far too obvious, and it may be many years before anything reaches the squadrons.

Standard ARM, AGM-78

Origin: General Dynamics Pomona Division
Propulsion: Aerojet (ATSC) Mk 27 Mod 4 boost/sustain solid motor
Dimensions: length 4,572mm (180in); body diameter 343mm (13.5in); span (rear fins, greater than strake wings) 1,092mm (43in)
Weight: at launch typically 635kg (1,400lb)
Performance: speed Mach 2.5; range (depending on launch height) up to 56km (35 miles)
Warhead: conventional blast/fragmentation, direct-action and proximity fuzes
Users: South Korea, USA (AF, Navy, Marines)

In September 1966 the Naval Air Systems Command contracted with Pomona Division of General Dynamics for an ARM having higher performance, longer range and larger warhead than Shrike, which at that time was giving indifferent results. Unlike Shrike the whole programme was developed in industry, the basis being the Standard RIM-66A ship-to-air missile. Flight testing took place in 1967-8; production of AGM-78 Mod 0 began in late 1968 and 10 years later had absorbed well over $300 million at a unit price initially in the neighbourhood of $128,000.

AGM-78 Mod 0 was carried by the Air Force Wild Weasel F-105F and G and the Navy A-6B and E. The missile flies on a dual-thrust motor, steering with tail controls and very low aspect ratio fixed wings. The AGM-78A

Below: Close-up of an AGM-62 Walleye about to undergo a captive flight test under the wing of an A-3B Skywarrior at Point Mugu back in 1967. Clearly visible are the four powered control surfaces on the four wings and the windmill turbogenerator.

Mod 0 of 1968 was fitted with the TI seeker used in Shrike. This was soon replaced by the Maxson broad-band seeker of the main (Mod 1) production version, AGM-78B. This has capability against search, GCI, SAM and other radar systems, and is intended to give the launch platform freedom to attack from any direction and turn away 'outside the lethal radius of enemy SAMs'.

Carrier platforms preferably have a TIAS (Target Identification and Acquisition System) able to measure 'specific target parameters' and supply these to the seeker head in the missile before launch. The Mod 1 missile is compatible with the APR-38 system carried by the USAF F-4G Wild Weasel which supplies this need. AGM-78C, D and D-2 have further-increased capability and reduced unit cost, but in 1978 production was not funded, (deliveries then about 700) and effort has since been devoted to improving missiles with field modification kits. Navy and Marine A-6E squadrons carry this missile, as would the Wild Weasel F-16.

Left: The larger of the two missiles carried by this F-4G is an AGM-78 Standard ARM (the other being a Shrike). An ALQ-119 ECM pod is also visible.

Below: One of the first carriers of the Standard ARM was the US Air Force Republic F-105G Thunderchief, the original Wild Weasel platform. Note the nose receiver windows.

Tacit Rainbow, AGM-136A

Origin: Northrop Corporation, Ventura Division, Newbury Park, California
Propulsion: one Williams International J400-404 turbojet rated at 109kg (240lb) thrust
Dimensions: length 2,540mm (100in); body diameter 360mm (14in); span 1,765mm (69.4in)
Weight: about 200kg (440lb)
Performance: typical level speed 966km/h (600mph); mission endurance up to 30 minutes
Warhead: large conventional type with impact fuze
Users: US Navy and (joint) Air Force, with NATO customers expected

Derived distantly from the family of BQM-74 Chukar target and reconnaissance RPVs the Tacit Rainbow anti-radar cruise missile was revealed at the April 1987 Navy League convention. Often called 'Son of HARM', it is launched in the general direction of hostile defence systems, stabilized by a Singer-Kearfott flight control system, whilst its Texas Instruments receiver searches for hostile radars. Like the British ALARM, which is much more compact, this Northrop missile stores the locations of all emitters and homes on its selected target up to minutes after the latter has been switched off.

Walleye, AGM-62

Origin: Martin Marietta
Propulsion: none
Dimensions: length (I) 3,440mm (135in), (II) 4,040mm (159in); body diameter (I) 317mm (12.5in), (II) 457mm (18in); span (I) 1,160mm (45.5in), (II) 1,130mm (51in)
Launch weight: (I) 499kg (1,100lb), (II) 1,089kg (2,400lb)
Performance: speed subsonic; range (I) 26km (16 miles), (II) 56km (35 miles)
Warhead: (I) 374kg (825lb), (II) based on Mk 84 bomb
Users: include Israel, USA

An unpowered glide bomb with TV guidance, AGM-62 Walleye was developed from 1963 by the NOTS at China Lake, assisted from 1964 by the Naval Avionics Facility. Intended to overcome the aircraft-vulnerability hazard of visual radio-command ASMs, Walleye quickly proved successful, and in January 1966 Martin was awarded the first production contract. This was later multiplied, and in November 1967 the need for Walleye in SE Asia resulted in Hughes Aircraft being brought in as second source. In 1969 the Navy described this missile as 'the most accurate and effective air-to-surface conventional weapon ever developed anywhere'.

Walleye 1 has a cruciform of long-chord delta wings with elevons, a gyro-stabilized TV vidicon camera in the nose, and ram-air windmill at the tail to drive the alternator and hydraulic pump. The pilot or operating crew-member identifies the target (if necessary using aircraft radar), aims the missile camera at it, focusses it and locks it to the target using a monitor screen in the cockpit. The aircraft can then release the missile and turn away from the target, though it must keep the radio link with the missile. In theory the missile should glide straight to the target, but the launch operator has the ability to break into the control loop and, watching his monitor screen, guide it manually into the target.

In 1968 the Navy funded several developments — Update Walleye, Walleye II, Fat Albert and Large-Scale Walleye among them — which led to the enlarged Walleye II (Mk 5 Mod 4) for use against larger targets. In production by 1974, Walleye II was deleted from the budget the following year and replaced by the first procurement of ER/DL (Extended Range/Data-Link) Walleye II (Mk 13 Mod 0). The ER/DL system was originally planned in 1969 to allow a launch and leave technique at greater distance from the target, the missile having larger wings to improve the glide ratio, and the radio data-link allowing the operator to release the missile towards the target and then, when the missile was much closer, acquire the target on his monitor screen, focus the camera and lock it on. Operations in SE Asia showed that it would be preferable to use two aircraft, the first to release the Walleye (if possible already locked on the approximate target position) and then escape and the second, possibly miles to one side, to update the lock-on point and monitor the approach to the target. Since 1978 about 1,400 I and 2,400 II missiles have been converted to ER/DL.

GUIDED WEAPONS

Eryx

Origin: Aérospatiale, Châtillon
Propulsion: low-thrust solid motor giving trajectory control through centre of gravity of the missile
Dimensions: length 905mm (35.6in); body diameter 160mm (6.3in)
Weight: 14kg (30.9lb)
Performance: speed rises steadily to 1,080km/h (671mph); range 25 to 600m (82 to 1,969ft)
Warhead: hollow charge, penetration
Users: France

Originally called ACCP (Anti-Char Courte Portée, or anti-tank short range), Eryx is fired gently from a Kevlar container with command to line-of-sight guidance using a flare on the missile and a charge-coupled device camera on the launcher. Most are for infantry, but Eryx is also to be deployed from helicopters and light attack aircraft.

Below: This infantry launcher is stencilled with the original designation of Eryx (ACCP). Photographs of the missile and its planned helicopter installation had not been released as this book went to press.

Right: Looking down on an MBB BO 105P helicopter, in service with the Federal German Army Aviation as the PAH-1 (anti-tank helicopter type 1). Six launch tubes for HOT missiles are visible (the maximum load). The stabilized sight is mounted on the cabin roof.

Hot

Origin: Euromissile GIE
Propulsion: SNPE Bugeat boost and infra cast double-base (Epictète) sustainer
Dimensions: length 1,275mm (50.2in); body diameter (max, warhead/guidance) 165mm (6.5in); span (wings extended) 312mm (12.3in)
Weight: at launch 25kg (55lb)
Performance: speed 900km/h (560mph); range 400 to 4,000m (1,312 to 13,123ft)
Warhead: hollow charge 6kg (13.2lb)
Users: Egypt, France, West Germany, Iraq, Kuwait, Libya, Saudi Arabia, Spain, Syria and two unnamed customers

This missile should really be Hottt (the name is often written all in capitals), because it is Haut-subsonique Optiquement Télé-guidé Tiré d'un Tube (high-sub-sonic optical remote-guided fired from a tube). Work began with joint Franco-German army re-quirements, studies by Nord and Bölkow in 1964, engineering development and prolonged fir-ing trials by Aérospatiale/MBB (which jointly formed Euro-missile) and the start of mass pro-duction in 1977. Each missile is delivered as a round of ammuni-tion in a sealed GRP tube.

The ignition signal fires the thermal battery, gyro and flares, gas pressure blowing the end-caps off the tube. The booster then fires inside the tube, burn-ing for 0.9 second and accel-erating the missile to the speed given in the data; the sustainer then takes over and maintains this speed over a further 17.4 se-cond burn, giving times of 8.7 seconds to 2,000m (2,185 yards), 12.5 seconds to 3,000m (3,280 yards) and 16.3 seconds to 4,000m (4,375 yards). The sus-tainer exhausts centrally where a single TVC spoiler can steer the missile. About 30-50m (100-165ft) from the launcher the safety system is deactivated to allow the sensitive fuze to detonate the head as soon as the streamlined nose skin is distorted. Penetra-tion is 700mm (28in) at 0° and 280mm (11in) at 65°.

Air-launched Hot serves with the German BO 105P helicopter (PAH.1) with six launch tubes, and Spain uses the BO 105C. France will have 160 SA 342M Gazelles, with four tubes each, as do several export customers. The SA 361H and various twin-engined Dauphin versions can carry eight, as does the Lynx, in all cases with stabilized magnify-ing night sights. Production of dawn-to-dusk systems proceeds at 800 rounds per month, but development and integration of night FLIR sights is a matter of urgency. Germany has adopted a TI system made under licence.

ANTI-TANK MISSILES

Below: Launching a HOT missile from an SA 342M Gazelle helicopter of the French ALAT (army light aviation).

Right: The installation of the HOT missile system in an MBB BO 105P anti-tank helicopter. The sight could be in the nose or on a mast.

HOT Installation

1 Gyro-stablilized magnifying sight.
2 Localizer (part of guidance equipment, detects IR tracer).
3 Steering indicator (artificial horizon).
4 Sight control unit.
5 Control selection unit.
6 Firing system.
7 Sight electronics box.
8 Electronics boxes for localizer, guidance, and launch ramp control.
9 Slaving electronics box.
10 Ramp selector switch units and cables.
11 Actuator.
12 Six launch ramps.
13 Two launch ramp supports.

HOT 2

1 Missile container plug.
2 Glass fibre tubular container.
3 Hollow charge warhead, ignition triggered by distortion of nose cone upon impact.
4 Fuze.
5 Sustainer motor.
6 Booster motor.
7 Guidance module containing decoder, gyroscope, battery, control wire, sustainer jet deflector, and IR tracer.
8 Thermal battery, pyrotechnically primed on firing.
9 Safety locking mechanisim.
10 Electrical connector system.
11 Arming wire.

Above: HOT 2 is certainly the most important anti-tank helicopter-launched missile currently in production in Europe.

PARS 3LR

Origin: EMDG (Euromissile Dynamics Group)
Propulsion: rocket motor
Dimensions: not yet finalized
Weight: not yet finalized
Performance: range 4,500m (14,464ft)
Warhead: exceptionally powerful
Users: the partner countries

In January 1980 the governments of Britain, France and West Germany signed a memorandum of understanding for the development by EMDG of a new generation of anti-tank missiles for the 1990s. EMDG comprises Aérospatiale, British Aerospace and MBB. Aérospatiale leads on the new infantry missile, BAe on the PARS 3LR long-range land version and MBB on the helicopter version. A high-subsonic or transonic missile, PARS 3LR will have passive infra-red homing guidance and will be suitable for use against both enemy armour and helicopters, in all weather. Engineering development was to begin seven years after the agreement, in 1987.

CHINA

Red Arrow (Hong Jian) 73

Origin: NORINCO, Beijing
Propulsion: boost/sustain solid rocket motor
Dimensions: length 868mm (34.2in); body diameter 120mm (4.72in); span 393mm (15.47in)
Weight: 11.3kg (24.9lb)
Performance: speed 430km/h (267mph); range 3,000m (3,280 yards)
Warhead: hollow-charge HEAT, penetration 500mm (19.7in), or 150mm (5.9in) at 65°
User: People's Republic of China

Superficially similar to the Soviet AT-3 'Sagger', apart from having smaller wings, this missile has manual command to line of sight guidance, using an optical sight and joystick. The warhead is armed 70 to 200m (230 to 655ft) after leaving the rail launcher and minimum range in the ground-launched mode is 500m (545 yards). A laser training simulator has been developed.

Red Arrow (Hong Jian) 8

Origin: NORINCO, Beijing
Propulsion: boost/sustain solid rocket motor
Dimensions: length 875mm (34.45in); body diameter 120mm (4.72in); span 320mm (12.6in)
Weight: 11.2kg (24.7lb)
Performance: speed 865km/h (537mph); range 100-3,000m (110-3,280 yards)
Warhead: hollow-charge HEAT, penetration 800mm (31.5in)
User: People's Republic of China

A tube-launched, optically-tracked, wire-guided missile, Red Arrow 8 uses the semi-automatic command to the line of sight guidance pioneered by Aérospatiale, in which a goniometer senses the direction of the missile's IR emission and automatically sends signals to keep it on the line of sight between the operator and target. Many features of this missile bear a close resemblance to the French Milan. It is not certain that an air-launched version exists, but the HJ-8 has been included because it is China's most advanced anti-tank missile and a helicopter version seems logical.

GUIDED WEAPONS

Above: An AT-2 'Swatter' fired from a surprisingly high-flying Mi-24 'Hind-D', probably of Soviet Frontal Aviation.

Right: This Polish-built (Soviet-designed) Mi-2 'Hoplite' helicopter is armed with four AT-3 'Sagger' missiles.

AT-2 'Swatter'

Propulsion: single-grain solid motor with inclined lateral nozzles
Dimensions: length 902mm (35.5in); body diameter 150mm (5.9in); span 660mm (26in)
Weight: at launch 25kg (55lb)
Performance: speed 540km/h (335mph); range up to 2,200m (7,218ft)
Warhead: hollow charge, pierces 600mm (23.6in)
Users: all Warsaw Pact countries, Afghanistan, Egypt, Syria

Bearing in mind that it was planned in the early 1960s and was in action in 1967, this second-generation anti-armour missile was a remarkable technical achievement, and it is still deployed in very large numbers. In particular it is often seen on the Soviet Mil Mi-8 'Hip-E', and Mi-24 'Hind-A' and 'Hind-D'.

It has a constant-diameter tubular body, with a blunt tail which before launch is connected to a multi-pin umbilical plug. The motor fires through diagonal upper and lower nozzles to accelerate the missile off a long rail launcher, which in the case of helicopter installations is under the body. Four rear wings have roll-control elevons, and the missile homes on the heat of its target detected by a sensitive nose seeker, driving two canard foreplanes, the missile rolling in bang/bang fashion to steer left/right. There are no guidance wires. Later missiles are only gradually replacing this prolific weapon.

AT-3 'Sagger'

Propulsion: boost motor with four diagonal nozzles, sustainer has central nozzle with jetevator TVC for steering
Dimensions: length 860mm (34in); body diameter 120mm (4.7in); span 460mm (18.1in)
Weight: at launch 11.3kg (24.9lb)
Performance: speed high subsonic; range 500 to 3,000m (1,640 to 9,843ft)
Warhead: hollow charge, 3kg (6.6lb), pierces 600mm (23.6in)
Users: all Warsaw Pact countries plus Afghanistan, Algeria, Angola, Egypt, Ethiopia, Iraq, Libya, Mozambique, Syria, Uganda, Vietnam, Yemen and Yugoslavia.

During the Middle East War in October 1973, two-man teams of Egyptian infantry opened what looked like small suitcases and inflicted on Israeli battle tanks casualties the like of which had seldom been seen on any battlefield. Ever since, the little missile codenamed 'Sagger' by NATO has been treated with great respect, though it is still a simple device with no tube launcher or any guidance other than optical sighting and wire command.

Called Malyutka in the Soviet Union, it was first seen in a Moscow parade in May 1965.

Since then it has been seen on many army platforms and it is also the usual anti-armour missile for helicopter use for export customers, including Poland's SM-2 and the Mi-8 'Hip-F'. The Mi-24 'Hind-A' can carry this missile on its four outboard launchers, firing from the hover or at low forward speeds.

The missile is accelerated by a boost motor just behind the warhead, and flies on a sustainer with jet-deflection steering. There are no aerodynamic controls, but the small wings can fold for packaging. A tracking flare is attached beside the body, and it is claimed that an operator can steer to 1,000m (1,095 yards) with unaided eyesight, and to three times this distance with the magnifying optical sight used in air platforms.

AT-6 'Spiral'

Propulsion: unknown type of rocket motor, probably dual-thrust solid
Dimensions: unknown, but length in region of 1,800mm (7in); body diameter 140mm (5.5in)
Weight: possibly about 32kg (70.5lb)
Performance: speed about 1,000km/h (620mph); range 7 to 10km (4.35 to 6.2 miles)
Warhead: large HEAT (high-explosive anti-tank), penetrates at least 650mm (25.6in) at 90°
Users: Most Warsaw Pact countries by 1983

At first, in 1977 when it was first identified, this tube-launched system was believed to use the same missile as AT-4 and AT-5, but by 1980 Western observers had realized that it was completely new. Unlike other Soviet anti-tank missiles this has been identified only in air-launched applications, carried by the Mi-24 'Hind-E' and, it is believed, the Su-25 'Frogfoot' close-support attack aircraft. The air-launched missile is believed also to have NATO designation AS-8.

It homes in on its target by radio command or laser guidance, the designator being either in the launch aircraft or aimed by friendly ground troops. The warhead is possibly of double-cone type and is judged able to knock out all known armour.

AT-X-?

During the past several years there has been a near-panic in NATO armies to find countermeasures against this supposed new anti-armour missile which has millimetre-wave guidance. By late 1982 this missile appeared to be little more than a rumour based on the Soviet Union's known work on such radars.

Below: The Mi-24 'Hind-E' can carry up to 12 AT-6 'Spirals' (but only racks fitted here).

SWEDEN

Bantam, RB 53

Origin: AB Bofors
Propulsion: Bofors dual-thrust solid motor
Dimensions: length 848mm (33.4in); body diameter 110mm (4.3in); span 400mm (16.75in)
Weight: at launch 7.6kg (16.75lb)
Performance: speed 303km/h (188mph); range 250m to 2,000m (820 to 5,562ft)
Warhead: hollow charge, Bofors 1.9kg (4.2lb)
Users: Sweden, Switzerland

Developed almost entirely by AB Bofors as a private venture from 1956, this is one of the smallest and lightest first-generation anti-tank missiles, and was notable for introducing a GRP airframe with folding wings to fit a slim container/launcher. In its simplest form for infantry the whole system, with one missile, weighs 20kg (44.0lb) with 20m (66ft) of cable to link the operator and launcher. If necessary the operator can add another 100m (328ft) of cable. Bantam has been fired from light aircraft such as

the SK61 Bulldog and Saab Supporter and Agusta-Bell 204 helicopter.

On leaving the launch box the wings flip open, their curved trailing-edge tips rolling the missile so that it can be steered by the trailing-edge spoilers sequenced by a pellet-spun gyro. The hollow-charge warhead has electrical double-skin fusing and can penetrate up to 500mm (19.7in). Sweden adopted Bantam as missile RB53 in 1963, and — despite having its indigenous Mosquito — Switzerland followed in 1967. Production continued until about 1978, and the missile remains in limited service.

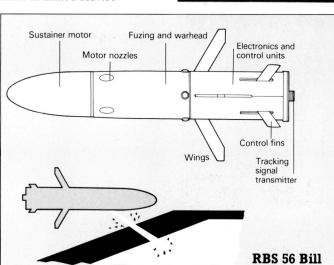

RBS 56 Bill

Below: Launch of one of the lightweight plastics RB 53 Bantam missiles from an Agusta-Bell AB 204 helicopter of the Swedish army aviation.

Above: The RBS 56 Bill is unique in that it is designed not to strike the target but to pass close above it, the diagonal jet from the shaped-charge

warhead then piercing the relatively light top armour. Note the unusual location of the sustainer rocket motor in the nose.

Above: The impressive detonation of an RBS 56 Bill tested against a main battle tank. This missile is triggered by a proximity fuze.

Bill, RBS 56

Origin: AB Bofors
Propulsion: Royal Ordnance dual-thrust solid rocket
Dimensions: length 900mm (35.4in); diameter 150mm (5.9in); span 410mm (16.1in)
Weight: about 16kg (35.3lb) with container
Performance: speed 720km/h (447mph); range 150 to 2,000m (492 to 6,562ft)
Warhead: obliquely-angled shaped-charge
User: Sweden

The RBS 56 Bill (pick) is due to enter service in the later 1980s after a development programme shared equally by Bofors and the FMV (Swedish matériel administration). The weapon is an advanced anti-tank missile which is fired, in its baseline ground-launched form, from a container tube fitted with a sight unit and mounted on a tripod. The design is characterized by a wide-diameter body with the rocket in the nose, exhausting through obliquely-disposed lateral nozzles about one-third of the way aft along the body; a centrally-mounted warhead and fuzing system; and small spring-out wings and control fins in the aftermost third of the body, which also contains the electronic and control units. The body terminates in a laser tracking signal transmitter, and the missile is wire-guided. The missile is designed to fly 1m (3.3ft) above the operator's line of sight, and the key to the Bill's capabilities is the shaped-charge warhead, which is fitted with a proximity fuze and angled to fire 30° downwards from the missile's centreline as the weapon overflies the target's most vulnerable upper surfaces. This allows the jet of gas and vaporized metal to burn through the target tank's thinnest armour. There is every likelihood that the Bill will be adopted for helicopter use.

USA

Hellfire, AGM-114

Origin: Rockwell International
Propulsion: Thiokol TX657 reduced-smoke 'all-boost' motor
Dimensions: length 1,626mm (64in); body diameter 178mm (7in)
Weight: at launch 44.84kg (98.86lb)
Performance: speed quickly builds to Mach 1.17, range 'far in excess of present anti-armour systems'
Warhead: Firestone 9kg (20lb) 178mm (7in) diameter hollow charge
User: USA (Army, initially)

A direct descendent of Rockwell's Hornet, this missile has applications against hard point targets of all kinds, though it is officially described as 'the USA's next-generation anti-armour weapon system'. Numerous development firings took place from 1971 before full engineering go-ahead was received in October 1976. It has semi-active laser homing with a very advanced seeker from Martin Marietta. The seeker has a Cassegrain telescope under the hemispherical glass nose sending signals to the electronics section with micro-processor logic. Steering is by four canard controls, and Hellfire can pull 13g at Mach 1.17. A former Under-Secretary of Defense, William J.

Above right: A longitudinal cross-section of the laser-homing seeker head of the Hellfire.

Right: A schematic diagram showing how Hellfires may be fired from behind cover against targets designated by lasers (blue lines).

Below: A McDonnell Douglas AH-64A Apache of the US Army armed with its 30mm gun and eight Hellfires. Up to 16 of the latter can be carried, making it the most powerfully armed helicopter in the Western world.

Hellfire Laser Seeker

1 Impact switch.
2 Spin torquer.
3 Video amplifier.
4 Sample and hold.
5 Pulse logic.
6 Decoder.
7 Mode control.
8 Power supply.
9 Mother board.
10 Interface board.
11 Impact switch.
12 Gyro.
13 Detector pre-amplifier.

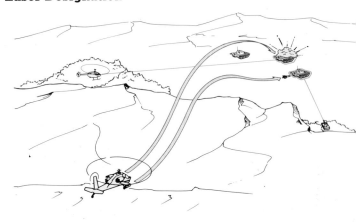

Laser Designation

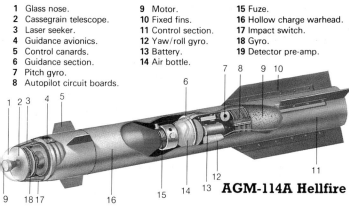

1 Glass nose.
2 Cassegrain telescope.
3 Laser seeker.
4 Guidance avionics.
5 Control canards.
6 Guidance section.
7 Pitch gyro.
8 Autopilot circuit boards.
9 Motor.
10 Fixed fins.
11 Control section.
12 Yaw/roll gyro.
13 Battery.
14 Air bottle.
15 Fuze.
16 Hollow charge warhead.
17 Impact switch.
18 Gyro.
19 Detector pre-amp.

AGM-114A Hellfire

Above: A simplified cutaway of the AGM-114A Hellfire missile. Colour is used to clarify the internal components and construction.

Perry, said 'This missile most often goes right through the center of the bull's eye.'

The primary carrier is the AH-64A Apache helicopter (16 rounds) but Hellfire has flown on the Cobra and the A-10A Thunderbolt II fixed-wing platform. Numerous Hellfires have been launched without prior lock-on, some of them in rapid-fire homing on different multiple targets using ground designators with individual coding. The missile notices the laser radiation in flight, locks-on and homes at once. IOC was achieved in 1984, by which time this missile had also been developed with 'launch and leave' IIR guidance, and with dual-mode RF/IIR guidance. The first 680 rounds were delivered before September 1984. By 1987 Hellfire, AGM-114A, had been deployed on the first hundred combat-ready Apaches, and on the Marines' SeaCobra and Super-Cobra, Lynx and Black Hawk.

Tow, BGM-71

Origin: General Motors-Hughes, Tucson
Propulsion: Hercules K41 boost (0.05s) and sustain (1s) motors
Dimensions: length 1,162mm (45.75in); body diameter 152mm (6in); span (wings extended) 343mm (13.5in)
Weight: (BGM-71A) 20.9kg (46.1lb)
Performance: speed 1,003km/h (623mph), range 500 to 3,750m (1,804 to 12,303ft)
Warhead: (BGM-71A) Picatinny Arsenal 3.9kg (8.6lb) shaped-charge with 2.4kg (5.3lb) explosive; see text for later
Users: include Canada, Denmark, Ethiopia, West Germany, Greece, Iran, Israel, Italy, Jordan, South Korea, Kuwait, Lebanon, Luxembourg, Morocco, Netherlands, Norway, Oman, Pakistan, Saudi Arabia, Spain, Sweden, Taiwan, Turkey, UK, US (Army, Marines), Vietnam and Yugoslavia

Often written TOW (Tube-launched, Optically-tracked,

Wire-guided), this weapon is likely to set an all-time record for guided-missile production.

Prime contractor Hughes Aircraft began work in 1965 to replace the 106mm recoilless rifle. The missile's basic infantry form is supplied in a sealed tube which is clipped to the launcher. The missile tube is attached to the rear of the launch tube, the target sighted and the round fired. The boost charge pops the missile from the tube, firing through lateral nozzles amidships. The four wings indexed at 45° spring open forwards, and the four tail controls flip open rearwards. Guidance commands are gener-

Right: Cutaway drawing of the original production version of TOW, BGM-71A. As before colours are used to clarify the internal arrangement. Later I-TOW and TOW 2 are almost identical internally.

Below: Firing a BGM-71A TOW anti-tank missile from a McDonnell Douglas 530MG Defender helicopter. The missile has only just left the launch tube yet its tail controls are almost fully deployed and the wings are unfolding. On this helicopter the sight system is on a rotor mast.

ated by the optical sensor in the sight, which continually measures the position of a light source in the missile relative to the LOS and sends steering commands along twin wires. These drive the helium-pressure actuators working the four tail controls in pairs for pitch and yaw. In 1976 production switched to ER (Extended Range) TOW with the guidance wires lengthened from 3,000m (9,843ft) to the figure given. Sight field of view reduces from 6° for gathering to 1.5° for smoothing and 0.25° for tracking. The missile electronics pack is between the motor and the warhead.

Tow reached IOC in 1970, was used in Vietnam and the 1973 Middle East war, and has since been produced at a higher rate than any other known missile. The M65 airborne TOW system equips the standard American attack helicopter, the AH-1S TowCobra and the Marines' twin-engine AH-1J and -1T improved SeaCobra, each with a TSU (telescopic sight unit) and two quad launchers. Other countries use Tow systems on the BO 105, Lynx, A109, A129, 500MD and other attack helicopters.

Hughes has developed a mast-

mounted sight (MMS) which uses the BAe Tow roof sight but with a TV down-tube, the whole mounted above the rotor hub of the 500MD. In late 1981 production began of the Improved Tow, with a new warhead triggered by a long probe, extended after launch to give 381mm (15in) stand-off distance for greater armour penetration. The shaped-charge head with LX-14 filling and a dual-angle deformable liner, is also being retrofitted to many existing rounds. By late 1982 Hughes was near mass-production of Tow 2, which has several I-Tow improvements plus a new head with the same diameter as the rest of the missile with a mass of 5.9kg (13lb) and an even longer (540mm/21.25in) extensible probe, calculated to defeat all tanks of the 1990s. Flight performance is maintained by a new double-base motor giving about 30 per cent greater total impulse. Both new missiles are for air-launch applications.

Total production of Tow 1 (1969-83) was 310,793. By February 1986 production of I-Tow was 39,924 and of Tow 2 33,454, both remaining in full production. They are in use from 12 types of helicopter.

BGM-71 Tow

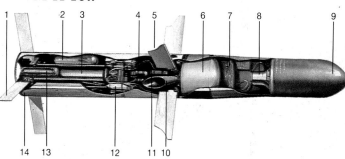

1 Flick-out control fins.
2 Gas bottle.
3 Launch motor (booster).
4 Batteries.
5 Flick-out wings.
6 Flight motor (sustainer).
7 Electronics.
8 Safety/arm unit.
9 Warhead.
10 Motor nozzle.
11 Gyro.
12 Control actuators.
13 Wire dispenser.
14 IR source (for missile tracking).

GUIDED WEAPONS

FRANCE

L4

Origin: DCN, Paris and ECAN, St Tropez
Propulsion: one electric motor driving contra-rotating propellers
Dimensions: length (including parachute stabilizer/retarder) 3,130mm (123.2in); diameter 533mm (21in)
Weight: 525kg (1,156lb)
Performance: speed 30kt (56km/h); range 5,500m (18,045ft)
Warhead: 100kg (220lb)
User: France

This lightweight torpedo is unusual amongst the air-launched species of anti-submarine weapons in having the 533mm (21in) diameter of full-calibre submarine-launched torpedoes, and was developed by the Direction des Constructions Navales specifically for airborne applications. The main launch platforms for the type are the Malafon ship-launched anti-submarine missile, patrol aircraft such as the Dassault-Breguet Atlantic (and forthcoming Atlantique), and larger anti-submarine helicopters such as the Aérospatiale Super Frelon. The torpedo is of basically conventional design and construction, and is intended for use against submarines moving at not more than 20kt. There are two variants of the L4, the earlier type being optimized for the attack of deep-dived submarines, and the later type for anti-submarine engagements in shallow water. After descent into the water under its stabilizing parachute, the torpedo undertakes a circular search pattern as its acoustic seeker listens for a target. As soon as such a target has been locked into the homing system the torpedo vectors in towards it, and the warhead is finally detonated by the inbuilt impact or acoustic proximity fuzes. The L4 has been modernized in recent years, and now has a claimed capability against submarines operating at any depth between periscope depth and 300m.

Above: L4 carried by a Super Frelon helicopter of the French Aéronavale, protecting the French missile submarines.

Below: Portly L4 torpedoes carried inside the fuselage weapon bay of an Atlantic maritime patrol aircraft. The L4 is claimed to be very quiet-running in operation.

Murène

Origin: ECAN, St Tropez, working with industry
Propulsion: one electric motor driving contra-rotating propellers
Dimensions: length (including parachute stabilizer/retarder) 2,960m (116.5in); diameter 324mm (12.75in)
Weight: 280kg ((617lb) without 15kg (33lb) parachute pack
Performance: speed 38kt (70km/h) for search and more than 53kt (98km/h) for attack; range many km; endurance (combined search and attack phases) 12 minutes; diving limits from 30 to more than 1,000m (100 to more than 3,280ft)
Warhead: 60kg (132lb) shaped-charge HE
Users: to be France and export customers

The Murène is now under development for service entry in

January 1991, and this torpedo is certainly the most advanced lightweight torpedo ever to have been developed in France, and possibly the world. The torpedo is aimed in the short term at the French forces, but clearly has enormous possibilities in the open world market. The Murène is being designed with a full capability against diesel-electric or nuclear submarines operating slowly and quietly over the continental shelf, or at speed and more noisily in the ocean depths. The electric motor is rated at more than 100kW (134hp), drawing current from a silver oxide/aluminium battery which uses sea water to dissolve the solid electrolyte. At the front of the torpedo are transducer arrays looking ahead, to the side and (to measure the depth of the water) down, as well as three powerful sonars emitting pure tones of FM pulses. Three microprocessors in the homing head compare possible target parameters, pick a target and

Left: Murène is currently being developed for service use in the 1990s. It will be a fast and versatile weapon.

Below: A cutaway drawing showing the internal features of the Murène torpedo. The shaped-charge warhead fires forward through the acoustic head and antenna arrays to pierce the target's hull.

1 Stator (propeller duct).
2 Propeller.
3 Rudder actuator.
4 Priming valve.
5 Auxiliary batteries.
6 Command central unit.
7 Nose (plane) antennas.
8 Side antennas.
9 Acoustic homing head.
10 Shaped-charge warhead
11 Motor/pump set.
12 Degaussing unit.
13 Electromechanical unit.
14 Electric motor.
15 Control surfaces.

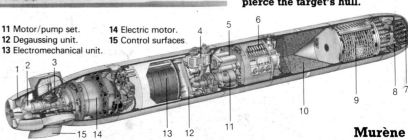

Murène

AIR-LAUNCHED TORPEDOES

bring the torpedo alongside the objective before turning it in to strike the target at the optimum angle with its 60kg (132lb) shaped-charge warhead, which is able to penetrate some 1.2m (3.9ft): at an angle of 50° the warhead has pierced a 20mm (0.8in) outer hull, 2m (6.6ft) of ballast water, 40mm (1.6in) of pressure hull and a further 300mm (11.8in). The Capitole main guidance system has four 16-bit Motorola 68000 microprocessors separate from the homing head. Later versions of the Murène are expected to be powered by a lithium/thionyl chloride battery.

A 244/S

Origin: Whitehead Moto Fides, Livorno
Propulsion: one electric motor driving contra-rotating propellers
Dimensions: length 2,700mm (106.3in); diameter 324mm (12.75in)
Weight: not revealed
Performance: speed 30kt (55.5km/h); range 6,500m (21,325ft)
Warhead: shaped-charge HE (high explosive)
Users: Italy and various export customers

The A 244 lightweight torpedo was designed as successor to the US Mk 44 type, and was conceived for use on warships and by aircraft (both fixed-and rotary-wing), with particular emphasis on the shallow-water capability required for its successful employment in the Mediterranean. In its air-launched form the torpedo is stabilized in flight by a parachute attached to the tail, the AG70 seeker unit being initiated as the torpedo enters the water. The A 244/S is a more advanced version carrying the CIACIO-S seeker unit with a choice of active or passive sonar. The CIACIO-S can separate the real target from decoys even in the presence of heavy acoustic reverberation by special signal modulation and processing, and can search through a substantial volume of water with self-adaptive pre-programmed patterns for the searching beams. Other features of the advanced seeker are pre-programmed combinations of signal-processing techniques, spatial filtering and the ability to inaugurate tactical manoeuvring that matches the torpedo to the changing situation.

Right: An Agusta-Bell 212ASW of the Marinavia releasing an A 244 while in contact via its Bendix AQS-13B dunking sonar. The stabilization chute is starting to deploy.

Below: A Whitehead A 244 torpedo seen on display at the 1987 Paris Air Show. This is the more advanced A 244/S version of the weapon.

GUIDED WEAPONS

Soviet torpedoes

Virtually nothing of a concrete nature has been published about Soviet torpedoes in general, and this applies perhaps most strongly to the weapons designed for carriage and delivery by Soviet maritime patrol aircraft and anti-submarine helicopters. It is generally believed that these air-launched weapons have a diameter of 406mm (16in), and that the torpedoes come in two basic lengths each fitted with a parachute retarder at the tail. The shorter models are in all probability medium-range weapons intended for use against submerged submarines, while the lengthier models are designed for longer-range operations against surface vessels as well as submarines. Some aircraft, including the Mil Mi-14 'Haze' helicopter and fixed-wing machines such as the Beriev M-12 'Mail', Ilyushin Il-38 'May' and Tupolev Tu-142 'Bear', may carry torpedoes of larger diameter and length for use against the escorts of US Navy battle groups. These more substantial weapons, with a

Above: The Il-28 'Beagle' is believed still to be in use by the AV-MF (Soviet naval air force) for torpedo training. Designation of the torpedo is not yet known.

diameter of 650 or 660mm (25.6 or 26in), may be capable of carrying a nuclear warhead, but the smaller weapons are generally reckoned to have conventional warheads. The light 406mm torpedoes carried by the Kamov Ka-25 'Hormone' and Kamov Ka-27 'Helix' anti-submarine helicopters are believed to possess a wire-guidance option, but the standard homing method is sonar (active or passive), though another possibility is wake-homing for the larger weapons. The fuzing system employs a magnetic proximity device backed by an impact system, the primary objective being to pierce the hull of a submarine or break the back of a surface vessel.

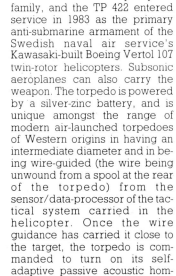

Above: The TP 42 is a typical lightweight electric torpedo with wire guidance. It is in production and in service with the Swedish navy.

Below: Basically the new TP 43 is a TP 42 with modern microprocessor control. It combines wire guidance with a new homing head.

SWEDEN

TP 42

Origin: FFV, Eskilstuna
Propulsion: one electric motor driving contra-rotating propellers
Dimensions: length 2,600mm (102.4in) with wire-guidance spool; diameter 400mm (15.75in)
Weight: 298kg (657lb)
Performance: speed 30kt (56km/h); range up to 20,000m (65,617ft) depending on speed
Warhead: about 50kg (110lb)
User: Sweden

TP 42 is the baseline designation of an important Swedish anti-submarine and anti-ship torpedo family, and the TP 422 entered service in 1983 as the primary anti-submarine armament of the Swedish naval air service's Kawasaki-built Boeing Vertol 107 twin-rotor helicopters. Subsonic aeroplanes can also carry the weapon. The torpedo is powered by a silver-zinc battery, and is unique amongst the range of modern air-launched torpedoes of Western origins in having an intermediate diameter and in being wire-guided (the wire being unwound from a spool at the rear of the torpedo) from the sensor/data-processor of the tactical system carried in the helicopter. Once the wire guidance has carried it close to the target, the torpedo is commanded to turn on its self-adaptive passive acoustic homing system. This is also activated if the wire guidance system should break, and controls the terminal phase. The onboard system correlates principles to provide accuracy under adverse sonar conditions. The weapon has 20 and 30kt speed options

(the higher option reducing range to 10,000m, 32,808ft), and speed changes can be made at operator command or be pre-set in the onboard guidance system. The TP 427 is an export version of the TP 422 with changes to the guidance and fuzing systems to avoid compromising Sweden's nationally vital anti-submarine operating frequencies.

TP43

Origin: FFV, Eskilstuna
Propulsion: one electric motor driving contra-rotating propellers
Dimensions: length 2,850mm (112.2in) with wire-guidance spool; diameter 400mm (15.75in)
Weight: 280kg (617lb) excluding 30kg (66lb) wire spool
Performance: speed 30kt (56km/h); range 20,000m (65,617ft) at 15kt
Warhead: 45kg (99lb) shaped-charge HE
User: Sweden

Entering service in 1987, the TP 43 series is based on the TP 42 family with improvement resulting mainly from the adoption of modular construction, a guidance package that makes use of digital microprocessing, inbuilt test equipment and special (classified) features to make possible attacks on quiet submarines operating in shallow water. The baseline air-launched version is the TP 432, which has greater tactical flexibility through the availability of three running speeds, including one considerably greater than that attainable by the TP 42 series, and provided for attacks on the new generation of high-speed nuclear attack submarines as well as more rapid engagement of slower boats. The air-launched version is fitted with a lighter (and therefore smaller) battery than the 350kg (772lb) ship-launched version, and thus cannot achieve the heavier variant's ranges of 30,000, 20,000 and 10,000m (98,425, 65,617 and 32,808ft) at 15, 25, or 35kts respectively, though the exact ranges of the air-launched model at these speeds remains undivulged for security reasons. The TP 43XO is the export version of the TP 43 family, and bears a relationship to the TP 432 identical to that of the TP 427 to the TP 422. The TP 43XO is also offered with the option of different propulsion systems to suit customers.

1 Warhead with homing head and (top) impact fuze.
2 Battery section with computer, processor and proximity fuze.
3 Wire dispenser drum, and main DC electric power supply.
4 Afterbody with motor, gearbox, control servo motors and flaps.
5 Tail with rudders, wire outlet and propellers.

TP 43

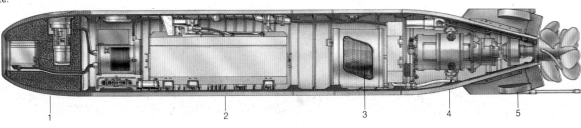

AIR-LAUNCHED TORPEDOES

Sting Ray

Origin: Marconi Underwater System, Waterlooville
Propulsion: no details revealed, but of a very high-energy type giving at least 8 minutes at full power
Dimensions: length 2,597mm (102.25in); diameter 324mm (12.75in)
Weight: 265kg (585lb)
Performance: speed 45kt (83km/h); range 11,100m (36,417ft)
Warhead: 40kg (88lb) shaped-charge HE
Users: UK and several export customers

The Sting Ray is generally regarded as the world's most advanced lightweight torpedo in current service, and is a highly capable weapon intended for launch by surface ships, aircraft (both fixed- and rotary-wing) and missiles such as the Australian Ikara. The torpedo is a highly versatile weapon capable of successful attacks on all types of submarine in both shallow and deep

waters. The key to this performance is a high-speed vehicle using pump-jet propulsion, sturdy construction to allow operations down to a depth of at least 1,000m (3,280ft) and an extremely sophisticated guidance package that includes a multi-mode multi-beam sonar and fully programmable digital computer to give dramatically enhanced target-acquisition and homing capabilities under all water conditions.

In its airborne role the torpedo is dropped under its retarding parachute only after the launch aircraft's onboard tactical system has fixed the basic position of the target. When it has entered the water and freed itself of the parachute, the Sting Ray sets up a pre-programmed search pattern designed to maximize the chances of target detection. As soon as the target has been acquired, the computer and ac-

tive/passive sonar make it all but impossible for the target to evade attack, the advanced software of the guidance and homing system allowing it to filter out background and decoy noise, and to make an interception rather than undertake the conventional tail-chase pursuit. Here the Sting Ray's speed makes it difficult for the target to outrun the weapon, which has a powerful shaped-charge warhead.

Below: Sting Ray just after launch from a Lynx HAS.Mk 2. Its agility means that it can counter virtually any evasive manoeuvre made by the target.

Above: Marconi's new Sting Ray, now in volume production, is probably the most effective lightweight torpedo in service in the world today. Here seen

mounted on a Pilatus Britten-Norman Defender, it is equally effective in the difficult sonar conditions of shallow water and the deep ocean.

141

GUIDED WEAPONS

Mk 44 Mod 1

Origin: various US contractors as well as overseas licensees
Propulsion: one electric motor driving contra-rotating propellers
Dimensions: length 2,560mm (100.75in); diameter 324mm (12.75in)
Weight: typically 233kg (514lb)
Performance: speed 30kt (56km/h); range 5,485m (18,000ft); diving limit 300m (985ft)
Warhead: 34kg (75lb) HE
Users: a total of 31 countries bought the Mk 44, but many of these no longer operate the type

The Mk 44 torpedo was accepted for service in 1956 in its Mk 44 Mod 0 initial variant, and was one of the most important lightweight anti-submarine torpedoes of the 1960s and early 1970s. The weapon had three primary applications. Firstly, it was used as an air-launched weapon from fixed- and rotary-wing launch platforms. Secondly, it was employed as a ship-launched weapon (using the Mk 32 tube system linked to the ship's underwater weapons fire-control system). And thirdly, it constituted one of the offensive payloads of the RUR-5A ASROC long-range anti-submarine rocket system. The weapon's battery is activated by sea water, and the acquisition range of the homing system is 650 yards (595m). The initial model has a weight of 193kg (425lb) and a length of 2,540mm (100.0in). Depth and course settings are entered into the guidance system

Below: A Mk 44 anti-submarine torpedo about to be carried on a practice mission by Royal Navy No 824 Sqn, from a Sea King HAS. Mk 5.

(via an umbilical cable) from the launch platform's fire-control system just before launch to provide this limited weapon with the maximum chance of getting into acquisition range of the target submarine. The slightly later Mk 44 Mod 1 has a few detail improvements in comparison with the Mk 44 Mod 0, but is not a significantly different weapon. The type was built in fairly substantial numbers, but is now rapidly disappearing from service even as a training weapon.

Above: Gradually being replaced by the SH-60B Seahawk, the Kaman SH-2F Seasprite is still the main US helicopter armed with the Mk 46 torpedo.

Below: Notable for the simplicity of its afterbody fins, the Mk 46 has electric propulsion to contra-rotating propellers. This example was photographed aboard an SH-3H Sea King at NAS Keyport, Washington.

Mk 46 Mod 1

Origin: Honeywell, Gould and Aerojet Electro Systems
Propulsion: one Otto monopropellant thermo-chemical engine driving contra-rotating propellers
Dimensions: length 2,590mm (102.0in); diameter 324mm (12.75in)
Weight: 230kg (508lb)
Performance: speed 45kt (83km/h); range 10,975m (36,000ft) at 15m (50ft) depth, decreasing to 5,485m (18,000ft) at 455m (1,500ft) depth
Warhead: 44kg (97lb) HE
Users: USA and 24 other countries

The Mk 46 programme was launched during 1960 when the need to supersede the obsolescent Mk 44 became fully apparent. The Mk 44 had not long been in service, but the threat posed to US Navy battle groups by a new generation of deeper-diving, faster and quieter Soviet submarines made it imperative that a more capable counterweapon be developed without delay. Thus there appeared the Mk 46, without doubt numerically and tactically the most important anti-submarine torpedo currently fielded by the Western nations and their allies. The original Mk 46 Mod 0 began to enter service in 1966, and differs from its successors in having a solid-propellant motor. This variant is 2,667mm (105.0in) long and weighs 258kg (568lb). The Mk 46 has been developed in several variants, the next of which was the Mk 46 Mod 1, which was introduced in 1967 with an Otto monopropellant engine because the solid-fuel motor of the Mk 46 Mod 0 had proved difficult to service. The Mk 46 Mod 4 is based on the Mk 46 Mods 1 and 2, but is fitted only in the Mk 60 CAPTOR (enCAPsulated TORpedo) anti-submarine weapon moored on the seabed at choke points on submarine transit routes. After it

has entered the water and discarded its retarding parachute, the Mk 44 is designed to initiate a helical search pattern, acquiring the target at a maximum range estimated at 595m (650 yards) before closing in for the kill. Though the Mk 46 is now a somewhat elderly design by the standards of this fast-developing technology, the onboard guidance system is sufficiently advanced to direct the weapon in repeated attacks in the event that the first attack fails. The most modern version of the family is the Mk 46 Mod 5 NEARTIP. This is a much-modified version developed by Honeywell to provide the weapon with a continued capability against Soviet submarines wearing 'Clusterguard' anechoic coatings to reduce their sonar reflection by some 33%. NEARTIP (NEAR-Term Improvement Program) torpedoes have been produced as such or converted from older weapons, and feature improved motors and control units, upgraded guidance systems for repeated attacks and, as a means of reducing the effect of 'Clusterguard' coatings, more senstive sonar transducers.

Below: Dropping a Mk 46 from an SH-2F Seasprite. The lanyard automatically deploys the parachute canopy.

Mk 50 Barracuda

Origin: Honeywell, Hopkins
Propulsion: one stored chemical energy propulsion system with a Garrett closed-cycle steam turbine driving a pump-jet
Dimensions: length 2,896mm (114.0in); diameter 324mm (12.75in)
Weight: 363kg (800lb)
Performance: speed more than 40kt (74km/h); range 13,715m (45,000ft); diving limit 600m (1,970ft)
Warhead: shaped-charge HE
Users: to be US Navy and probably NATO countries

The Mk 50 Barracuda is an advanced weapon entering production in 1987 after development from 1975 as the Advanced Light-Weight Torpedo. The ALWT was planned specifically as successor to the Mk 46 series (including the Mk 46 Mod 5 NEARTIP), and is thus designed for ship and aircraft (both fixed- and rotary-wing) launch platforms. The weapon is intended to counter the latest fast-running, deep-diving Soviet submarines, and as such can be considered the American counterpart to the British Sting Ray torpedo.

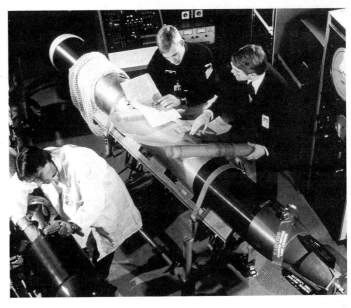

Capabilities demanded of the new weapon, in comparison with those of the Mk 46, were greater range, speed and maximum depth (all needed for attacks on the latest types of Soviet submarine) plus improved active/passive sonar capability allied to an extremely advanced computer guidance system. The Mk 50 should enter service in about 1990, and noteworthy aspects of the design are a good depth capability (though still not to the depths attainable by the

Above: Honeywell and US Navy personnel during acceptance testing of a prototype Mk 50 Barracuda. Note the absence of propellers; this torpedo is driven by a sea-water pump jet system.

latest Soviet submarines) without loss of range, and a self-adaptive guidance system based on the AYK-14 digital computer to allow minimum-energy interceptions and the possibility of multiple attacks.

GUIDED WEAPONS

The first aerial guided missiles were developed in World War I, but only for use against surface or naval targets. The concept of the AAM (air-to-air missile) had hardly dawned at the start of World War II, largely because of the extreme difficulty of developing a workable system. The first to be attempted – and they were built in large numbers and very nearly deployed in service – were the German Hs 298 and X-4. Both had basic shortcomings, and post-war research by the victorious Allies concentrated initially on radar guidance of missiles capable of flying at supersonic speed to intercept enemy aircraft. Almost all had SARH (semi-active radar homing), in which the target aircraft is 'illuminated' by the radar of the missile-armed fighter, and its missiles home on the radiation which they can detect being scattered or reflected back from the target.

A few AAMs had active radar, being equipped with their own radar transmitter with which they could lock-on to the target aircraft. This demands a very large, heavy and expensive missile, which in turn needs a large fighter. Moreover, it is difficult for such a large missile to lock-on to the correct target at the limit of its effective range, and there is often a need for some kind of mid-course guidance, followed by very careful IFF (identification friend or foe) locks to ensure, first, that the missile does lock-on to the enemy aircraft, and second, that it can never lock-on to a friendly one. It is also essential for the SARH missiles always to have receivers precisely coded to reject all radar signals except those emanating from its own launch aircraft. Were this not the case, errant AAMs could home on friendly aircraft that find themselves caught in hostile radars!

In 1950-51 two close-range missile families were in final development in the USA which were to have a major influence on future AAM design. One, the GAR-1 (AIM-4) Falcon, was not only small, fast and agile, but it was developed in many forms with different guidance systems. Some of the Falcons were IR-homing missiles; in other words, they homed on the heat emitted by enemy aircraft. The other missile, GAR-8 (AIM-9) Sidewinder, represented a major technical and economic breakthrough. No longer was each missile a large and impressively costly package of high-technology engineering. Though Sidewinder lacked little in quality control, its basic concept was 'Make it simple and cheap'. This in turn promised to be a route to reliability, as well as capturing world markets.

Sidewinder was little more than a piece of piping, of 5in (127mm) diameter, stabilized in flight by four fins each

Above: Short-range AAMs such as these AIM-9L Sidewinders on a Sea Harrier have autonomous capability once launched, and thus provide useful offensive and defensive capability on all types of aircraft.

Left: A neat contrast of old and new, the former epitomized by the Lightning F.Mk 6 with the limited AA armament of two Firestreak AAMs, and the latter characterized by the Phantom FGR.Mk 2 with the altogether more impressive fit of four Sparrows and four Sidewinders.

Above right: An older solution to the air interception problem was the AIR-2 Genie, a massive unguided rocket with command-detonated nuclear warhead. Together with its launch platform, the F-106, the Genie is now disappearing from service.

Right: The basic design of the Sidewinder may now be getting on for 40 years old, but constant development has kept the missile well up to the forefront of AAM technology. This is a launch from a USMC F/A-18 Hornet.

incorporating a slipstream-driven flywheel (called a Rolleron). The rear section housed the simple solid rocket motor. Amidships was a blast/fragment warhead. Near the nose was a section carrying four control fins, spaced at 90° round the missile, driven by gas pressure from a solid-fuel generator. These fins could be swivelled to steer the missile instantly in any direction. Right in the nose was a IR (infra-red) seeker cell, extremely sensitive to any heat radiation falling on it. The cell was mounted at the focus of a gimbal-mounted optical telescope inside the transparent nose of the missile, so that any IR 'seen' by the missile would be magnified and focussed on the sensitive cell (which in most versions of the missile was cooled to increase its sensitivity). The principle of operation was that the optical system would be steered to focus the incoming IR radiation on the seeker cell, and the angular movement of the optics would be magnified and used to tell the control system how to steer the missile.

Any IR-homing missile has several major advantages over a radar homer. One is that, as it is passive (non-emitting), its approach cannot be detected by the enemy, who also need have no warning of being picked up by any hostile radar or other emitting system. Most important of all, the SARH missiles demand illumination of the target all the time the missile is in flight, right up to final closure and interception of the target. As fighter radars are nose-mounted, this means that the fighter, even though it may have identified the enemy aircraft long before and launched its missile, still has to keep on suicidally flying towards the enemy, whilst broadcasting its presence with a powerful radar. No surer way could be devised of getting one's self shot down.

In contrast, the IR-homer is a passive weapon of what is called the 'fire and forget' type. The moment it has positively locked-on to the the enemy it can be launched; and the moment it has been launched it can be forgotten. The fighter can at once turn away and start engaging a fresh target, secure in the knowledge that the previous missile will home on its target by itself. Of course, early IR homers tried to home on the Sun, or on the Sun's reflection in a lake or greenhouse, or on many other sources of heat. They were also often erratic in their behaviour, and failed to achieve positive lock unless fired from close range directly astern of a target aircraft in full afterburner, presenting an ideal juicy target. Today's IR-homing AAMs are hundreds of times more sensitive and discriminatory. Their guidance systems use newer sensitive materials, better optics and special devices to make the missile ignore all radiation except that actually emitted by the target. And no aircraft, no matter how cunningly it may be designed according to stealth principles, can avoid emitting IR radiation in proportion to the power of its engines.

The latest IR-homing AAMs are even able to home on enemy aircraft from dead ahead, or from any other angle. Known as all-aspect missiles, they have already – in the Falklands campaign, for example – racked up an impressive record of kills. Whereas in the Vietnam war many AAMs scored a kill ratio as low as from 8 to 26 per cent – in other words, at times, out of 100 AAMs fired, 92 failed to bring down the target – the AIM-9L Sidewinder in the Falklands scored 77 per cent (20 kills out of 26 firings). And, compared with what can be achieved today, the AIM-9L is a very old and outdated missile, though still one of the best in service.

In the author's view, the passive fire-and-forget yet positively locked-on IR missile, or a possible successor using some other wavelength such as the optics of the human eye, will continue to offer such advantages over all active systems that it must remain the preferred type. Nevertheless, major customers ouch as the US Air Force and Navy continue to favour the radar-guided missile for longer-range interception, though in improved forms. Some are very sensibly designed to home on emissions in RF (radio frequency) bands from the enemy aircraft. The simplest target on which to home is obviously the enemy's main radar, but most combat aircraft (other than stealth designs) offer numerous emitters, any of which could in most circumstances provide acceptable homing signals. Most future AAMs under development, of which details are known, carry receivers coded to radars carried either in the launching fighter or in the missile itself.

145

GUIDED WEAPONS

Piranha, MAA-1

Origin: CTA Instituto de Atividades Espaciais; production by D.F. Vasconcelos Co
Propulsion: solid motor from Army Imbel Piquete plant
Dimensions: length 2,720mm (107in); body diameter 150mm (5.9in); fin span 652mm (25.7in)
Weight: at launch 86kg (190lb)
Performance: speed over Mach 2; range 16km (10 miles)

Below: A drawing of the underside of the long-bodied Shenyang J-8 I fighter, showing installation of two drop tanks and two PL-2 air-to-air missiles. The PL-2A is similar but has a later IR seeker with a tapered nose.

Warhead: HE 12kg (26.5lb)
User: Brazil

The Brazilian air force (originally partnered by the army and navy which both withdrew in 1977) has been developing this AAM since early 1976. Its homing head has a cooled IR detector, and the auto-pilot uses proportional navigation applied via canard controls. The warhead has DA and proximity fuzes.

The first captive trials on a Xavante took place in 1983, followed by live firing from an F-5E in 1985. The missile is broadly similar to a 'second generation' Sidewinder, though body diameter is greater. The Piranha is to be used on Brazil's version of the AMX.

CAA-2

This missile, currently known only by its American designation, is virtually the Chinese version of the European AIM-132A ASRAAM. At least it looks outwardly similar, for it is a wingless dogfight AAM with rear control fins. It exists in IR and SARH forms, and has been seen in service on the J-7 fighter. Details and name remain unknown.

PL-2 (Pili 2)

Origin: exported by CPMIEC, Beijing
Propulsion: smokeless solid rocket motor
Dimensions: length 2,880mm (110in); body diameter 120mm (4.72in); fin span 530mm (20.9in)
Weight: 70kg (154lb)
Performance: speed Mach 2; range 5-7.8km (3.1-4.85 miles)
Warhead: 11.3kg (25lb)
Users: China (AF and Navy) and export customers

First seen in the mid-1960s, the Pili 2 is the Chinese copy of the Soviet K-13A (SB-06), itself deriv-

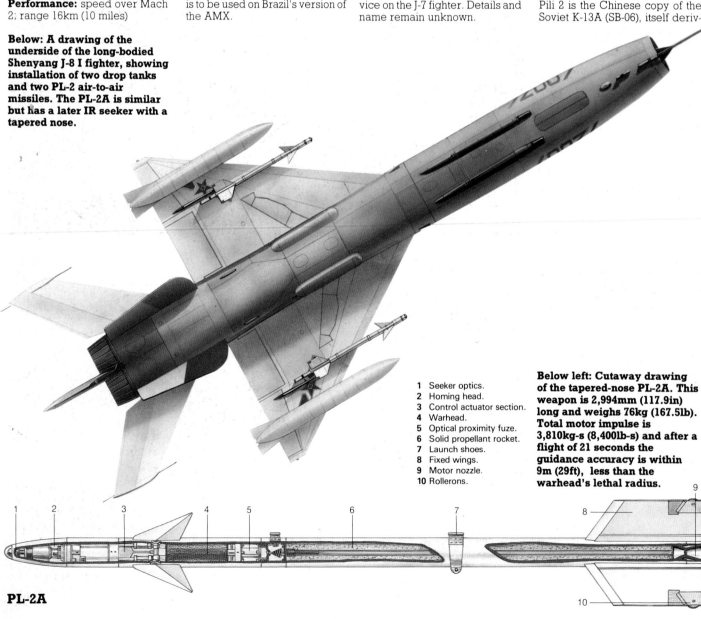

1. Seeker optics.
2. Homing head.
3. Control actuator section.
4. Warhead.
5. Optical proximity fuze.
6. Solid propellant rocket.
7. Launch shoes.
8. Fixed wings.
9. Motor nozzle.
10. Rollerons.

Below left: Cutaway drawing of the tapered-nose PL-2A. This weapon is 2,994mm (117.9in) long and weighs 76kg (167.5lb). Total motor impulse is 3,810kg-s (8,400lb-s) and after a flight of 21 seconds the guidance accuracy is within 9m (29ft), less than the warhead's lethal radius.

PL-2A

AIR-TO-AIR MISSILES

ed from AIM-9B Sidewinder. At first called CAA-1 by NATO, it has been produced in large numbers, giving way in the 1970s to Pili-2A (PL-2A) with an improved IR seeker giving greater lock-on range of up to 10km (6.2 miles).

PL-5B (Pili 5B)

Origin: exported by CATIC, Beijing
Propulsion: advanced solid motor
Dimensions: length 2,892mm (113.9in); body diameter 127mm (5in); fin span 657mm (25.87in)
Weight: 85kg (187.4lb)
Performance: burn-out speed Mach 4.5; maximum range 16km (10 miles)
Warhead: blast/fragmentation with IR fuze or continuous-rod with RF fuze, lethal radius 10m (33ft)
User: China

Disclosed in 1986, this AAM appears essentially to be a copy of AIM-9L and similar long-span models of Sidewinder, even to the point of having the same body diameter. Seeker refrigeration is by compressed air (not nitrogen), and the dead zone around the Sun is given as 16°. The Pili 5B is in service on 'a variety of aircraft'.

PL-7 (Pili 7)

No data have yet been published for this AAM, which combines PL-2A basic design with the aerodynamics of Matra Magic. It has cropped delta canard fins, closely followed by Magic-shape fixed fins downstream. Several features of the body also correspond with those of the French missile. Lock-on within the entire rear hemisphere can be achieved between range limits of 500m (1,640ft) and 14.4km (9 miles). The warhead weighs 12kg (26.45lb).

Above: With growing confidence the People's Republic aircraft industry is showing off its wares in the West. This PL-2A was mounted on the Xian FT-7 Airguard advanced trainer (derived from the MiG-21) at the 1987 Paris airshow.

Right: PL-7 missiles displayed with a Nanchang A-5C attack aircraft (plus tanks and rocket launchers).

Below: Portrait of the PL-5B. This missile can sustain a 30g turn, and the warhead lethal radius is in all cases well in excess of 10m (33ft).

Magic

1 IR homing head.
2 Guidance electronics.
3 Rate gyro.
4 Umbilical.
5 Battery.
6 Launcher adapter.
7 Motor.
8 Leading-edge sawcut.
9 Motor nozzle.
10 Warhead.
11 Proximity fuze.
12 Control surface.
13 Actuator.
14 Fixed winglet.

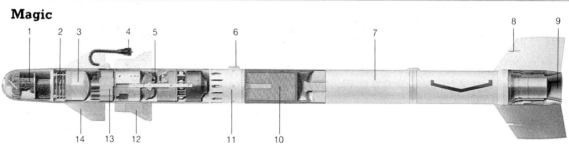

Left: The shapes and proportions of a Magic look quite different seen from almost end-on. The carrier aircraft is a delta-wing Mirage.

Above: Cutaway of a Magic, so arranged that aerodynamic surfaces are seen squared-on, not at 45°. Bright colours are used for clarity.

FRANCE

Magic, R.550

Origin: SA Matra, Vélizy-Villacoublay
Propulsion: SNPE Romeo (Magic 1) or Richard (Magic 2) Butalane high-impulse solid motor
Dimensions: length 2,770mm (109in); body diameter 157mm (6.2in); span 668mm (26.3in)
Weight: at launch 89.8kg (198lb)

Performance: speed about Mach 3; range 0.32-10km (0.2-6.2 miles)
Warhead: conventional rod/fragmentation, 12.5kg (27.6lb) with all-sector proximity fuze or impact-loop detonation
Users: total of 16 countries by late 1986; not listed by Matra but including Abu Dhabi, Argentina, Ecuador, Egypt, France, Greece, India, Iraq, Kuwait, Libya, Oman, Pakistan, Saudi Arabia, South Africa, Syria and United Arab Emirates

Alone among European companies Matra took on the Sidewinder in head-on competition and has not merely achieved technical success but has also

IOC was reached in 1975, since when production at Salbris built up to 100 per month. Unit price is in the order of $15,000, and about 8,000 rounds have been delivered.

In 1984 production switched to the Magic 2. This has a new motor (see data) and a more sensitive multi-element IR seeker giving all-aspect engagement capability. The head can be slaved to the radar of the Mirage 2000 as an alternative to autonomous operation. The warhead has a new proximity fuze. Several countries (mainly Mirage 2000 customers) have ordered Magic 2.

MICA

Origin: SA Matra, Vélizy-Villacoublay
Propulsion: advanced solid motor with TVC
Dimensions: length 3,110mm (122in); diameter 152mm (6in)
Weight: 110kg (243lb)
Performance: burn-out speed Mach 4; range 'from a few hundred metres to 50km (31 miles)'
Warhead: advanced conventional
User: France (and probably widespread exports)

The Missile d'Interception et de Combat Aérien is fully funded by the French goverment and is planned as the most important AAM for the period after 1993. In almost every respect it promises to be an outstanding missile, combining virtually all the capabilities of ASRAAM and AMRAAM and in some ways being superior to both.

Aerodynamically, MICA has wings of extremely low aspect ratio, forming mere strakes along the sides of the body. The distinctive control fins at the rear are for use at extreme range after motor burn-out, control during powered flight being by TVC using a motor jet-deflection system. In the dogfight mode the missile is locked-on before launch, and has outstanding power of manoeuvre (exceeding the 50g of Magic) from the moment of laun-

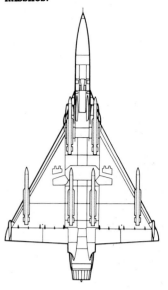

Below: The future standard air-to-air armament of the Mirage 2000 will be six MICA missiles.

ch, to pull round to engage a target in almost any direction other than astern of the launch aircraft. There is a choice between an advanced multi-cell IR seeker and an active radar, in each case 'fully protected against enemy countermeasures'. At medium and longer ranges the MICA cruises under a strapdown inertial system, with a receiver for a target update from the launch fighter if this is necessary. Without a data-link update the mid-course guidance continues until, near the target, the missile switches on its own seeker. MICA has a multi-target capability, and even the IR version is described as all-weather.

The first proof of concept round was fired in October 1982, and full developement started in 1985. MICA is also the basis for ground-to-air and ship-to-air versions, and is expected to arm the Mirage 2000 (six missiles), Rafale B ACT and ACM versions, and probably fighters of foreign design.

Below: MICA has wings of extremely low aspect ratio (essentially strakes), and control surfaces at the tail of unusual shape.

established export customers and an output rate exceeding that of any other AAM ever produced in Western Europe. Wisely the weapon was made installationally interchangeable with Sidewinder, but the design requirements were greater than those of presently available versions of the US missile, including launch anywhere within a 140° rear hemisphere at all heights up to 18,000m (59,000ft) and with limitations at higher altitudes; ability to snap-fire at ranges down to 300m (984ft); ability to fire from a launch platform flying at any speed (no minimum) up to over 1,300km/h (808mph) whilst pulling up to 6g; ability to pull 50g in manoeuvres; and ability to cross in front of the launch aircraft only 50m (164ft) ahead.

The IR guidance uses the SAT AD.3601, the PbS seeker being cooled prior to launch by a liquid nitrogen bottle in the launch rail. Its output drives the electric control section with four canard fins stationed immediately downstream of four fixed fins with the same span as the tips of the controls. The tail fins are free to rotate around the nozzle. Propulsion is by an SNPE Romeo single-stage composite-DB motor which gives high acceleration for 1.9sec. The warhead weighs 12.5kg (27.6lb), of which half is the explosive charge detonated

Above: An extraordinary amount of smoke attends the firing of a Magic 2, in this case from a Mirage 2000 of EC 1/2 escadre.

by IR proximity and DA fuzes.

Matra began development as a company venture in 1968, receiving an air ministry contract in 1969. After various simpler air trials a missile with guidance was fired from a Meteor of the CEL against a CT-20 target in a tight turn on 11 January 1972. On 30 November 1973 a Magic was fired from a Mirage III in an extreme test of manoeuvrability.

GUIDED WEAPONS

Above: SA 342M Gazelle helicopters of the French ALAT (army light aviation) will in future carry twin launch tubes for Mistral snapshoot

IR-homing missiles. These versatile weapons can be used against a variety of targets, including most types of aircraft.

Below: Mistral has a 'sharp pencil' type nose, four small flick-out fins and a double row of IR fuze windows around the forebody.

Mistral

Origin: SA Matra, Vélizy-Villacoublay
Propulsion: boost/sustain solid rocket motor
Dimensions: length 1,880mm (70.9in); diameter 90mm (3.54in)
Weight: 17kg (38lb)
Performance: speed Mach 2.6; range 300-6,000m (1,000ft-3.7 miles)
Warhead: 3kg (6.6lb)
User: France plus exports

This neat missile is the air-launched version of the SATCP (French initials for surface-to-air, short range), a very advanced tube-launched weapon of fire-and-forget type. AATCP, named Mistral, is almost the same round but fired from a twin-tube launcher with flick-open eyelid nose doors. It is carried by helicopters either for self-defence or as an aggressive air-combat weapon. The IR seeker, which has multiple flat transparent panes like those of the Firestreak, can be cued onto the target before launch, and its scanning pattern is also pre-selectable. The helicopter turns away immediately the missile is fired, the Mistral thereafter accelerating very rapidly to cover 3km (1.86 miles) in 5 seconds whilst manoeuvring to destroy a target pulling 8g. The warhead has a laser proximity fuze. Depending on mission and other stores helicopters can carry up to eight Mistrals, ready for instant firing using a roof or mast sight, or a helmet sight.

R.530

Origin: SA Matra, Vélizy-Villacoublay
Propulsion: Hotchkiss-Brandt/SNPE Antoinette motor with Plastargol filling (8,500kg/18,740lb boost for 2.7 sec followed by 6.5 sec sustain) or SNPE Madeleine with Isolane propellant giving higher performance.
Dimensions: length (radar) 3,284mm (129.3in), (IR) 3,198mm (125.9in); body diameter 263mm (10.35in); span 1,103mm (43.43in)
Weight: at launch (radar) 192kg (423.3lb), (IR) 193.5kg (426.6lb)
Performance: speed Mach 2.7; range 18km (11 miles)
Warhead: Hotchkiss-Brandt, two types each of 27kg (60lb), either pre-fragmented or continuous rod; both proximity and DA fuzed
Users: Argentina, Australia, Brazil, Colombia, France, Iraq, Israel, Lebanon, Pakistan, South Africa, Spain, Venezuela (many no longer active, and most in process of replacement)

In 1957 work began on this completely new weapon which has enjoyed a long life. Abandoning twist-and-steer, Matra reverted to cruciform delta wings and tail controls, two of the wings having ailerons for roll control. Having experience of various guidance systems, the air ministry and Matra still could not make up their minds and at first conducted trial firings with either SARH or IR homing. Both types became established in production and the R.530 can be carried in pairs, one missile being a heat-homer with an infra-red seeker and the other a radar-homer.

The two homing heads, which can if necessary be exchanged by a user squadron to suit circumstances on operations, are the SAT AD.3501 infra-red seeker, claimed to have all-aspect capability including head-on, and the EMD AD.26 matched to the Cyrano IV radar of the Mirage F1. A slightly different receiver is used by the Aéronavale for missiles carried by the F-8E(FN) Crusader, with APQ-94 radar.

Though an indifferent performer, with an unimpressive record of firing trials, R.530 had no evident rival and cleaned up a 14-nation market with some 4,400 rounds sold at termination in 1980, at a typical price of $44,000.

For many years SA Matra considered various improved versions and updates, but in the event the company wisely decided to scrap the R.530 entirely and start again with a completely 'new generation' missile which has today matured as the Super 530 family. This is described in the next entry.

Below: Two elderly Mirage IIIE attack fighters of the 13th Wing, that on the right being armed with a Matra R.530 AAM (the other has an Armat anti-radar ASM).

Super 530

Origin: SA Matra, Vélizy-Villacoublay
Propulsion: SNPE Angèle Butalane high-impulse (composite CTPB) solid motor, 2-second boost and 4-second sustain
Dimensions: length 3,540mm (139.4in); body diameter 263mm (10.35in); span (wing) 500mm (19.7in), (tail) 900mm (35.43in)
Weight: (530F) 250kg (551lb), (530D) 265kg (584lb)
Performance: speed Mach 4.6; range (530F) 35km (22 miles), (530D) over 40km (25 miles)
Warhead: Thomson-Brandt fragmentation, 30kg (66lb)
Users: not announced but export orders from 10 countries including Mirage 2000 customers

By January 1971, when development of this missile started, Matra was a mature AAM producer able to take a studied look at the requirements and secure in the knowledge that R.530 would probably remain in production almost a further decade. Though to a slight degree based on the R.530, as reflected in the designation, this is in fact a totally new missile marking very large advances in flight performance and offering doubled acquisition distance and effective range and also introducing snap-up capability of 7,600m (25,000ft), since increased to 9,000m (29,500ft), believed to exceed that of any other AAM other than Phoenix.

From the start only one method of guidance has been associated with Super 530, SARH. This uses the EMD Super AD.26, matched with the Cyrano IV radar of the Mirage F1. Electric power comes from a silver/zinc battery with 60-sec operation. Thomson-Brandt developed the Angèle propulsion motor, with Butalane composite propellant of much higher specific impulse than that of earlier French motors. This can accelerate the missile rapidly to Mach 4.6, thereafter sustaining approximately this speed to sustainer burnout. Wings are not necessary at this speed, but Super 530 does have four wings of very low aspect ratio, manoeuvring by the cruciform of tail fins which have an unusual shape. It can pull 20g up to 17,000m (56,000ft) and 6g at 25,000m (82,000ft).

The homing head was test-flown in September 1972, and an inert missile airframe was air-launched in July 1973. Firing trials from a Canberra of the CEV began in 1974, progressing to trials with guidance in 1975. Firing trials from a Mirage F1 C began at Cazaux in 1976, and evaluation firing at CEAM was initiated during 1975, targets in 1978 including the supersonic Beech AQM-37A.

Super 530F, the version for the Mirage F1, entered service in December 1979, and more than 1,490 rounds had been ordered by late 1986. In 1985 production began on the Super 530D (D for Doppler) matched to the RDI radar of the Mirage 2000. This version has improved snap-down performance and is claimed to be a true all-weather, all-sector, all-altitude AAM.

Below: Side elevation of the Super 530 (both versions generally similar).

Bottom: Mirage 2000 from Les Cigognes squadron with two Super 530D and two Magic 2.

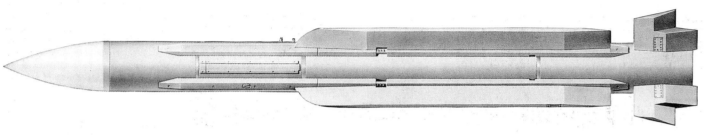

Python 3

Origin: Rafael Armament Development Authority
Propulsion: Rafael solid motor
Dimensions: length 3,000mm (118in); body diameter 160mm (6.25in); fin span 860mm (33.9in)
Weight: 120kg (264.5lb)
Performance: claimed superior in speed, turn radius and range to AIM-9L Sidewinder (range 0.5-15km/0.3-9.3 miles)
Warhead: conventional rod-type, 11kg (24lb)
User: Israel

First exhibited at the 1981 Paris air show, this AAM has been developed as a successor to Shafrir 2, and is claimed to surpass its predecessor in all respects. Rafael is responsible for most parts of Python 3 including the new IR seeker cell (housed in a slightly tapering forebody), which is claimed to have exceptional sensitivity and a wider look-angle than that of most other IR-homing missiles (it is described as an all-aspect weapon). The delta canard controls are large, as are the fixed tailfins which are sharply swept on both leading and trailing edges, and which carry roll-control aerodynamic surfaces and slipstream-driven rollerons. The Python 3 can be operated in a choice of boresight, uncaged or radar-slaved modes, and in combat over the Lebanon in 1983 achieved results 'comparable with the AIM-9L'.

Above: Rafael call the Python 3 canard controls the fins (620mm span), the rear fins being called wings. The rollerons pivot freely.

Below: Close-up of the Python 3 homing head, showing the Cassegrain type optical telescope for focussing the heat on the sensor.

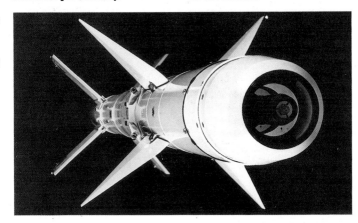

Right: A corresponding view of the earlier Shafrir, which had a generally similar telescope system.

Below: Cutaway drawing of the Rafael Shafrir. As in other cutaways, bright colours are used for high contrast.

Bottom: An IAI Kfir C7 of the Israeli air force with six Mk 82 bombs, two tanks and two Shafrir AAMs which are carried for self-defence.

1 IR-transparent cap.
2 Cassegrain telescope.
3 IR seeker cell.
4 IR fuze windows.
5 Circuit boards.
6 Guidance electronics.
7 Canard controls.
8 Actuator for horizontal (pitch) canards.
9 Warhead.
10 Cross-section of solid motor propellant.
11 Fin.
12 Rolleron.

Shafrir

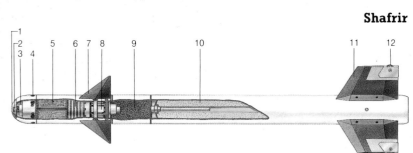

Users: Chile, Israel, South Africa, Taiwan, and from four to 10 other (undisclosed) countries

Development of this wholly Israeli AAM, derived by Rafael Armament Development Authority from early Sidewinders, was started in 1961. All models have a Cassegrain optical system behind a large hemispherical nose, pneumatic control fins, and fixed wings indexed in line and containing recessed rollerons similar to those of the Sidewinder. The most fundamental difference introduced with the Israeli weapon is a substantial increase in body diameter. Simplicity was the keynote throughout, and a price of $20,000 has been quoted.

Mk 1 did not complete development, but Mk 2 entered Chel Ha'Avir service in 1969, and in subsequent fighting is credited with the destruction of over 200 aircraft. Of these more than half were destroyed during the brief Yom Kippur war in October 1973, claimed to indicate an SSKP of 60 per cent. Mk 2 is carried on a pylon adapter, which can also carry alternative weapons.

Shafrir

Origin: Rafael Armament Development Authority
Propulsion: solid motor
Dimensions: length 2,470mm (97in); body diameter 160mm (6.3in); span 520mm (20.5in)
Weight: at launch (Mk 2) 93kg (205lb)
Performance: speed supersonic; range 5km (3.1 miles)
Warhead: conventional 11kg (24.3lb) containing 4kg (8.8lb) of explosive plus pre-fragmented bodies, with row of IR fuze windows around nose and also DA fuze

When the seeker locks-on, the pilot is informed both visually and aurally. The Mk 2 homes by lead-collision using proportional navigation. This model is used by the Chel Ha'Avir on Mirages and Kfirs, and also by several export customers. Mk 3 has been under test for several years and has a later guidance and control section; it is called Python 3.

ASRAAM, AIM-132A

Origin: BBG, a consortium led by British Aerospace and Bodensee Gerätetechnik
Propulsion: advanced solid motor
Dimensions: not disclosed but probably smaller than Sidewinder
Weight: probably lighter than typical Sidewinder
Performance: range limits probably to be about 1 to 15km (0.6-9.3 miles); speed over Mach 3
Warhead: probably small
Users: probably to include West Germany, UK, USA and most other NATO countries

The obvious need for a completely new close-range AAM was made more acute by the progressive obsolescence of the AIM-9 family and cancellation of the German Viper and British SRAAM. After years of talking, the decision was taken at Government level to develop an ASRAAM (said as a word, the acronym meaning Advanced Short-Range AAM) in Europe for use by NATO. The memorandum

Below: Dummy ASRAAM and Sky Flash missiles carried by the British Aerospace EAP demonstrator (hoped to lead to the EFA).

of understanding was signed by the USA, France (which has merely a watching brief), the UK and West Germany. Following a 'pre-feasibility' stage which lasted to the end of 1981, the three actively participating governments authorized BAe Dynamics and BGT, the team leaders, to proceed to the feasibility study stage, leading into 1983. Project definition extended through 1986, with engineering development lasting beyond 1990 and production deliveries beginning in 1992. The intention is that AIM-132A shall be made under licence in the USA, despite continued development of Sidewinder.

The programme had its inception in a 1970 British requirement, QC.434, calling for a wholly new and very advanced dogfight AAM. This was met by the British Aerospace Taildog (later called SRAAM), a brilliant and wholly successful AAM which should have been the first member of a family to include SAMs and ASMs. Completely wingless, it was fired from multiple tubes which in a stealth fighter could be internal. TVC (thrust-vector con-

trol), using semaphore-arm spoilers in the motor exhaust, enabled sharp turns to be made from the moment of launching. It was possible to engage targets flying far off alongside the launch aircraft, and one test shot nearly hit the nose of the trials Hunter aricraft! Other features included an advanced IR seeker and pilot helmet sight.

In typically British fashion this worldbeating programme was first reduced to the status of a mere technology demonstrator, in 1975, and finally killed off altogether, just after the demonstration of a swivel-nozzle motor. In its place came the multinational memorandum of understanding, which has contrived to downgrade the technology and progressively add to the timescale and, thus, the overall cost. One of the major crippling factors is the political insistence that ASRAAM must fit existing Sidewinder launchers, precluding tube launch or multiple internal carriage, now or in the future. A second was the choice of tail fin controls in place of TVC with a swivelling nozzle, precluding manoeuvres until the missile has

accelerated well ahead of the launch aircraft. A third questionable choice was cancellation of a superb millimetric-wave active radar seeker, which was completely developed by GEC Marconi Avionics and fully met all the NATO requirements.

Thus by 1992 ASRAAM will hopefully emerge from its chrysalis as a tail-fin missile with IR guidance; and there are still, in 1987, arguments about whether the MSU (missile support unit), needed to refrigerate the seeker, should be on the launcher or in the missile. At least one can hope that the repeated choice of a design solution offering what appears to be a lower technical risk (at the cost of lower performance) will result in continued adherence to costs and schedules, though the latter are hardly demanding when viewed against the timescale hoped for in 1970.

Below: AIM-132A ASRAAM fits the Sidewinder shoe on the side of the Tornado pylon. It should offer good all-aspect performance with low life-cycle costs.

GUIDED WEAPONS

ITALY

Aspide

Origin: Selenia Industrie Elettroniche Associate SpA
Propulsion: solid motor developed from Rocketdyne Mk 38 by Difesa e Spazio
Dimensions: length 3,700mm (145.67in); body diameter 203mm (8in); wing span 1,000mm (39.37in)
Weight: at launch 220kg (485lb)
Performance: speed Mach 4; range 50-100km (31-62 miles)
Warhead: Difesa e Spazio 33kg (72.75lb) fragmentation
User: Italy

Though a wholly Italian development, and the largest single missile programme in the country, this impressive weapon was designed 'to be compatible with

Below: Cutaway drawing of the Selenia Aspide in its AAM version. As usual, colour is used for clarity; for example, 'cut edges' are depicted red. In its SAM version the wings are larger.

Bottom: The F-104S Starfighter interceptors of the AMI (Italian air force) carry both Sparrow and Aspide, interfaces being similar. This one has Aspide 1As fitted.

Aspide (AAM version)

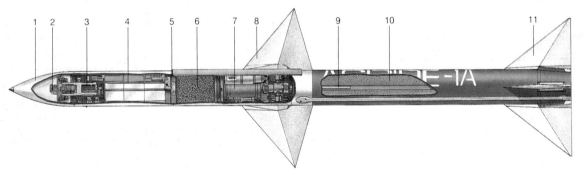

1 Radome.
2 Electroformed radar antenna.
3 Gyro and guidance section.
4 Microwave microelectronics.
5 Main fuze.
6 Warhead.
7 Control power section.
8 Four moving control wings.
9 Igniter.
10 Solid motor.
11 Fixed fins.

154

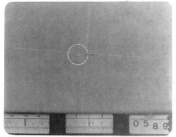

Above: A fine rear view of an F-104S parked on the flightline of the Reparto Sperimentale Volo (flight test establishment) at Pratica di Mare. Both the large AAMs are Aspides. The fuselage pylons, here empty, can carry Sidewinders, as seen in the photograph at the foot of the facing page, for shorter-range engagements.

Above: A dramatic sequence of four (from a greater number) frames from a high-speed ciné film showing a test of an Aspide from Salto di Quirra range. The target was an Aérospatiale CT-20 jet drone (centred in cross). The missile, without warhead, is ringed prior to striking and destroying the target.

systems using Sparrow'. This extends to AAM applications, for which the immediate application is the Italian air force F-104S Starfighter originally tailored to AIM-7E, and several surface-launched applications. The Italian SAM system using this missile is named Spada in its mobile land form, and a different ship-to-air system is named Albatros. Similar to Sparrow in basic configuration, Aspide is powered by an advanced single-stage motor by SNIA-Viscosa Difesa e Spazio (which made the motors for Italian Sparrows) giving higher thrust and a speed of Mach 4 at burn-out. The all-round performance is claimed to exceed that of even AIM-7F, and the guidance is likewise claimed to have significant advantages over that of the American missile. Matched with an I-band monopulse fighter radar, it is said to have greater ECCM capability,

to offer increased snapdown performance, and to be markedly superior at very low altitudes. The seeker aerial system is driven hydraulically. The radome and forebody are described as redesigned for more efficient operation at hypersonic speeds, and in the AAM role the moving wings have extended tips with greater span. The fragmentation warhead is ahead of the wings. Following carry-trials in 1974 and prolonged static testing of the seeker, firing trials at Salto di Quirra, Sardinia, begain in May 1975. By 1977 completely representative Aspide missiles, including the AAM version, had completed qualification firings and production began in 1978. Final verification trials took place in 1979-80. The AAM is replacing Sparrow in the Italian air force, carried by the F-104S ASA. It could also be a possible missile for Italian Tornados.

AAM-1

Origin: Mitsubishi Heavy Industries
Propulsion: solid motor
Dimensions: length 2,600mm (102.4in)
Weight: at launch 70kg (154.3lb)
Performance: speed supersonic; range 7000m (22,966ft)
Warhead: fragmentation
User: Japan (Japan Air Self-Defense Force)

Almost a direct copy of AIM-9E Sidewinder, this AAM was developed in 1960-9 by Mitsubishi Heavy Industries for use by F-86F, F-104J and F-1 fighters of the JASDF. In 1969-71 a total of 330 rounds were delivered and these have subsequently been in the JASDF inventory alongside larger numbers of Sidewinders. AAM-1 is unofficially reported to be slightly shorter (2,600mm/ 102in) and lighter (70kg/154lb) than most Sidewinders, and to have the modest range of 7km (4.3miles).

IR-AAM

As a result of Japan's policy of revealing virtually nothing about its armed forces' weapons, hard information about the IR-AAM (Infra-Red Air-to-Air Missile) is almost totally lacking. In 1981 Mitsubishi Heavy Industries was awarded a contract by the Japan Development Agency's Technical Research and development Institute for the development and pre-production manufacture of this new air-to-air missile. The IR-AAM uses technological experience gained by the company with the AAM-1 and discontinued AAM-2. The latter was a development (1972-79) of the AAM-1 with all-aspect collision-course guidance using an infra-red seeker developed by Nihon Electric. Some 60 AAM-2 development missiles were fired, but the IR-AAM programme now offers usefully greater tactical advantages.

V3 Kukri

Origin: Armscor, Pretoria
Propulsion: 2-stage solid motor
Dimensions: length 2,940mm (115.75in); body diameter 127mm (5in) canard span 420mm (16.53in); tail fin span 530mm (20.9in)
Weight: at launch 73kg (162lb)
Performance: speed Mach 2+; range 300-4,000m (1,000ft-2.5 miles)
Warhead: fragmentation
Users: South Africa and 'selected export customers'

Development of this South African AAM began in 1971, and the initial V3A version went into production in 1975. Though generally similar to earlier dogfight AAMs, and as far as possible compatible with Sidewinder and Magic mechanical and electrical interfaces, V3 has many novel features. The most visible one is that the canard controls are not symmetrical, one plane having simple delta canards and the other (at 90°) having fixed delta canards in front and movable so called 'double delta' controls at the rear. The IR seeker is refrigerated by a compressed clean-air system housed in the launcher and its optics are under a transparent hemisphere. V3 is a twist-and steer missile, the tail fins being free to rotate round the rear of the double-base motor; the delta controls govern roll and the tandem group of surfaces control pitch. The pilot cues the missile using an off-boresight helmet sight for rapid acquisition.

Though V3A is still operational it was replaced in production in 1979 by V3B. This has a helmet sight with wider limits on designation angle, a more sensitive IR seeker with greater look angle and an upgraded motor. V3B immediately went into service on the Mirage III and F1, and since 1982 an export version, known as the Kukri, has been available.

Below: A V3 Kukri, showing the unique asymmetric arrangement of canard control fins and fixed canard fins.

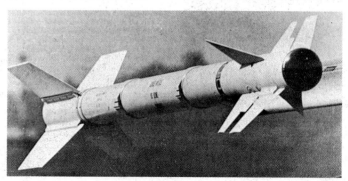

GUIDED WEAPONS

AA-2 'Atoll'

Propulsion: solid motor resembling those used in Sidewinder, nozzle diameter 80mm (3.15in)
Dimensions: length (IR) about 2,800mm (110in), (radar) about 3,100mm (122in); body diameter 120mm (4.72in); span (early AA-2 canard) 450mm (17.7in), (AA-2-2 canard and all tails) 530mm (20.9in)
Weight: at launch (typical) about 70kg (154lb)
Performance: speed about Mach 2.5; range 6.5km (4 miles)
Warhead: blast-fragmentation, 6kg (13.2lb)
Users: include Afghanistan, Algeria, Angola, Bangladesh, Bulgaria, China, Cuba, Czechoslovakia, Egypt, East Germany, Finland, India, Iraq, Laos, Libya, Morocco (stored), Mozambique, North Korea, Peru, Poland, Romania, Somalia, Soviet Union, Syria, Uganda, Vietnam, Yemen (both), Yugoslavia

Right: A Sukhoi Su-22 'Fitter-J' attack aircraft of the Libyan Arab Air Force photographed by the US Navy in 1981. It is carrying two K-13A (AA-2 'Atoll') AAMs.

Below: This Libyan MiG-23MS 'Flogger-E' fighter was photographed on the same occasion in August 1981. All four of its missiles are of the short-nosed regular AA-2 type with infra-red seeker.

Unlike most Soviet weapons this AAM is beyond doubt a copy of a Western original, the early AIM-9B Sidewinder. When first seen on 9 June 1961, carried by various fighters in an air display, it was almost identical to the US weapon. Since then it has followed its own path of development, and like Sidewinder has diversified into IR and SARH versions. Body diameter is even less than that of Sidewinder, and so far as is known all the IR models have the nose-to-tail sequence of AIM-9B. The 6.0kg (13.2lb) warhead is a BF type with smooth exterior.

Believed to be designated K-13A or SB-06 in the Soviet Union, several early versions have been built in very large numbers as standard AAM for most models of MiG-21, which carry two on large adapter shoes (which house the seeker cooling system in later models) on the underwing pylons. Licence production by the MiG complex of Hindustan Aeronautics has been in progress since the early 1970s (it is thought for the Indian air force only, the navy using the Matra Magic). In addition, virtually the same missile is (or was) produced in China, as the Pili-2 (which see).

About 1972 it became evident that a second and much longer version of the missile was in use. This received the NATO designation AA-2-2 'Advanced Atoll', though there is no evidence that it is actually more advanced in design. The extra length is combined with an opaque conical nose, and it has long been assumed (or known) that this is the SARH version, the extra length being occupied by the radar receiver and antenna system. Of course, this version cannot be carried except by aircraft with a compatible target-illuminating radar. Surprisingly, 'Atolls' have not been identified with different improved shapes of canard fin, as has Sidewinder. Production probably ceased about 1977, when the AA-8 'Aphid' began to enter service in quantity.

AA-3 'Anab'

Propulsion: probably solid motor
Dimensions: length (both versions) about 3,600mm (142in); body diameter 280mm (11in); span 1,300mm (51in)
Weight: at launch about 275kg (600lb)
Performance: speed about Mach 2.5; range (IR) about 19km (12 miles), (radar) at least 24km (15 miles)
Warhead: unknown but probably large
Users: include East Germany (not operational), Soviet Union

This second-generation AAM was the first large long-range all-weather missile to reach the PVO, which it did at about the time dummy examples were displayed carried by an early Yak-28P interceptor at Tushino at the 1961 Soviet Aviation Day display. At that time it was at first thought by the West to be an ASM, but it was eventually identified as an AAM carried in both IR and SARH versions usually one of each. The carriers are the Yak-28P (in all versions except trainers), Su-11 and Su-15/21. All these aircraft have the radar called 'Skip Spin' by NATO, a much more capable installation than those associated with the earlier AAMs and probably derived from the Scan Three fitted to the Yak-25. Believed to be designated RP-11, it operates in I-band between 8,690/8,995 MHz at peak power of 200 kW, with a PRF of 2,700/3,000pps and pulse-width of about 0.5 microsec. It is assumed that CW illumination is provided for missile homing.

This missile has four very large rear wings, whose narrow-chord trailing-edge controls are probably ailerons. Thus the canard surfaces, indexed in the same plane as the wings, move as two pairs for pitch and yaw only.

By early 1987 there was no information on either type of homing head, the motor has a single central nozzle, and may have boost-sustainer portions, and the warhead is amidships, with a proximity fuze. An AA-3-2

Above: Airbrakes open, this Sukhoi Su-21 'Flagon-F' is armed with AA-3s outboard and small AA-8s inboard.

'Advanced Anab' has been identified since 1972, but how it is 'advanced' has not become public. The Yak-28P is believed to have been withdrawn to reserve and training units, and the Su-11 is also gradually being phased out of first-line PVO service, but this missile remains the primary armament of the Su-21 deployed in large but dwindling numbers by the Soviet Union in 1971-4.

AA-5 'Ash'

Propulsion: probably solid motor
Dimensions: length (IR) 5,500mm (216.5in), (radar) 5,200mm (204.7in); diameter 305mm (12in); span 1,300mm (51in)
Weight: at launch about 390kg (860lb)
Performance: speed about Mach 3; range (IR) about 21km (13 miles), (radar) about 55km (35 miles)
Warhead: unknown but probably large, perhaps 45kg (100lb)
User: Soviet Union

This large AAM was developed in 1954-9 specifically to arm the Tu-28P long-range all-weather interceptor, and genuine missiles were seen carried by a development aircraft of this family at the 1961 Aviation Day display at Tushino. (This aircraft had a very large ventral bathtub believed to house side-looking or early-warning radar, not seen subsequently.) Early versions of Tu-28P, at first mistakenly reported

Above right: The giant Tupolev 'Fiddler' normally carries IR-homing AA-5 missiles on the inboard pylons and the radar type outboard.

Right: A row of AA-5 missiles, apparently all of the semi-active radar species, about to be loaded aboard Tu-128 'Fiddler' interceptors.

as 'Blinder' but corrected to 'Fiddler', carried two of these missiles on underwing pylons.

So far as one can tell, they were SARH guided, associated with the 'Big Nose' radar of the carrier aircraft, a very large and powerful I-band radar which had no counterpart operational in the West until the AWG-9 of 1974. The missile is matched to the radar in scale, being larger than any Western AAM. For many years Western estimates of AA-5 range were ludicrously low, but they are creeping up and may now be about half the true value for the radar version. This missile has giant delta wings indexed in line with four tail controls.

Early Tu-28Ps are thought to have entered PVO service soon after 1961, filling in gaps around the Soviet Union's immense frontier. By 1965 the Tu-128 was being armed with the newly introduced IR version of this missile. This aircraft has four underwing pylons carrying the IR version, with Cassegrain optics behind a small nose window, on the inners and the SARH model, with opaque (usually red-painted) conical nose on the outers. Early versions of MiG-25 'Foxbat' interceptor were also armed with this missile, usually one of each type. It is not known whether these aircraft also had 'Big Nose' or an early model of 'Fox Fire' radar. This large but obsolescent weapon remains in the IA-PVO inventory as the standard armament of the Tu-128 Fiddler, the production aircraft, which (despite repeated rumours of an interceptor version of the Tu-22 'Blinder') has no known replacement offering the same combat radius.

AA-7 'Apex'

Propulsion: advanced boost/sustain solid motor
Dimensions: length (radar, only known version) 4,600mm (181in); body diameter (front) 195mm (7.7in), (main section) 223mm (8.8in); span 1,050mm (41.4in)
Weight: at launch about 320kg (705lb)
Performance: speed about Mach 3; range (radar) estimated from 15-35km (9.3-21.75 miles)
Warhead: 40kg (88lb)
Users: include Czechoslovakia, East Germany, India, Libya, Soviet Union, and an increasing number of other countries

This important missile is aerodynamically slightly similar to the AA-5 'Ash'. Indeed it has been suggested it is a successor, though it is considerably slimmer and much smaller. The large cylindrical body rides on four large delta wings and four rear control fins indexed in line around the nozzle of the motor. The newer weapon is, however, somewhat smaller, and has a totally different front end. Curiously, the body diameter is reduced over almost the first metre from the tip of the nose, so the guidance section has to fit in a constricted portion.

Though this family of missiles has been seen on the MiG-25, it is chiefly used to arm the MiG-23MF (but not the MiG-23MS export version which has a non-compatible radar). There is an IR version, designated R-23T, and an SARH type designated R-23R.

While a smaller diameter may not reduce IR seeker performance it obviously must restrict the diameter of the receiver aerial in the SARH model. In fact, there may not be any SARH dish, because surrounding the guidance section are four projections which were at first wrongly iden-

AA-6 'Acrid'

Propulsion: unknown but probably solid motor with very long-burn sustainer
Dimensions: length (IR) 5,800mm (228in), (SARH) 6,290mm (248in); body diameter 400mm (15.7in); span 2,250mm (88.6in)
Weight: at launch (both) about 700kg (1,650lb)
Performance: speed about Mach 4; range (IR) about 25km (15.5 miles), (radar) about 80km (50 miles)
Warhead: unknown but US estimate 60-90kg (132-200lb), blast-fragmentation
Users: include Libya and Soviet Union, possibly Algeria and Syria

Largest AAM in the world, this awesome weapon family was designed around 1959-61 originally to kill the B-70 Valkyrie (which instead was killed by the US Congress) and entered PVO service as definitive armament of the Mach 3.2 MiG-25 'Foxbat-A' interceptor. With four missiles, two IR-homers on the inner pylons and two SARH on the outers, this aircraft is limited to Mach 2.8. It is, of course, totally a straight-line aircraft at such speeds, and in its original form was not intended for any kind of close encounter with hostile aircraft. Since 1975 developed versions with many changes have emerged able to withstand about +6g at Mach 2 and armed with AA-6 and AA-7 missiles.

Like the Tu-28, the MiG-25 was intended to detect targets at long range, using the Markham ground-air data link to give a cockpit display based on ground surveillance radars, switching to its own 'Fox Fire' radar at about 160km (100 mile) range. This equipment, likened to an F-4's AWG-10 in character but greater in power, includes CW aerials in slim wingtip pods to illuminate the target for the SARH missiles, which could probably lock-on and be fired at ranges exceeding 100km (62 miles); both pulse/CW power and receiver-aerial size are considerably greater than for any Sparrow and closely similar to AWG-9/Phoenix.

The IR version has much shorter range, though there is no reason to doubt that current Soviet technology is increasing IR fidelity as is being done elsewhere. 'Acrid' has a large long-burning motor, giving a speed generally put at Mach 4 (the figure of 2.2 in one report is nonsense) and manoeuvres by canard controls, with supplemen-

tary ailerons (possibly elevons) on all four of the cropped delta wings. The latter have the great area needed for extreme-altitude interception, for the B-70 cruised at well over 21,000m (70,000ft); but early 'Acrid' missiles did not have look-down capability. Soviet films suggest that, when the range is close enough, it is usual to follow national standard practice and ripple missiles in pairs, IR closely followed by SARH. The two homing heads are typically dissimilar, the IR model having a rounded transparent nose and the radar type an opaque cone. This missile is being replaced by AA-9 'Amos'.

Above: A Libyan MiG-25 seen over the Mediterranean in August 1981 armed with two AA-6 'Acrids'. Both appear to be of the radar type.

Left: A MiG-23 of the so-called 'Flogger-G' type, armed with two R-23 (AA-7 'Apex') and two dogfight AAMs, that on the right side being an R-60 (AA-8 'Aphid'). The R-23R has a pointed nose.

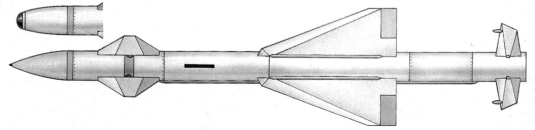

Below: The two versions of the standard medium-range AAM, the Soviet R-23 series (called AA-7 'Apex' by NATO). R-23R has a pointed nose, while the IR-homing R-23T has a blunter transparent nosecap. There are apparently nose and tail controls.

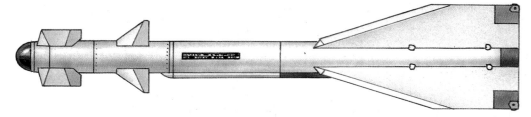

tified by Western observers as extra control surfces but which in fact are almost cetainly SARH receiver aerials working on an interferometer principle (as do the four aerials spaced around the nose of the Sea Dart missile). It should be possible to home on the signals received by these four shallow fin-like projections, and dispense with the need for an internal radar dish. At the same time, the reason for the reduced diameter of the forebody of this missile is obscure, unless it is to provide an area-ruled ogival platform to carry the four blade aerials. Immediately to the rear, at the upstream end of the full-diameter section, a dark ring probably locates the windows of the proximity fusing system. The tail controls are cropped at the tips at an angle appropriate to about Mach 3, and carry near the tips forward-facing bullet fairings similar to those on the wings and control fins of certain other Soviet anti-aircraft missiles. The only really puzzling thing about AA-7 is its very poor performance, which may simply be yet another case of the West's childish wishful thinking. There is no evident reason why this missile should not have performance appreciably greater (in range, ceiling and manoeuvrability) than most versions of Sparrow, its nearest Western counterpart. The 'High Lark' J-band radar of most MiG-23 interceptors is a set in the 150kW class with a plate aerial of about 0.76m (30in) diameter. If the low estimates of AA-7 range are accurate, one explanation might be devotion of much of the missile body to duplicated guidance methods in each round, with extremely sophisticated ECCM circuits to ensure that the homing lock is never broken. The only alternative is a sharp upward revision of the estimated flight performance. AA-7 was probably developed by the Soviet Union in 1971-4.

AA-8 'Aphid'

Propulsion: advanced boost/sustain motor, probably solid
Dimensions: length (IR, only known version) 2,150mm (84.6in); body diameter 120mm (4.72in); span 400mm (15.75in)
Weight: at launch about 55kg (121b)
Performance: speed about Mach 2.5; range (IR) estimated 0.5-5.5km (0.3-3.5 miles)
Warhead: estimated at 7-9kg (15-20lb)
Users: include East Germany, India, Libya, Soviet Union, probably others including most MiG-23 users

Supplementing and eventually probably to replace the vast stock of AA-2 'Atoll' close-range missiles, this interesting weapon is one of the smallest guided AAMs ever built, and is being produced in extremely large quantities as the air-combat missile of the PVO, FA and AV-MF. First seen, together with the R-23R (AA-7) in 1976, it will probably remain important into the next century. Somewhat similar in shape and size to the USAF Hughes Falcon of 30 years ago, AA-8 is a technically novel canard with delta wings right at the tail (resembling grossly broadened versions of the tail fins of the 'Atoll' family), canard delta control fins and, at the extreme nose and immediately ahead of the control fins, four rectangular blades of very low aspect ratio and with span considerably less than that of the controls. These are believed to be fixed aerodynamic surfaces to enhance combat manoeuvrability, but they are by no means obviously linked for this purpose with the movable fins as are the two sets of surfaces in the French Matra Magic missile, and it is possible that the fixed blades serve a different function concerned with guidance or ECM.

The only known R-60 (Soviet designation) has a hemispherical glass nose for an IR seeker, though some Western reports state that there is also an SARH model. Almost certainly the propulsion is of the boost-coast type, and it may have better manoeuvrability than any other AAM over ranges up to about 8km (5 miles). A black stripe between the guidance section and motor almost certainly locates the proximity fuze for the warhead. This was originally estimated at barely half the size of the warhead carried by all current models of Sidewinder, but has been revised upwards. This AAM is carried by the MiG-21, MiG-23 (on body pylons), Yak-38 and probably other types of aircraft including the Su-21 and Su-25.

Above: The best drawing yet to appear in the West of the very small dogfight AAM called R-60 (NATO name AA-8 'Aphid'). It has widely spaced fixed and moving canard fins and large wings.

Left: Two Yak-38 (NATO 'Forger') jet-lift V/STOL fighters each armed with R-60 (AA-8 'Aphid') close-range dogfight AAMs. The pylons can also carry gun pods or rocket launchers.

Below: An excellent picture of a MiG-29 (NATO'Fulcrum') armed with pairs of R-60 close-range AAMs outboard and large AA-10 missiles inboard under each wing. Further illustrations of AA-10 appear overleaf.

Left: A diagram (on a smaller scale than the others) of the mighty AA-9, whose true designation is unknown.

Below: Two pairs of tandem AA-9 missiles carried beneath the fuselage of a MiG-31 (NATO 'Foxhound').

AA-10 'Alamo'

Propulsion: rocket
Dimensions: generally similar to R-23R (AA-7)
Weight: probably similar to R-23R (AA-7)
Warhead: unknown
User: Soviet Union

AA-9 'Amos'

Propulsion: unknown, but probably a large single-charge solid rocket
Dimensions: length 4,200mm (165in); body diameter 410mm (16.1in); span (wings) 1,300mm (51in), (controls) 1,800mm (71in)
Weight: at launch about 580kg (1,280lb)
Performance: speed about Mach 3.5; range (SARH) see text
Warhead: large conventional or nuclear, possibly 80kg (176lb)
User: Soviet Union

Fascinating on the score of both its exceptional body diameter and its configuration, this AAM was first reported by the US Department of Defense in 1978, when it was said to have performed well in prolonged lookdown/shoot-down tests at Vladimirovka. A little later Washington stated that AA-9 (NATO designation) had scored impressive kills or simulated (within lethal radius) kills against small cruise missiles flying at various heights down to only 50m (200ft), after initial acquisition from the test aircraft (modified MiG-25s) at heights of around 6,000m (19,685ft).

AA-9, the Soviet designation of which is not yet known, is the armament of the MiG-31 'Foxhound', which carries two pairs under the fuselage and probably has the capability of carrying four more under the wings (as an alternative to other weapons). This missile has the greatest body diameter of any AAM in history, the obvious reason for this being in order to accommodate the largest possible SARH receiver dish in the nose. No IR version of this missile has been seen. Indeed it may be that the nose radar is of the active type. In either event, the range can hardly be less than 130km (80 miles), and may well be similar to that of the smaller US Navy

Phoenix. The official US range estimate of 40km (25 miles) is obviously nonsensical, though doubtless this missile can be fired from such a range.

In configuration AA-9 is unique, though it has a faint similarity to that of Phoenix. There are no forward aerodynamic surfaces or projections, though much of the body is covered with black lines which are probably flush radio aerials for reference measure-

ments and the proximity fuze. Aft of the body's mid-point are the four long-chord wings which are almost rectangular but with swept leading edges. Immediately to the rear, touching the wings, are the four rectangular control surfaces, projecting far beyond the wing tips. All the evidence points to AA-9 being a weapon of tremendous speed and range intended for stand-off interceptions.

Until April 1987 the only available source of information on this extremely important new AAM was US Department of Defense drawings, showing an appearance resembling the R-23R (AA-7 'Apex'). In that month the Norwegian Air Force released a superb picture of a Sukhoi Su-27 'Flanker' carrying six examples of this missile (two in tandem under the fuselage, two under the deep engine nacelles and two under the intermediate wing pylons (outboard and tip pylons were empty). This missile, which probably has a range in the region of 48km (30 miles), has a unique canard configuration utterly unlike R-23R and bearing only a faint resemblance to the obsolescent AA-3 'Anab'. The startling feature is the use of longspan canard controls having inverse taper. They are attached to a control ring at the forward end of the giant motor section, which has a diameter greater than the

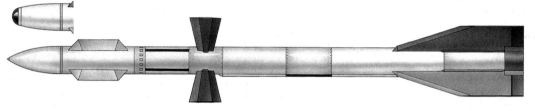

Above: Though still slightly speculative, these diagrams show the two versions of the new Soviet AAM known to

NATO as AA-10 'Alamo'. As usual, the radar version has a pointed nose and the IR variant a blunt one.

Below: An Su-27 (NATO 'Flanker') armed with short and long radar AA-10s and (outboard) IR-homing AA-10s.

nose guidance section. On the latter are four blades similar to those on other Soviet AAMs, and the nose differs according to whether guidance is by IR or semi-active radar. Four large fins are at the tail; they generally resemble those of AA-3 'Anab' but it is not known if they have that missile's trailing-edge controls. Obviously the radar version of this missile has full lookdown/shoot-down capability.

AA-11 'Archer'

Propulsion: rocket
Dimensions: unknown, but possibly similar to R-60 (AA-8)
Other data: possibly similar to R-60 (AA-8)
User: Soviet Union

First mentioned by the US Department of Defense in 1986, but not shown in an artist's impression as this book went to press in 1987, AA-11 is an important new close-range dogfight missile carried by the MiG-29 and Su-27. It may be fair to consider it a replacement for the R-60 (AA-8 'Aphid'), though this is speculation. Some authorities state that this AAM can also be carried by the MiG-23 and MiG-25 interceptor versions.

SA-7 'Grail'

Propulsion: dual-thrust boost/ sustain solid motor
Dimensions: length 1,350mm (53.25in); body diameter 70mm (2.75in); fin span 200mm (7.9in)
Weight: at launch about 9.2kg (20.3lb)
Performance: speed Mach 1.5; range 0.8-5km (0.5-3 miles)
Warhead: conventional fragmentation, 2.5kg (5.5lb), graze and DA fuzes
Users: in AAM role Soviet Union, Yugoslavia and possibly other countries

The SA-7 'Grail' was originally a SAM for use by infantry. A rudimentary weapon, it has IR homing which cannot be relied

Below: This US Department of Defense sketch of Kamov's 'Hokum' shows SA-7 'Grail' inboard of what appear to be AA-2 (K-13A) 'Atoll' AAMs.

upon to achieve lock-on to an approaching aircraft, though the seeker has been progressively improved. Over 50,000 rounds have been exported to at least 22 countries, and it is a favoured terrorist weapon. As in other countries the Soviet Union has used this SAM as a self-defence weapon for helicopters, twin and four-barrel pods having been seen since 1981 mounted on various types of Mi-24 'Hind' and on Yugoslav Gazelles.

No details are yet available of the way targets are acquired, but anti-armour Mi-24 versions are well equipped with sighting and weapon cueing systems. The seeker of land-based SA-7 missiles is uncooled, so aircraft installation problems should be minimal.

RBS 70

Origin: Saab Bofors Missile Corporation, Sweden
Propulsion: Bofors solid boost motor; IMI (UK) solid sustainer
Dimensions: length 1,320mm (52in); body diameter 106mm (4.17in); span (fins extended) 320mm (12.6in)
Weight: at launch (bare missile) 15kg (33lb); (with launch tube) 22kg (48.5lb)
Performance: speed supersonic; range 5km (3 miles)
Warhead: pre-fragmented 1kg (2.2lb), with optical proximity and DA fuzes
Users: not yet available

The RBS 70 was produced by AB Bofors (then, in 1974-8, not associated with Saab) as a SAM for use by infantry, with advantages over earlier man-portable

Above: A quad RBS 70 installation mounted on a British Lynx helicopter. The video tracker can use the same optical system as the laser.

weapons in this class. The missile is popped out of its tube by a short-burn motor which drops off just beyond the mouth of the tube. Fins and midposition wings unfold and the sustainer then accelerates the round to well beyond Mach 1. Guidance is by riding a laser beam held on the target: any deviation from the beam is sensed and processed by an on-board computer which sends signals to the control fins. By 1980 the RBS 70, whose development was part-funded by Switzerland, was in the hands of troops in Sweden and Switzerland.

In 1981 a Lynx helicopter was exhibited carrying on a left-side pylon a four-round launcher (another would be mounted on the right side) for an AAM version. The system would include a Saab Helios roof-mounted sight with auto-handover after launch of the chosen round(s). With the helicopter hull-down, only the sight being visible to the enemy, the control unit boresights the video tracker to the target aircraft so that the laser can designate the target through the same optical window. Alternatively, target designation can be from a remote friendly laser, the helicopter remaining passive.

RB 73

Propulsion: rocket boost followed by Volvo Flygmotor ramjet derived from RRX1 and produced with foreign partner (probably Aérospatiale or Marquardt)
Dimensions: generally similar to Sky Flash (see entry under UK)

Weight: probably similar to Sky Flash
Performance: cruising speed Mach 4 to Mach 5; range over 100km (62 miles)

As noted in the entry on the UK Sky Flash, Britain has all the ingredients necessary for an active-radar Sky Flash which would offer tremendous advantages and probably cost less than half as much as the American AMRAAM. The Swedish government was in April 1987 about to go ahead on a joint programme, initially funded at SKr 1.5 billion, on a missile designated RB 73 (British designation had been Sky Flash 90). Volvo Flygmotor, with long experience of supersonic ramjets for missile propulsion, has proposed that RB 73 should also incorporate this form of propulsion, far more efficient in terms of fuel burn and range than a rocket. RB 73 would probably be ready in 1992, in time to arm the Saab JAS 39 Gripen.

Sky Sword

Origin: Chung Shan Institute of Science and Technology
Data: similar to AIM-9G/H Sidewinder
User: Taiwan

The first live example of this IR-homing AAM was fired from an F-5E on 18 May 1986, achieving a hit on a Firebee target drone. Sky Sword is planned as an indigenous replacement for Sidewinder in the Chinese Nationalist air force, and it bears a close external resemblance to AIM-9G/H. No further details were available in mid-1987.

UNITED KINGDOM

Firestreak

Origin: DH Propellers, (now British Aerospace)
Propulsion: solid motor amidships with tube to nozzle
Dimensions: length 3,188mm (125.5in); body diameter 222mm (8.75in); span 746.8mm (29.4in)
Weight: at launch 136kg (300lb)
Performance: speed about Mach 3; range 1.2-8km (0.75-5 miles)
Warhead: conventional 22.7kg (50lb) with IR proximity fuze system
User: UK (RAF)

Originally codenamed Blue Jay, this AAM reached IOC in 1958. Development had begun seven years previously, the prime contractor being assisted by the RAE, RRE and RARDE, and with Mullard playing a central role in the IR guidance. Guided rounds were fired from 1954. In 1955 a Venom launched a pre-production Blue Jay against a Firefly U.9, and about 100 rounds were then fired at the WRE from Avon-Sabres against Jindiviks. In 1958 the missile was named Firestreak, and entered service with the Sea Venoms of 893 Sqn RN (two missiles), followed by the Javelin FAW.7 (four) with 33 Sqn RAF in August 1958. Subsequently various subtypes served with the Sea Vixen FAW.1 and 2 of the RN (four) and all marks of Lightning (two) of the RAF, Saudi Arabia and Kuwait.

Several thousand rounds were produced, ending in 1969. Operational interceptors had a slaving unit which pointed the IR Cassegrain telescope to look at the target held by the fighter's radar. Another unique feature was the eight-sided glass nose, like a sharp pencil. Error signals commanded proportional navigation by tail controls driven by long push-pull rods from actuators in the forebody fed with air from a toroidal bottle near the

motor nozzle! The air also drove a turbo-alternator. The seeker cell and potted electronics were cooled by nitrogen from the fighter. Nearing the target, two rings of IR sensors located behind glass windows ahead of the wings locked-on to the target to form a two-beam proximity fuze feeding target bearing and range and, at the correct point, detonating the warhead surrounding the motor tube. Firestreak eventually achieved an SSKP of 85 per cent when fired within a 3,050m (10,000ft) radius to the rear of the target. A few survive into the late 1980s but are being phased out with the Lightning.

Red Top

Origin: Hawker Siddeley Dynamics (now British Aerospace)
Propulsion: single-stage solid motor
Dimensions: length 3,320mm (130.6in); body diameter 222mm (8.75in); span 908mm (37.75in)
Weight: at launch 150kg (330lb)
Performance: speed at burn-out Mach 3.2; range up to 12km (7.5 miles)
Warhead: conventional fragmentation 31kg (68.3lb)
User: UK (RAF)

Originally called Firestreak Mk IV, this was a rationalized Firestreak with the components reassembled in a more logical arrangement, and with a completely new seeker head, motor and warhead to give very much greater lethality. The basic requirement, of late 1956, was to produce a missile not confined to the ±15° squint angle of first-generation IR seekers, and, by developing a seeker itself able to home on the target's jet or other hot parts, attack successfully from any direction. As early as 1958 an American publication reported that 'Red Top . . . has a 68lb conventional warhead and a range of 14,000 yards, with a cooled lead telluride cell receiving in a 4 to 5 micro range'. Though slightly garbled, this disclosed valuable information which at the time was highly classified, and

Left: Withdrawn from service in the 1960s, the Gloster Javelin heavy interceptor carried four Firestreaks in its later versions (this example is an FAW. Mk 9).

even today no details of the seeker may be given.

In the course of development the missile was redesigned with an untapered forebody to accommodate a larger warhead. The improved motor gave a speed of just over Mach 3 at burn-out, while the nose was redesigned as a full-diameter glass hemisphere. Wings and tail controls were completely redesigned with greater area, and with planform and section profile matched to Mach 3, greater altitudes and much greater lateral acceleration. The powerful warhead, of a new type, had a later IR fuzing system in advance of any other AAM system of the late 1950s. It was positioned as a single package ahead of the wings, while the control group was relocated next to the control fins.

Development was rapid and successful, and by late 1964 Red Tops were being issued to No. 74 Sqn, whose Lightnings were being upgraded with a larger vertical tail to counter the slightly larger side area of the new missile. At the same time Red Top was issued to the first RN squadron equipped with the Sea Vixen FAW.2, 899 Sqn, replacing the Firestreak on four wing pylons. The Red Top was subsequently improved in small details and remains in limited service.

Above: Early English Electric Lightnings of RAF No 111 Sqn showing (near) Red Top and (on the aircraft in the rear) Firesteak.

Below: Live Red Tops carried by a Lightning F.Mk 3 of RAF No 29 Sqn, which later re-equipped with Phantoms. Note the fixed FR proble.

Sky Flash

Origin: British Aerospace, Hatfield
Propulsion: Aerojet or Rockwell Mk 52 PB/AP solid motor
Dimensions: length 3,680mm (145in); body diameter 203mm (8in); span 1,020mm (40in)
Weight: at launch 193kg (425lb)
Performance: speed Mach 4; range 50km (31 miles)
Warhead: AIM-7E type 30kg (66lb) continuous-rod pattern, with proximity and DA fuzes
Users: Sweden, UK (RAF, possibly RN later)

Before the US industry developed its own monopulse seeker for Sparrow, the UK industry began such work in 1969, leading to a brilliant series of test firings in November 1975 and production delivery to the RAF by BAe Dynamics in 1978. Originally XJ.521, and later named Sky Flash, this missile is a -7E2 with a completely new MSDS homing head operating in I-band with inverse processing by all-solid-state microelectronics. The warm-up time has been reduced from about 15 seconds to less than 2 seconds. The short range of the basic -7E2 is considered acceptable for European conditions, though the -7F motor could be fitted if needed.

The trials programme from Point Mugu is judged the most successful of any AAM in history: more than half the missiles actually struck their targets, often in extremely difficult conditions of glint or evasive manoeuvres, while the miss-distance of the remainder averaged 'about one-tenth that of most radar-guided AAMs'. Moreover, the warhead is triggered by a deadly EMI active-radar fuze placed behind the seeker, the warhead being behind the wings.

Sweden adopted Sky Flash as RB 71 for the JA 37 Viggen. Sky Flash is carried by RAF Phantoms in the interception role and is matched with Foxhunter radar on the Tornado F.3 interceptor. Sky Flash Mk 2 was unfortunately abandoned by the British government at an advanced stage in early 1981, neatly destroying work which had put the BAe/MSDS team ahead of the world. Instead the American AMRAAM will be

made under licence and used by European NATO nations. Sweden is upgrading its missiles to RB 71A standard with a new motor and improved guidance.

Under the terms of the 1980 memorandum of understanding BAe is prohibited from working on any rival to AMRAAM. Despite this it is hoped that an updated Sky Flash can be made available to meet the needs of a large global market for a BVR (beyond visual range) missile. Called Sky Flash 90, the new version has simple strapdown inertial mid-course stabilization followed by active terminal homing using a proven GEC Marconi radar. There is no need at

medium ranges for mid-course updating. The Sky Flash 90 will also have thinner wings and an improved rear end to reduce drag. The immediate customer is Sweden (see RB 73 entry), but because no CW guidance is needed the Sky Flash 90 is expected to appeal to many other countries.

Right: Sweden's Saab JA37 Viggen is seen here armed with two RB 71 Sky Flash missiles.

Below: The BAe Tornado F.Mk 3 (an F.Mk 2 prototype is shown) was lengthened in order to accommodate pairs of Sky Flash AAMs in tandem.

GUIDED WEAPONS

Right: Starstreak is at present used in SAM roles but has colossal potential as an AAM. The main body fins extend after launch.

Starstreak

Origin: Shorts Missile Systems Division, Belfast
Data: generally not publishable
User: initially (UK)

Starstreak, the next generation beyond Blowpipe and Javelin, is in full development as a close air-defence weapon system (SAM) for troops and ships. It can also be used in the air-to-air role, and its combination of virtues makes it a system without parallel. Briefly, the Starstreak system comprises an environmental canister from which is fired a hypervelocity (possibly Mach 4.5) missile comprising a central body on which ride three high-KE (kinetic energy) explosive darts. The laser guidance and extremely brief flight time make the system essentially immune to counter-measures, and the fact that after burn-out of the high-thrust motor the three darts hold a fixed formation makes for the greatest possible lethality. As an AAM the S.14 Starstreak would probably be fired from reloadable quadruple boxes.

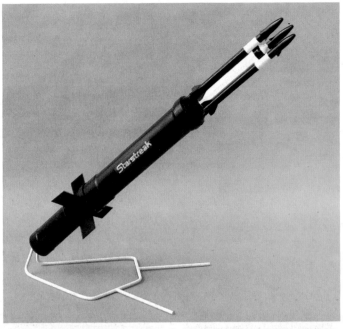

AAAM

Origin: contractor to be determined, but from industry of the USA
Propulsion: could be rocket, pulse rocket, ramjet or hybrid
Dimensions: proposal from General Dynamics Pomona would be 3,660mm (144in) long
Weight: proposal from GD Pomona would weigh 163kg (360lb)
Warhead: not designed but conventional
User: US Navy

In 1984 the US Navy planned to launch development of a new Advanced AAM (AAAM) to replace the AIM-54 Phoenix as long-range armament of the F-14 Tomcat into the later 1980s. The decision was then delayed for two years pending consideration of a so-called Outer Air Battle Report dealing with defence of the fleet against aerial threats. At last an RFP (request for proposals) was issued in March 1987, followed by a Demo and Validation phase award to two finalist contractors later in 1987. Full-scale development would follow around 1990,

Above: In this computer simulation of a Starstreak attack, the three high kinetic energy explosive darts have just separated from the launcher.

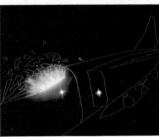

Above: The Starstreak warheads maintain a fixed formation right through to target impact. Guidance is by laser.

for entry into Navy service around 1995, considerably later than planned.

As far as possible the Navy is leaving engineering features open to the contractors, to encourage competition and ensure the maximum incorporation of new and advanced technology. It does, however, expect that terminal guidance will be with the aid of a multi-mode seeker, such as a combination of radar, IR and EO (electro-optical) guidance. It is hoped the missile will weigh less than 295kg (650lb), be of less than 229mm (9in) diameter and cost $600,000-750,000. The cost is obviously a ridiculously optimistic hope, because today's less advanced AIM-120A is coming out at almost $3 million. AAAM is hoped to be undetectable at launch and, of course, to be able to home on targets in an environment of sophisticated countermeasures. It is hoped the F-14D will be able to take-off or land back on a carrier whilst carrying eight AAAMs.

In April 1987 two of the principal AAAM bidders, Hughes Aircraft and Raytheon Co, announced that they were forming a joint-venture partnership called H & R Co to compete for the AAAM programme. This was in response to a 20 March 1987 Navy RFP for the demonstration/validation phase of the programme which required contrac-

tor teaming (collaboration). The two companies announced that the solutions put forward by them had proved to be wholly compatible, each having selected dual-mode radar and IR guidance as well as ramjet propulsion. Should the H & R missile be selected for full-scale development, Raytheon will have responsibility for radar guidance and fusing and Hughes for IR guidance and the on-board data processor. McDonnell Douglas Astronautics would be principal subcontractor, responsible for the missile airframe design and ramjet propulsion. As well as the Grumman F-14 and McDonnell Douglas F/A-18 the new missile is to be compatible with many other aircraft including the Grumman A-6 attack bomber and the USAF's McDonnell Douglas F-15. It is to replace the AIM-54 Phoenix in production 'in the late 1990s'.

AMRAAM, AIM-120A

Origin: Hughes Aircraft, Missile Systems Group
Propulsion: advanced internal rocket motor, details and contractor not yet decided
Dimensions: length 3,580mm (141in); body diameter 178mm (7in); fin span 635mm (25in)
Weight: at launch 152kg (335lb)
Performance: speed about Mach 4; maximum range in excess of 48km (30 miles)
Warhead: expected to be lighter than 22kg (50lb)
Users: to include USAF, USN, USMC, Germany (West) and UK (RAF and possibly RN)

Originally called BVR (Beyond Visual Range) missile, the Advanced Medium-Range AAM is the highest-priority AAM programme in the United States, because AIM-7M is becoming long in the tooth and is judged urgently in need of replacement in the 1980s by a completely new missile. AMRAAM is a joint USAF/USN programme aimed at producing a missile having higher performance and lethality than any conceivable advanced version of Sparrow, within a package that is smaller, lighter, more reliable and cheaper. AMRAAM will obviously be matched with later versions of F-14, -15, -16, and -18 equipped with programmable signal processors for Doppler beam-sharpening and with advanced IR sensors able to acquire individual targets at extreme range. The missile would then be launched automatically on inertial mid-course guidance, without the need for the fighter to illuminate the target, the final terminal homing being by a small active seeker. The task clearly needed a very broad programme to investigate not only traditional sensing and guidance methods but also new ones such as target aerodynamic noise, engine harmonics and laser scanning to verify the external shape and thus confirm aircraft type. Multiple-target and TWS are required, and AMRAAM will have a high-impulse motor giving rapid ac-

Below: An F-16 can detect a hostile aircraft, launch an AMRAAM and then take evasive action.

Fire and Forget

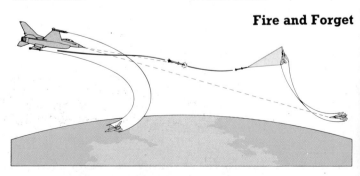

celeration to a Mach number higher than 4, with subsequent manoeuvre by TVC and/or tail controls combined with body lift, wings not being needed.

The original list of five competing groups was narrowed to two in February 1979, and at the end of 1981 Hughes was picked over Raytheon to build 94 test missiles, with options on 924 for inventory plus follow-on production (which is currently to be split between two contractors, Raytheon becoming second source).

By late 1982 the AMRAAM (always pronounced as a word) was well into firing trials, fully guided rounds doing well against increasingly tough targets at Holloman and Pt Mugu. Midcourse guidance is Nortronics inertial, and the small Hughes active terminal radar now uses a TWT (travelling-wave tube) transmitter. In 1980 West Germany and the UK signed a memorandum of understanding assigning AMRAAM to the USA and ASRAAM to the two Euro-

pean nations. Since then work has gone ahead on integrating the US missile into the RAF Tornado F.3 and Luftwaffe F-4F upgrade. No European rival is countenanced.

By 1985 AIM-120A was in deep trouble, mainly because of severe cost overruns but also because of delays. No test round was fired into a hostile ECM environment until October 1986! By this time some of the problems were approaching a solution, and low-rate production was approv-

ed for Fiscal Year 1987, 105 rounds by Hughes and 75 by Raytheon, costing $537.4 million or about four times the 1978 planned price. For FY1988 the production will be 630, shared 55-45, and IOC (initial operational capability) is now due in October 1989.

Total USAF buy is planned to be 17,000, with another 7,000 for the Navy. No information has been given on the numbers or work-sharing of missiles for NATO European countries.

AIM-120A AMRAAM

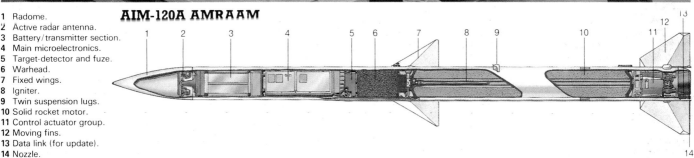

1 Radome.
2 Active radar antenna.
3 Battery/transmitter section.
4 Main microelectronics.
5 Target-detector and fuze.
6 Warhead.
7 Fixed wings.
8 Igniter.
9 Twin suspension lugs.
10 Solid rocket motor.
11 Control actuator group.
12 Moving fins.
13 Data link (for update).
14 Nozzle.

Top: A May 1987 picture of AIM-120A AMRAAM missiles in the new Hughes final checkout area at the Tucson plant in Arizona. Note overhead conveyor.

Above: Cutaway of AIM-120A AMRAAM, using bright colours for clarifying the components. The 23kg (50lb) warhead is of the blast-fragmentation type.

Left: Test launch of a prototype AMRAAM from an F-16A in 1981. An AIM-9J Sidewinder is on the wingtip.

been studied for many years. Indeed in 1979 Vought Corporation even held a contract to develop hardware for an ASAT system to be operational by 1985. This comprised a space interceptor, launched from an F-15 fighter, so accurate that it would unfailingly destroy its satellite target by direct collision. Trajectory control was effected by a ring of 56 small rocket thrusters around the mid-section (it will be appreciated that aerodynamic control surfaces are ineffective in space). Two ITVs (instrumented target vehicles) were placed in orbit on 12 December 1985, but the whole programme has been delayed by a moratorium imposed by the US Congress, despite the growth of the SDI.

Little more appeared to happen until on 10 March 1987 USAF Brigadier-General Robert R. Rankine Jr told a news conference the threat of Soviet reconnaissance satellites had become so great that ASAT was being restructured and extended, the altitude limit being raised from the previous 926km (575 miles) to 2,775km (1,725 miles). Funding is being made available in the Fiscal Year 1989 budget for assessment of a more powerful booster for the F-15 ASAT (Miniature ASAT) or adoption of a new vehicle launched from the ground and based on the Pershing II missile. In other testimony the USAF said 15 ASAT weapons were available from previous funding. All are tubular missiles with aerodynamic stabilizing fins at the tail, a high-impulse motor, a seeker in the nose (various wavelengths are being studied, but most are based on laser technology) and at least one ring of trajectory control thrusters amidships.

According to US testimony the Soviet Union already has an operational ASAT capaibility, testing the booster most recently in February 1987. It is not publicly known if this is air-launched.

ASAT

Origin: Vought Corporation, Dallas
Propulsion: Lockheed SR75-LP-1 solid rocket booster, and Altair III solid rocket sustainer
Dimensions: length 5,400mm (212.66in); body diameter 503mm (19.8in)
Weight: at launch 1,194kg (2,632lb)
Performance: speed hypersonic; range 1,000km (620 mile) orbital altitude
Warhead: Vought kinetic-energy Miniature Vehicle
Users: to be USA (AF)

First of a new family of air-launched weapons, ASAT should really be termed not an AAM but an air-to-space missile (though acronym ASM is already used). The Anti-SATellite missile has

Above: A remarkable photograph showing the ASAT test launch from an F-15 on 13 September 1985. The main rocket motor has just ignited, and the missile is climbing to begin an interception trajectory. Today the ASAT has had to grow physically in order to intercept much higher.

Below: The first carry trials flight of an ASAT vehicle, under a modified F-15. The 1984 test used an ASAT similar to those fired in 1985.

Falcon, AIM-4

Origin: Hughes Aircraft; some models licensed to Saab-Scania of Sweden
Propulsion: solid motor (various suppliers), some with boost/sustain charges
Dimensions: see separate table of variants
Weight: see separate table of variants
Performance: see separate table of variants
Warhead: various 13-18kg (29-40lb) with proximity fuze (AIM-26A, 1.5kT nuclear)
Users: Canada, Finland, Greece, Japan, Sweden, Switzerland, Taiwan, Turkey, USA (AF, ANG)

Above: A Swedish Saab J35F 'Filip' interceptor armed with four RB 27 missiles — Hughes Falcon AAMs built in Sweden under licence.

Below: In the Convair F-106A Delta Dart interceptor the Falcon missiles are carried in an internal weapon bay and swung out on hinged arms.

The first guided AAM in the world to enter operational service, Falcon was created by a new team. In 1947 the USAF asked for bids on a radar-based fire-control system for manned interceptors, and a guided AAM for the following interceptor generation. Both packages were won by Hughes Aircraft. By 1955 the family of fire-control systems had included the E-9, fitted to the F-89H, with a new computer and software for guns, FFARs or guided missiles. Subsequently the more advanced MG-10 followed for the supersonic F-102, the MG-13 for the F-101 and the semi-automated MA-1 for the F-106. All were matched to the missile Hughes created, at Culver City, and put into production at a new plant at Tucson in 1954. Called Falcon, it was later re-styled AIM-4.

The airframe, about the size of a man, contained a large proportion of GRP construction. Accelerated at about 50g by a single-charge Thiokol solid motor it had a hemispherical nose radome flanked by receiver aerials like small nose fins, giving SARH proportional navigation and steering by elevons on the trailing edges of the delta wings. Most early installations were internal, three being housed in the tip pod on each wing of the F-89H and J, and six fitting the weapon bay of the F-102A. Both reached IOC with Air Defense Command in mid-1956. Later that year the first IR Falcon, AIM-4B, entered service with a glass nose, followed by AIM-4A (radar) with larger controls carried well behind the wings. The AIM-4C had a better

IR seeker able to lock-on against a wider range of ambient temperatures. The IR missiles were popular in permitting the interceptor to break away as soon as the missile(s) had been launched (though, as in the Soviet Union, it was common doctrine to fire one missile with each type of guidance to ensure a kill). These early Falcons accounted for three-quarters of the total production.

In 1958 deliveries began of AIM-4E Super Falcon. It introduced a longer-burning motor, advanced SARH guidance with a new receiver behind a pointed radome of new material, long wing-root fillets and a more powerful warhead. In May 1959 the Tucson plant switched to the -4F with a new motor having boost/sustainer charges, improv-

ed SARH guidance with greater accuracy and ECCM provision, and airframe modifications including a white moistureproof sleeve over the fore-body and a 102mm (4in) metal probe on the nose to form a weak oblique shock. A few weeks later came AIM-4G with -4F airframe and a new IR seeker able to lock-on to smaller targets at greater ranges.

In 1960 came a dramatic development. The AIM-26 was developed to give high SSKP in head-on attacks. IR was judged inadequate in such engagements, and because of the reduced precision of SARH it was decided to use a much more powerful warhead. AIM-26A was fitted with almost the same nuclear warhead as Genie, triggered by four active-radar proximity-fuze aerials almost

flush with the body ahead of the wings. The body had to be of greater diameter, and a larger motor was necessary. The AIM-26B followed, with large conventional warhead, and this was exported as HM-55 and licence-built by Saab-Scania as RB 27. Today about 800 of the M26B model are the only Falcons left in USAF Aerospace Defense Command service. The Swiss Flugwaffe uses the HM-55 on the Mirage IIIs matched with Hughes Taran radar.

In 1958 Hughes began work on a fourth-generation fire-control and AAM system to arm the F-108 Rapier. The ASG-18 radar was used for mid-course guidance and target illumination over ranges exceeding 161km (100 miles), and the missile, then called GAR-9, was also given IR terminal homing. Propulsion was by a Lockheed storable liquid rocket giving hypersonic speed, so that the wings became mere strakes along the body. In 1959 this large AAM, still called Falcon, was transferred to the proposed YF-12A 'Blackbird' research interceptor with which it conducted much basic fact-finding in advanced interception techniques.

The final production Falcon was the AIM-4D of 1963. The only Falcon tailored for anti-fighter combat, it was a crossbreed combining the small airframe of early models with the powerful motor and advanced IR seeker of the -4G. The result is a fast and effective short-range missile. More than 8,000 -4As and -4Cs have been remanufactured to this standard.

THE FALCON FAMILY												
1947	1950	1962	Export	Sweden	Guidance	Length	Diameter	Span	Launch wt	Speed	Range	Production
XF-98	GAR-1	AIM-4	—	—	SARH	1.97m (77.8in)	163mm (6.4in)	508mm (20.0in)	50kg (110lb)	M2.8	5 km (5 miles)	4,080
—	GAR-1D	AIM-4A	—	—	SARH	1.98m (78.0in)	163mm (6.4in)	508mm (20.0in)	54kg (120lb)	M3	9.7 km (6 miles)	12,100
—	GAR-2	AIM-4B	—	—	IR	2.02m (79.5in)	163mm (6.4in)	508mm (20.0in)	59kg (130lb)	M3	9.7 km (6 miles)	16,000
—	GAR-2A	AIM-4C	HM-58	RB 28	IR	2.02m (79.5in)	163mm (6.4in)	508mm (20.0in)	61kg (134lb)	M3	9.7 km (6 miles)	13,500 (inc. 1,000 HM and
—	GAR-2B	AIM-4D	—	—	IR	2.02m (79.5in)	163mm (6.4in)	508mm (20.0in)	61kg (134lb)	M4	9.7 km (6 miles)	4,000 3,000 RB)
—	GAR-3	AIM-4E	—	—	SARH	2.18m (86.0in)	168mm (6.6in)	610mm (24.0in)	68kg (150lb)	M4	11.3 km (7 miles)	300
—	GAR-3A	AIM-4F	—	—	SARH	2.18m (86.0in)	168mm (6.6in)	610mm (24.0in)	68kg (150lb)	M4	11.3 km (7 miles)	3,400
—	GAR-4A	AIM-4G	—	—	IR	2.06m (81.0in)	168mm (6.6in)	610mm (24.0in)	66kg (145lb)	M4	11.3 km (7 miles)	2,700
—	XGAR-11	XAIM-26	—	—	SARH	2.13m (84.0in)	279mm (11.0in)	620mm (24.4in)	91kg (200lb)	M2	8 km (5 miles)	c100
—	GAR-11	AIM-26A	—	—	SARH	2.14m (84.25in)	279mm (11.0in)	620mm (24.4in)	92kg (203lb)	M2	8 km (5 miles)	1,900
—	GAR-11A	AIM-26B	HM-55	RB 27	SARH	2.07m (81.5in)	290mm (11.4in)	620mm (24.4in)	119kg (262lb)	M2	9.7 km (6 miles)	2,000 (inc. 400 HM and
—	GAR-9	AIM-47A	—	—	SARH/IRTH	3.2m (126.0in)	335mm (13.2in)	838mm (33.0in)	363kg (800lb)	M6	213 km (115 miles)	c80 800 RB)
—	—	XAIM-4H	—	—	ALH	2.03m (c80in)	168mm (6.6in)	610mm (24.0in)	73kg (160lb)	M4	11.3 km (7 miles)	c25

Genie, AIR-2A

Origin: Douglas Aircraft Co
Propulsion: Thiokol solid motor, 16,600kg (36,600lb) thrust
Dimensions: length 2,946mm (116in); body diameter (except warhead) 445mm (17.5in); span (fins extended) 1,016mm (40in)
Weight: at launch 373kg (822lb)
Performance: speed Mach 3.3; range 8-10km (5-6.2 miles)
Warhead: W25 1.5 kiloton nuclear
Users: USA (AF)

Though it is an unguided rocket, this can be classed as an AAM. Development was begun by Douglas Aircraft in 1955, as soon as LANL (Los Alamos Nuclear Laboratory) could predict success with the warhead. The first live missile was fired from an F-89J at 4572m (15,000ft) over Yucca Flat, Nevada, on 19 July 1957. The rocket was detonated by ground command, and USAF observers standing unprotected at ground zero (ie directly under the burst) suffered no ill effects. A training missile, with a white-cloud spotting charge instead of a warhead, was called Ting-a-Ling and is now ATR-2A.

Genie is carried by the F-106. The Hughes fire-control system tracks the target, assigns the missile, commands the pilot to arm the warhead, fires the missile, pulls the interceptor into a tight turn to escape the detonation, and finally triggers the warhead at the correct moment. Lethal radius is over 305m (1,000ft). Missile propulsion is by a Thiokol TU-289 (SR49) motor of 16,600kg (36,600lb) thrust. Flick-out fin-tips give the missile stability, and correct roll and gravity-drop. Several thousand Genies had been built when production ceased in 1962; the improved TU-289 motor remained in production to 1982.

Above: One of the earliest US Air Force F-4C Phantoms is seen here in 1966 carrying Genies on its inboard wing pylons, plus four Sparrows.

Below: An AIR-2A Genie nuclear rocket, with fins retracted, about to be loaded aboard the special test F-106A Delta Dart interceptor.

Phoenix, AIM-54

Origin: Hughes Aircraft
Propulsion: Aerojet (ATSC) Mk 60 or Rocketdyne (Flexadyne) Mk 47 long-burn solid motor
Dimensions: length 4,010mm (157.8in); body diameter 380mm (15in); span 925mm (36.4in)
Weight: at launch 447kg (985lb)
Performance: speed Mach 5+; range over 200km (124 miles)
Warhead: continuous-rod 60kg (132lb) with proximity and impact fuzes
Users: USA (Navy), Iran (484 supplied)

The most sophisticated and costly AAM in the world, this missile provides air defence over an area exceeding 31,000km^2 (12,000 square miles) from near sea level to the limits of altitude attained by aircraft or tactical missiles. But it can be fired only from the F-14 Tomcat and costs more than $1 million.

Following the classic aerodynamics of the Falcon family, Phoenix was originally AAM-N-11, and Hughes Aircraft began development in 1960 to replace the AIM-47A and Eagle as partner to the AWG-9 for the F-111B. This advanced fire-control system was the most capable ever attempted, and includes a very advanced radar (derived from the ASG-18 carried in the YF-12A) of high-power PD type with the largest circular aerial (of planar type) ever carried by a fighter. It has look-down capability out to ranges exceeding 241km (150 miles), and is backed up by an IR tracker to assist positive target identification and discrimination. AWG-9 has TWS capability, and an F-111B with the maximum load of six Phoenix mis-

Phoenix Flight Test

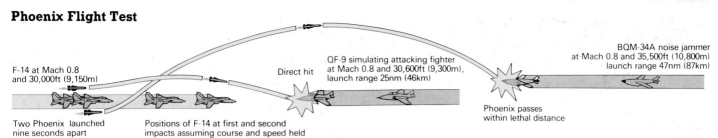

F-14 at Mach 0.8
and 30,000ft (9,150m)

Two Phoenix launched
nine seconds apart

Positions of F-14 at first and second
impacts assuming course and speed held

Direct hit

QF-9 simulating attacking fighter
at Mach 0.8 and 30,600ft (9,300m),
launch range 25nm (46km)

Phoenix passes
within lethal distance

BQM-34A noise jammer
at Mach 0.8 and 35,500ft (10,800m)
launch range 47nm (87km)

siles could engage and attack six aircraft at maximum range simultaneously, weather conditions and target aspect being of little consequence; indeed the basic interception mode assumed is head-on, which is one of the most difficult at extreme range.

Propulsion is by a long-burning Rocketdyne (Flexadyne) Mk 47 or Aerojet Mk 60 motor, giving a speed to burn-out of Mach 3.8. Combined with low induced drag and the power of the large hydraulically-driven tail controls, this gives sustained manoeuvrability over a range not even approached by any other AAM, despite the large load of electrical battery, electrical conversion unit, autopilot, electronics unit, transmitter/receiver and planar-array seeker head (all part of the DSQ-26 on-board guidance) as well as the 60kg (132lb) annular blast fragmentation warhead with Downey Mk 334 proximity fuze, Bendix IR fuze and DA fuze.

Hughes began flight test at PMTC in 1965, using a DA-3B Skywarrior, and achieved an interception in September 1966. In March 1969 an F-111B successfully engaged two drones, and subsequently the Phoenix broke virtually all AAM records including four kills in one pass (out of a six-on-six test, there being one no-test and one miss), a kill on a BQM-34A simulating a cruise missile at 15m (50ft), and a kill on a BQM-34E flying at Mach 1.5

tracked from 246km (153 miles), the Phoenix launched at 204km (127 miles), and impacting 134km (83.5 miles) from the launch point. The first AWG-9 system for the F-14A Tomcat, which replaced the F-111B, was delivered in February 1970. Production of Phoenix AIM-54A at Tucson began in 1973, since when output averaged about 40 per month until 1978; it then slowed and ended in 1980 at 2,566 rounds.

Since late 1977 production missiles have been of the AIM-54B type with sheet-metal wings and fins instead of honeycomb structure, non-liquid hydraulic and thermal-conditioning systems, and somewhat simplified engineering.

In 1977 Hughes began a major effort to produce an updated

Phoenix to meet the needs of the 1990s. This missile, AIM-54C, has totally new all-digital electronics, more reliable and flexible in use than the analog unit, with a solid-state radar replacing the previous klystron tube model. Accuracy is improved by a new strap-down inertial reference unit from Nortronics, and ECCM capability is greatly enhanced. Another improvement is a new proximity fuze developed by the Naval Weapons Center. Hughes delivered 15 engineering models from summer 1980, the first firing (head-on against a QF-4, the missile being in the semi-active mode throughout) being successful on 2 June 1980. Then followed 30 pilot-production rounds in the second half of 1981, with full production following

Above: Schematic diagram showing two tests of Phoenix missiles in 1973, both in the face of hostile countermeasures. In one the missile passed within lethal distance of a BQM-34 drone; the other achieved a direct hit on a QF-9 Cougar (former Navy jet fighter). Neither of the targets was manoeuvring.

from mid-1982 with about 450 delivered as this book went to press.

There is a possibility AIM-54A missiles may be updated. Meanwhile, to spur competition in Phoenix production, the Navy is arranging for a second source to share manufacture, and Raytheon will compete for orders starting in Fiscal Year 1989.

Left: This F-14A (BuNo 160010) was photographed with wings fully swept whilst armed with the maximum load of six AIM-54 Phoenix missiles. It serves with squadron VF-32 aboard the carrier *JFK*.

Below: Cutaway drawing of the AIM-54A Phoenix (the new AIM-54C is similar). This is the only Western AAM that remotely approaches the size and power of several types of Soviet AAM.

1 Radome.
2 Planar array active radar antenna.
3 Proximity fuze antenna (one of four spaced at 90°).
4 Warhead.
5 Fuzing unit.
6 Fixed wings.
7 Umbilical connector.
8 Moving control fins.
9 Nozzle.
10 Rear detection antenna.
11 Hydraulic power unit.
12 Autopilot.
13 Electric converter.
14 Rocket motor.
15 Guidance section.

Above: The awesome launch and motor ignition of an AIM-54 Phoenix from an F-14A Tomcat of VF-84 Jolly Rogers squadron of the US Navy. Not many Phoenix are actually fired during training.

AIM-54 Phoenix

Sidewinder, AIM-9

Origin: original design by US Naval Weapons Center, China Lake; commercial production by Philco (now Ford Aerospace) and later GE, today shared by Ford Aerospace (most versions, currently -9L and -9P) and Raytheon (-9L and -9M)

Propulsion: solid motor (various, by Rockwell, Aerojet or Thiokol, with Aerojet Mk 17 qualified on -9B/E/J/N/P and Thiokol Mk 36 or reduced-smoke TX-683 qualified on -9L/M)

Dimensions: see variants table

Weight: see variants table

Performance: see variants table

Warhead: (B/E/J/N/P) 4.5kg (10lb) blast-fragmentation with passive IR proximity fuse (from 1982 refitted with Hughes DSU-21/B active laser fuse), (D/G/H) 10.2kg (22.4lb) continuous rod with IR or HF proximity fuse, (L/M) 11.4kg (25lb) advanced annular blast-fragmentation with active laser IR proximity fuse

Users: (all versions) Argentina, Australia, Belgium, Brazil, Canada, Chile, Denmark, West Germany, Greece, Iran, Israel, Italy, Japan, South Korea, Kuwait, Malaysia, Morocco, Netherlands, Norway, Pakistan, Philippines, Portugal, Saudi Arabia, Singapore, Spain, Sweden, Taiwan, Tunisia, Turkey, UK (RAF, RN), USA (all services)

One of the most influential missiles in history, this slim AAM was almost un-American in development for it was created by a very small team at NOTS China Lake, operating on the proverbial shoestring budget. Led by Dr. W.B. McLean, this team was the first in the world to attack the problem of passive IR homing guidance, in 1949, and the often intractable difficulties were compounded by the choice of an airframe of only 127mm (5in) diameter, which in the days of vacuum-tube electronics was a major challenge.

In 1951 Philco was awarded a contract for a homing head based on the NOTS research and today, 36 years later, the guidance team at Newport Beach, now called Ford Aerospace and Communications, is still in production with homing heads for later Sidewinders. The first successful XAAM-N-7 guided round was fired on 11 September 1953. The first production missiles, called N-7 by the Navy, GAR-8 by the USAF and SW-1 by the development team, reached IOC in 1956.

These early Sidewinders were made of sections of aluminium tube, with the seeker head and control fins at the front and four fixed tail fins containing patented rollerons at the back. The rolleron is similar to an air-driven gyro wheel, and one is mounted in the tip of each fin so that it is spun at high speed by the slipstream. The original solid motor was made by Hunter-Douglas, Hercules and Norris-Thermador, to Naval Propellant Plant design, and it accelerated the missile to Mach 2.5 in 2.2 seconds.

The beauty of this missile was its simplicity, which meant low cost, easy compatibility with many aircraft and, in theory, high reliability in harsh environments. It was said to have 'less than 24 moving parts' and 'fewer electronic components than the average radio'. At the same time, though the guidance method meant that Sidewinder could be carried by any fighter, with or without radar, it was erratic in use and restricted to close stern engagements at high altitude in good visibility. The uncooled PbS seeker gave an SSKP of about 70 per cent in ideal conditions, but extremely poor results in bad visibility, cloud or rain, or at low levels, and showed a tendency to lock-on to the Sun, or reflections from lakes or rivers.

The pilot energized his missile homing head and listened for its signals in his headset. It would give a growl when it acquired a target, and if it was nicely positioned astern of a hot jetpipe the growl would become a fierce strident singing that would rise in intensity until the pilot let the missile go. Plenty of targets had early Sidewinders up their jet-pipes in the 1950s, but real-life engagements tended to have the wrong target, or the wrong aspect, or the wrong IR-emitting background. In October 1958, however, large numbers of Sidewinders were fired by Nationalist Chinese F-86s against Chinese MiG-17s, and 14 of the latter were claimed in one day. This was the first wartime use of AAMs.

Nearly 81,000 of the original missile were built in three almost identical versions which in the new 1962 scheme were designated AIM-9, -9A and -9B. Nearly all were of the -9B form, roughly half produced by Philco (Ford) and half by Raytheon. A further 15,000 were delivered by a European consortium headed by BGT, which in the late 1960s gave each European missile a new

Right: Italy's Agusta A129 Mangusta attack helicopter can carry self-defence AIM-9Ls in addition to its quad TOW launchers.

Below: US Marine Corps F/A-18A Hornet (161248) with tanks, bombs, Lantirn pods and AIM-9M Sidewinders.

THE SIDEWINDER FAMILY

Model	Guidance	Length	Control fin span	Launch wt	Mission time	Range	Production
AIM-9B	Uncooled PbS.25° look, 70 Hz reticle. 11°/sec tracking	2830mm (111.4in)	559mm (22.0in)	70.4kg (155lb)	20 sec	3.2 km (2 miles)	80,900
9B FGW.2	CO₂ cooling, solar dead zone reduced to 5°	2908mm (114.5in)	559mm (22.0in)	75.8kg (167lb)	20 sec	3.7 km (2.3 miles)	15,000
AIM-9C	Motorola SARH	2870mm (113.0in)	630mm (24.8in)	84.0kg (185lb)	60 sec	17.7 km (11 miles)	1,000
AIM-9D	N₂ cooled PbS, 40° look, 125 Hz reticle, 12°/sec tracking	2870mm (113.0in)	630mm (24.8in)	88.5kg (195lb)	60 sec	17.7 km (11 miles)	1,000
AIM-9E	Peltier-cooled PbS, 40° look, 100 Hz reticle, 16.5°/sec tracking	3000mm (118.1in)	559mm (22.0in)	74.5kg (164lb)	20 sec	4.2 km (2.6 miles)	5,000 (ex-9B)
AIM-9G	As -9D plus SEAM	2870mm (113.0in)	630mm (24.8in)	86.6kg (191lb)	60 sec	17.7 km (11 miles)	2,120
AIM-9H	As -9G plus solid-state, 20°/sec tracking	2870mm (113.0in)	630mm (24.8in)	84.5kg (186lb)	60 sec	17.7km (11 miles)	7,720
AIM-9J	As -9E plus part-solid-state	3070mm (120.9in)	559mm (22.0in)	78.0kg (172lb)	40 sec	14.5 km (9 miles)	10,000 (ex-9B)
AIM-9L	Argon-cooled InSb. fixed reticle, tilted mirror system	2850mm (112.2in)	630mm (24.8in)	85.3kg (188lb)	60 sec	17.7 km (11 miles)	16,000² 3,500
AIM-9M	As -9L, better motor and ECCM	2850mm (112.2in)	630mm (24.8in)	86.0kg (190lb)	60 sec	17.7 km (11 miles)	7,000
AIM-9N	As -9E plus part solid-state	3070mm (120.9in)	559mm (22.0in)	78.0kg (172lb)	40 sec	14.5 km (9 miles)	23,000
AIM-9P	As -9N plus reliability improvements	3070mm (120.9in)	559mm (22.0in)	78.0kg (172lb)	60 sec	17.7 km (11 miles)	—
AIM-9R	As -9M with new guidance	2850mm (112.2in)	630mm (24.8in)	87.0kg (193lb)	60 sec	19.3 km (12 miles)	

seeker head of BGT design known as FGW Mod 2. This has a nose dome of silicon instead of glass, a cooled seeker and semiconductor electronics, and transformed the missile's ability to lock-on in adverse conditions. The Swedish designation for the missile is RB 24.

By 1962 SW-1C was in use in two versions, AIM-9C by Motorola and AIM-9D by Ford. This series introduced the Rocketdyne Mk 36 solid motor giving greater range, a new airframe with tapered nose, long-chord controls and more swept leading edges on the tail fins, and new guidance. Motorola produced the -9C for the F-8 Crusader, giving it SARH guidance matched to the Magnavox APQ-94 radar, but this odd man out was unreliable and was withdrawn (see Side-

Below: For many years the European-built AIM-9L will be the only close-range AAM carried by RAF Tornado F.3s.

Above: This Brazilian prototype of the AMX is yet another type that relies on the 9L/9M Sidewinder.

arm). In contrast, -9D was so successful it formed the basis of many subsequent versions. The new guidance section introduced a dome of magnesium fluoride, a nitrogen-cooled seeker, smaller field of view, and increased reticle speed and tracking speed. The control section introduced larger fins, which were detachable, and high-power actuators fed by a longer-burning gas generator. The old 4.54kg (10lb) warhead with passive-IR fuse was replaced by a 10.2kg (22.4lb) annular blast-fragmentation head of the continuous-rod type, fired by either an IR or HF proximity fuse.

AIM-9E was fitted with a Ford seeker head with Peltier (thermo-electric) cooling, further-increased tracking speed and new electronics and wiring harnesses, giving increased engagement boundaries especially at low level. AIM-9G has so-called SEAM (Sidewinder Expanded Acquisition Mode), an improved -9D seeker head, but was overtaken by -9H. The latter introduced solid-state electronics, even faster tracking speed, and double-delta controls with increased actuator power, giving greater manoeuvrability than any previous Sidewinder as well as limited all-weather capability. AIM-9J is a rebuilt -9B or -9E with part-solid-state electronics, detachable double-delta controls with greater power, and long-burning gas generator. Range is sacrificed for high acceleration to catch fast targets. There are -9J-1 and J-3 improved or 'all new' variants. A major advance came with -9L, with

which NWC (as NOTS now is) at last responded to the prolonged demands of customers and the proven accomplishments of BGT. The latter's outstanding seeker head developed for the Viper was first fitted to AIM-9L to give Alasca (All-Aspect Capability), a great missile that was used merely by West Germany as a possible fall-back in case -9L failed to mature. AIM-9L itself, in full production from 1977, has long-span pointed delta fins, a new guidance system and an annular blast-fragmentation warhead sheathed in a skin of pre-fragmented rods, triggered by a proximity fuse in which a ring of eight GaAs laser diodes emit and a ring of photodiodes receive.

About 16,000 of the -9L series were expected to be made, some by a new BGT-led European consortium which this time includes BAe and companies in Norway and Italy. Pilot production deliveries began in 1981, and BAe received its first production contract (for £40 million) in February 1982. No European missiles had reached British squadrons in April 1982 and 100 -9Ls were supplied for use by Harriers and Sea Harriers in the South Atlantic from US stocks, gaining 25 known victories. The Swedish designation is RB 74. Production by a Japanese consortium (led by Mitsubishi) continues.

AIM-9M is a revised -9L. AIM-9N is the new designation of J-1 (all are -9B or -9E rebuilds) The AIM-9P is a rebuild of -9B/E/J, and additional -9P missiles are being made from new.

Under the terms of a 1980 memorandum of understanding, the AIM-132 ASRAAM is to be the new standard NATO close-range AAM. Despite this, development of future versions of Sidewinder is continuing, the next generation being AIM-9R. Originally called AIM-9M Improved, the -9R has a totally new IIR (imaging IR) seeker which has demonstrated reliable lock at ranges far exceeding those of previous versions. It also dispenses with the refrigeration (missile support) system, which in today's USAF versions is inside the missile and in Navy missiles inside the launcher shoe. Ford and Raytheon have prepared to go into production with -9R in 1988.

Below: Some Sidewinders have a smokeless motor, but this USAF F-16A has been almost obscured by a 9J.

Sidewinder Guidance Sections

	AIM-9B: 80,900 produced by Philco and GE and c15,000 by European consortium; 10,000 + updated by Ford.
	AIM-9C/D: 9C SARH model by Motorola (1,000 +), 9D with better IR/speed/manoeuvre, 950 + by Ford for US Navy.
	AIM-9E: 9B rebuilt with new cooled wide-angle seeker, about 5,000 for USAF by Ford (Aeronutronic).
	AIM-9G/H: 9G improved 9D with off-boresight lock-on (2,120 Raytheon, USN); 9H solid-state (3,000 Ford AF).
	AIM-9L/M: 9L 3rd generation all-aspect (Ford and Raytheon, also Europe); 9M improved ECCM/motor (Raytheon).
	AIM-9J/N: J rebuilt B/E with new front end (Ford c14,000 for AF); N (formerly J1) further improved (c, 7,000).
	AIM-9P improved B/E/J or new production, new motor/fuze and better reliability, c13,000 by Ford for USAF.

GUIDED WEAPONS

Sparrow, AIM-7

Origin: (AIM-7E,-7F,-7M) Raytheon Company, USA, with second-source production (-7M) by GD Pomona and licence-manufacture (-7M) by Mitsubishi, Japan
Propulsion: (-7E) Aerojet or Rockwell Mk 52 Mod 2 PB/AP solid motor, (-7F,-7M) Hercules or Aerojet Mk 58 high-impulse solid motor
Dimensions: length (E, F) 3,660mm (144in), (M) 3,680mm (145in); body diameter 203mm (8in); span 1,020mm (40in)
Weight: at launch (E) 205kg (452lb), (F, M) 228kg (503lb)
Performance: speed (all) about Mach 4; range (E) 44km (28 miles), (F, M) 100km (62 miles)
Warhead: (E) 30kg (66lb) continuous-rod warhead, (F, M) 40kg (88lb) Mk 71 advanced continuous-rod warhead, in each case with proximity and DA fuzes
Users: (AAM use only) West Germany, Greece, Iran, Israel, Italy, Japan, South Korea, Spain, Turkey, UK (RAF), USA (AF, Navy, Marines)

Considerably larger than other contemporary American AAMs, this missile not only progressed

through three fundamentally different families, each with a different prime contractor, but late in life mushroomed into totally new versions for quite new missions as an ARM (Shrike) and a SAM (two types of Sea Sparrow).

Sperry Gyroscope began the programme as Project 'Hot Shot' in 1946, under US Navy BuAer contract. By 1951 Sperry had a contract for full engineering development of XAAM-N-2 Sparrow I, and the suffix I was added because by that time there was already a Sparrow II. The first representative guided flight tests took place in 1953. This missile was a beam rider, with flush dipole aerials around the body which picked up the signals from the fighter radar beam (assumed to be locked-on to the target) and drove the cruciform delta wings to keep the missile aligned in the centre of the beam. At the tail were four fixed fins, indexed in line with the wings. Propulsion was by an Aerojet solid motor, and missile assembly took place at the Sperry-Farragut Division which operated a Naval Industrial Reserve plant at Bristol, Tennessee.

IOC was reached in July 1956, and Sparrow I was soon serving in the Atlantic and Pacific Fleets, and with the Marine Corps.

In 1955 Douglas obtained limited funding for Sparrow II, as

1 Radome with CW receiver.	6 PB/AP motor.
2 Discrete-component electronics.	7 Fixed fins.
3 Autopilot.	8 Reference antenna (along sides).
4 Moving wings.	9 Improved radome.
5 Warhead.	10 Slotted antenna for doppler radar.
	11 Solid-state electronics.
	12 Increased-power controls.
	13 Larger high-impulse motor.
	14 Axial instrumentation tunnel.

AIM-7E Sparrow
AIM-7F/7M Sparrow

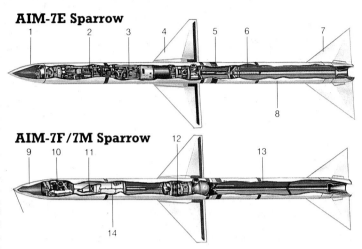

main armament for the proposed F5D-1 Skylancer. Amazingly, however, the company did not switch to SARH guidance but to fully active radar, and this was tough in a missile of 203mm (8in) diameter, a figure common to all Sparrows. In mid-1956 the Navy decided to terminate Sparrow II, but it was snapped up by the Royal Canadian Air Force as armament for the Arrow supersonic interceptor. After severe

Above: No successive generations of the same missile show a greater increase in capability than AIM-7E (top) and AIM-7F/7M. Apart from the new radar a key feature was compact electronics.

difficulties Prime Minister Diefenbaker cancelled Sparrow II on 23 September 1958, and the Arrow itself the following February.

Three years previously Raytheon had begun to work on Sparrow III, taking over the Bristol plant in 1956. Sparrow III uses almost the same airframe as Sparrow II but with SARH guidance. By the mid-1950s Raytheon had become one of the most capable missile companies, possibly because its background was electronics rather than airframes. It built up a missile engineering centre at Bedford, Massachusetts, with a test base at Oxnard (not far from Point Mugu), California; production of Sparrows was finally shared between Bristol and a plant at South Lowell, near Bedford.

Most of the airframe is precision-cast light alloy. Early Sparrow III missiles had an Aerojet solid motor, not cast integral with the case, and introduced CW guidance. AIM-7C, as it became, reached IOC in 1958 with Demons of the Atlantic and Pacific fleets. AIM-7D introduced the Thiokol (previously Reaction Motors) prepackaged liquid motor, and was also adopted by the Air Force in 1960 as AIM-101 to arm the F-110 (later F-4C) Phantom. All fighter Phantoms can carry four Sparrows recessed into the underside of the fuselage, with target illumination by the

Above: A fully armed F-15 Eagle fighter of the USAF showing both types of AAM currently carried. Four AIM-7M Sparrows nestle against the flanks of the fuselage, while AIM-9L Sidewinders ride on the lateral shoes beside the underwing pylons.

THE SPARROW FAMILY

1950 designation	1962	Guidance	Length	Span	Launch wt	Range	Production
AAM-N-2 Sparrow I	AIM-7A	Radar beam riding	3.56m (140in)	0.99m (39in)	141kg (310lb)	8 km (5 miles)	c2,000
AAM-N-3 Sparrow II	AIM-7B	Active radar homing	3.66m (144in)	0.99m (39in)	191kg (420lb)	?	c100
AAM-N-6 Sparrow III	AIM-7C	SARH CW	3.66m (144in)	1.02m (40in)	172kg (380lb)	40 km (25 miles)	2,000
AAM-N-6A/AIM-101	AIM-7D	SARH CW	3.66m (144in)	1.02m (40in)	200kg (440lb)	40 km (25 miles)	7,500
AAM-N-6B	AIM-7E	SARH CW	3.66m (144in)	1.02m (40in)	205kg (452lb)	44 km (28 miles)	25,000
—	AIM-7F	SARH CW solid-state	3.66m (144in)	1.02m (40in)	228kg (503lb)	100 km (62 miles)	3,000
—	AIM-7M	SARH CW solid-state	3.68m (145in)	1.02m (40in)	228kg (503lb)	100 km (62 miles)	1,800 +

used by US troops, or the much more effective Stinger-POST (passive optical seeker technique) which replaces the simple IR homing by an advanced two-colour (IR and UV) guidance using the latest IRCCM logic circuits and with a unique rosette scan which significantly enhances target detection.

This version is intended for all battlefield helicopters, and since early 1982 studies have also included the A-10A and Alpha Jet fixed-wing aircraft. A fire-and-forget weapon, Stinger is issued as a certified round in its sealed launch tube and requires no attention between delivery and launch. The basic launcher houses the seeker coolant reservoir and modular electronics, and can be stacked three or four deep, giving a maximum of 16 rounds. For high-speed aircraft a faired launcher is available, enclosing the twin missile tubes. The pilot has a recticle sight or HUD, control panel and a select/uncage/ fire control on his cyclic stick, launch being made when the acquisition tone is heard in his headset.

Originally a company initiative, air-to-air Stinger received DoD funding from 1981. Nevertheless, despite the clear (indeed urgent) need, and interest from many quarters, the US Army failed to approve the ROC (required operational capability) during prolonged study. Not until September 1984 did the Army authorize development of a Stinger kit for the OH-58C/D helicopters, allowing two years for a task that appeared already to have been completed. Operational testing took place in September 1986. Meanwhile, despite having picked Sidewinder, the Marine Corps is studying Stinger as armament for its OV-10A and V-22 Osprey.

Below: RAF technicians attend to an AIM-7E2 Sparrow in its recess under a Phantom FGR.2. One wing is missing.

Above: A blue band marks the location of the Mk 71 continuous-rod warhead of an AIM-7M Sparrow launched from an

F-15A of the USAF (NORAD) 318th Fighter Interceptor Squadron at McChord AFB, Washington state.

Stinger, AIM-92A

Origin: General Dynamics Pomona Division
Propulsion: tandem Atlantic Research solid motors, high-thrust launch motor and longer-burn flight motor
Dimensions: length 1,524mm (60in); body diameter 69.85mm (2.75in); span (fins extended) 91.4mm (3.6in)
Weight: at launch 13.6kg (30lb); complete twin launch installation with electronics and cooling system 45kg (99lb)
Performance: speed Mach 2+; range up to 4.8km (3 miles)
Warhead: Picatinny Arsenal fragmentation, 3kg (6.6lb)
User: US Army initially

From the well-known Stinger infantry SAM, GD Pomona is developing a range of other weapons, including the MLMS (multipurpose lightweight missile system). MLMS uses either the standard Stinger, as now widely

Below: ATAS (air-to-air Stinger) with launcher, adapter, joystick, coolant bottle, a typical roof-mounted sight, launcher electronics and interface box.

APQ-72, APQ-100, APQ-109, APQ-120, or APG-59 (part of AWG-10 or -11) radar. In the Italian F-104S Starfighter the radar is the Rockwell R-21G/H, and in the F-14 Tomcat the powerful Hughes AWG-9. The AIM-7D as also the basis for PDMS Sea Sparrow.

AIM-7E, the next version (also used in the NATO Sea Sparrow system), uses the Rocketdyne free-standing solid motor with Flexadyne propellant (Mk 38), which gives a slightly increased burn-out speed of Mach 3.7. The warhead is of the continuous-rod type, the explosive charge being wrapped in a tight drum made from a continuous rod of stainless steel which shatters into about 2,600 lethal fragments. DA and proximity fuses are fitted. Many thousands of -7E missiles were used in Vietnam by F-4s, but, owing to the political constraints imposed on the American fighters, were seldom able to be fired. Accordingly, AIM-7E2 was developed with shorter minimum range, increased power of man-

oeuvre and plug-in aerodynamic surfaces requiring no tools. The AIM-7C, D and E accounted for over 34,000 missiles.

Introduced in 1977, AIM-7F has all-solid-state guidance, making room for a more powerful motor, the Hercules Mk 58, giving further-enhanced flight speed and range, as well as a larger 40kg (88lb) warhead. Claimed to lock-on reasonably well against clutter up to 10 db, -7F is compatible with CW PD radars (and thus with the F-15 and F/A-18), and has a conical-scan seeker head. In 1977 GD Pomona was brought in as second-source supplier and with Raytheon delivered missiles split roughly between the Navy and the Air Force.

In 1982 both contractors switched to AIM-7M, developed by Raytheon. This has an inverse-processed digital monopulse seeker giving greatly improved results in adverse conditions. GD's first contract was for 690, following 3,000 of the -7F type. The Sparrow has now reached the end of its life.

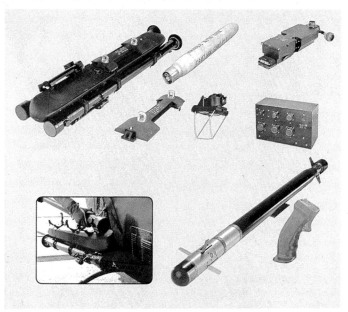

MACHINE GUNS AND CANNON

In 1914 the first fighters were built with pusher engines so that the pilot, or a second crew-member, could fire a machine gun forwards without hitting the propeller. This established the concept of the trainable (often but stupidly called a 'flexible') machine gun, mounted on an aircraft and able to be aimed independently. A year later, in 1915, the true fighter was born when a way was found to fix a machine gun to fire straight ahead, missing the blades of a tractor propeller. In 1934 Britain's Air Ministry and RAF worked out that future combats would need no fewer than eight machine guns, in order to obtain a lethal number of bullet strikes in the short time an enemy aircraft was expected to be in the fighter's sights. By 1941 as many as 12 machine guns were being fitted, all firing ahead, while virtually all large bombers were protected by guns mounted in power-driven turrets.

From the earliest days of air warfare the large-calibre cannon had been used, able to fire various kinds of explosive ammunition with far greater lethality than even a group of bullets. The drawback of the cannon was usually its huge size, ponderous weight, tremendous recoil force, very low rate of fire and limited supply of ammunition (some were loaded by hand, like a field gun). By World War II the shell-firing cannon had overcome most of these drawbacks, and the standard armament of British fighters had switched to four guns of 20mm calibre, while the US fighters tended to adopt a middle course with six heavy machine guns of 12.7mm (0.5in) size. Many bombers continued to fit power-aimed guns, often of 20mm or 23mm calibre, and such guns are still carried by aircraft of the Soviet Union.

Today the pivoted or turreted gun is rare, and seen mainly on helicopters where it can be brought to bear very quickly to fire on ground targets. Helicopter guns of this kind are mounted not on top but underneath, and in some recent installations, such as the AH-64A Apache, the gun is hung completely exposed in the open air.

Almost all other modern aircraft guns are fixed to fire ahead. They may be designed into the aircraft, as is the case with almost all modern fighters, or they can be installed together with their ammunition and electrical control system inside a streamlined nacelle, commonly called a pod, which is hung on standard 356mm (14in) or 762mm (30in) mounts like any other externally carried store. Pods can turn almost any aircraft, including piston and turboprop trainers, into a kind of 1980s version of the Spitfire, but they are generally held to lack the accuracy of a fuselage-mounted gun, and firing them often causes the aircraft to dip nose-down, throwing it off target.

In the Soviet Union the fast-firing GSh-23L cannon (possibly other types as well) has been installed in external pods on pivoted mounts so that, while the pod stays aligned fore-and-aft, the gun can be tilted downwards. This makes it possible to keep firing on ground targets for longer periods than would be possible with a gun firing straight ahead.

A further change in gun installations has been that, as the lethality and firing rate of individual guns has increased, so has the number needed in each aircraft dropped. Whereas virtually all fighters in the decade after World War II had at least four guns, today few have more than one. A single modern gun can be apparently devastating in its effect, and in particular it can consume heavy large-calibre ammunition with such a voracious appetite that keeping more than one such gun fed would be a severe embarrassment. Even as it is, attack helicopters with a single cannon commonly fly with the ammunition tank only partly filled.

Thus, guns have naturally tended to become more powerful and more effective over the years, and they have also been made very much more reliable. During World War II there were often quite long periods when the MRBF (Mean number of Rounds fired Before Failure, i.e. unwanted stoppage of the gun's action) was no higher than 50 or 60. It was for this reason that the Spitfire IB, with two 20mm Hispano cannon, almost damned the whole idea of cannon in the minds of RAF Fighter Command. Today guns made by General Electric and McDonnell Douglas Helicopter Co. achieve an MRBF of 15,000 or more.

One of the chief reasons for the enhanced reliability of modern guns is that they keep each fresh round of ammunition

Above: Developments in the capability of barreled weapons for aircraft have been steady, and paralleled throughout by improved ammunition types matched to weapon and, increasingly, to role.

Right: A highpoint in aircraft weapon design has been the externally-powered General Electric 'Gatling' principle. Such a weapon is the three- or six-barrel GECAL 50 seen here in its three-barrel form.

Right: Combat operations in the 1960s reaffirmed the value of the aircraft cannon. The Phantom was designed without such a weapon, but was soon modified to accept an SUU-23 podded 20mm Vulcan such as that under the centreline of this Phantom FGR.Mk 2.

Below: Another externally-powered weapon type is the Hughes (now McDonnell Douglas Helicopters) Chain Gun type. This is better suited to lower rates of fire, and is seen here in the form of the M230 30mm cannon carried by the AH-64A Apache for the area fire role.

under positive control at all times. Even in a 9g manoeuvre each shell case is held firmly and exactly positioned as it enters the gun, is fired and is then ejected from the action. Powered conveyors feed the ammunition and carry away the spent cases, either dumping the latter overboard or conveying them back to the ammunition tank. The latter is becoming the preferred method, because it avoids damage to the aircraft: once a spent case has been dumped overboard it is obviously no longer under control, and the airflow round a speeding jet is not only extremely powerful but it often moves in unexpected directions.

Of course, it would be nice if one could do away with the case entirely, and this leads into brief consideration of the recent technical development of aircraft guns. Though there have been countless different kinds of action, or 'lock', for rapid-fire automatic weapons – most of them originally patented from 20 to 50 years before they were put to real use – it is hard to escape from the basic concept of an oscillating member called a breech-block or bolt, held in guideways or cam slots inside a fixed casing to which the barrel is attached. Some guns use two superimposed barrels, fired simultaneously, while others use twin barrels fired alternately by bolts linked by a kind of see-saw mechanism. Certainly the most (literally) revolutionary gun of recent years is the family of guns developed by General Electric in Vermont

during the Korean War (1950-3) and popularly known as Gatling guns because, though having nothing else in common with the guns developed by Dr Gatling well over 100 years ago, they have multiple barrels fired in succession

The first of these guns, the M61A1 of 20mm calibre, is today by far the most important aircraft gun in the non-Communist world. Among its advantages are very high rate of fire, compactness and exceptional reliability. Barrel life is also enhanced because each barrel fires only a small proportion of the rounds. From the original M61, developed under the name Project Vulcan, GE has derived a range of related guns far more diverse than any previous 'family' of automatic weapons, with calibres from 5.56mm (0.22in) to 30mm and with the number of barrels selected according to the desired rate of fire. Some are self-powered by the energy released by the firing of each round, while others are driven by the onboard electric, hydraulic or pneumatic system. With the bigger guns the horsepower needed at maximum firing rate is considerable.

One of the many innovations introduced with the M61 gun is linkless feed. Previously, virtually all production aircraft automatic guns of less than 37mm calibre had been fed with ammunition in which successive rounds are connected by links, the cases serving as hinges like a bicycle chain or tank track. A few guns withdraw the rounds, fire them and then reinsert the empty cases in the links to return a linked belt to the magazine. Most simply dump links overboard, or try to shoot the loose links into a collector box. GE's linkless feed conveys the ammunition along a flexible guideway under power, one guideway bringing live rounds to the gun and a second conveying the spent cases back to the magazine.

Looking at a traditional round of ammunition one can see it wastes space. It has a circular cross section and tapers. So-called telescoped ammunition makes much better use of the space by fitting the projectile almost completely inside the case. The West German firm Heckler & Koch have done better still by making the case not round but square, wasting no space at all, but this ammunition is used so far only in infantry weapons.

Undoubtedly, future guns will use a square-section propellant charge inside a combustible case, totally consumed during firing so that nothing is left to be disposed of. The rival alternative scheme feeds nothing but the projectiles to the gun: as each round is rammed into the chamber a metered dose of liquid propellant is squirted in behind it and fired.

MACHINE GUNS AND CANNON

Fabrique Nationale (Browning) M3P

Origin: Fabrique Nationale, Herstal
Calibre: 12.7mm (0.5in)
Length: 1,653mm (65in)
Weight: 29 to 35kg (64 to 77lb) depending on barrel
Rate of fire: variable between 900 and 1,100 rounds per minute by use of a special back plate group
Muzzle velocity: 850 to 920m (2,789 to 3,018ft) per second depending on ammunition type

The M3 series of heavy machine guns for aerial use was developed during World War II as a faster-firing version of the Browning M2, which was rated at between 750 and 850 rounds per minute. The later weapon offered the same levels of mechanical safety and reliablity as the initial gun, but with a markedly higher rate of fire. FN in Belgium is now one of the main manufacturers of these weapons, and the M3M is the version intended for use in helicopter doors with pintle mounts such as the Belgian FN ETNA MPS 1050 and the Italian

Below: A typical helicopter-type mounting for the FN-built 12.7mm (0.5in) Browning.

Aerea DGP (Door Gunner Post). The latter weighs 70kg (154lb) complete with its gun, and has 100 rounds of ready-use ammunition on the mounting and another 400 to 1,000 rounds off it depending on the helicopter type.

The M3P is the standard version for fixed installations, and incorporates such features as a firing solenoid, flash suppressor, a device to prevent 'cook offs' and different barrel options. The most recent round developed for this still-important weapon is the FN 169 Armour-Piercing Explosive Incendiary type, which possesses a complete round weight of 112g (3.95oz) and a projectile weight of 43g (1.52oz) including the penetrator of heavy alloy, which is located just behind the explosive/incendiary filling that occupies the nose of the projectile. This projectile is designed to penetrate the side armour of armoured personnel carriers at a range of 700m (765 yards).

FN HMP

1 Removable muzzle flash-hider.
2 Suspension lugs.
3 Main breech mechanism.
4 Adapter module (to match aircraft installation).
5 Trigger-operated solenoid firing unit.
6 Elevation/windage adjustment.
7 Ammunition feed tray and channel.
8 Magazine (250 rounds).

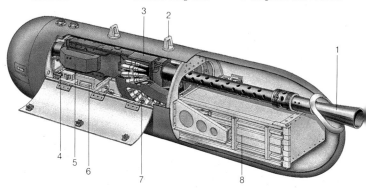

Above: Cutaway of the FN HMP (heavy machine gun pod), a recent mount for a gun basically 70 years old in design yet still of great importance.

Below: This McDonnell Douglas (formerly Hughes) 500 MD Defender has an HMP on the right side and twin TOW missiles on the left.

GUNS AND PODS

Above: This Agusta-Bell 412 has an HMP with the MRL (multiple rocket launcher) beneath, plus a MAG 60/40 machine gun mounted above.

FN ETNA HMP

Origin: Fabrique Nationale, Herstal
Weight: loaded 116kg (256lb)

The ETNA HMP is FN's basic podded installation of the M3P for light tactical aircraft flying at speeds up to Mach 0.75. The 12.7mm (0.5in) machine gun runs almost the complete length of the pod, and its muzzle and associated flash suppressor emerge through a port in the upper side of the pod's nose. The other main items are the 250-round magazine located under the barrel in the forward part of the pod, the collector for spent cases located to the side of the action opposite the feed, and the electro-mechanical safety and cocking device located on the left of the receiver so that the weapon can be cocked only after the aircraft has taken safely to the air. The pod's dimensions include an overall length of 1,810mm (71.25in) and a diameter of 420mm (16.54in). The HMP can also be upgraded in offensive power by the addition on its lower side of an MRL 70 launcher with four 69.85mm (2.75in) unguided rockets. The combination of rockets and a 'fifty' machine gun provides even very light tactical aircraft with a very potent punch.

FN ETNA TMP-5

Origin: Fabrique Nationale, Herstal
Weight: loaded 108kg (238lb)

This is the podded installation of two MAG 60/40 machine-guns for carriage by helicopters and light tactical aircraft. The two guns are installed side-by-side in the upper portion of the pod's forward section, with their muzzles and associated flash suppressors protruding into the outside air, on an elastic cradle arrangement to reduce the recoil forces transmitted to the pod structure and thence to the aircraft. In the space between the guns and the skin of the pod, and extending to the rear of the pod, are the two magazines, each holding 500 rounds of linked ammunition. The spent cases are ejected inwards by each gun and collected in a central container. Like the HMP pod, the TMP-5 is controlled electrically, and features an electro-hydraulic safety and cocking system so that the potential hazards of gun arming on the ground can be avoided, and in-flight stoppages cleared. The pod's dimensions include a total length of 1,900mm (74.8in), a width of 422mm (16.8in) and a height of 425mm (16.7in).

The FN ETNA CMP is a simple development of the TMP-5 to add a reconnaissance capability. The

Below: ETNA equipment on a McDonnell Douglas (Hughes) 530 MG Defender helicopter includes Stingers, rocket pods and the HMP and TMP pods.

Above: In this installation the FN MAG 58 (60/40) is installed in the LFP, standing for light floor pintle. Note the ammunition box and bag for collecting the empty cases.

only major change is the addition of a 35mm camera built into the lower side of the nose, which is deepened to provide the required volume. The carriage of two identical pods (one under each wing) allows stereoscopic images to be built up, with consequent tactical advantages through far more detailed analysis. The pod's overall dimensions are identical with those of the TMP-5, but weight is increased slightly to 114kg (251lb).

FN MAG 60/40

Origin: Fabrique Nationale, Herstal
Calibre: 7.62mm (0.3in)
Length: 1,255mm (49.4in) with flash suppressor
Rate of fire: 1,000 rounds per minute
Muzzle velocity: 840m (2,756ft) per second

The FN MAG (more properly the MAG 60/40) is the aerial version of the MAG 58 rifle-calibre machine gun widely used by ground forces in many parts of the world. The weapon is gas-operated, and fed from a metal-link belt, and one of its chief advantages in the close-support and fire-suppression role is its component commonality with the ground-based version. Naturally enough, ammunition supply is rarely a problem, for the weapon uses the standard 7.62mm x 51 rounds of the ground-based MAG 58. The weapon can be fitted on a variety of helicopter door installations, usually on pintle mounts such as the Belgian FN ETNA AFSA II (complete with ammunition box and combined link plus case collector), but is also widely employed in podded installations for carriage by helicopters and fixed-wing light tactical aircraft.

MACHINE GUNS AND CANNON

Above: Avibras Helicopter Armament System, comprising the MAG 60/40 machine gun mounted above the LM-70-19 rocket launcher, on a Bell 205.

BRAZIL

Avibras gun pods

Avibras has studied several pods for external mounting of cannon and machine guns. One model is in service with the Brazilian air force mounting twin FN MAG 7.62mm (0.3in) machine guns. The company has also developed an integrated Helicopter Armament System comprising rockets (which see) plus a pivoted FN MAG.

CHINA

Chinese cannon

The People's Republic of China has developed from Soviet originals (which see) two basic types of aircraft cannon, which are available for export.

The 23mm gun is available in several forms. The Type 1 is a lighter model intended for fixed or pivoted (turret) mounting. Weighing 39kg (86lb), it fires Type 1 HEI or HEI-tracer ammunition at 800-950 rounds per minute with a muzzle velocity of 680m (2,231ft) per second. The Type 2 is a heavier model for fixed installations. Weighing 43kg (94.8lb) it fires Type 2 API or HEI ammunition at 1,200 rounds per minute with a muzzle velocity of 705m (2,313ft) per second. The Type 2H is fitted with a long perforated muzzle brake; this gun weighs 47kg (103.6lb).

The 30mm gun is Type 1 only. It fires a 0.418kg (14.8oz) projectile at a muzzle velocity of 795m (2,608ft) per second. The rate of fire is not given, but is probably similar to that of the Soviet NR-30.

In 1986 China revealed the existence of a new 23mm aircraft cannon. This is a six-barreled Gatling weapon.

Above: Chinese 23mm Type 2, with barrel life of 6,000 rounds and recoil force not exceeding 2,600kg (5,732lb). It is based on a Soviet gun.

FRANCE

GIAT (DEFA) 552A

Origin: GIAT, St Cloud
Calibre: 30mm
Length: 1,660mm (65.4in)
Weight: 81kg (179lb)
Rate of fire: 1,300 rounds per minute

The first important French jet fighter, the Dassault Ouragan, inevitably had a World War II-type armament of four 20mm Hispano 404 cannon, installed under the forward fuselage. The 12th development Ouragan was used for armament trials, and it was fitted with two of the first flight-cleared DEFA 30mm revolver cannon. In April 1951 the French government ordered 17 development aircraft of the more advanced Mystère II design, and Nos 6, 7 and 9 were fitted with the DEFA 541, first of the DEFA guns to reach pre-production status. No 17 had the broadly similar Hispano 603, which did not go into production. The DEFA was picked for the production Mystère IIC, and from that time onwards virtually every French fighter has had two DEFA cannon, though of progressively improved sub-types, typically with 125-150 rounds per gun. The first production Dassault Mirage IIIC was so cripplingly restricted in internal stowage volume that the SEPR.844 booster rocket was fed with furaline fuel carried in two tanks occupying the gun ammunition bay. This meant that the sole armament was a single R.511 or AA.20 missile, the worst example of 'combat persistence' in history. Later the booster rocket became a rarity, and all subsequent Dassault fighters have had a broadly similar twin-30mm installation in the lower fuselage at the wing roots. DEFA guns have also been widely used in foreign aircraft, including the Israeli IAI Kfir and Lavi, Argentine FMA

Above: Underside of the gun area of a Dassault Mirage F1.C showing the muzzle channels for the DEFA 552A guns and air louvres.

Below: 30mm ammunition on display together with the latest of the DEFA (GIAT) range of fighter guns, the Type 554.

Pucará Charlie, Brazilian version of the AMX and versions of the Spanish CASA C-101. IAI in Israel and Atlas/Armscor in South Africa are two foreign licensees for the DEFA 552/553 (it was officially stated at the unveiling of the Atlas Cheetah in July 1986 that all armament of this aircraft is of South African origin). All these guns fire ammunition virtually identical (apart from details of the belt links) to that fired by the British Aden.

The original DEFA 552, which entered production in 1954, was the French counterpart of the British Aden and likewise derived from the German MG213C, and using a similar five-chambered revolving cylinder. In 1971 production switched to the DEFA 552A (550-F2A), which among other things introduced a chromed barrel having an authorized life of 5,000 rounds. Both these guns use standard Aden/DEFA ammunition, fed by belt to either side. Cases are ejected on the same side as the feed and links on the opposite side. Ignition of each round is electric, and a pyrotechnic cartridge is provided to recock the gun in the event of any stoppage.

GIAT (DEFA) 553

Origin: GIAT, St Cloud
Calibre: 30mm
Length: 1,660mm (65.4in)
Weight: 81kg (179lb)
Rate of fire: 1,300 rounds per minute

The DEFA 553, which entered production in 1968, is an improved version of the DEFA 552A, with more flexible electro-mechanical control and with a new barrel made of nitrochrome steel. MTBF is increased to 4,000 rounds. The control system has four settings: off (inhibited), continuous fire, burst of 0.5 second, and burst of 1 second. Production continued in 1987 for numerous French and foreign aircraft. Total production of the 552/553 series exceeds 11,000.

GIAT (DEFA) 554

Origin: GIAT, St Cloud
Calibre: 30mm
Length: 2,010mm (79.1in)
Weight: 85kg (187lb)
Rate of fire: (air-to-air) 1,800 rounds per minute or (air-to-ground) 1,100 rounds per minute
Muzzle velocity: 820m (2,690ft) per second

The DEFA 554 entered production in 1979. It is a major redesign of the basic French aircraft cannon, and offers higher performance whilst firing unchanged ammunition. Feed can be from either side without modification, and the gun has similar electro-

mechanical controls to the DEFA 553. Two are fitted to the Dassault-Breguet Mirage 2000 and the Brazilian version of the AMX. The DEFA 554 is also suitable for mounting in the CC420 pod which can also accommodate the DEFA 552/552A and DEFA 553.

GIAT M.621

Origin: GIAT, St Cloud
Calibre: 20mm
Length: 2,207mm (86.9in)
Weight: 47kg (103.6lb)
Rate of fire: choice of 740 or 300 rounds per minute
Muzzle velocity: depending on type of round 980-1,030m (3,215-3,379ft) per second
Ammunition weight: projectile 100g (3.5oz)

Like the DEFA cannon, the M.621 was originally developed at the MAT (Manufacture Nationale d'Armes de Tulle). With an average recoil force of only 400kg (882lb), it is suitable for

light aeroplanes and for pivoted or fixed mounting on light helicopters. With a muzzle brake in place of the flash eliminator, and using a shock-absorbing mount, recoil is reduced to 250kg (551lb). The cannon takes standard M56 (M61-type) ammunition, in all versions with steel or brass case, fed by belt from

Above: Uncowled mount of a GIAT M.621 cannon on an AS 355M₂ light helicopter.

either side and with cases and links discharged to the side or downward. The M.621 is available in a pod which, with 150-round belt, weighs 170kg (375lb).

Above: Another helicopter installation of an M.621, this time on a Gazelle, with a 7 x 70mm rocket launcher on the opposite side.

Below: Simplified cutaway of the GIAT M.621 gun pod, which is used chiefly on aeroplanes rather than on helicopters. The shape of the

pod has been specifically designed to achieve a low coefficient of drag, in this case less than 0.22. Reloading takes between 2 and 4 minutes.

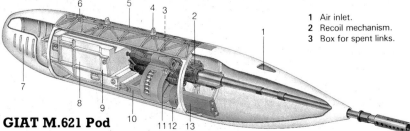

GIAT M.621 Pod

1 Air inlet.
2 Recoil mechanism.
3 Box for spent links.
4 Suspension lugs.
5 Structural beam.
6 Umbilical plug connector.
7 Ventilation louvres.
8 Ammunition box.
9 Access door.
10 Ammunition feed duct.
11 Case ejection chute.
12 Recocking unit.
13 Main electrics box.

MACHINE GUNS AND CANNON

GIAT 30/781

Origin: GIAT, St Cloud
Calibre: 30mm
Length: 1,870mm (73.6in)
Weight: including 10kg (22.5lb) of control electronics 65kg (143lb)
Rate of fire: up to 750 rounds per minute
Muzzle velocity: 1,025m (3,363ft) per second
Ammunition weight: projectile 275g (9.7oz)

GIAT 30/791B

Origin: GIAT, St Cloud
Calibre: 30mm
Weight: 110kg (242.5lb)
Rate of fire: 300/600, 1,500 or 2,500 rounds per minute
Muzzle velocity: 1,025m (3,363ft) per second
Ammunition weight: projectile (typical) 275g (9.7oz).

Above: The HAP version (1985 model) of the proposed Franco-German Eurocopter, which if built would have a Type 781B cannon under the nose.

Below: Designed expressly for future helicopters, the Type 781B cannon is a much lighter weapon than most guns firing high-energy 30mm.

The 30/791B is a new gun developed to meet the requirements of the Dassault-Breguet Rafale B in all its versions. Firing 20-790 (30 x 150) ammunition, with electric hot-wire ignition, the gun is symmetrical and arranged for left or right feed. Firing rate is set by electrical command, with optional fire patterns, for 0.5-second or 1-second bursts, or continuous fire. The links are stripped before the rounds enter the gun, and following a malfunction the gun is automatically recocked. The ammunition includes an HE/AP/Incendiary round which is safe for the first 20m (66ft) of trajectory, is triggered by a 2mm aluminium sheet and self-destructs.

This new lightweight cannon has been developed to arm helicopters (notably the French HAP version of the proposed Franco-German Eurocopter) and light aeroplanes, with internal or pod mounting. It has a single feed for 30 x 550 ammunition, and is claimed to offer long life and outstanding reliability, and a complete training capability without the need to fire. Recoil is only 612kg (1,350lb) (compared with 2,755kg/6,074lb for the 30/791B), and the operator can select single shots or bursts of varied lengths at selected rates.

Left: Though it fires the same high-velocity 30mm ammunition as the 781B, the Type 791B is a heavier gun of the revolver type, giving a much higher rate of fire. It is one of the fastest-firing single-barrel cannon.

Below: The Dassault-Breguet Rafale A prototype has a DEFA 554 30mm gun in the left side of the fuselage, alongside the engine duct. In a production Rafale B this would be replaced by a GIAT 791B, though the installation would look similar.

GERMANY

BK27

Origin: Mauser-Werke Oberndorf
Calibre: 27mm
Length: 2,300mm (90.55in)
Weight: 100kg (220.5lb)
Rate of fire: selectable at 1,000 or 1,700 rounds per minute
Muzzle velocity: 1,025m (3,363ft) per second
Ammunition weight: projectile 260g (9.17oz)

This totally new single-barrel gun with revolving-cylinder feed was developed under one of the three prime contracts in the NAMMA (Tornado) programme, the others being for the aircraft and engine. Diehl and Dynamit Nobel developed and produce the ammunition (comprising AP, APHE, HE, TP and TP-F), which is belt-fed from either side and electrically fired. A particular feature of the Bordkanone 27 is its high muzzle velocity, which is classified.

In retrospect it is possibly unfortunate that NAMMA, the NATO MRCA Management Agency set up by the three governments to act as their executive and contractual interface for the Panavia Tornado programme, issued no guidelines to IWKA-Mauser Werke Oberndorf regarding compatibility with existing NATO ammunition. As a result there now exists the almost ludicrous situation in which this important gun uses ammunition just 3mm too small in calibre for the enormous stocks of 30mm

Above: Forming a unique calibre, making no attempt at inter-operability of ammunition, the BK27 x 145 is a gas-operated revolver cannon.

Above right: All IDS versions of Tornado have two BK27 x 145 guns, one on each side of the fuselage. This aircraft comes from JaboG 31 'Boelcke' wing.

Below: The Alpha Jet can have a 30mm DEFA gun pod or the BK27 x 145 pod (as on this aircraft).

Aden/DEFA ammunition, which is now also used by the gun of the McDonnell Douglas AH-64 Apache helicopter, and just 2mm too large for the new NATO standard high-power 25mm ammunition which is used by the GAU-12/U and British Aden 25 and likely to be widely adopted for other Western aircraft. The original application for the BK27,

the IDS version of Tornado, has two guns in the lower fuselage each with an ammunition box of 180 rounds. The ADV version, produced for the RAF as the Tornado F.3 and also for Oman and Saudi Arabia, has the starboard (right-hand) gun only. The Tornado ECR (Electronic Combat and Reconnaissance), for the West Germany air force, has no guns. Other applications for this gun include the Dassault-Breguet Alpha Jet A light close-support aircraft of the Luftwaffe (centreline jettisonable pod with 150 rounds) and the Swedish Saab JAS 39 Gripen multi-role fighter (single gun mounted internally in lower left side of fuselage with 200 rounds).

MK30F

This Mauser 30mm gun was developed for ground applications, such as the Wildcat flak vehicle, but it also exists in a form suitable for aircraft application. It fires belt-fed ammunition at 800 rounds per minute at a muzzle velocity of 1,100m (3,600ft) per second, and for its calibre is very powerful.

Rh202

This Rheinmetall 20mm gun is used mainly in land and sea applications, but has also been developed for use from aircraft including helicopters. A single-barrel gas-operated weapon, it fires all standard 20mm ammunition at rates normally between 800 and 1,000 rounds per minute but selectable to 600 rounds per minute if desired, with a muzzle velocity in the general range 1,050-1,100m (3,445-3,3600ft) ps.

Left: MBB is testing the BO 105 FFCA (fixed forward-firing cannon installation). The gun is a 20mm Rh202, mounted centrally and fed by the black chute.

MACHINE GUNS AND CANNON

ITALY

P/N 781 586

Origin: Aerea SpA, Milan
Length: complete pod 1,750mm
(68.9in)
Weight: loaded 84kg (185lb)

This pod carries two FN 7.62mm
(0.3in) machine guns, each with
500 rounds. The pod is hung on
NATO 356mm (14in) lugs and
may be jettisoned. Cases and
links may be ejected or retained
in the pod.

MTP

Origin: Aerea SpA, Milan
Length: 1,800mm (70.9in)
Weight: fully loaded pod 175kg
(386lb)

The Multi-Task Pod houses any
standard aircraft 12.7mm (0.5in)
machine gun, with 250 rounds,
plus six 70mm (2.75in) rockets. It
is hung from NATO 356mm (14in)
lugs, and provides for inflight
recocking of the gun.

**Below: Aerea helicopter/
aeroplane pods include (from
the left) the 7.62mm twin pod,
the MTP and the HL-18-50
rocket launcher. The latter is
described in the section
dealing with rockets.**

**Above: Yet another modern use
for the ancient '50 calibre
Browning', the Aerea DGP
provides a seat for the gunner
and a chute for spent cases.**

DGP

Origin: Aerea SpA, Milan
Weight: complete 70kg (154lb)

The Door Gunner Post is an installation for an FN/Browning
12.7mm (0.5in) gun in the doorway of a helicopter. The ammunition box holds 100 rounds, with
other boxes within reach. Spent
cases are ejected via a chute and
links collected in a net bag. The
gunner remains seated even
when firing at an angle of 70°
downwards.

SOUTH AFRICA

GA1

Origin: Armscor, Pretoria
Calibre: 20mm
Length: 1,780mm (70.1in)
Weight: 39kg (86lb)
Rate of fire: 700 rounds per
minute
Muzzle velocity: 720m (2,362ft)
per second

The GA1 is a modernized version
of the German MG151 of World
War II. A wide range of belted
ammunition can be fed from
either side, with electric ignition,

and the gun is claimed to be simple and light. The Rattler system
is a servo-assisted pivoted mount
for helicopters, with gunner seat,
ammunition supply and optical
sight system. It has been tested in
the prototype Alpha XH-1.

Fighter gun

Armscor has stated it is self-
sufficient in aircraft armament,
and the company is known to be
producing a gun for fighters.
Almost certainly it is an advanced DEFA 30mm weapon made
under licence.

SOVIET UNION

UB-12.7

Calibre: 12.7mm (0.5in)
Weight: typical UBK 21.5kg
(47.4lb)
Rate of fire: 1,000 rounds per
minute (varies with model)
Muzzle velocity: 860m (2,822ft)
per second

Many sub-types of Universal
Beresin have been produced
since 1940, and the UBK (unsyn-

**Above: Some versions of the
Soviet Mi-24 (such as this
'Hind-A') have a UBT 12.7mm
in the nose position.**

chronized fixed) version is still found in such aircraft as the MiG-15UTI. The pivoted UBT is installed in helicopters as a fire-suppression weapon with limited secondary capability against helicopters.

4 x 12.7

Designation is not yet known of the four-barreled 12.7mm (0.5in) gun fitted to most versions of the Mi-24 'Hind' helicopter in a power-operated chin turret. It presumably fires standard belt-fed ammunition, probably at a cyclic rate selectable at up to at least 4,000 rounds per minute. Again, the primary role is fire-suppression (including that of light flak vehicles when AP ammunition is fired), and a more effective anti-helicopter capability is possible.

Below: A four-barrel gun is fitted to most attack versions of the Mi-24.

NR-23

The family of 23mm guns designed jointly by Nudel'man and Rikhter has been produced in enormous numbers in several versions which in general replaced the NS series and B-20

weapons. A typical NR-23 weighs 39kg (86lb) and fires at 850 rounds per minute. This gun is made in China as the Type 23-1. In the PV-23 system similar guns are widely used in tail turrets for bomber, tanker, transport and related types of aircraft, though often the later AM-23 is used in turrets, firing at 1,300 rounds per minute. The 43kg (94.8lb) AM-23 is made in China as the Type 23-2.

Below: The Soviet M-4 'Bison' has twin NR-23 turrets with a remote sighting system which was developed from that designed for the Boeing B-29.

Above: The neat recessed installation of a GSh-23L twin-barrel gun in a MiG-21bis.

GSh-23L

A recent application of the pioneer Gast principle, in which the breeches of two guns are interlinked mechanically so that each in effect drives its partner, the weapons of the GSh-23 series are outstanding guns weighing about 72kg (158.7lb) and firing standard 23mm ammunition at up to 3,000 rounds per minute. In the GP-9 pack a single gun is installed together with 200 rounds of ammunition. There is also an external pod in which the gun is pivoted so that it can be depressed to fire on surface targets with the aircraft flying approximately level. A completely different external pod is carried by the Sukhoi Su-21 interceptor. Twin fixed guns are mounted internally in the IAR-93/Orao Romanian/Yugoslav aircraft.

6 x 23

No designation is yet known for the 'Gatling' type gun fitted to the MiG-23BN and MiG-27 attack aircraft. The consensus of Western opinion is that it is of 23mm calibre and has six barrels. It is mounted semi-externally, but with the ammunition box inside the fuselage.

Above: Flame blasts from the NR-30 muzzle brake of a Pakistani F-6 (MiG-19SF).

NR-30

Virtually a scaled-up NR-23, this gun of 30mm calibre entered service in 1954 and is still found in four subtypes in many tactical aircraft. Though lighter than rival 30mm weapons at only 66kg (145.5lb), the NR-30 guns are far more powerful and fire 410g (14.5oz) projectiles at up to 1,000 rounds per minute with a muzzle velocity of 780m (2,560ft) per second. Usually a large combined muzzle brake and flash hider has to be installed; it is common for the muzzle flame to be deflected above and below in wing-root installations.

2 x 30

No designation is yet known for the twin-barrel gun fitted inside the left side of the nose of the Sukhoi Su-25. It is believed to be of 30mm calibre, and may even fire special ammunition more powerful than normal (Soviet 30mm ammunition already being very much more powerful than Aden/DEFA ammunition). The installation suggests that the gun is longer than the NR-30.

6 x 30

No designation is yet known for the gun fitted inside the left wing root of the Mikoyan-Gurevich MiG-29, inside the belly of the Sukhoi Su-24 and, probably, to the Su-27. The consensus of Western opinion is that it is of 30mm calibre and has six barrels. In each installation the ammunition tank must be extremely large, and in the MiG-29 the feed must pass across the top of the left air inlet duct.

MACHINE GUNS AND CANNON

Uni-Pod 0127

Uni-Pod 0127

1 200 rounds capacity magazine.
2 14in suspension lugs.
3 Recoil damper.
4 Ejection chute for spent links.
5 Ejection chute for spent cases.
6 Charger unit.
7 Air ventilation outlet.
8 Compressed air bottles (part of gun charger system).
9 Access pipe for cocking tool.
10 Feed chute.
11 Cal 0.50in M3 Browning machine gun.

Origin: FFV, Linköping
Length: 1,916mm (75.4in)
Weight: loaded 118kg (260lb)

This pod houses a Browning M3 gun of 12.7mm (0.5in) calibre and a belt of 220 rounds. It is for use on helicopters and light aeroplanes including jet trainers. Cases and links may be ejected or collected, and the latest version has inflight recocking and a rounds-counter.

Above: This cutaway shows salient features of the Swedish Uni-Pod, with M3 Browning. In the version illustrated the cases and links are dumped overboard through chutes.

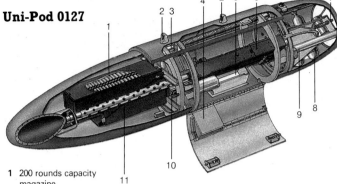

Above: Twin FFV Uni-Pod 0127s are fitted to this military MBB BO 105 CB helicopter. These pods give useful forward-firing firepower (though such an old gun cannot equal the performance of modern weapons) and are self-contained.

Below: Swedish air force conscripts servicing the 30mm Aden pod from an AJ37 Viggen. A compressed-air hose is used to recock the gun. The picture was taken at the F7 Skaraborgs wing at Såtenäs.

Aden pod

Origin: FFV, Linköping
Length: 3,850mm (151.6in)
Weight: loaded 364kg (802lb)

This pod, carried by AJ37 Viggen and Sk60 (Saab 105) aircraft, houses an Aden Mk 4 gun, 150 (option of 200) rounds of 30mm ammunition, and the electrical control system. The pod is attached by a variety of standard fittings.

KAA

Origin: Oerlikon-Bührle, Zurich
Calibre: 20mm
Length: 2,690mm (105.9in)
Weight: 88kg (194lb)
Rate of fire: 1,100 rounds per minute
Muzzle velocity: 1,040-1,100m (3,412-3,600ft) per second

The KAA is one of a family of guns specifically developed to arm tactical helicopters. Guns may be pintle-mounted in the doorway or externally, or mounted in a fixed cradle on each side or on the centreline. In either event the result is a highly capable armament fit with a wide range of air-to-surface and air-to-air capabilities.

Below: Particularly heavy armament for a 'Huey', this AB 205 has paired TOW missiles plus the Oerlikon GBH-A01 gun system. The gun is a 25mm, fed from ammunition boxes inside the fuselage.

KAD

Origin: Oerlikon-Bührle, Zurich
Calibre: 20mm
Length: 2,744mm (108in)
Weight: 68kg (150lb)
Rate of fire: about 850 rounds per minute
Muzzle velocity: about 1,040m (3,412ft) per second

The KAD is a lighter helicopter gun with a slightly slower firing rate than the KAA. As with the other guns of this family, ammunition types are AP, APDS-T, HEI, SAPHEI and TP, all available with or without tracer.

Above: Westland Lynx armed with the 20mm Oerlikon KAD in a fixed mounting.

KBA

Origin: Oerlikon-Bührle, Zurich
Calibre: 25mm
Length: 3,105mm (122.24in)
Weight: 112kg (247lb)
Rate of fire: 570 rounds per minute
Muzzle velocity: 1,100-1,360m (3,600-4,462ft) per second

This 25mm gun has exceptional power, stemming from its tremendous muzzle velocity, which varies with projectile weight from 150g (5.3oz) for APDS-T up to 180g (6.35oz) for other species. As in the case of the KAA and KAD, the ammunition belt is fed from a container inside the helicopter, one magazine per gun.

Above: The Oerlikon KCA is one of the most powerful of all single-barrel cannon.

KCA

Origin: Oerlikon-Bührle, Zurich
Calibre: 30mm
Length: 2,691mm (105.94in)
Weight: 136kg (300lb)
Rate of fire: 1,350 rounds per minute
Muzzle velocity: 1,030m (3,379ft) per second

This 30mm fighter gun, used in the JA37 Viggen, has a single barrel and four-chamber revolver cylinder which the pneumatic cocking system cycles three times to charge all chambers before the gun is fired. Ammunition is considerably more powerful than the Aden/DEFA type, the projectile weighing 360g (12.7oz) and having a high muzzle velocity resulting from a propellant charge weighing twice as much as the projectile. This gives short flight times and flat trajectories. Ammunition types are AP, HEI, SAPHEI and TP.

Hispano Mk 5

Origin: BMARC Ltd, Grantham (and Hispano-Suiza SA)
Calibre: 20mm
Length: 2,052mm (80.8in)
Weight: 42kg (92.6lb)
Rate of fire: 580-640 rounds per minute
Muzzle velocity: 840m (2,788ft) per second

Nearly 99,000 'Hispano' cannon, essentially all in 20mm calibre, were made in the UK from 1939. Large numbers, mostly of the Mk 5 type with a shorter barrel, are still in worldwide service. Ammunition, including AP, HEI, ball and tracer, is percussion-fired.

Aden Mk 4

Origin: Royal Ordnance, Small Arms Division
Calibre: 30mm
Length: 1,590mm (62.6in)
Weight: 87kg (191.8lb)
Rate of fire: 1,200-1,400 rounds per minute
Muzzle velocity: 790m (2,592ft) per second

During World War II the pre-eminent British fighter design team had been that of Supermarine Division of Vickers-Armstrongs, and their first jet, the Attacker, retained the standard late-wartime armament of four 20mm Hispano Mk 5 in the wings. With the swept-wing Swift the 30mm Aden was specified, and it appeared essential to put this heavier gun in the fuselage. At first there was room for only two, but with the Swift F.2 an extra pair was installed, the wing inboard leading edge being extended forward to accommodate the ammunition. This caused unacceptable pitch-up when pulling g at high speed and played a major role in terminating the programme and causing the decline of the company. Supermarine also built a large twin-jet naval fighter, the two versions differing mainly in that the Model 508 was designed for four Adens and the Model 529 for four of the smaller Hispanos. Eventually this led to the Scimitar, which was the first aircraft to have four Adens installed conventionally under the nose, individually removable. The contemporary RAF night fighter, the Gloster Javelin, had such an enormous and thick wing that (having originally been planned with a 94mm/3.7in or 114mm/4.5in recoilless gun in the fuselage) it entered service with four Adens in the wings outboard of the main landing gears. The rival de Havilland D.H.110 had similar armament in the fuselage, but by the time it had become the Navy's Sea Vixen the guns had been judged obsolete and replaced by packs of FFARs. The first and only British supersonic fighter, the Lightning, thus emerged at a time of much argument over guns. The Mks 1, 1A and 2 all had an Aden Mk 4 on each side of the cockpit (they put out quite a flash at night). The Mk 3 dispensed with guns, as did the T.4 and T.5 trainers; but by the time the F.6 came along the RAF had begun to recognize that guns had some value and adopted the twin-Aden pack, which could be fitted into the front of the enlarged belly tank, which BAC had originally developed for export customers, it was also fitted to the rebuilt F.2A. In the tiny Folland Gnat an Aden was mounted in the fuselage side, its muzzle in the lip of the engine inlet; remarkably, its use did not cause engine problems and several gun victories were later scored by Indian Gnats. Another export user of the Aden was Sweden, which put M/55 Adens into the 80°-swept inboard wings of the Saab J35 Draken. In the final production version, the J35F 'Filip', electronics replaced the left-hand gun; soon there was pressure for the other gun to be restored, and many Drakens have flown with extra guns in external pods.

Derived directly from the wartime MG213C, the Aden got its name from Armament Development Enfield, though Royal Armament R&D Establishment at Ft Halstead also played a major role. Like the German original, it has a single barrel indexed at the 12 o'clock position on a five-chambered revolving feed cylinder. The gun is operated by a gas-driven slide, firing is by 26V electrics, and cocking and charging the cylinder before opening fire is pneumatic. Adens were first used in the Hawker Hunter, in which four barrels remained with the aircraft while the four breech units and empty ammunition boxes were winched out as a single package and replaced. In such aircraft is the Jaguar, Gnat, Marut and Draken the gun is mounted internally. In the Harrier two Mk 4 guns, each with up to 130 rounds, are scabbed on the underside of the fuselage. The Mk 5 Straden was a rapid-fire version which has been overtaken by the Aden 25.

Below: The Aden gun pods (seen here on a Sea Harrier FRS.1) have some effect as lift-improvement devices. Each contains the gun and its ammunition, and is detachable.

MACHINE GUNS AND CANNON

Right: The newly available Aden 25 fits the same mounting points as the 30mm gun. For an increase in weight of less than 10 per cent it offers three times the kinetic energy. Cases and links are ejected.

Aden 25

Origin: Royal Ordnance, Small Arms Division
Calibre: 25mm
Length: 2,285mm (90in)
Weight: 92kg (202.8lb)
Rate of fire: 1,650-1,850 rounds per minute
Muzzle velocity: 1,050m (3,445ft) per second

Derived from the 30mm Straden, this new gun fires the more powerful NATO 25mm ammunition in a gun as far as possible installationally interchangeable with the older 30mm gun. A significant change is that the ammunition is percussion-fired, eliminating electromagnetic hazards. BAe and Royal Ordnance are together perfecting the design of a scabbed-on pod for the Harrier GR.5; each of the two pods houses one gun and 100 rounds (the ammunition is longer than the 30mm type and has greater case diameter). The two pods with full ammunition weigh 430kg (948lb).

Right: The MBB/Kawasaki BK 117A-3M typically has eight anti-tank missiles (TOW or HOT) and a Lucas turret. Here the turret is shown with a streamlined casing, fitted with a gun with a plain muzzle.

Below: Lucas Aerospace developed the helicopter gun turret as a company venture, in an amazing example of private enterprise by a British company which deserves to find an increasingly wide market. It would in the longer term pay to use a modern gun such as the GECAL 50.

Helicopter Gun Turret

Origin: Lucas Aerospace, Actuation Division, Wolverhampton
Gun: Browning 12.7mm (0.5in)

Lucas has produced this turret for fitting in the chin position on helicopters. Armed with a traditional Browning gun, it has hydraulic elevation to +20°/±45° and azimuth movement of ±120°, at rates up to 80° per second. Aiming can be slaved to helicopter sensors, or sighting systems or a helmet sighting system. The installed turret would be designed to match the helicopter, with a close-fitting casing and an integral or remote magazine.

Below: The Lucas turret has been designed for minimum depth, to ease installation as a modification to existing helicopters whilst minimizing drag and vulnerability, and to avoid injury to the crew in a crash landing. In this installation (in a UH-1) no streamlined casing is used.

Lucas Helicopter Gun Turret

1 Ammunition feed.
2 Geared ring (mounted on floor of helicopter).
3 Hydraulic connectors which allow turret to traverse.
4 400 rounds capacity magazine.
5 Valve block.
6 Gearbox.
7 Hydraulic motor for azimuth movement.
8 Re-cocking/charging actuator (to discharge round in the event of a misfire).
9 Recoil damper.

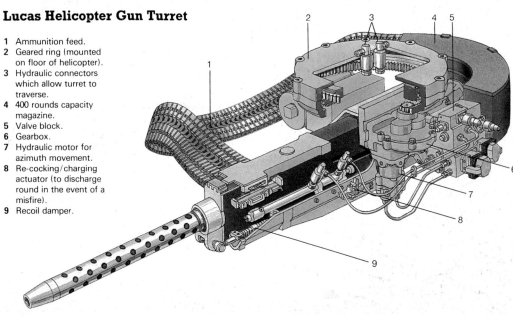

Browning rifle-calibre

Origin: original design by J.M. Browning and made by Colt's Patent Fire Arms Co., later widely licensed (including UK and Belgium)
Calibre: 7.62mm (0.30in) or 7.7mm (0.303in)
Length: 980mm (38.6in)
Weight: typical 10kg (22lb) but varying slightly with model
Rate of fire: 1,200 rounds per minute
Muzzle velocity: 720m (2,362ft) per second

Amongst the many older weapons that still play a useful part in the air armament field, generally as trainable weapons in helicopter doors, is the Browning 7.62mm (0.3in) rifle-calibre weapon. This is often of the standard M1919A4 ground variety, but occasionally encountered is the specialized M2 aircraft version. The M1919 series is based closely on the M1917 machine gun, but fitted with an air-cooled barrel in place of the earlier weapon's water-cooled variety. This contributes to the weapon's comparatively light weight of 14.1kg (31lb), and other advantages of the weapon are a good rate of fire (500 rounds per minute), extreme reliability, and feed from a boxed 250-round linked belt. Ammunition and parts supply offer no problems as the M1919 series is still in very widespread service.

The definitive aircraft version (for use in fixed and trainable installations) is the M2, which is basically similar to the M1919A4 but evolved from the M1917 via the M1918, M1918A1, M1919, M1921 and M1922, which all introduced lightened components in an effort to boost rate of fire to 1,200 rounds per minute. This weapon was extensively used in the 1920s, 1930s and 1940s, slowing giving way to the larger 'fifty-caliber' machine gun.

Browning M2/M3

Origin: original design by J.M. Browning and made by Colt's Patent Fire Arms Co., later widely licensed including UK
Calibre: 12.7mm (0.5in)
Length: typically 1,460mm (57.5in)
Weight: typical 29kg (64lb)
Rate of fire: (M2) 750-850 or (M3) 1,200 rounds per minute
Muzzle velocity: 820-850m (2,690-2,790ft) per second depending on ammunition

Very large numbers of these famous guns are still in use, and several factories are still producing new examples, the most important being FN in Belgium.

This basic design of gun has been deployed in such numbers over so long a period that it merits a brief further discussion. In 1918 it was already apparent that rifle-calibre guns were becoming ineffective against 'modern aeroplanes in which vital parts are armoured'. General John J. Pershing, C-in-C of the American Expeditionary Forces in Europe, personally cabled the Army Ordnance Department calling for the urgent development of an aircraft machine gun having a calibre of at least 12.7mm (0.5in) and muzzle velocity not lower than 823m (2,700ft) per second. There was at this time already the 11mm (0.43in) Vickers, and considerable amounts of 11mm ammunition were available. The Ordnance Board had already studied an 11mm Browning, but when it received Pershing's directive it authorized development of a new 12.7mm gun, with highest priority on aircraft use, secondly as a water-cooled ground gun and thirdly as a tank machine gun. Design was handled by John M. Browning at Winchester Arms Co. and Fred T. Moore at Colt Patent Fire Arms Co., to whom a contract was awarded. The original Browning Cal 0.50 Model 1921 suffered from various deficiencies, notably overheating and (like the early weapon) inability to feed from the right side. In 1927-32 Dr (later Colonel) S.G. Green improved the gun into the Model M2, with a universal receiver for left or right feed and a longer and heavier barrel matched to more powerful ammunition, yet having much longer life. In the Depression money was tight but the US Navy came to the rescue with funds, and after further improvements the M2 was a mature and extremely reliable weapon by World War II when production was shared by no fewer than nine manufacturers. In 1946 development was completed on the M3, in which by numerous often small changes the rate of fire was increased by 50 per cent, typically from 800 to 1,200 rounds per minute. This remained in production for US fighters until 1955, and together with the HB (Heavy Barrel) ground gun is still manufactured by FN Herstal SA in Belgium, and spares are made by numerous companies throughout the world. Most of the many thousands of guns in current use are reconditioned M2s, usually incorporating new barrels. Several companies in at least four countries manufacture compatible ammunition.

Above: The B-52D had a Bosch Arma MD-9 tail turret (here with covers off) with four 'fifties'. Today's B-52G has similar guns in the ASG-15.

Below: A hand-aimed Browning HB (heavy barrel) 0.5in mounted on the right side of a 'Huey' with floodlights.

MACHINE GUNS AND CANNON

Above: Originally known as the Emerson MiniTAT (Tactical Aircraft Turret), the FTS is seen here in the fully extended position under a Bell UH-1N (Bell 212). Various kinds of sight can be used.

limit its firing is halted and its partner is increased from 2,400 to 4,200 rounds per minute to maintain the volume of fire. The elevation limits are +15° to -90°. Each gun has 3,000 rounds stored in a drum.

Emerson FTS

Origin: Emerson Electric, St Louis
Weight: exclusive of gun and ammunition 62.6kg (138lb)

Originally called MiniTAT, the Flexible Turret System can be readily fitted to any light helicopter without (it is claimed) structural modification. It carries a General Electric M134 (7.62mm/0.3in Minigun), fed with ammunition from boxes in the fuselage. The mount is electrically aimed in any direction and with elevation limits of +10° to −70°.

Emerson M28

This helicopter armament system comprises a chin turret mounting an M134 Minigun and an M129 grenade-launcher. The 7.62mm (0.3in) gun fires at 2,000 or 4,000 rounds per minute to 1,370m (4,500ft); the M129 fires up to 300 grenades of 40mm calibre to the same range at 420 rounds per minute. Azimuth limits are 114° left or right, and elevation limits +17.5°/−50°

Emerson M21 MAMEE

This helicopter armament system comprises two M134 Miniguns and two M158 rocket pods each with seven 70mm (2.75in) rockets. The guns traverse from 70° outboard to 12° inboard, and when either gun reaches the inboard

Above: Many early AH-1G and related sub-types of HueyCobra have been fitted with the Emerson M28 armament system. This chin turret is seen here with an M134 Minigun nearer the camera, with an M129 launcher for 40mm grenades on the further side.

Left: In this version of the Emerson M21 MAMEE the rocket launcher is not the seven-tube but the 19 x 70mm variety (there are several of these). The flexible ammunition feed conveyor can be seen linking the gun with the ammunition drum on top.

GE M134, GAU-2B/A Minigun

Origin: General Electric Company, Burlington, Vermont
Calibre: 7.62mm (0.3in)
Length: 802mm (31.56in) with motor
Weight: 30.4kg (67lb)
Rate of fire: selectable 2,000 or 4,000 rounds per minute or alternatively 3,000 or 6,000 rounds per minute
Muzzle velocity: 869m (2,850ft) per minute

A natural derivative of the famed M61 Vulcan guns, but on a much smaller scale of size, the Minigun has been made in large numbers for incorporation in various helicopter armament systems and pods for light attack and trainer aircraft.

The Minigun's operating system is based on a barrel assembly (externally powered by a two-speed electric motor) to rotate round a common axis, each of the six barrels having its own bolt assembly operated by a follower-fitted cam that moves in a cam path machined into the rotor assembly. The movement of

Above: The General Electric A/A49E-3 external Minigun mount for the UH-1N (and other helicopters) is dominated by the ammunition tanks.

Left: The Sikorsky UH-60A Black Hawk, standard tactical helicopter of the US Army, is normally unarmed, but this example has a pintle-mounted Minigun on each side.

Below: Night firing of the SUU-11B/A Minigun pods of an AC-47 'Puff the Magic Dragon', the Vietnam gunship.

Minigun pod

General Electric produces a standard external pod for the Minigun, with designations SUU-11B/A (USAF) and M18A1 (Army). Hung on 356mm (14in) NATO lugs, it has a length of 2,159mm (85in), and weighs 147kg (324lb) loaded with 1,500 rounds of ammunition, linkless feed system and electrical control package. Cases are ejected overboard downwards.

this follower turns the rotor's basically circular movement into the bolt's essentially fore-and-aft movement; this controls the cycle of chambering, firing and extracting one round per barrel per complete rotation. Thus even at the Minigun's maximum rate of 6,000 rounds per minute each barrel fires only 1,000 rounds, giving the exceptional life of about 100,000 gun rounds. This rotary action also has the beneficial effect of reducing internal loads on the gun, thereby increasing reliability, and the use of an external power system obviates the need for a cocking and re-cocking system as dud rounds are automatically ejected. This last also enhances the weapon's utility in remotely-controlled installations. The electric motor has two speeds, giving the choice of firing rates. The feed is linkless, rounds supplied to the magazine in linked belts being automatically delinked as they are loaded.

The designation GAU-2B/A is used for the basic US Air Force weapon, the equivalent designation for the US Army version, which has generally a 4,000-round per minute rate, being M134 Minigun. The type has proved extremely successful in the role of suppressing ground fire of various types.

Above: The GAU-8/A is probably the most powerful aircraft gun. Here propellant smoke spews from an A-10A Thunderbolt II which is also carrying HOBOS and Paveway 'smart' attack weapons.

Below: Specialist ground crew of the USAF 354th Tactical Fighter Wing at Myrtle Beach AFB, South Carolina, prepare to operate the massive 30mm loading system of an A-10A. Over a ton of ammo is carried.

GE GAU-8/A Avenger

Origin: General Electric Company, Burlington, Vermont
Calibre: 30mm
Length: complete gun system 6,400mm (252in)
Weight: complete gun system with loaded ammunition drum 1,723kg (3,800lb)
Rate of fire: selectable 2,100 or 4,200 rounds per minute
Muzzle velocity: 1,066m (3,500ft) per second

From the outset the GAU-8/A was designed for killing tanks and other hard-skinned ground targets, and because of its size and power it was clear that any future CAS (close air support) aircraft armed with it would have to be virtually designed around the gun. In the A-10A the gun fills the entire lower central part of the fuselage, the enormous ammunition drum extending back 6.4m (nearly 21ft) from the muzzle, almost touching the front of the forward tank in the mid-fuselage. Because of the gun's power and recoil forces it was desirable to place the axis of the firing barrel (at the six o'clock position on the gun) on the aircraft centreline.

This in turn required the nose landing gear to be offset to the right side of the aircraft. Each round of Staballoy ammunition weighs 690g (1.52lb), and the AP projectiles 354g (0.78lb), both values very much greater than for previous 30mm ammunition. The depleted uranium Staballoy, cheaper and much easier to fabricate than the tungsten previously used for AP cores, has proved entirely satisfactory and caused no problems in service. A typical attack procedure is for two A-10As to fly low-level orbits of about 1,220m (4,000ft) diameter, breaking off on each to fire a 1-second burst (about 70 rounds) with the fixed sight set to 1g at a range of 1,220m (4,000ft). Each orbit takes around 16 seconds and causes speed to bleed off, and after the second circle it is usual to retire to build up speed and reassess the situation. By this time only about 140 of the 1,350 rounds will have been fired. There is clearly a basic problem in aiming accurately at sufficient targets to use up the ammunition whilst at the same time standing at least 610m (2,000ft) away from the target area to avoid the most intense defensive fire. This attack mode also does not take into account the profusion of close-range SAMs that equip all Soviet front-line motor-rifle regiments.

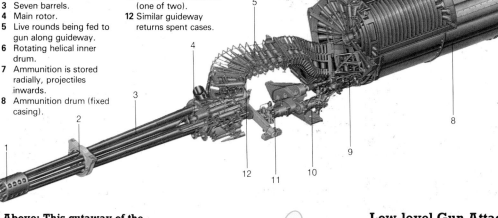

GAU-8/A Avenger

1 Muzzle assembly and blast suppressor.
2 Front mount (selected to adjust harmonization of barrels).
3 Seven barrels.
4 Main rotor.
5 Live rounds being fed to gun along guideway.
6 Rotating helical inner drum.
7 Ammunition is stored radially, projectiles inwards.
8 Ammunition drum (fixed casing).
9 Drive gearbox to drum and linkless feed.
10 Drive shafts from hydraulic motors.
11 Hydraulic drive motor (one of two).
12 Similar guideway returns spent cases.

Above: This cutaway of the GAU-8/A shows features which are repeated on a smaller scale of size in most of the 'Gatling' type General Electric aircraft guns. In this installation, in the A-10A, a very large quantity of ammunition (over 1,100 rounds) is carried.

The complete GAU-8/A gun system is the biggest and most powerful ever built for aircraft; its muzzle horsepower is many times greater than that of World War II 75mm or 105mm (2.95 or 4.13in) guns, and dozens of times greater than that of wartime rapid-fire cannon. It was designed specifically for the tank-killing role in the Fairchild A-10A, and as noted above fires specially high-energy armour-piercing ammunition with a penetrator core of depleted uranium. Other rounds in the linkless feed from the 1,174-round storage drum are HEI and TP. The drum is linked to the gun via a two-way feed which returns cases to the drum. An indication of the scale of this gun is afforded by the fact that choosing aluminium as the case material saves 373kg (600lb) on the weight

of the loaded drum. The gun has seven barrels driven by dual hydraulic motors, a single motor giving the half-speed firing rate. The seven-chamber revolver drum is normally empty, except when the gun is firing. On release of the trigger, rounds already in the gun are reversed out again into the feed system. Despite this, within 0.55 second of again pressing the trigger the gun is firing at maximum rate. The gun is exceptionally accurate, and barrel life is a minimum of 20,000 rounds.

Low-level Gun Attacks

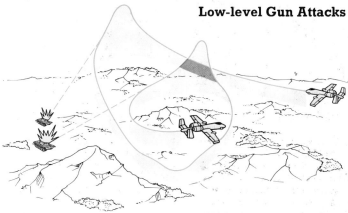

Above: Here shown with its row of access covers open, the bay housing the A-10A's gun and ammunition has a length of 6.4m (21ft). As the mighty gun has to be on the centreline, the nose landing gear had to be offset to the right side of the aircraft.

Left: As explained on the facing page, A-10As make fairly brief firing runs during which only small amounts of ammunition can be used. On each run the pilot zooms up to between 61m (200ft) and 152m (500ft).

Left: Looking up at the underside of a US Marine Corps AV-8B Harrier II. A bulge links the two pods to convey ammunition (right hand pod) to the GAU-12/U gun (left). Aerodynamic strakes are added to increase the effectiveness of the pods as lift-improvement devices.

Above: The bare GAU-12/U gun, seen without its 11.1kW (15hp) pneumatic drive motor, is mostly just the five barrels. General Electric state that MRBF (mean rounds before failure) exceeds 100,000 shots. Such reliability and life has never been achieved before.

GE GAU-12/U Equaliser

Origin: General Electric Company, Burlington, Vermont
Calibre: 25mm
Length: 2,134mm (84in)
Weight: 125kg (275.5lb)
Rate of fire: usually 3,600 rounds per minute but can be set at up to 4,200 rounds per minute
Muzzle velocity: 1,100m (3,600ft) per second with slight variations for different ammunition

First of the Vulcan family to fire the high-power standard NATO 25mm ammunition, the GAU-12/U is a five-barrel weapon driven by a pneumatic motor turned at 9,000rpm by engine bleed air and geared down to the rear of the gun. Ammunition comprises API, APDS, HEI and TP. In the AV-8B Harrier II a magazine of 300 rounds is scabbed on the right side of the aircraft's belly. A bridge connects the linkless feed to the gun, which occupies an outwardly similar pod on the left side. These pods also act as LIDs. The crossover bridge also houses the drive shaft for the magazine feed system. Cases are ejected.

MACHINE GUNS AND CANNON

Above: The GPU-5/A is a self-contained pod housing the GAU-13/A gun, which is a lightened four-barrel version of the GAU-8/A. The ram-air inlet in the nose, next to the muzzle aperture, provides pneumatic drive power. Compared with 20mm, the 30mm ammo offers four times the kinetic energy at twice the range.

GE GAU-13/A

Origin: General Electric Company, Burlington, Vermont
Calibre: 30mm
Length: 2,794mm (110in)
Weight: 153.8kg (339lb)
Rate of fire: variable up to 3,000 rounds per minute
Muzzle velocity: 987 (API) or 1,037m (3,238 or 3,400ft) per second

The GAU-13/A is a lightweight derivative of the massive GAU-8/A, using four barrels instead of seven and possessing many advanced features. It uses the same high-pressure giant-size ammunition, and the action incorporates the same reverse-clearing oper-

ation which quickly removes rounds already in the gun each time the trigger is released. The gun has bleed-air or stored pneumatic drive, with microprocessor control, and in USAF service it is carried externally in the GPU-5/A pod to give fighter and attack aircraft an anti-armour capability. The GPU-5/A is 4.3m (169in) long, weighs 862kg (1,900lb) complete with 353 rounds of ammunition, and carries the ammunition in two helical layers (surrounding the gun) which convey the live rounds and fired empties in an endless linkless conveyor system as in the GAU-8/A. The pod is completely self-contained and is designed for supersonic speeds.

GE 225

Origin: General Electric Company, Burlington, Vermont
Calibre: 25mm
Length: 2,210mm (87in)
Weight: with feeder and drive system 81.6kg (180lb)
Rate of fire: variable up to 2,000 rounds per minute
Muzzle velocity: HEI 1,097m

(3,600ft) or APDS 1,341m (4,400ft) per second
Ammunition: 25mm Bushmaster family

This versatile gun uses the twin-barrel Gast principle (see 'Pre-1920' section) in which an oscillating lever fires a round in one barrel whilst extracting the case from the other. A rear cam multiplies the reciprocating motion and imparts controlled acceleration to the bolts. A single shaft and sprocket feed the linked-belt ammunition to both barrels from either side of the gun; cases are ejected downwards. The GE225 can be self-powered, or driven externally (2.2kW/3hp at 750 rounds per minute, 18.6kW/25hp at 2,000 rounds per minute). Live rounds are automatically cleared at the end of each burst. In helicopter mounts, such as the Bell AH-1S chin turret, a soft mount minimizes recoil forces.

Below: The GE 225 is not a 'Gatling' but has twin fixed barrels. It fires very high velocity Bushmaster-type 25mm ammunition. It could be fitted to a future LHX helicopter.

GECAL 50

Origin: General Electric Company, Burlington, Vermont
Calibre: 12.7mm (0.5in)
Length: 1,181mm (46.5in)
Weight: three barrels 30kg (66lb), six barrels 43.5kg (96lb)
Rate of fire: three barrels up to 4,000 rounds per minute, six barrels up to 8,000 rounds per minute
Muzzle velocity: 884m (2,900ft) per second

This company-developed gun promises to find a wide range of applications throughout the world, because it fires all standard US and NATO ammunition of this calibre. Technically it is a typical member of the Vulcan family derived from the M61. Few guns are so flexible and versatile. The GECAL 50 can be self-powered by gun gas, or have electric, hydraulic or pneumatic drive. It can be fed from any direction with linked or linkless ammunition. It can have three or

Above: Making a fantastic contrast with the ancient 'fifty-calibre Browning', the GECAL 50 fires the same ammunition but at many times the (selectable) rates and MRBF. This one is on a UH-60A.

Below: Two lightweight GE guns for helicopter pintle mountings. The small one is a 7.62 Minigun; the bigger weapon the GECAL 50 in its more common version which has three barrels.

six barrels, depending on the rate of fire desired, and the barrel length can be anything from 915m to 1,295mm (36in to 51in) to allow ballistic performance optimized to the mission. When used with linked ammunition the gun has a delinking feeder. Gun clearing is accomplished by a declutching feeder with linked ammunition and through gun reversal in linkless systems. A unique feature, which GE may introduce on other guns, is a 'controlled burst' firing rate control which almost instantly reaches the full cyclic rate and then stops the burst after about 10 rounds, all of which impact the target virtually simultaneously. Among the wide range of types of ammunition is an M17 tracer round visible to a range of about 1,600m (5,250ft).

The GECAL 50 is marketed as an internal gun, or as a conformal or external podded gun, but its chief immediate applications are expected to be in helicopters and other VTOL aircraft. It is likely to be a standard fit on several versions of the Bell/Boeing V-22 Osprey, set to 2,000 rounds per

minute and fed with 1,200 rounds in a linkless feed system which retains the spent cases. Pintle-mounted versions using linked ammunition would be used in door gun positions. The gun can be field-stripped by one man in a few minutes without tools, and its predicted reliability is not less than 50,000 mean rounds between failures.

GE M195/M35

The M35 is an installation of a Vulcan-type six-barrel gun under the left weapon sponson of AH-1G helicopters of the US Army. The gun, the M195, is basically an M61 gun with a different drive, reduced rate of fire of 750 to 1,000 rounds per minute, and with blast deflectors on the muzzles of 1,026mm (40.4in) barrels. The 950 rounds are carried in boxes on the left and right sides of the helicopter and fed by a linked belt. The total system weight with ammunition is 530kg (1,168lb).

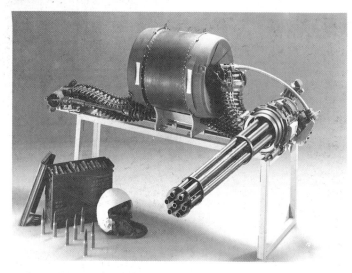

GE M61 Vulcan

Origin: General Electric Company, Burlington, Vermont
Calibre: 20mm
Length: 1,875mm (73.8in), (SUU pods) 5,055mm (199in)
Weight: (M61A1) 120kg (265lb), (GAU-4) 125kg (275lb), (SUU-23/A pod, empty) 489kg (1,078lb), (SUU-23/A pod, with 1,200 rounds) 785kg (1,730lb)
Rate of fire: maximum 6,600 rounds per minute; can be set to 6,000 or 4,000
Muzzle velocity: 1,036m (3,400ft) per second

The US General Electric Company began studying the design of cannon for USAF fighter aircraft in 1950. Its office at Burlington, Vermont, contracted to develop a new gun using the principle of multiple barrels first used in the mid-19th century by Dr Gatling. This offers several advantages. As each barrel is at a different part of the firing cycle, the whole firing process can be carried out simultaneously in all the barrels, so that if there are (say) six barrels, then rate of fire can be multiplied by six. Moreover, this can be done without any increase in the heating or wear of the individual barrels. The only drawback is the high rate of consumption of ammunition, and a general need for large feed magazines.

The Gatling had been cranked round by hand, but the General Electric Project Vulcan guns, which were first fired in pre-production form in 1953, needed much greater drive power. The original form of Vulcan gun had six barrels firing standard 20mm ammunition. This was fed by long linked belts, and though the gun appeared from very early in development to be unexpectedly reliable, the unprecedented rate of fire caused severe problems with the belts. Links broke, stretched or jammed, and link disposal was often difficult. Development soon began on a completely new linkless feed, and by 1956 it was clear that each aircraft installation would have to

Above: Bench assembly of the M61A1 gun installation in the F-16 Fighting Falcon. The power-drive from the drum feeds up to 515 rounds of ammunition to the offset gun.

Righ: Grey smoke spews from the offset gun port of an F-16A Fighting Falcon as it makes a straffing run on a ground target. The pilot aims with the assistance of his electronic head-up display.

be individually tailored. Since then General Electric has designed more than 30 quite different Vulcan installations. They include externally powered and self-powered guns, in fixed and trainable mounts, fed by linked belts or linkless feed systems.

All versions of the gun are basically similar. The most common is the M61A1 family, driven by the aircraft's hydraulic or, in a few cases, electrical power system. At full rate about 35hp is needed to drive the gun and linkless feed. The six identical barrels are attached to the drum-like breech rotor which revolves (anticlockwise when viewed from behind the gun) inside the

Above: USAF armament tradesmen start reloading the ammunition drum of an F-15 Eagle. The 20mm belt enters next to the right front Sparrow missile attachment.

stationary breech housing. The latter has a deep elliptical slot machined on its inner wall in which run six cam followers, one on the breech of each barrel. As the barrels rotate, the followers are thus driven linearly into and out of the associated breech, successively chambering, firing and extracting the rounds. At the muzzle end the barrels are clamped together, there being a choice of clamps giving slightly different

barrel angles and thus more varied dispersion patterns.

The GAU-4 self-powered version is driven by energy from the exploding propellant charges. The gun is initially fired by an electrically operated inertia starter (or, in older models, a powerful spring) which starts the barrels revolving. Four of the six barrels incorporate gas bleeds to pipe very hot high-pressure gas to drive a piston and rotary drive mounted between the barrels ahead of the action. The gas power is sufficient also to drive the ammunition feed systems.

Standard M50 ammunition is primed electrically. Many types of projectile are available, including HE, HEI, AP, AP-T and ball. Most installations feed the ammunition without links. Ammunition, usually from 650 to (in the F-111, when installed) 2,084 rounds, is stored in a large drum. From this is a conveyor belt housed in a strong flexible duct. In some installations spent cases are not discharged overboard but are returned to the drum via a second flexible guideway with its own conveyor. Inside the loaded drum the rounds are stored between paddle-like radial partitions. A central rotor in the form of a giant helix, or Archimedean screw, then moves the fresh rounds from the drum into the conveyor in a multi-stage operation. This screw rotor is driven via a high-power flexible coupling from the gun, and the gun also drives the belt conveyors inside the feed guideways.

The first service installation was in the Lockheed F-104, in which the gun is low in the left side of the fuselage. It was found that a single gun was amply

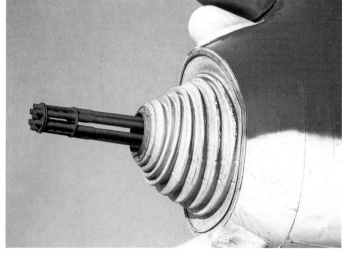

powerful enough, and there was no need for a second. In any case the bulk and weight of the installation are considerable. Many later fighter installations followed, most along similar lines. In almost all cases the gun was offset to left or right of the aircraft centreline, and in more recent aircraft, such as the F-14, F-15 and F-16, the correct amount of rudder(s) is applied automatically to counter undesired yaw caused by the offset recoil when the gun is fired. Thus, the fighter can stay on-target without pilot action.

One of the earliest installations was the tail defence of the B-58 Hustler supersonic bomber. For this the T-171 version was developed, looking like the sting of a wasp and capable of limited angular movement to cover a cone pointing aft from the tail. The gun and feed in this aircraft were self-contained, but aimed-manually with radar assistance by the third crew-member. The other tail-defence installation is in the B-52H, in which case the T-171 is installed in a more conventional spherical-mount turret, with aiming-guidance radars immediately above. This effective installation is still in service, but the B-52G retains its turret mounting four 0.5in guns.

General Electric also developed two closely related types of external pod mounting, the SUU-16/A and SUU-23/A. These differ only in the sub-type of gun fitted. The earlier 16/A houses the

M61A1, with external power provided by a ram-air turbine. This is hinged out from the side of the pod immediately prior to firing. It runs up to speed within 1 sec, but at airspeeds below 650km/h (304mph) low turbine power results in reduced firing rate, and in any case its use increases drag and causes a small additional loss in airspeed over and above that due to recoil. The 23/A houses the self-powered GAU-4 gun, with an electric inertia starter. Aft of the gun is the drive system to the single conveyor feeding from a 1,200-round drum. Cases are dumped overboard, and on each cessation of firing a few (usually five) live rounds are dumped in order to clear the breeches and prevent a cook-off. Large numbers of these pods are in service, one user being the Phantom FGR.2s of the RAF. They provide devastating firepower, but accuracy is not quite as good as that of an internal gun, and this was the chief reason for the clamour for an internal gun for the F-4 Phantom during the Vietnam war, a demand satisfied by the F-4E.

GE has developed numerous derived versions of these incredibly successful weapons, as well as many multi-barrel guns in smaller and larger calibres, as described separately.

Above: Lacking an internal gun, the Phantom FG.1 and FGR.2 of the Royal Air Force can be fitted with the SUU-23/A pod, which houses a self-powered GAU-4 gun.

Below: The SUU-16/A is the M61 pod housing the version of the gun powered by a ram-air turbine. The latter drops down into the slipstream as soon as the gun is fired.

1 Electrical control group.	7 Rear gun support.
2 Ammunition drum.	8 Feed conveyor.
3 Linkless feed drum cover.	9 Return conveyor.
4 Exit unit.	10 M61A-1 gun.
5 Turbine actuator.	11 Front gun support.
6 Suspension lug.	12 Feeder.

13 Rounds counter.	
14 Clutch and brake.	
15 Ram-air turbine.	
16 Turbine door.	
17 Drive shaft.	
18 Conveyor drive.	

The SUU-16/A Gun Pod

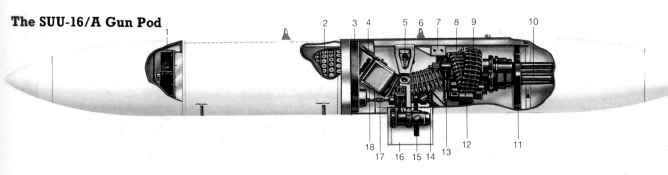

GE M197

Origin: General Electric Company, Burlington, Vermont
Calibre: 20mm
Length: 1,892mm (74.5in)
Weight: 66kg (145lb)
Rate of fire: selectable 400-3,000 rounds per minute
Muzzle velocity: 1,036m (3,400ft) per second

The M197 is very loosely half an M61A1 Vulcan, and uses many common parts. It fires standard M50-series ammunition, which can be fed either via a linkless conveyor or from a traditional linked belt. All current M197s need a 2.2kW (3hp) external drive. This gun entered production in 1969, and its chief application has been in the Universal Turret; it also fits the Lightweight Gun Pod GPU-2/A. These installations are the next two entries.

Left: Loosely regarded as half an M61 Vulcan, the M197 is a neat 20mm weapon. It is used in the Universal Turret.

GE Universal Turret

Described as a fourth-generation system, this is an advanced version of the turret produced for the Bell AH-1J and AH-1T Sea-Cobras; today it is in production for the AH-1S of the Army. The chin turret is electrically driven via two servo motors at slewing and elevation rates of 60° per second, the limits being 110° left and right, and +21°/50° up/down. Logic units link the turret to any of a variety of sighting and control stations, and the installation includes an integrated feed system. In the AH-1S the turret is armed with the M197, set to fire at 750 or 1,500 rounds per minute, but it can also operate the 7.62mm (0.3in) Minigun, 30mm XM188 and 30mm M230 Chain Gun. The ammunition capacity is normally 750 rounds of 20mm (as in the AH-1S) or 500 rounds of 30mm.

GE GPU-2/A

Origin: General Electric Company, Burlington, Vermont
Length: 3,040mm (119.7in) with motor
Weight: about 270kg (595lb) with full ammunition
Ammunition capacity: 300 rounds

Otherwise known as the Lightweight Gun Pod, the GPU-2/A is an extremely effective and compact pod suitable for suspension from any standard mounts on a helicopter or aeroplane. It contains an M197 three-barrel 20mm gun (which see), set to fire at 750 or 1,500 rounds per minute, together with an ammunition storage system, linkless feed and case ejection chute. At the rear is a Ni/Cd battery which can drive the gun and feed up to three complete magazine loads without recharge (the battery can be recharged from the aircraft if power is available). No special tools are required for reloading or for changing barrels, both of which can be done with the pod on the aircraft. The main user is the US Navy.

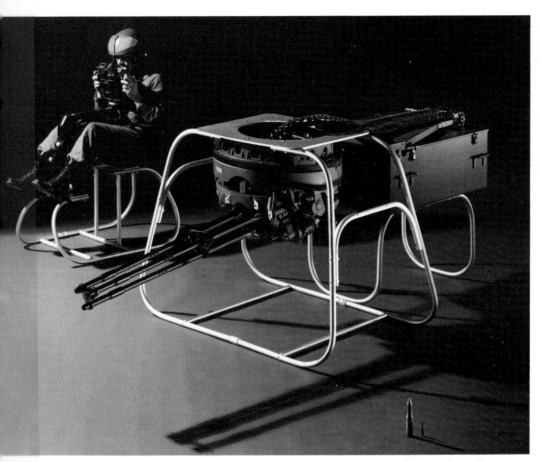

30mm calibre which fires Aden/ DEFA ammunition. This has a lower muzzle velocity than most US ammunition, and the gun has relatively short barrels. It is thus compact and light, completely interchangeable with the M197, and suitable for fixed or turreted applications on helicopters or light aeroplanes. The rate of fire can be selected at a level causing no resonance effects to the vehicle.

GE XM214

Origin: General Electric Company, Burlington, Vermont
Calibre: 5.56mm (0.22in)
Length: 686mm (27in)
Weight: with drive 15kg (33lb)
Rate of fire: selectable up to 10,000 rounds per minute
Muzzle velocity: 990m (3,250ft) per second

Latest of the many descendants of the M61A1, the XM214 is easily the smallest, firing the same compact M193 rounds as the M16 rifle. Its rate of fire is the highest of any gun ever put into production, though bursts of as few as three rounds can be fired. There are six barrels, and the six bolts and firing pins are all driven by a single mainspring. When the trigger is released, feeding of the linkless ammunition stops instantly, and rounds in the gun are fired off in the final split second to empty the gun. Drive is by Ni/Cd battery, aircraft electric or hydraulic supply, or self-power using gun gas. Most applications are expected to call for firing rates between 400 and 6,000 rounds per minute, and the XM214 offers an unusual combination of safety, reliability and maintainability features, with no need for tools or timing procedures.

Above: The General Electric Universal Turret System is seen here with the M197 fitted, and the gunner seated at his optical sight.

Left: The Bell AH-1T Improved SeaCobra of the US Marine Corps is fitted with an electrically operated chin turret armed with an M197 cannon.

Below: The XM188 fires 30mm ammunition much less powerful than that of the GAU-8/A and GAU-13/A. It suits helicopters.

GE XM188E1

Origin: General Electric Company, Burlington, Vermont
Calibre: 30mm
Length: 1,440mm (56.7in)
Weight: 50kg (110lb)
Rate of fire: selectable up to 2,000 rounds per minute
Muzzle velocity: 792m (2,600ft) per second

Yet another offshoot from the classic M61A1 Vulcan, the XM188E1 is a three-barrel gun of

MACHINE GUNS AND CANNON

Right: The Bell UH-1H 'Huey' with the pintle-mounted M60 was by far the commonest combination of its kind in the Vietnam war. One gun could be mounted on each side.

Below: Early UH-1B and C helicopters were often armed with the M16 armament subsystem in which two remotely aimed M60 machine guns were combined with M158 7 x 2.75in launchers.

M60

Origin: design by US Army with industrial participation and manufacture by Maremont
Calibre: 7.62mm (0.3in)
Length: 1,111mm (43.75in)
Weight: typically 10.5kg (23.2lb)
Rate of fire: 600 rounds per minute
Muzzle velocity: 853m (2,800ft) per second

After World War II the US Army spent many years trying to develop a good general-purpose machine gun. Despite having such excellent German prototypes as the MG42 and FG42 success proved elusive, and to this day the weapon that resulted,

Above: The OV-10 Bronco LARA (light armed reconnaissance aircraft) saw action in Vietnam with four M60 guns firing ahead from its sponsons (stub-wings for carrying weapons). The dropped stores here are Marceye IV dispensers each with FM-56A/B fuzes.

the M60, has never been a complete success. It is a gas-operated belt-fed weapon with an air-cooled barrel, which is difficult to change though this must be done frequently, and whose change brings a new gas cylinder and foresight (and bipod, if fitted). The M60C and D were much used in Vietnam from helicopters, and even today the M60 is important. Helicopter guns usually have twin spade grips, with ammunition supplied from a box on the cabin floor.

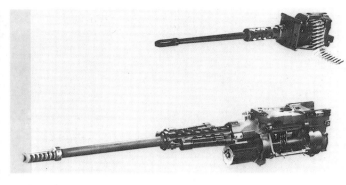

Above: The two members of the MDHC Chain Gun family used in aircraft are the big M230 and small EX-34.

MDHC EX-34

Origin: McDonnell Douglas Helicopter Co, Culver City
Calibre: 7.62mm (0.3in)
Length: 889mm (35in) with flash suppressor
Weight: 13.15kg (29lb)
Rate of fire: 550 rounds per minute
Muzzle velocity: 856m (2,810ft) per second

The EX-34 is a logical scale-down of the M230 Chain Gun to rifle calibre. Though experimental versions can fire at 1,000 rounds per minute, the production guns normally fire at 550-570 rounds per minute, which is considered a good compromise for accurate aiming and ammunition consumption. Reliability is claimed to be 'several orders of magnitude better than any comparable weapon of this calibre'. The EX-34 is the gun used in the same company's HGS-55 armament system fitted to the company's Model 500 Defender family of light attack helicopters (see separate entry).

MDHC HGS-55

Origin: McDonnell Douglas Helicopter Co, Culver City
Calibre: 7.62mm (0.3in)
Weight: loaded 98.9kg (218lb)

This helicopter gun system is based on the M27 but uses the company's own EX-34 Chain Gun, which is extremely reliable but much slower-firing than the M134 of the M27 system. The gun mount and drive system are little changed, and the ammunition supply of 2,000 rounds is unchanged. The HGS-55 provides accurate firepower against point targets out to a range of 900m (2,950ft).

Below: A fine portrait of a Bell OH-58A Kiowa scout helicopter of the US Army fitted with the M27E1 armament subsystem. The M134 Minigun (pp188-189) is trainable in elevation only, the whole helicopter being slewed or steered to bring the gun on target. A 2,000-round ammunition box is carried inside the cabin.

MDHC M27E1

Origin: McDonnell Douglas Helicopter Co, Culver City
Calibre: 7.62mm (0.3in)
Weight: loaded 106.6kg (235lb), without ammunition 48.5kg (107lb)

One of the most reliable of all helicopter gun systems, the M27 was developed (by the then Hughes Helicopters) to adapt the GE M134 Minigun to the OH-6A and OH-58A scout helicopters. The gun is pivoted in elevation only, with limits of +10°/−24°. A supply of 2,000 rounds is fed by link belt, and MDHC developed the split-beam rangefinder sight. By withdrawing three pins the gun can be removed.

MDHC Mk 4 Mod 0

Origin: McDonnell Douglas Helicopter Co, Culver City
Weight: loaded 630kg (1,389lb), without ammunition 357kg (787lb)

The Mk 4 gun pod houses the Mk 11 Mod 5 gun and 750 rounds of 20mm ammunition, the latter stored in a rotary magazine and fed via dual chutes. Cases and links are ejected overboard downwards. The pod can be hung from 356mm or 762mm (14in or 30in) mounts, and is cleared for supersonic flight. The Navy fitted 829 production pods in 1965-7, and this store is also carried by Israeli A-4s.

MDHC Mk 11 Mod 5

Origin: McDonnell Douglas Helicopter Co, Culver City
Calibre: 20mm
Length: with loader 1,990mm (78.35in)
Weight: mechanism 63.5kg (140lb), barrels 23.1kg (51lb), loader 20.4kg (45lb) and total 108.8kg (240lb)
Rate of fire: normally either 700 or 4,200 rounds per minute

This unusual gun is part-gas, part-recoil operated and is fed with two linked belts of M50 or M100 ammunition which enter from both left and right sides simultaneously. Rounds are fed by the loader into an eight-chambered revolver cylinder and are fired down the upper and lower twin barrels, which are indexed at the 12 o'clock and 6 o'clock positions. Rounds are rammed, fired and ejected simultaneously, the cases being relinked before being ejected. The gun has seen service only in the Mk 4 pod (next entry).

MACHINE GUNS AND CANNON

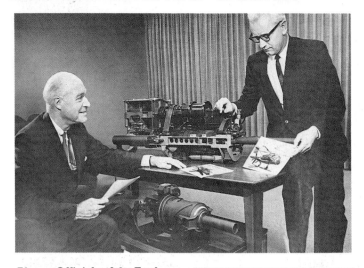

Above: Officials of the Ford Aerospace & Communications Aeronutronic division discuss the M129 grenade launcher. The cannon (the XM140) in the rear remained a prototype.

MDHC M129

Origin: McDonnell Douglas Helicopter Co, Culver City
Calibre: 40mm
Weight: 20.4kg (45lb)
Rate of fire: 400 rounds per minute
Muzzle velocity: 240m (787ft) per second

The M129 is a standard launcher of 40mm grenades, firing with considerable accuracy to a range of some 2,200m (7,220ft). Ammunition is spiral-wound in the container and fed by linked belt. The projector is electric-motor driven, and incorporates a hydrospring recoil-reducing system. This launcher is the weapon in the XM8 installation (facing page).

MDHC M230

Origin: McDonnell Douglas Helicopter Co, Culver City
Calibre: 30mm
Length: 1,638mm (64.5in), with muzzle brake 1,889mm (74.4in)
Weight: total gun system 55.9kg (123lb)
Rate of fire: 625 rounds per minute
Muzzle velocity: 792m (2,600ft) per second

First of the famous Chain Gun family, originally developed when the company was Hughes Helicopters, the M230 is a single-barrel lightweight gun with a unique rotating bolt mechanism driven by an external 4.8kW (6.5hp) motor and chain. The gun fires from an open bolt, without chargers, feeders or any auxiliary devices, and the external power and precise control at all times over every part and every round makes for smooth operation and unique reliability. The M230 can fire US M789/799 as

Above: The unrivalled multiple sensor group of the TADS/ PNVS of the AH-64A with the M230 Chain Gun below.

Below: The M230 Chain Gun is a notably robust item of kit, which in the AH-64A is completely exposed under the fuselage in all weather.

well as Aden/DEFA ammunition. It can fire from linked belts, but the three helicopter applications use a linkless feed.

It should be emphasized that the M230 exactly meets the US Army's requirements as the gun of the McDonnell Douglas AH-64A Apache. Many other guns were available, including the GE M188 three-barrel 30mm gun firing at up to 2,000 rounds per minute. But high rates of fire tailored to air-to-air applications are not the optimum for attacks on surface targets, and 30mm ammunition is extremely heavy. The 625 rounds per minute fire rate is by no means the cyclic limit for the M230, but the best compromise for this application. The prototype gun was first fired in April 1973, and three years later about 250,000 rounds of XM552 and XM639 ammunition had been fired through variously differing Chain Gun prototypes. Then in 1976 the gun was rechambered to take Aden/DEFA ammunition and the US M788/789/ 799 counterpart. This resulted in today's M230, which was adopted as the gun to arm the Apache.

McDonnell Douglas Helicopter (then Hughes) designed the entire Area Weapon System comprising the gun, its mounting and ammunition supply. The gun is installed completely exposed, hanging from a lightweight turret with electric drive slaved to the helicopter's sensors or the

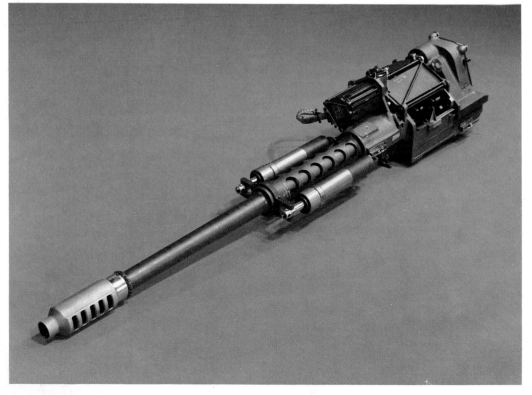

crew's IHADSS (Integrated Helmet And Display Sighting System), with the aid of which either crew-member can cue a sensor or the gun to aim exactly wherever he is looking. Azimuth limits are 100° left or right (normally locked central) and 11° up to 60° down (the gun being spring-loaded to reside normally in the 11° up position) A giant box of 1,200 rounds is located in the bottom of the fuselage directly under the main rotor. The linkless feed supplies ammunition along the left side of the helicopter, the empty cases being returned via a mirror-image duct on the right-hand side.

In a crash the whole gun installation is designed to be thrust up between the cockpits without injury to the crew. Base Ten Systems contribute avionic subsystems: the gun control box, which controls gun firing, the ammunition feed and dynamic braking of the gun drive motor, the rounds counter and the magazine controller. Lear Siegler supplies the turret control box which compensates for recoil and, by re-aiming the gun 10 times per se-

Right: The M230 Chain Gun installation in the AH-64A is shown here in colour. The ammunition is stored in a 1,200-round flat box near the helicopter's centre of gravity. Unlinked rounds are fed along the right side by an endless conveyor system.

cond, puts it exactly back on target after the firing of each round.

The M230 Chain Gun's most important application is in the AH-64A Apache helicopter. This Area Weapon System houses 1,200 rounds of M789 ammunition, fed by a linkless conveyor which has a return transporter for

Above: An AH-64A Apache attack helicopter of the US Army, showing its gun in the rest position, barrel 11° up.

Below: The M230 was originally designed by Hughes specifically for the AH-64A helicopter. It was modified to fire Aden/DEFA rounds.

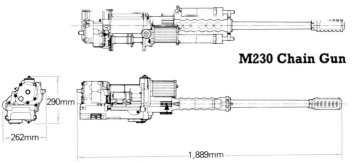

M230 Chain Gun

290mm

262mm

1,889mm

Chain Gun Installation

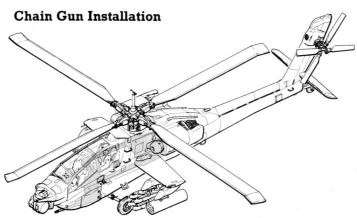

empty cases. System weight is 684kg (1,509lb), or 265kg (585lb) empty. In the AH-1S Cobra a similar feed/return system is used, with capacity of 426 rounds. System weight is 340kg (749lb) loaded and 195kg (430lb) empty. In the Cobra the firing rate is raised to 725 rounds per minute. In the HGS-30 Light Combat Helicopter system, as fitted to the MD-500 Defender, a single linkless conveyor feeds 200 rounds, cases being ejected. This system weighs 179kg (395lb) loaded and 109kg (240lb) empty. The cyclic rate of the gun is reduced to 300 rounds per minute.

MDHC XM8

Origin: McDonnell Douglas Helicopter Co, Culver City
Weight: loaded 108kg (238lb), without ammunition 54.4kg (120lb)
Elevation limits: +10°/—24°

The XM8 is the grenade-launcher partner of the M27E1 gun system, both being quick change systems in which the firing unit is removed by undoing three quick-release pins. The installation feeds 150 rounds of belted M384 (grenade) ammunition, no boost or feed being required. An optical beam-splitter reflex sight is used.

MACHINE GUNS AND CANNON

Pontiac M39E

Origin: design by Illinois Institute of Technology, followed by Ford Motor Co., and manufacture by Pontiac Division of General Motors
Calibre: 20mm
Rate of fire: 1,600 rounds per minute
Muzzle velocity: 870m (2,850ft) per second

Like almost all major countries the USA copied the Mauser MG213C revolver cannon after World War II, and the M39 was the result. The design team at the Illinois Institute of Technology introduced more changes than in the other copies, the chief one being that the barrel was mounted low down and indexed in line with the cylinder chamber at the 6 o'clock rather than 12 o'clock position. Gas operation, a five-chamber cylinder and electric detonation were retained. In 1950, when many prototypes had been fired, development was passed to Ford Motor Co, and pressure of the Korean War resulted in urgent production orders being given to Pontiac.

The M39 became available from production in late 1954, and by chance this was just at the time that General Electric was reaching the definitive stage with its even more revolutionary Vulcan multi-barrel gun. The existence of the GE gun was to have a profound influence on the market for the more traditional M39: had it not been for Northrop's purely private venture in doggedly pushing ahead with the N-156 Freedom Fighter, the M39 might have had limited impact and few customers.

Air fighting over Korea had at last convinced the USAF that six 'fifties' were no longer adequate as fighter armament, but the Mikoyan-Gurevich MiG-15's giant slow-firing cannon did not seem a good answer either. Even at this early time it was widely considered that all guns were likely to be no more than temporary stop-gap weapons which would be rendered obsolete by the availability of guided air-to-air missiles. It was partly for this reason that the considerable body of opinion in favour of adopting a gun of 30mm calibre failed to carry the day. The 20mm calibre won because of the enormous stocks of ammunition held, and the (erroneous) belief that all guns would probably be withdrawn within 10 years. Taking the North American F-86 Sabre as an example, while all regular day fighter-bomber versions continued with traditional armament, the radar-equipped F-86D all-weather interceptor exchanged guns for a modest box of FFARs linked with a complex automatic fire-control system. This was not cleared for export, and so the otherwise similar F-86K for

Left: Sole active application today of this gun, the M39A2 arms the F-5E Tiger II, this example of which is painted in simulated WarPac markings with an Aggressor unit. The gun is mounted on its side, so that the barrel is aligned with the most inboard chamber in the revolver cylinder.

Below: The muzzles of the twin M39 cannon are menacing in this head-on view of an F-5E of the USAF 527th TFW (Aggressors) based at RAF Alconbury. Like the later F/A-18 Hornet the guns are on top of the fuselage.

NATO air forces had to be fitted with the simpler APG-37 radar matched to gun armament, and instead of six 12.7mm M3s this version was armed with four M24 cannon of 20mm calibre, basically the old Oerlikon-derived Colt. But the final fighter-bomber version for the USAF, the F-86H, switched over to four cannon at Block 5 (No 114) and in this case the new M39 gun was specified. This was the first aircraft in service with the fast-firing revolver cannon. On the other hand, the US Navy had no claim on the M39, and retained the traditional cannon on such aircraft as the FJ Fury series, F3H Demon, F4D Skyray,

F8U Crusader and A4D Skyhawk, the final model being the Mk 12.

On the other hand the USAF did plan to use the M39E in all its new day fighter-bombers, and it started with the first two design in its supersonic 'Century' series, the North American F-100 and McDonnell F-101. Both had four guns each with 200 rounds, but in the big F-101A and C the lower right gun was normally removed to make room for Tacan. Then the brilliant Vulcan gun matured and was adopted as the M61, and from the Lockheed F-104 this became the standard US fighter gun, with one exception. This was

Northrop's family of lightweight fighters. As authorized by company president Whitley Collins in 1958 this was designed by Welko Gasich with no internal armament whatsoever, carrying just a Sidewinder AAM on each wingtip and various external stores (including a gun pod if necessary) on three pylons. When this aircraft was finally adopted as the F-5 in October 1962 the specification called for two M39A2 guns, each with 280 rounds, and these have been on every F-5A and F-5E since; two-seaters usually have a single gun. This has greatly extended the M39's active life.

Left: Rearming an F-100D Super Sabre. This was one of the first applications of the M39 gun at the start of the 1950s. The four guns are installed at an angle, to suit the feed of the belts of ammunition. The normal quantity of ammunition was 200 rounds per gun.

Below: Another view of an F-100D Super Sabre, showing the arrangement of four M39A cannon in the lower part of the forward fuselage. The rearming access panel has been removed and the armament specialist is preparing the guns for the next mission over South East Asia in the 1960s. Note Snakeye bombs.

Tround 12.7

Origin: Tround International, Phillipsburg, New Jersey
Calibre: 12.7mm (not circular, see text)
Weight: bare gun 25.85kg (57lb)
Rate of fire: set to 1,250 rounds per minute
Muzzle velocity: 975m (3,200ft) per second

For many years the Tround company has been developing guns using revolutionary ammunition in which a trochoid (hence the name, derived from 'triangular round') section projectile is fired from inside a surrounding case of moulded polycarbonate. The case is strong enough to need no surrounding barrel chamber, so the guns need no reciprocating parts, the Tround being fired behind the barrel. Indeed one tround could have several projectiles, all fired down separate barrels. The current 12.7mm (0.5in) gun is on test by the US Navy and is hoped to lead to a production gun of 20mm calibre. An eight-barrel Tround has sustained a firing rate of 20,000 rounds per minute. Clearly the potential is tremendous, but as this book went to press the company had still not achieved acceptance, despite excellent results on test.

GLOSSARY

A

AA Anti-Aircraft

AAAM Advanced Air-to-Air Missile

AALAW Advanced Air-Launched Anti-Armour Weapon

AAM Air-To-Air Missile

ACCP *Anti-Char Courte Portée* (short-range anti-tank [missile])

ACM Advanced Cruise Missile

ACMT Advanced Cruise Missile Technology

active emitting its own signals, which are reflected from the target and thus enable the missile to home on a passive target by its own efforts

ACV Air-Cushion Vehicle

ADSM Air Defence-Suppression Missile

AFV Armoured Fighting Vehicle

ALARM Air-Launched Anti-Radiation Missile

ALCM Air-Launched Cruise Missile

ALWT Advanced Light-Weight Torpedo

AMD Avions Marcel Dassault

AMRAAM Advanced Medium-Range Air-to-Air Missile

ANS *Anti-Navire Supersonique* (supersonic anti-ship [missile])

AP Armour-Piercing

APDS Armour-Piercing Discarding Sabot

APHE Armour-Piercing High Explosive

API Armour-Piercing Incendiary

APT Armour-Piercing Tracer

ARM Anti-Radiation (Radar) Missile

ASAT Anti-Satellite

ASCC Allied Standards Co-ordinating Committee (a NATO body tasked with agreement on terminology and other language problems, and with the assignment of reporting names to Warsaw Pact hardware)

ASM Air-to-Surface Missile

ASMP *Air-Sol Moyenne Portée* (medium-range air-to-surface [missile])

aspect ratio slenderness of a two-dimensional surface (square of span divided by area)

ASRAAM Advanced Short-Range Air-to-Air Missile

ASV Anti-Surface Vessel

ASW Anti-Submarine Warfare

ATF Advanced Tactical Fighter

AT/AP Anti-Tank/Anti-Personnel

ATGW Anti-Tank Guided Weapon

ATSC Air Technical Service Command (US)

AWACS Airborne Warning and Control System

B

bang/bang control system with only two states: on and off; thus a bang/bang control surface is in either the neutral centre position or driven quickly to the limit of its travel

BAT *Bombe d'Appui Tactique* (tactical attack bomb)

beam rider a vehicle equiped with a radio receiver and control system which automatically tends to keep the vehicle travelling along the centre of a coded radar beam

BF Blast Fragmentation (warhead which relies for effect on blast and the fragments of a thick-walled casing or central rod)

BGT Bodensee Geräte-Technik

BKEP Boosted Kinetic-Energy Penetrator

BLU Bomb Live Unit

booster propulsion motor imparting large thrust for a short time, to give high acceleration at the beginning of the flight

BTL Bell Telephone Laboratories

burnout point at which a missile's propellants have been totally consumed

BVR Beyond-Visual-Range

C

cannon continuous-fire weapon similar to the machine gun but firing explosive shells; the minimum practical calibre for such weapons is 15mm (0.59in)

CAPTOR enCAPsulated TORpedo

CAS Close Air Support

Cassegrain optics Use of two parabolic mirrors to magnify (concentrate) IR or optical radiation

CBU Cluster Bomb Unit

CEAM *Centre d'Experiences Aériennes Militaires* (centre for military air evaluation) (French)

CEL *Centre d'Essais des Landes* (Landes test centre) (French)

CEP Circular Error Probable, the radius of the circle within which half the missiles fired at a target are statistically likely to impact

CEV *Centre d'Essais en Vol* (flight test centre) (French)

CLOS Command to Line Of Sight

closed bolt/breech gun firing system in which the round is ready in the chamber with the bolt fully closed when the trigger is operated; the system gives a short locking period, but there is the risk of a 'cook-off'

CMC Cruise Missile Carrier

CSRL Common Strategic Rotary Launcher

CSW Conventional Stand-off Weapon

CW Continuous-Wave (radiation, as distinct from pulsed radiation)

CWW Cruciform-Wing Weapon

cyclic rate of fire the maximum rate at which an automatic weapon can fire without regard to the practicalities of acceleration to rate, cooling and ammunition supply

D

DA Direct Action

DB Double-Base (rocket propellant)

DEFA *Direction des Etudes et Fabrications d'Armement* (directorate for the study and manufacture of weapons) (French)

DEW Directed-Energy Weapon

DGP Door Gunner Post

DoD Department of Defense

Doppler radar radar whose operation depends on the apparent change of frequency caused by relative velocity between the radar and target

DTE *Direction Téchnique des Engins* (technical directorate for missiles) (French)

dual-thrust rocket which starts operating at a high (boost) thrust and then operates for a prolonged period at a low (sustain) thrust

DVK *Deutsche Versuchs-anstalt für Kraftfahrzeug und Fahrzeugmotoren* (German Research Establishment for Vehicles and Vehicle Motors)

E

ECCM Electronic Counter-Counter Measures

ECM Electronic Counter Measures

EMD Electronique Marcel Dassault

EO Electro-Optical

ESD Electronique Serge Dassault

EW Electronic Warfare

F

FFAR Folding-Fin Air(craft) Rocket

FLIR Forward-Looking Infra-Red

FM Frequency-Modulated

FPB Fast Patrol Boat

frequency agile radio or radar whose operating frequency automatically hops and jumps in seemingly random manner to confuse the enemy, or which can be positively controlled in accordance with a prior programme

G

gas operation in relation to self-loading and/or automatic weapons, the term gas operation connotes a system whereby propellant gas is tapped from the barrel between the chamber and muzzle to actuate a piston mechanism that drives the system which unlocks the breech of the weapon, extracts the spent case, drives the breech block back against a powerful spring, and then allows the spring to drive the block forward again, in the process chambering a fresh round

gathering the phase just after the launch of a beam-riding or other missile which has to be gathered into a narrow radar beam or optical line of sight

GBU Glider Bomb Unit

GCI Ground-Controlled Interception

GD General Dynamics Corporation

GE General Electric Company

GIAT *Groupement des Armements Terrestres* (industrial group for land weapons) (French)

gimballed mounted on pivots so that it can tilt in any direction

GLCM Ground-Launched Cruise Missile

GP General-Purpose

GPU Gun Pod Unit

GRP Glass-Reinforced Plastics

H

HARM High-speed Anti-Radiation Missile

HE High Explosive

HEAT High Explosive Anti-Tank

HEI High Explosive Incendiary

HMP Heavy Machine gun Pod

homing automatically flying towards the target

HVM Hyper-Velocity Missile

I

ICBM Inter-Continental Ballistic Missile

IFF Identification Friend or Foe

IHE Improved High Explosive

IIR Imaging Infra-Red

interferometer device for measuring with individual wavelengths; thus a radar can be produced with receiver aerials sensitive to successive pulses or continuous-wave peaks

IOC Initial Operational Capability

IR Infra-Red (i.e. heat)

IRCCM Infra-Red Counter-Counter Measures

IRCM Infra-Red Counter Measures

J

JASDF Japanese Air Self-Defence Force

K

kT kiloton, i.e. explosive yield equivalent to that of 1,000 tonnes of TNT

L

LAL Launch-And-Leave (missile)

LANL Los Alamos Nuclear Laboratories

LF Low-Frequency

LGB Laser-Guided Bomb

LID LIft Improvement Device

LOAL Lock-On After Launch

LOBL Lock-On Before Launch

lock-on ability of certain tracking systems (radar, infra-red and optical) to search for a target and, having found one, to cease search and instead continuously track that target

look-down ability of certain radars to be detect and track targets flying at low level despite the fact that the ground is so close behind them when seen from higher altitude

LOS Line of Sight

LOV Low-Observable Vehicle

LR-SOM Long-Range Stand-Off Missile

M

machine gun continuous-fire weapon firing ball ammunition (solid projectiles); the maximum practical calibre for such weapons is 14.5mm (0.57in)

MDAC McDonnell Douglas Astronautics Company

MDHC McDonnell Douglas Helicopter Company

MICA *Missile d'Interception et de Combat Aerien* (interception and air combat missile)

mid-course over most of the missile's flight, i.e. all except the launch (including gathering if applicable) and terminal phases

MIT Massachusetts Institute of Technology

MLMS Multi-purpose Lightweight Missile System

MoD Ministry of Defence

monopulse radar technique in which four overlapping beams (two azimuth and two elevation) give zero output voltage for a target exactly in their centre

MRBF Mean rounds between failures, a measure of a gun's reliablity

MSDS Marconi Space and Defence Systems

MT megaton, i.e. explosive yield equivalent to that of 1 million tonnes of TNT

MTP Multi-Task Pod

N

NDRC National Defense Research Committee

NEARTIP NEAR-Term Improvement Program

Ni/Cd Nickel/Cadmium

NOTS Naval Ordnance Test Station

NWC Naval Weapons Center

INDEX